Networking
Technologies

A Complete Guide to Passing the Novell CNE Exam

Dr. Andres Fortino, P.E.
Arnold Villeneuve, Master CNE

McGraw-Hill

New York   San Francisco   Washington, D.C.   Auckland   Bogotá
Caracas   Lisbon   London   Madrid   Mexico City   Milan
Montreal   New Delhi   San Juan   Singapore
Sydney   Tokyo   Toronto

McGraw-Hill

*A Division of The **McGraw-Hill** Companies*

©1996 by The McGraw-Hill Companies, Inc.

pbk   1 2 3 4 5 6 7 8 9 DOC/DOC 9 0 0 9 8 7 6

Product or brand names used in this book may be trade names or trademarks. Where we believe that there may be proprietary claims to such trade names or trademarks, the name has been used with an initial capital or it has been capitalized in the style used by the name claimant. Regardless of the capitalization used, all such names have been used in an editorial manner without any intent to convey endorsement of or other affiliation with the name claimant. Neither the author nor the publisher intends to express any judgment as to the validity or legal status of any such proprietary claims.

Library of Congress Cataloging-in-Publication Data
Fortino, Andres G.
    Networking technologies : a complete guide to passing the Novell
CNE exam / by Andres Fortino & Arnold Villeneuve.
        p.   cm.
    Includes index.
    ISBN 0-07-912312-0 (p)
    1. Electronic data processing personnel—Certification.   2. Novell
software—Study and teaching.   I. Villeneuve, Arnold. II. Title.
QA76.3.F67 1996
004.6—dc20   96-15802
                                                         CIP

McGraw-Hill books are available at special quantity discounts to use as premiums and sales promotions, or for use in corporate training programs. For more information, please write to the Director of Special Sales, McGraw-Hill, 11 West 19th Street, New York, NY 10011. Or contact your local bookstore.

Acquisitions editor: Jennifer Holt DiGiovanna
Editorial team: Robert E. Ostrander, Executive Editor
            Sally Anne Glover, Book Editor
            Jodi L. Tyler, Indexer
Production team: Katherine G. Brown, Director
            Wanda S. Ditch, Desktop Operator
            Brenda S. Wilhide, Computer Artist
Design team: Jaclyn J. Boone, Designer   9123120
            Katherine Lukaszewicz, Associate Designer   WK2

To my beloved teacher, Elizabeth Clare Prophet.
AGF

To my love, Jan Larabie; I wouldn't be me without you.
AV

Contents

Contents

Acknowledgments

This book is the product of a dozen years of association with many colleagues who have supported us in perfecting our knowledge of data communications and networking technology. Our gratitude goes out to all of them.

First to my friend and coauthor, Arnold, who was a first-rate teammate in producing this book and the Learning Tree course this book is based on. Then a great thanks to all those wonderful folks at Learning Tree International who put out the best educational product on the planet. Thank you to John Moriarty, Rick Adamson, Francesco Zamboni, Karen Snyder, Beverly Voight, Stu Ackerman, Bruce Wadman, and Lori Sheridan. A special thanks to Eric Garen and David Collins for creating Learning Tree and giving us the privilege of working in their company. We wish to thank all our Learning Tree students who over the years helped us shape the seminar and this book.

A special thanks goes to our colleagues Dr. Karanjit Siyan, Tim Watts, Peter Rybaczyk, Gary Yarus, Randy Ahrens, and many other instructors who informed us, taught our seminar, and in general enjoyed this wonderful technical field with us.

Our gratitude rightly extends to our acquisitions editor, Jennifer Holt DiGiovanna, who had great faith in us.

Finally, I wish to acknowledge the selfless work of my wife, Kathleen, who served as my editor and cheerleader. It was truly a joint project, and the credit belongs to her as much as to the author. Thank you for your patience and understanding, dear.

AGF

I would like to express my sincere thanks to Andres Fortino for providing me with the opportunity to coauthor this book, and for the doors that have been opened as a result.

AV

1
Computer network
and services

7
Build a network

2
Transmission media
and network hardware

6
Network management

Introduction
to
networking
technologies

3
Data communications

Standards

Models

Protocols

5
Popular protocol suites

4
The OSI model layers

x

Introduction

Networking Technologies: A Complete Guide to Passing the Novell CNE Exam covers the entire spectrum of technology used for implementing computer-based networks. The book takes a systematic approach in presenting this massive body of knowledge. It starts with an introduction to general network computing concepts and then proceeds to cover in detail each area of importance that you will need to understand, starting with cables and working up to the server-based applications accessed by users.

The information contained within is also geared to provide you with everything you need to pass the Novell NetWare Networking Technologies Certified NetWare Engineer exam, but it doesn't stop there. Each chapter is concluded with a combination of study questions, a workshop, and reference study sheets. The authors have included additional details on areas of emerging technologies that you need to be aware of. Finally, the closing chapter of the book walks you through the building of a departmental network to discover how different components are used as the network grows into an enterprise network with Internet and mainframe connections.

Chapter 1 is an introduction to computer networks and the services they provide. The main objective in this chapter is to present all the basic network components or elements, including an historical perspective on computer development. Today's networks are becoming more complex as we rush to integrate systems made by different vendors in different decades, yet provide seamless integration to the end user. The chapter presents a high-level perspective on computer networks and lays the foundation for other chapters to go into more detail on the technology that is used to implement networks.

Chapter 2 starts with the lowest level of computer components. Before computers communicate with each other, they need to be physically connected in some manner. Media and network hardware are the components that bind a network together. Without them, the computers on people's desks would not be able to attach to networks. A wire is not always required. In certain cases the transmission medium is a radio link with no existing wire. All the different types of media used to connect local area networks and how they work are covered in this section. In addition to wireless-based networks, this chapter explores satellite, infrared, and laser connections.

The local area network connectivity solutions are just one part of the story. Wide area networks (WANs) are required to connect across town or across the country. An investigation of the telephone system and the services offered by telephone providers is needed to understand WAN technology. The chapter also describes new approaches to telephone services such as ISDN. Since the existing telephone system was created and is intended to support voice communications only, we need devices to send out data over voice lines. X.25 is the heart of a class of network services called public switched data networks. In this chapter, there is a description of internetworking devices. The function of these devices is described in depth in later chapters.

Chapter 3 covers the concepts associated with network models and protocols and the associations and organizations responsible for establishing and maintaining them. *Protocols* are rules for communication between computers and are one of the three elements of computer networking. In this chapter we review one of the most important concepts of the computer networking industry—the Open Systems Interconnection (OSI) reference model. In subsequent chapters, we go into the OSI model in greater detail.

Chapter 4 provides you with a well-rounded understanding of the seven layers of the OSI reference model. It is a very useful tool for analyzing and understanding data communication systems. The OSI model is important because all of the communications protocols in use today (NetWare's IPX/SPX, the Internet's TCP/IP, and even IBM's SNA) can be mapped to functions that each layer of the model represents.

The seven layers of the OSI reference model are described in chapter 3. However, in chapter 4, each layer will be further analyzed by defining its purpose, identifying and describing the technology topics that are associated with that layer, and the methods used with each topic. The word "topic" is the Novell designation for characteristics or issues involved with that layer. We make use of that terminology to help you be more successful in passing the CNE exam.

Chapter 5 covers the most popular protocol stacks or suites within the networking industry. Chapters 1 through 4 talk about the topics and methods that are used throughout the networking industry. In chapter 5, we explore the most popular protocol solutions that facilitate the network communications process. As we proceed through this chapter, we will relate each of the topics or methods to the associated protocols within the stack or suite so that you can better understand their purpose and function. Finally, we review some of the less-used but equally important protocols implemented throughout the industry.

At the beginning of chapter 5, we review the need for rules in data communication and the relationship between models and protocols. The first protocol reviewed will be the IEEE Project 802 because most network protocol families function on top of the IEEE 802 series of protocols. The chapter then covers the most popular networking protocol stacks in use today. Finally, a review of several emerging communication protocols is done at the end of the chapter.

Once your network is put together, it doesn't stop changing. As it changes, problems invariably occur. In its bare essentials, network management is fire fighting at a distance. Some part of the network goes down, and the network administrator must identify the location of the outage and what to do to fix it. To accomplish this most-essential task well, a network administrator must have a wide variety of tools and techniques. Some activities must be done well in advance of any outages, such as configuration and performance management. Others, such as security and accounting, are often done after the fact. And the most important task, fault management, must be performed quickly and effectively at the moment of the outage. The models, tools, techniques, and schemes for effective network management are considered in chapter 6.

In chapter 7 we bring all the technologies together as we build a network from the ground up. While looking at all the components individually and developing an understanding of their functionality is important, it helps if we can acquire an appreciation of when we might use a specific technology. We follow the activities of an International Technologies research engineer as the organization's network is first installed and grows to an enterprise network.

Chapters 1 through 7 are the main parts of the book. However, the learning doesn't stop there. The appendices provide valuable reference information as well. Appendix A is a comprehensive section on network rules for implementing Ethernet and Token Ring networks. Appendices B and C provide the answers to concept review and study questions found at the end of each chapter. Appendix D is a listing of vendor resources. (Make sure to check out the Web page included on the CD-ROM that corresponds to appendix D.) Appendix E contains all the solutions to the International Technologies workshops. Appendix F is a list of standards organizations and how to contact them, appendix G lists acronyms and appendix H lists all of the resources and software included on the CD-ROM that comes with the book.

We know you will find the information in this book useful, not just in preparing for your Certified NetWare Engineer exam, but also long after you have obtained CNE and have started working with computer networks.

Enjoy the book!

Andres Fortino and Arnold Villeneuve

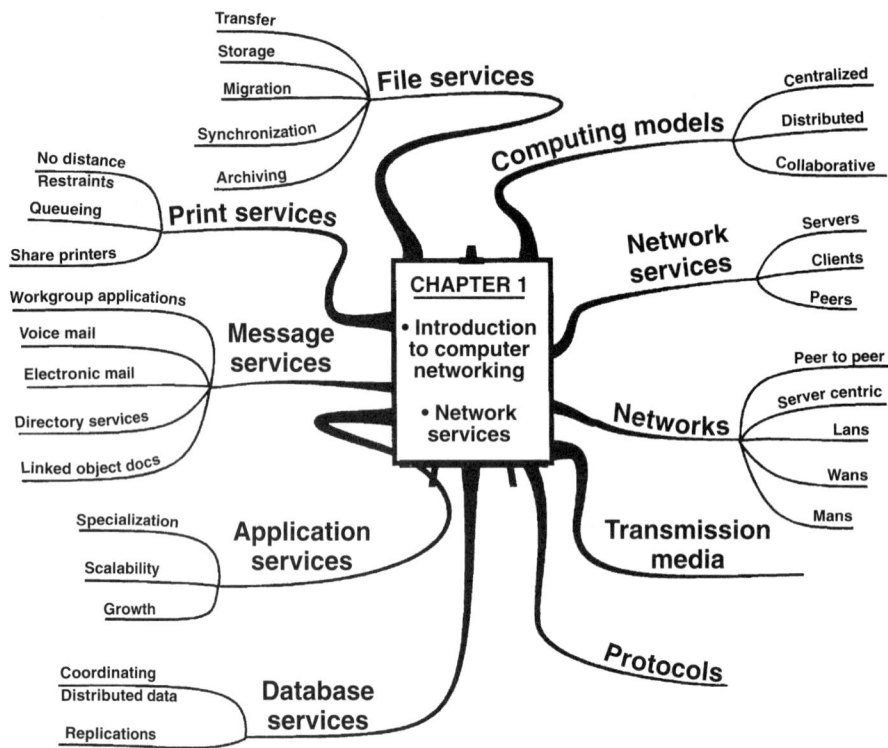

1

Computer networks and services

⇨ Introduction

Chapter 1 covers the Novell CNE exam objectives that deal with the introduction to computer networks and the services they provide. A broader objective in this chapter is also to introduce you to all the basic network components, including a historical perspective on computer development. Today's networks are becoming more complex as we rush to integrate systems made by different vendors and provide seamless integration to the end user. This chapter is a high-level perspective on computer networks and lays the foundation on which other chapters will build. Those chapters go into more detail on the technology that is used to implement networks.

⇨ CNE exam objectives

➢ Define networking.

➢ Describe centralized computing, distributed computing, and collaborative computing.

➢ Define and contrast the classifications of local area network (LAN), metropolitan area network (MAN), and wide area network (WAN).

➢ Define and contrast enterprise and global networks.

➢ Identify and describe the three basic networking elements.

⇨ Elements of computer networking

The definition of networking can be viewed as the sharing of information (i.e., data) and services (i.e., printing). However, one must not confuse the term "networking" as it is commonly viewed in today's computer environment. The sharing of information and services by groups of users occurred in the early days of computing as it does now. How the network is implemented to provide access to the data and services, and the type of computer processing it uses, is what differentiates these networks and will be the focus of the discussion in most of this chapter.

The evolution of computing

See Fig. 1-1.

Figure 1-1

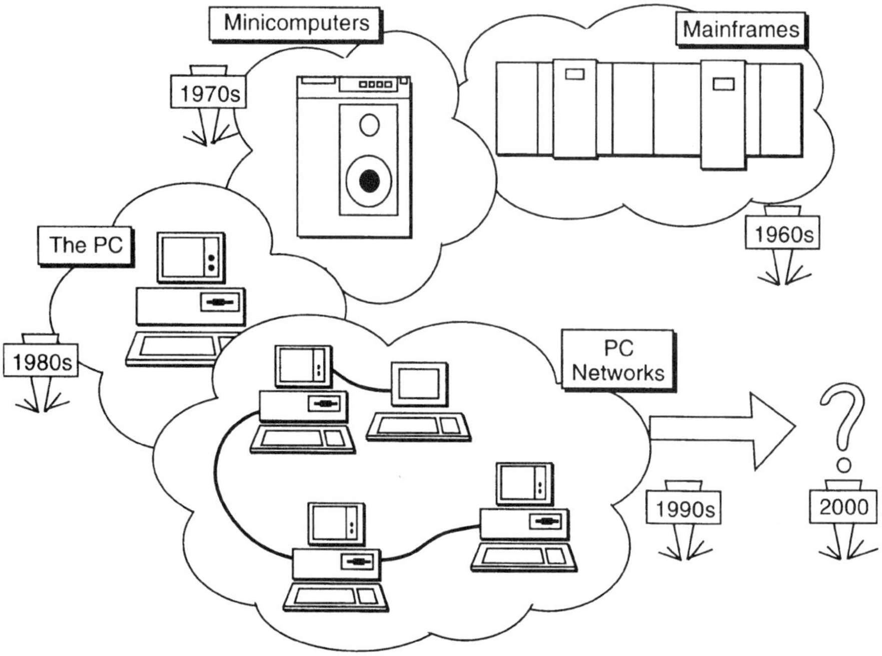

The evolution of computing. Learning Tree International

A brief history of computing

Today's computer network technology has evolved from developments made over the last 40 years. During this time, several stages of computer evolution have been identified:

> ➢ Prenetwork computing.

> ➢ Minicomputers and the development of the network.

> ➢ Personal computers.

> ➢ Computer networks.

> ➢ Present and future trends—multivendor networks.

As you study computers and the networks that connect them, you will see that these stages are not distinct or separate from each other in most organizations, but instead are joined together to meet overall business data-processing needs. For example, you find that many organizations have newer computer networks through which users access older computer-based processing systems (sometimes referred to as legacy systems).

✳ Prenetwork computing

Prenetwork computers were originally very expensive, room-sized machines. They were based on tube technology like that in old television sets; integrated circuits were still only on the drawing board. Prenetwork computers evolved in the 1960s as mainframe systems and were popularized by International Business Machines (IBM).

One of the main characteristics of mainframe technology is its use of centralized processing. We will study computer processing concepts in more detail later in this chapter. In this scenario, however, all processing is done by a central processing unit or CPU. Many terminals are used to access the applications and data at the same time. These terminals were originally directly connected to the mainframe system. The terminals did not do any processing of their own; instead they displayed characters on a terminal screen and sent typed characters to the mainframe via the terminal keyboard. Furthermore, they could only access applications available on the system they were directly connected to. Mainframes did not talk to other mainframes, or more appropriately, they were not networked.

A final comment about the early days of prenetwork computing development is that the equipment was proprietary to each specific vendor. If you purchased an IBM mainframe, you had to buy IBM terminals and peripherals such as printers to connect to it. Therefore, computer system components were vendor specific and proprietary.

✳ Minicomputers and the development of the network

Several stories have been recounted as to why the minicomputer was developed, but certainly my favorite states that it was for marketing purposes. Whether it is true or not, the assumption was highly probable when you consider that early mainframe systems were more expensive than most organizations could afford to purchase outright, let alone pay to maintain. Also, within many organizations, decisions were made at a departmental level.

The minicomputer was the answer. Smaller than the mainframe generation before it, it was less expensive and required fewer resources to operate and maintain. The market from a vendor's perspective was now considerably bigger.

While these new systems were now in the reach of many organizational departments, the requirement still remained—access to corporate data across departmental lines. Spurred on by this requirement, vendors such as IBM and Digital Equipment Corporation (DEC) developed the capability to connect the smaller systems together into a network configuration. The term local area network (LAN) was coined in the 1970s, before the computers the term is commonly associated with.

However, minicomputers inherited several characteristics from the mainframe era, primarily centralized processing and the use of terminals for access. As with its predecessor, minicomputer equipment was also vendor specific, and one could not mix and match components from one vendor's system with components from another vendor.

✳ The personal computer

Much maligned in the early days as a toy for electronics hobbyists, the personal computer has risen to significantly change the way we do business. And unlike earlier computer developments, the personal computer has made its way into the average home.

Stories are now legendary about early personal computer developments, with the first ones appearing in hobby magazines as early as 1979. However, in 1981 IBM introduced the IBM PC, which started a revolution, not to mention a multibillion dollar industry. Compared to the mainframe and minicomputer, the personal computer was an inexpensive, single-user machine.

Perhaps unfortunately for IBM, the personal computer the company implemented was not proprietary, and many other manufacturers soon started to build lower-priced systems and peripherals. However, it is also this one small yet important factor that probably lead to the explosion of technology that we have all witnessed in this area.

The most significant change in the evolution of computing occurred at this stage with the introduction of distributed computing. Each personal computer is more than just a dumb terminal. Each computer is accessed directly by one user at a time. That's because there is only one keyboard and display unit connected to each CPU system. The personal computer also came equipped with its own file storage device and could support peripherals such as printers. There was no need to be connected to a mainframe, as the computer could do its own application processing and data storage.

The introduction of the personal computer also started many spinoff industries, the most prominent of which was software development. And with personal computers being more accessible to the average person, software applications were developed and distributed much more quickly than in traditional computer environments. In many early cases, the software was available free of charge as hobbyists shared their labors.

✳ **The computer network**

During the early to mid-1980s, and more so in the 1990s, personal computers were interconnected to form LANs. In some cases they were even connected to existing mainframe and minicomputer-based LANs to emulate the terminals that were originally used to access the older legacy systems. The 1990s has often been referred to as the decade of the LAN.

File-server-based networks such as Novell NetWare were developed and became popular during this stage. Unlike the minicomputer-based LANs that used terminal and hosts with centralized computing, file-server-based LANs employed other personal computers to act as a central repository for data storage and other services. Because the file servers were based on personal computers interconnected to other personal computers, distributed computing was still very much employed as a means of processing.

Finally, unlike the original implementation of the personal computer that was based on the concept of a single user accessing the application or data on an individual basis, the implementation of personal-computer-based LANs required advancements in software. In particular, the system now had to keep track of multiple users accessing the application or data that resided on one centrally located file server.

❊ Present and future developments—multivendor networks

As computers evolved, end users began to demand the ability to interconnect systems in a seamless manner. Regardless of the type of computers they had on their desks, they wanted to be able to access any other type of computer system in their organization, which is no small feat in many instances. Users wanted systems that were more open. Government was the biggest promoter of open systems technology and helped develop many standards and protocols that are still in use today.

Two key terms were coined to introduce the concepts associated with interconnecting systems from different vendors: internetworking and interpretability.

At a basic level, internetworking is really the ability to connect one type of computer (i.e., a personal computer) to another different type of computing system (i.e., a minicomputer). However, the personal computer in this instance must use communication methods that the minicomputer host is familiar with (i.e., terminal emulation). In addition, the personal computer looks like just another terminal to the minicomputer host. So in the end, the client requesting the service must talk to the host providing the service as just another terminal that the client is used to dealing with. When the personal computer in question talks to the minicomputer, it is emulating a minicomputer terminal to the degree that the minicomputer does not differentiate the personal computer from a standard terminal.

Interpretability, on the other hand, allows different hosts to communicate with each other in their native mode. Building on the example just discussed, the personal computer uses drive letters (i.e., hard disk drive C:) to reference storage devices, or folders if it is an Apple Macintosh. Using interpretability, the same personal computer that was just emulating a minicomputer terminal would now be able to copy files to the minicomputer using a drive letter or folder format that was native to its way of referencing storage devices. In this latter format, the minicomputer host providing the service now appears as an extension of the personal computer resources, as opposed to another type of computer system.

With the capability to communicate from different computing platforms using either of the previous methods, the personal computer is no longer restricted to the resources that it has directly connected. The personal computer now becomes both the resources it provides directly, plus those available throughout the network. "The network is the computer" therefore becomes a very appropriate term as we move into multivendor networks. The services available on the network become an extension of the personal computer.

The concept of implementing interconnectivity and interpretability of different types of computing system platforms introduces the concept of cooperative computing. In cooperative computing, both centralized and distributed computing can be employed in a single processing request.

What does the future hold? Tighter integration of, and cooperation between, different computing systems employing each system for its area of specialization, with higher levels of cooperative computing.

Different computing methods

Now that we have provided you with a brief evolution of the stages of computing, it is appropriate to elaborate on the types of computer processing models that are employed in the different scenarios. In the previous text, we have referred to the following computing models: centralized, distributed, and cooperative. Here we will describe in more detail the specific characteristics of each.

The classical computing scenario—centralized computing

See Fig. 1-2.

Figure 1-2

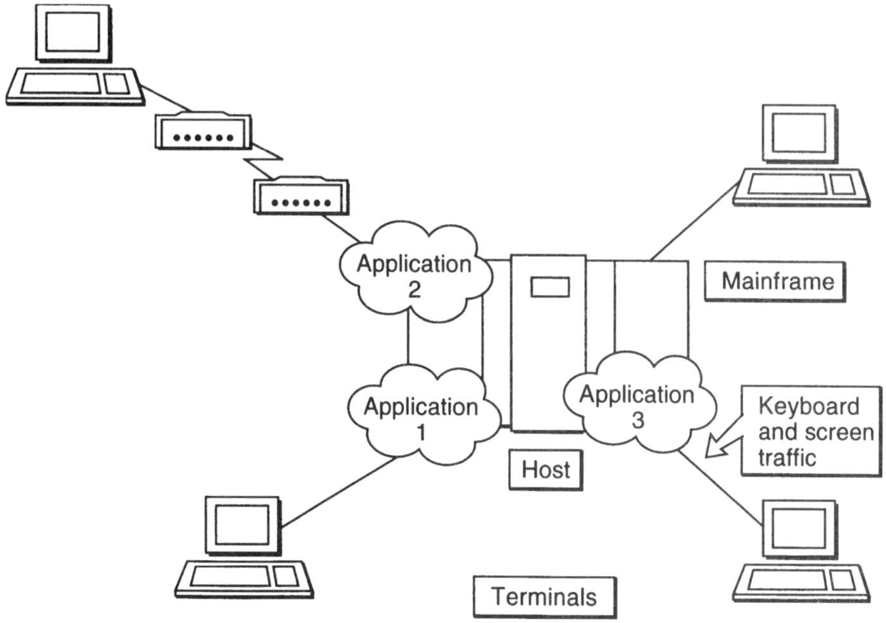

Centralized computing. Learning Tree International

⇨ Characteristics of centralized computing

In centralized computing, all processing is done at the host computer. The host can be accessed by many terminals at the same time (multiuser), and it can run many applications simultaneously (multitasking). Terminals do not do any processing in a centralized computing system, and they have appropriately been labeled as "dumb terminals." The terminal passes its request onto the host CPU by sending requests from its keyboard. The host application processes the requests and send the answer back to the terminal as characters to be displayed on its screen. Connected terminals can be local via direct connection or remote via telephone lines. The host, therefore, acts as a central repository for application, data, and backups.

Because the host does all the computing for terminals, it is also responsible for maintaining access privileges and security. Access to the host is managed through login and password control. Once connected to the host, further access control can be provided on a per-application basis.

In our earlier discussion of prenetwork computing, we state that the terminal received character information from the host to be displayed on the terminal's screen, and the terminal forwarded character information to the host via its keyboard. Because the communication between the host and its terminals is character based, traffic generated by the terminals uses a low data rate. The low data rates in question are usually between 1200 to 9600 bits per second or bps (more on bps in chapter 2).

On the surface, one would think that a low data rate is a limitation in centralized computing, but this is not necessarily the case. A human could not type fast enough to fill up a 1200-bits-per-second communication line. Why is this? Each alphabet character takes at least seven bits to be represented, and usually eight in a mainframe environment. Therefore, to completely use up a 1200-bits-per-second transmission line, the user would need to type in approximately 150 characters (or letters) per second:

$$\frac{1200 \text{ bits per second}}{8 \text{ bits per character}} = 150 \text{ characters per second}$$

⇨ Modern computing scenarios— distributed and cooperative

As the computer industry evolved, two additional types of computing methods were developed: distributed and cooperative. Distributed computing was implemented with the introduction of personal computers. Cooperative computing, or collaborative computing as it is sometimes referred to, really began when minicomputers and mainframes started to work together on processing tasks. However, cooperative computing is generally referred to as a combination of distributed and centralized processing systems working together. Let's look at these in more detail.

⇨ Distributed computing

See Fig. 1-3.

Figure 1-3

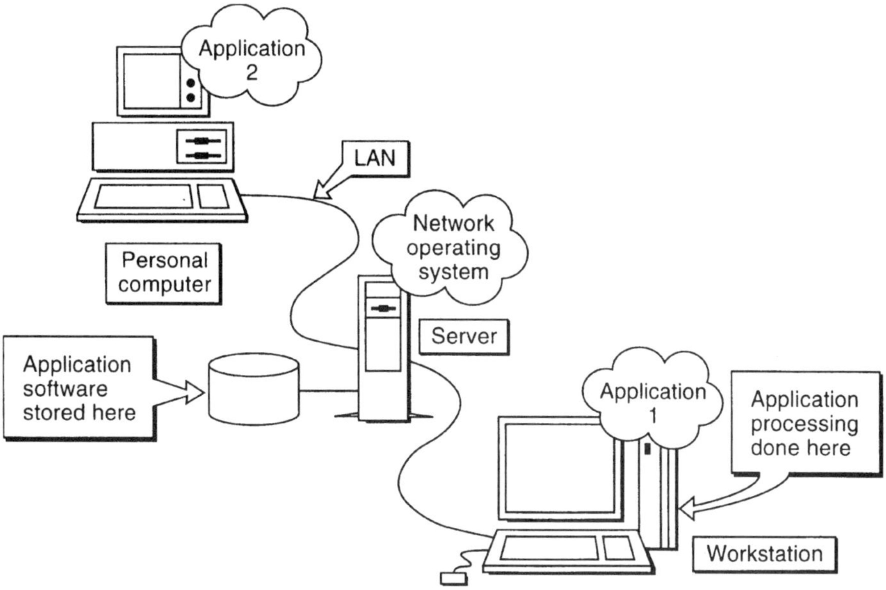

Distributed computing. Learning Tree International

✳ Characteristics of distributed computing

Distributed computing was really introduced with the advent of personal computers. The idea that a user could work on a personal computer and have it process only that user's requests was termed distributed because each computer had its own CPU. A group of users could work on individual computers to complete processing tasks such as working on a spreadsheet or word-processing application.

As we saw with the evolution of computing, distributed processing systems were then interconnected to allow for the sharing of information, as was already done on mainframes and minicomputers. However, even in a networked configuration where many personal computers were sharing information on a centrally located file server, the distributed processing model was still implemented because each system had its own CPU. Dumb terminals did not do their own processing. This type of network was commonly referred to as a file-server-based network. A personal computer was dedicated to providing services, usually file and print, to other personal computers.

To summarize, there are three main elements of a distributed computing system:

> File server or server.

> Workstation or client.

> Data rate requirements.

The file server or server provides for a central location of applications and data. It is controlled by a network operating system (NOS). The NOS manages server resources such as file system, printers, and communications. Finally, the server serves clients or workstations and cannot be used to access end user applications or data directly. End users' applications and data must by accessed via client workstations. Note: Peer-to-peer networks are discussed later.

Example file server network operating systems

> Novell NetWare.

> Banyan Vines.

> Microsoft Windows NT Server.

> IBM LAN Manager.

Workstations or clients can be various types of personal computers such as IBM-compatible PCs, Apple Macintosh, Unix workstations (both Intel or Motorola RISC-based) and Power PCs. Although the clients are connected to and can access their applications from the file server, the processing of the application is still done by the local CPU. The personal computer, in fact, downloads the application (WordPerfect, Lotus) from the file server's disk drive over the network to its own internal memory for processing.

The file server resources are seen as an extension of the personal computer's own resources. This extension of resources is done with software running at the workstation or client and is sometimes referred to as the workstation operating system (WOS), local operating system (LOS), or just plain disk operating system (DOS). Because the file server resources are seen as easily as local resources, applications and data can reside in either place and still be accessed by that client.

Finally, the workstation is a client of the server. Services are provided to the client workstation by the server. In this scenario, clients do not access each other's resources directly. They can only share resources available to them from a common server.

Data rate requirements are the last element of networked distributed computing. Under this scenario, a client on the network can go to a server and request a large application file to be downloaded to its local memory for processing. We are essentially moving a file from one computer to another. Once loaded, the client might not need to talk to the server again for additional resources for some time, perhaps not until it needs to save some data created by the application it just downloaded. The amount of data and the speed at which it must be transferred require very high and bursty data rates. Generally speaking, distributed network systems will employ network communication links that provide greater than 1 megabits per second (Mbits/sec) bandwidth capability (once again, more on Mbits/sec in chapter 2).

⇨ Cooperative computing

See Fig. 1-4.

✳ Characteristics of cooperative computing

Cooperative computing is sometimes also referred to as collaborative computing or client/server computing. With cooperative computing, one host (i.e., a personal computer, minicomputer, or mainframe) will run an application that requires processing support from an application running on another host. The two programs work in a client/server relationship to produce the end result or answer to the processing task.

Figure 1-4

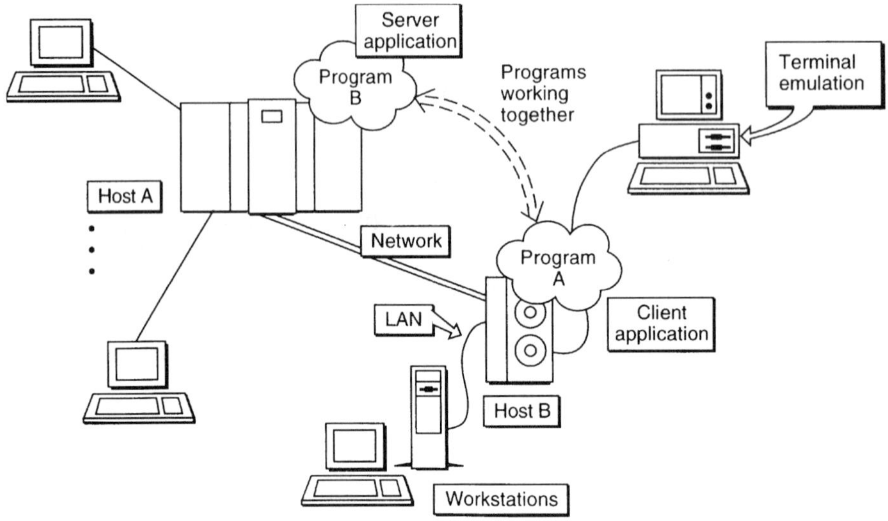

Cooperative computing. Learning Tree International

At least two computer systems are required for cooperative processing: one to run the client front-end application and one to run the database engine application. The client will formulate a question using a structured query language (i.e., how many staff are making more than $50,000.00). The client will then forward the question to the server host running the database engine for processing. The database engine application will then process the request searching the database for all records that meet this criteria. In this scenario, the database server is doing all the searching and sorting of the database, while the client CPU waits idle for a response. When the database server has compiled its answer, it forwards it back to the client for viewing.

There are several advantages to this form of processing, and they are salability and reduced network traffic: salability because we can install a database server with the appropriate processing power to processing large, computing-intensive requests, and reduced network traffic because only the question and final answer need to be communicated over the network. However, data rate needs can vary greatly in this area, depending on how well the client/server applications have been designed, although they are generally low.

An interesting aspect of cooperative computing is that both centralized and distributed processing systems can be employed together for processing. Also, dumb terminals connected to a centralized-processing-based host can make requests that will require support from applications running on distributed systems. This sometimes leads to the difficulty of determining which type of processing is actually being implemented—centralized or distributed. The answer can be found by looking at the specific application and determining which CPU is processing that actual application. In other words, the type of processing employed is determined by looking at the system that is running the application in question.

Type of computer networks

As we interconnect the different types of computing systems and processing models together, we can categorize the resulting entities into two groups: local area network and wide area network. Criteria used to categorize the networks generally include size, boundaries covered, data rates, and costs, although these distinctions are beginning to blur. Here we will review the characteristics of each, noting that the following chapters will discuss in detail the technologies and techniques that are implemented for each.

Local area network

See Fig. 1-5.

※ **Ownership**
One of the most prominent characteristics of a LAN is that you or your organization owns it. If you want to make changes to it, you simply go ahead and implement them. By owning it, you also determine to a large degree what the LAN will look like and what equipment you will use.

※ **Distance**
A LAN covers short distances. By this we mean within a building or at a campus site connecting several buildings. A typical LAN will connect all the computers within one office or offices spread over several floors in a corporate building.

Figure 1-5

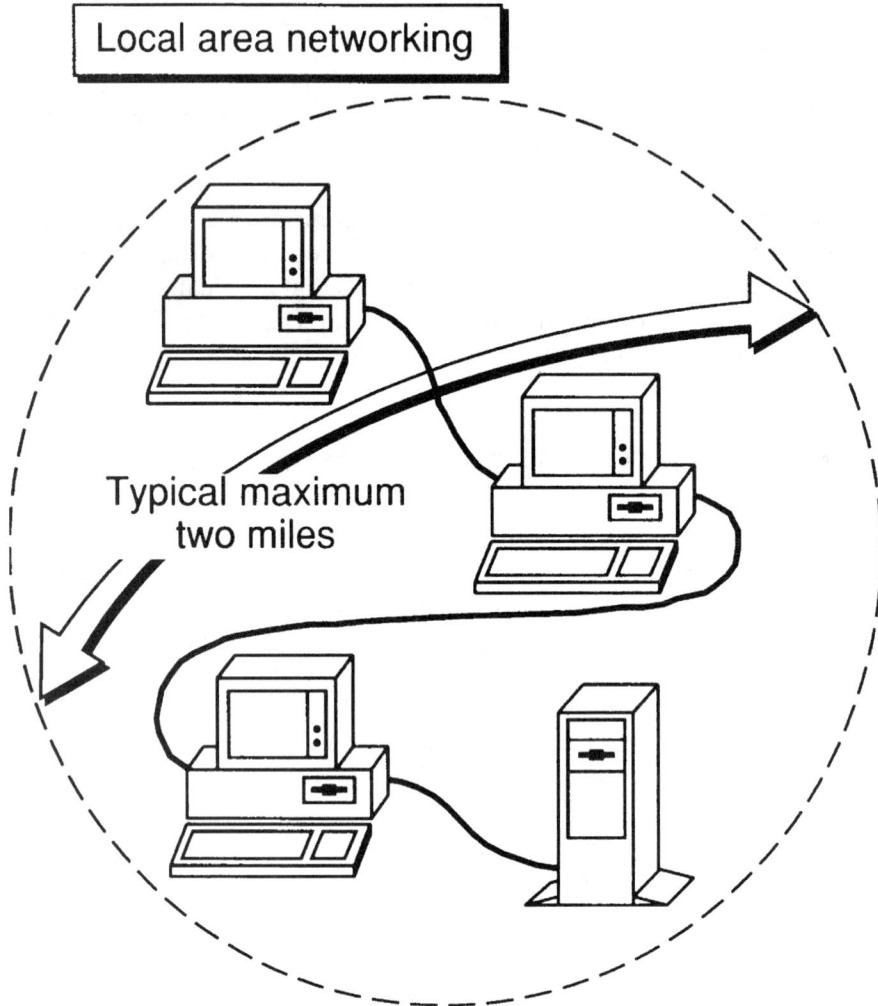

Local area network characteristics. Learning Tree International

❋ **Transmission media**

To interconnect all your computers together, you have many choices available to you. You can use a solid cable made out of wire (coax, twisted pair) or fiber optic, or you can employ devices that use radio waves, infrared light signals, or laser beams. While you have many media selections available, most LANs tend to use one media type for ease of operation and maintenance.

✳ Protocols

Protocols are like languages and rules of conduct and are used to allow computers to communicate to each other. As with the media, you have many choices as to the protocols you can use in your LAN. You can also use several protocols to communicate with different types of hosts on your network. Examples of protocols are Ethernet, Token Ring, ARCNET, and FDDI.

✳ Data rates

Before we state what the data rates usually are for a LAN, let's briefly review the type of traffic that is occurring over the network transmission media. We described earlier that a client workstation will download an application from the file server over the network. These applications can be very large in size taking up hundreds and even thousands of bytes of computer memory. On a stand-alone personal computer, applications are usually accessed from the internal hard disk drive which is quite fast.

We now move to downloading that same application from a file server. As a result, we need a fast enough data rate to get the entire application load in a reasonable amount of time before the user gives up. Therefore, data rates on LANs have always tended to be high, somewhere between 1 to 100 megabits per second (Mbits/sec). The current average networks use between 10 and 16 megabits per second data rates.

⇨ Metropolitan area network

See Fig. 1-6.

Metropolitan area networks (MANs) tend to be larger than LANs in that they cover larger boundaries or areas. While similar LAN technology is employed, MANs also employ different hardware and transmission media devices to achieve the wider distance coverage. In addition, MANs might only interconnect network sites on an as-required basis. MANs are usually a combination of LAN and WAN technology.

Figure 1-6

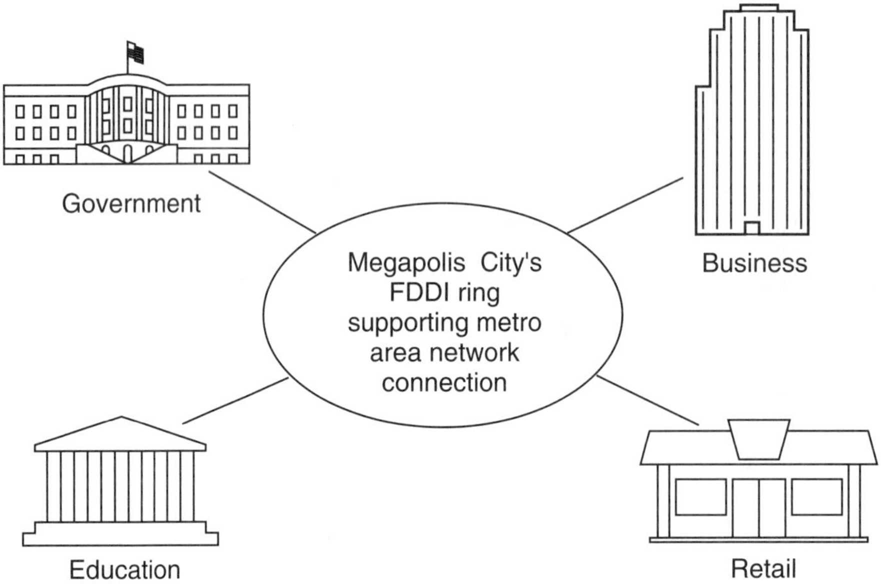

Metropolitan area network. Infomentat Inc.

✳ Ownership

Because we are now starting to cover larger distances, most often around or across an entire city, third-party interconnect companies (i.e., telephone companies) are brought in to facilitate the connection. These companies will use their own network infrastructure to interconnect your corporate networks or LANs.

✳ Media

Fewer media choices are available and are usually dictated by the interconnecting provider or telephone company. Choices usually include copper cable or fiber optics.

✳ Protocols

As with LANs, many protocols are available for MANs. In some cases, the hardware chosen will allow for the support of the same protocols you use within LAN environments (Ethernet, Token Ring, FDDI). In other cases you might have your protocols packaged inside of your interconnect provider's supported protocols.

❋ Data rates

MAN data rates can support the same high rate as LANs (100 Mbits/sec). However, they also support lower rates (down to 0.5 Mbits/sec) than typically found in LAN networks.

⇨ Wide area networks

See Fig. 1-7.

Figure 1-7

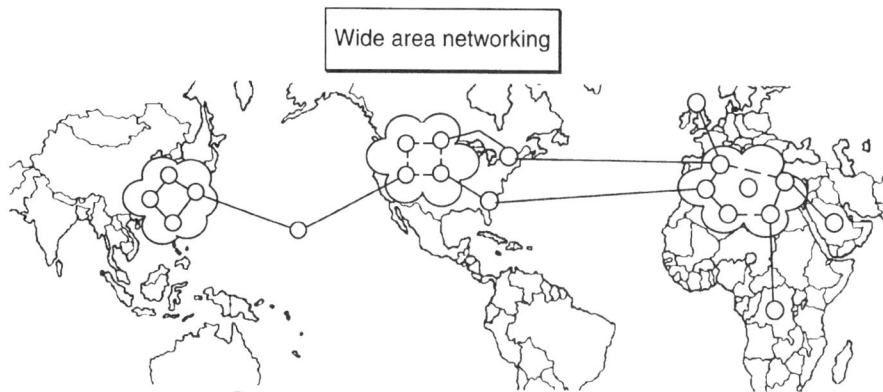

Wide area networking

- **Covers long distances**
- **Few media choices: telephone lines**
- **Protocols: X.25, TCP/IP**
- **Limited bandwidth: 2400 bits/sec, 64 kbits/sec**

Wide area network. Learning Tree International

❋ Ownership

Wide area networks are owned by interconnection providers such as telephone companies (AT&T, MCI, Sprint, Bell Canada, Unitel). These companies sell access to their networks for voice and data transmission. Our access to their networks is dictated by the types of service offerings they have and our data traffic requirements.

❋ Distances

Wide area networks cover longer distances, including across the country and around the world.

* **Transmission media**

  Because the interconnection companies own the networks, we generally tend to have little choice over what type of transmission media they use to transport our data traffic. Also, most telephone networks in place are still fairly old and use copper telephone lines, although this is changing rapidly with the implementation of fiber optics.

* **Protocols**

  Here again the interconnect company determines which protocols are available for you to connect your networks, and the choices are limited. TCP/IP and X.25 are the most common ones, although many new protocols and communication standards are being developed, like Integrated Services Digital Network (ISDN), ATM, Frame Relay, and SONET.

* **Data rates**

  Historically, data rates of WANs have tended to be low. Rates of 2400 bits/sec to 64 kilobits/sec were most common. Again, significant changes are taking place in this area, and the data rate lines between LANs, MANs, and WANs are becoming blurred. (See Fig. 1-8.)

⇨ Related network classifications

As networks are implemented within and throughout organizations, two additional distinctions have been developed to further identify network categories: enterprise and global networks. Although not always the case, these additional classifications are sometimes reserved for referring to WAN categories.

⇨ Enterprise networks

See Fig. 1-9.

Enterprise networks connect different parts of a large organization or company but do not connect the organization in question to other companies. Enterprise networks are used to provide access to shared

Figure 1-8

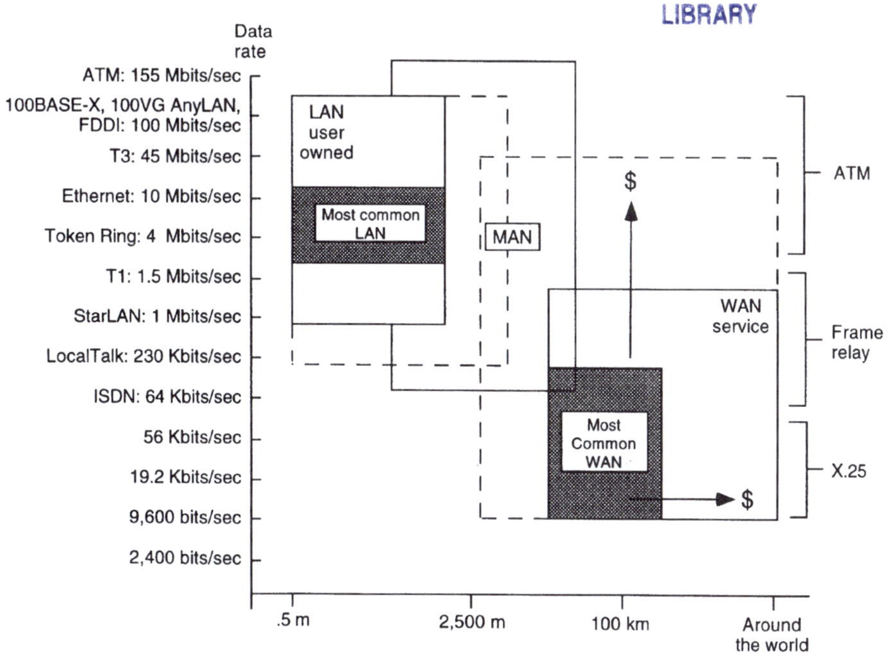

LANs, MANs, and WANs. Learning Tree International

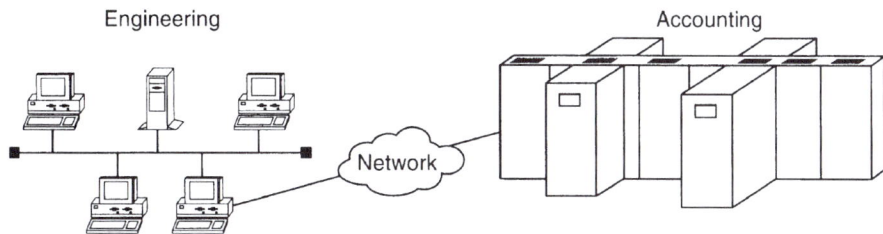

Figure 1-9

Enterprise networks. Learning Tree International

resources across departmental lines. They can also be used to connect branches and departments back to a central office computer system, usually a mainframe host. Enterprise networks do not cross country boundaries. Finally, both LAN, MAN, and WAN technology can be employed in this network distinction or classification.

An example of an enterprise network would be an organization that has offices in New York (head office), New Jersey (administration), Los

Angeles (development) and Dallas (sales). The main systems in New York and New Jersey are interconnected through MAN technology, and Los Angeles and Dallas connect back to the head office in New York through WAN technology. Each site has one or more department-based LANs.

Global networks

See Fig. 1-10.

Figure 1-10

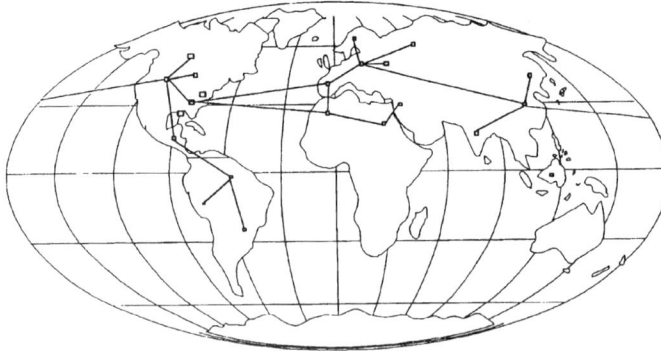

Global networks cross national, commercial, and government boundaries

Global networks. Learning Tree International

The global networks' designation is used in particular whenever an organization's network crosses national, commercial, and government boundaries. These networks are capable of supporting activities like international currency exchanges (banks, finance companies), electronic data interchange (EDI), and international time zone synchronization. The last characteristic of a global network is that it can span several organizations.

An example of a global network would be a superstore of retail goods. The store will have clerks monitoring shelf inventory levels of products they sell. As the clerk enters the number of products available for resale, the number is compared to a predetermined minimum inventory level in the store's main computer system. If it is below the minimum, the store issues a request for more inventory from the superstore warehouse. The warehouse computer system gathers all the orders for a specific product and sends an electronic data interchange order directly to the manufacturer of the product, listing which stores require reshipments and the number of items needed. The manufacturer could be in the same country or on the other side of the globe. The manufacturer then ships the needed items directly to each store and sends an invoice via electronic data interchange directly to the superstore head-office accounting department. The superstore pays for the received items via electronic funds transfer.

⇨ The elements of networking

The basic elements involved in computer networking can be reduced to three. However, this simplification should not understate the importance of developing a clear and concise understanding of them, for the rest of this book is based on these three areas. Every aspect of computer networking can be grouped under the following elements:

1 Pathway.

2 Rules.

3 Sharing.

See Fig. 1-11.

✳ Pathway

At the base of every network is a pathway, a way to get information moved from one computer to another. The pathway can be considered the lowest common denominator on the network. It is at this level that we use transmission media and electronic signals to physically connect stations together. Transmission media include physical cable or wireless technologies to transmit signals to one another. It is important to note that while you might be able to transmit signals to another workstation, this is no guarantee that the applications running on the workstation will be able to understand the message your signals are carrying.

Figure 1-11

Activity	Component	Characteristic
Sharing	Network services	Communications between individual components, typically applications
Rules	Protocols	Rules and conventions to facilitate the communications process
Pathway	Media and signals	Elements of signal transmission including media

The elements of networking. Learning Tree International

The pathway deals with the type of cable or wireless technology, the way this media is physically connected to the computer system, and how the signal is actually transmitted on the cable or through the air.

When you place a phone call to someone, you establish a pathway between the two of you. To do so you use the telephone (connecting device) and the telephone company's cables (transmission media).

❋ Rules

In the computer world, there is no margin for error. Therefore, strict rules must be defined and adhered to by communicating entities. Rules use protocols and conventions to ensure that the communication process is facilitated successfully. These same protocols and conventions are also used to determine when communications are not completed successfully.

Protocols are like languages in that they allow us to communicate with each other. However, they also determine how we speak to each other—when you speak and when I speak.

Following the previous example with the telephone call, once someone answers the phone, you need to ensure that you are speaking the same language. When two people talk, there is usually a polite, formal convention (although not always followed) that when one person talks, the other person listens. If both speak at the same time, the convention and protocols assist us in trying to recover the conversation to a point at which we can start again. Computers work the same way but are more exacting with the rules.

✳ Sharing

The purpose of the network is to share services or resources. Basic network services include file and printer sharing. There are also many other types of services that can be made available on the network. At this top level of the network, services are provided by accessing applications running on the service provider or server. To access a service, a workstation client needs to use a requester or redirector application.

A distinction can therefore be made between the three types of entities providing or requesting services:

1 Servers providing the services.

2 Clients requesting the services.

3 Peers that can both provide services to other clients and request services of other servers.

An important distinction is made here to emphasize that the services are not computers themselves but rather the applications that run on the computers (servers, clients, and peers).

Continuing on with our telephone call example, imagine we have just called an operator in another country. At this stage, the telephone companies have established a physical connection (pathway) between our two telephones, the operator speaks our language (rules), and now we are going to ask for directory assistance (sharing of information).

In this example, we are the client and the operator is the server working in a server/centric relationship. However, if the operator asked us what the weather was like where we are, we would be providing the operator (client) with a service, and we would assume the role of server (peer to peer).

In summary, networking applies to the ability to share information and resources (services). Networking is employed in LANs, MANs, and WANs to accomplish the previously discussed tasks. Three elements are required to implement a network: a pathway between two computers, rules to facilitate the communication process, and a service to be shared. In the next section we will review what kinds of services a network can provide.

⇨ Computer network services

> ➤ Define the roles of clients, servers, and peers as they relate to computer networks.

> ➤ List and describe several network services.

> ➤ Identify and describe the functions and other aspects associated with network services.

> ➤ Identify the appropriate network services for a given organizational scenario.

> ➤ Given a centralized or distributed network architecture, determine how a specified network service is affected.

⇨ Components of a network

❈ Server components
The term server is very appropriate as we talk about the systems on the network that share resources as they service our request for access to the information or service. Servers fall into several categories, including file servers, print servers, and database servers, to name a few.

A file server shares data and applications that are stored on its storage subsystem. A print server allows clients to access printers located on the network. And a database server is a specialized file server for storing and processing database files (database engines). Several other potential server services will be explored later.

✳ **Client components**

Clients, or workstations, are personal computers that access the resources on the network. As stated previously, the network resources are provided by the servers. Client systems come in many varieties and platforms, including IBM-compatible PCs, Apple Macintoshes, and Intel and Motorola-based Unix systems.

Clients, however, don't necessarily have to be personal computers. Any device that talks to a server for resources or services can be considered a client. For example, a security monitoring device that authorizes access for someone by referring to a server's access list can also be considered a client.

✳ **Peers**

Peers are computers on the network that can perform both the function of server and client. They can also do this simultaneously. Using Novell Personal NetWare (NetWare Lite), a personal computer can be in use by a user running an application locally while also allowing another user on the network to copy files to its hard disk drive or access its local printer.

⇨ PC network categories: File-server-centric networks and peer-to-peer networks

The types of networks that these three component or entities might reside on include "peer-to-peer" and "server-centric" networks.

✳ **File-server-centric networks**
See Fig. 1-12.

Figure 1-12

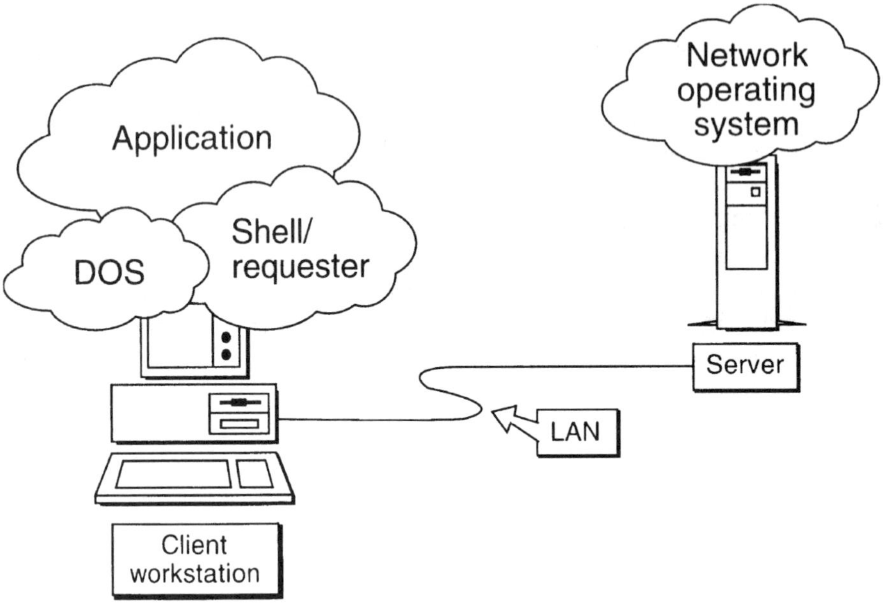

Anatomy of a PC network: file server centric. Learning Tree International

File-server-centric components and services In server-centric networks, each computer entity takes on a specific role in the communication process. One computer entity will take on the role of file server or server and is dedicated to doing only that role. To access a server's resources, the other entity must act as a client using a redirector or requester application.

Examples of server-centric networks include:

➢ Novell NetWare 3.x and 4.x.

➢ Banyan Vines.

➢ IBM LAN Server.

➢ Microsoft Windows NT (Application Server).

✳ **Peer-to-peer networks**
See Fig. 1-13.

Figure 1-13

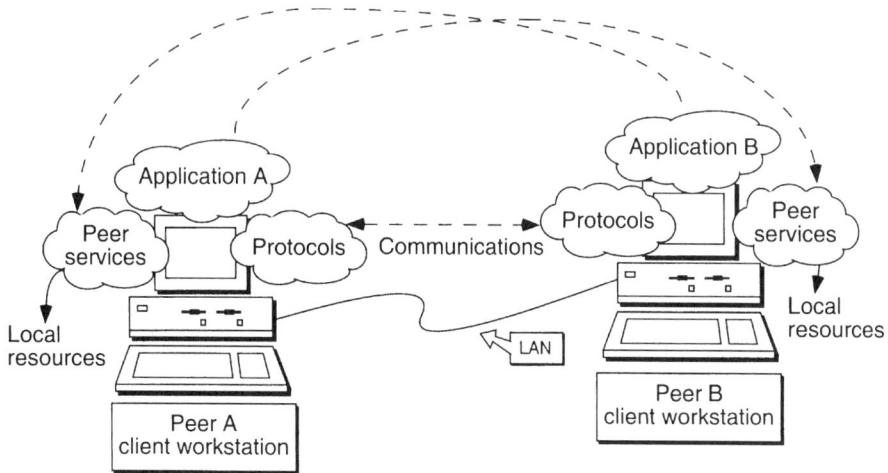

Anatomy of a PC network: peer to peer. Learning Tree International

In peer-to-peer networks, an entity can act as both a server and a client at the same time. An example of a peer-to-peer network is when you are using your personal computer to access an application and data, and, at the same time, another user is accessing your hard disk drive's file system over the network. The software you use on both personal computers will facilitate this communication process and sharing of services. Example software packages include:

➤ Microsoft Windows for Work groups.

➤ Artisoft Lantastic.

➤ Novell Personal NetWare (Lite).

➤ Microsoft Windows NT.

Of the two types of networks, server-centric implementations have tended to be the most popular in terms of ease of use, market share, and installed base.

Summary table of centralized versus distributed network services

See Fig. 1-14.

Figure 1-14

Characteristic	Centralized services	Distributed services
Typical type	File-server based	Peer to peer
Control of resources	Centralized	Decentralized
Server specialization	Network operating system on server	Peer to peer; no server specialization
Typical products	NetWare, LAN Server, VINES, NTAS	Windows for Workgroups, Macs, Windows NT
Benefits	Better resources security and protection; faster data sharing; record and file locking; easier management	No single point of failure; good use of client resources
Concerns	Server is single point of failure	Security and management of resources is difficult
Application	Larger departmental and enterprisewide networks	Small workgroups (6–7 computers)

Centralized versus distributed network services. Learning Tree International

⇨ Functions of a server

See Fig. 1-15.

✳ File services

See Fig. 1-16.

File services provide the ability to store, retrieve, transfer, and archive data files. Files are of many different types, including applications, text data, graphic or image, and sound files. Also, with the implementation of graphical user interfaces, data and application files have increased in size significantly. Keeping them on a central file server allows you to access and move them around on the network faster. Part of the capability of the network operating system (NOS) is to ensure that file services are accessed by many users without a conflict. To accomplish this task, the file service will provide file and record-locking features. Although file services are usually available on a NOS, they are not

Figure 1-15

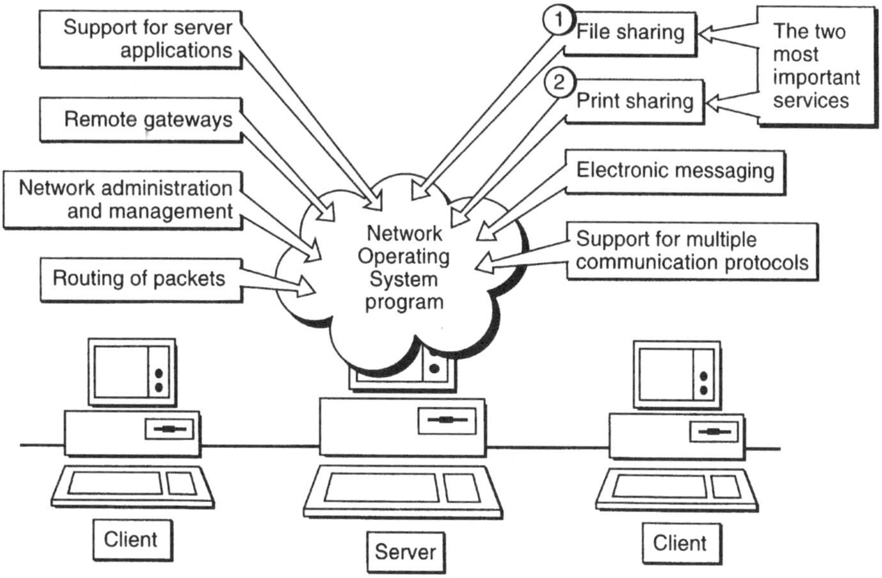

Functions of a server. Learning Tree International

Figure 1-16

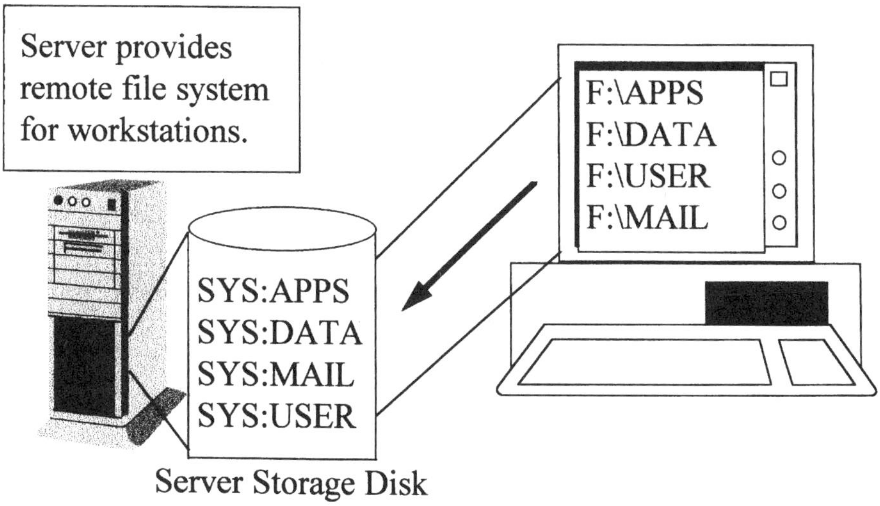

File services. Infomentat Inc.

Although file services are usually available on a NOS, they are not always required, as some servers provide services other than filing.

The file service might also act as simply a store-and-forward system, where it simply receives a file, stores it temporarily, and then transfers it on to its next destination. This form of file service is used heavily in electronic (e-mail) systems. Data migration also uses store-and-forward techniques to move infrequently used files from a server hard-drive disk onto a lower-cost storage device such as an optical disk or tape unit. Data migration employs three types of storage devices. Online storage is a fast local-server hard disk drive. Nearline storage is a slower local storage system such as an optical disk drive. Off-line storage supports media like tapes that are usually taken out of the device that is local to the server (i.e., tape unit).

A more recent example of the store-and-forward feature of file services is file update synchronization. This technique stores files in several places and uses time and data stamp comparisons to copy the most recent file to other systems. File update synchronization is very useful for mobile or nomadic computing when users work on files while traveling but wish to ensure that updated copies are moved to their personal storage areas. Applications such as NetWare Directory Services and Lotus Notes uses forms of file update synchronization.

The advantages of using file services on a server are central storage of shared data, centralized backup (archiving) of crucial data, and efficient use of computer hardware. Centralize management of access to (or denial of) a file is also a main feature of file services. However, the greatest disadvantage often sighted about centrally located file services is the "having all your eggs in one basket" syndrome. All of your crucial files are on one server, and if the server providing the file service is unavailable, clients cannot access the data.

✳ **Print services**
See Fig. 1-17.

Print services is the second of two main services that most servers provide (file services being the first). Print services allow clients to access shared printers distributed throughout the network. A print server receives a print job from a client and spools or queues the job in

Figure 1-17

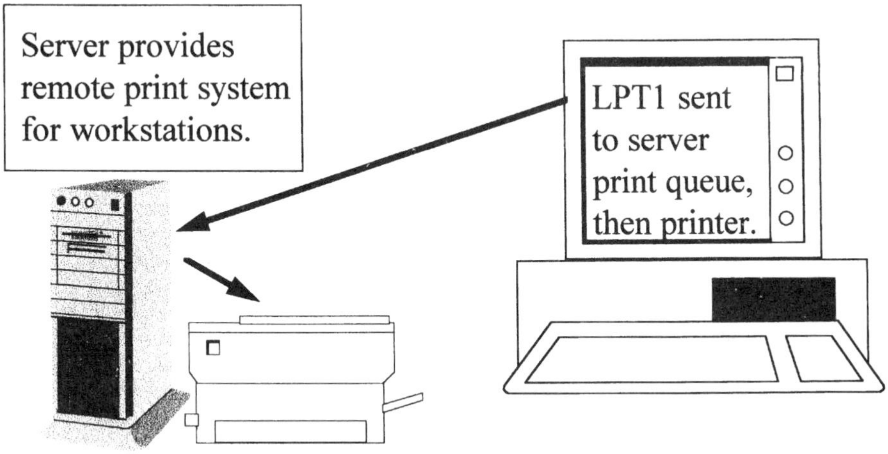

Server provides remote print system for workstations.

LPT1 sent to server print queue, then printer.

Print services. Infomentat Inc.

the form of a file on the server's hard disk drive. Each spool or queue is serviced by one or more printers. The print server monitors the availability of the printer and, when free, forwards the print job to the printer, usually over the network pathways. By sharing printer devices, we increase efficient use of hardware and can also share expensive, high-end equipment such as color printers and plotters.

Another major advantage of print services is that they eliminate distance limitations. When used on LANs, MANs, and WANs, network print services can allow a user to submit a print job anywhere in the organization, regardless of its physical location.

Printer services also include shared fax services. Special hardware and software allow users to print to a fax queue. The print server then forwards the fax job to a modem for transmission to a remote fax. Many new systems are available that provide dedicated fax services on the network, but these devices have been classified as print servers because users are still required to print the document in order to have it faxed.

A common capability of print services is to allow multiple platforms (Unix, DOS/Windows, Macintosh) to share printers throughout the network. Under this scenario, a Unix workstation can submit a print job to a Unix system spool and in turn have the job sent to a NetWare print queue/printer.

⇨ Message services

See Fig. 1-18.

Figure 1-18

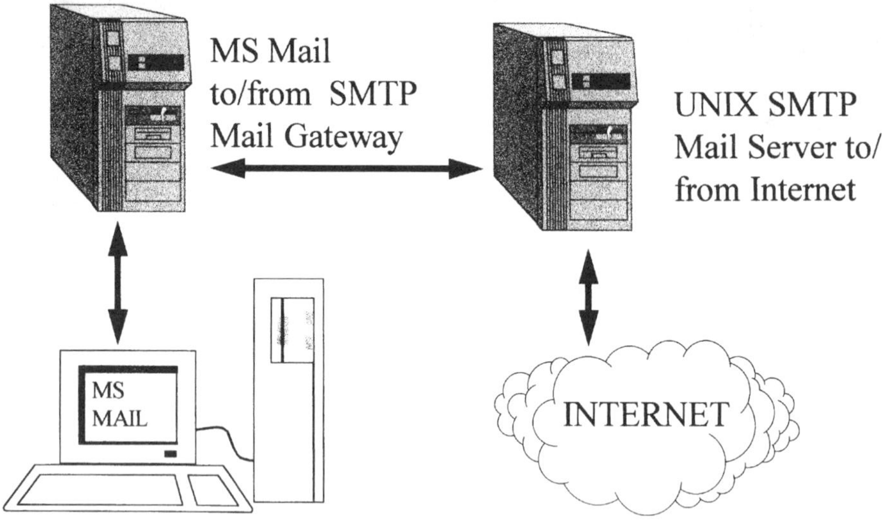

Message services. Infomentat Inc.

Message services provide the following benefits on a network:

1 Share mail messages and files.

2 Integrate voice mail capability with existing electronic mail.

3 Access object-oriented applications distributed throughout the network.

4 Use work-flow-based applications.

5 Manage network user and device address directories.

Message services make use of the server's file service store-and-forward capability. The main aspects of message services are the transmission, reception, and storage of a variety of document formats: text, binary files (compiled applications), digitized voice and video, and graphics. Electronic mail (e-mail) is the most popular example of a message service. However, voice mail (sound files) can also be stored and forwarded by message services.

This type of service also goes beyond your basic store-and-forward systems. It allows applications to actively share a variety of document and file types. Word processors can route forms to be completed by other users on the network. The message server is responsible for routing the form to the appropriate user on the network. The form might include links to graphic images or voice-annotated files that the recipient can pull up upon request. This is called work flow management.

Object-oriented document linking or embedding is used to facilitate this form of functionality. Object-oriented applications are programs that call upon other applications to facilitate the request. An example of this feature is common in messaging applications today like Microsoft Mail or Novell Groupwise, where you receive a mail message with an attached word-processing or spreadsheet document. When the attached document is selected for viewing with the e-mail application, the associated document application (word processing or spreadsheet) is automatically started. In effect, a message is sent to the operating system to start the application. Workstation operating systems and applications are moving quickly towards the object-linking technology.

Message services accomplish much of their functionality through addressing and as a result need to continually update directory databases containing this information. Directory services maintain lists of resources available on the network, including users. The information is stored in database files and distributed on servers located throughout the network. Directory services use file synchronization methods to distribute database file updates to other servers. With this feature, a user can access the directory to find out where a particular resource is located. In turn, the directory service can be used to determine if the user has sufficient rights to access the resource. Examples of directory services include Novell's NetWare Directory Services and Banyan Vines Street Talk.

Figure 1-19

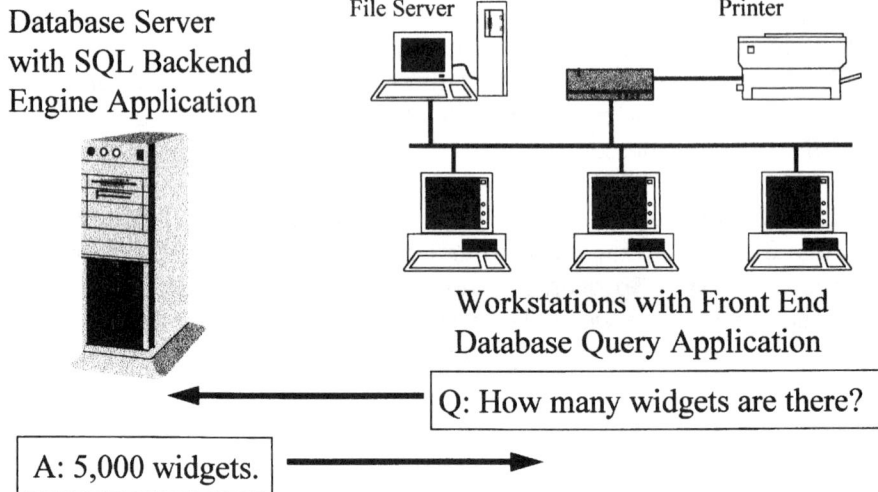

Database Server with SQL Backend Engine Application

File Server

Printer

Workstations with Front End Database Query Application

Q: How many widgets are there?

A: 5,000 widgets.

Database services. Infomentat Inc.

✳ Database services

See Fig. 1-19.

Database services are used mainly in client/server database systems. With database services, database files are stored on a dedicated server. However, clients do not access the database files directly. Instead, they forward a request or question to the database service. Their question is processed by the server's CPU, and only the answer is returned to them.

Network database servers provide several advantages:

1 Allow for specialized systems that are tuned towards intensive database functions to store, search, and retrieve database records.

2 Act as a centralized or distributed repository for data.

3 Manage data security.

4 Increase database access performance.

5 Reduce network traffic.

6 Provide multiplatform (Unix, DOS, Macintosh) access to data.

To understand how client/server database services work and why they are advantageous in network environments, we need to look at how older database systems work. Original databases, when used on a network, were only acting in a file service method. The client accessed the database application from a server and made a request. If the request required searching for specific records, each record in the database had to be transmitted from the server over the network to the client for processing. All records that met the criteria were forwarded back to the server and saved in a temporary file, where an index was also created. The client then accessed the file from the server. The main point is that the client had to process each record and created a lot of network traffic to accomplish this.

As stated initially, with client/server database services, the client only has to formulate the request. This is usually done with a structured query language (SQL) capable client front-end application. The database service server processes the request and does not have to be the same type of computer as the client. The server can be a special, multiprocessor-based server with lots of memory and fast hard disk drives dedicated to this task. There is reduced network traffic because only the question is forwarded, and the final answer or initial parts of it are sent back to the client.

There are two aspects of network database services: coordinating distributed and replication. Banks are a good example of companies that use distributed data as a way of separating information processing between departments. With this type of network database service, data is controlled by one department but shared with other departments. Although the data might be distributed and stored in different areas of the organization's network, it appears as one large corporate database. However, information in specific areas of the database are designated as being controlled by a particular group. So that although other departments will be able to access the data, only the "owner group" can actually change the data.

Replication is a database service technique that has become popularized by applications like Lotus Notes. Local data is much faster to access than remote data. With replication, a duplicate of the database is stored at other database servers on the network and is updated as changes occur in the original database file. A more advanced level of replication allows for local copies of the database records to be updated and individually forwarded or synchronized with the master or original database.

※ **Application services**
See Fig. 1-20.

Figure 1-20

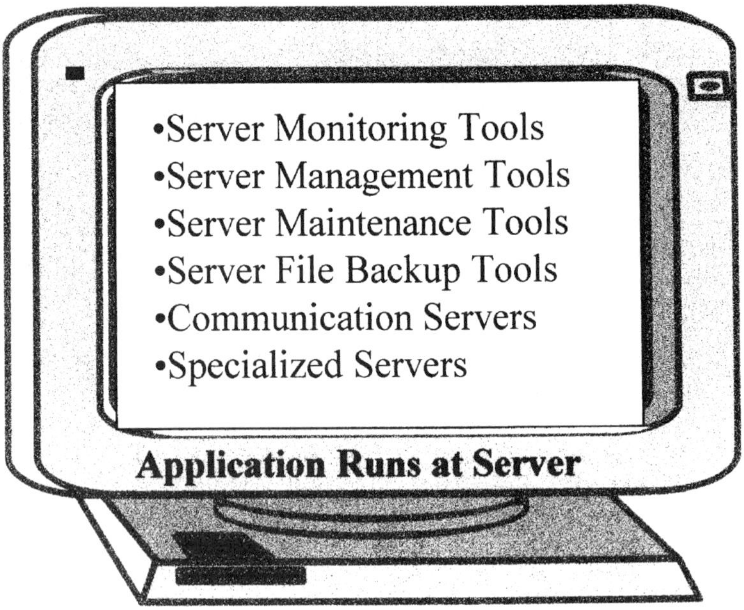

•Server Monitoring Tools
•Server Management Tools
•Server Maintenance Tools
•Server File Backup Tools
•Communication Servers
•Specialized Servers

Application Runs at Server

Application services. Infomentat Inc.

Application services share processing power by computers running cooperating components of an application on different machines or platforms. In this sense, it is similar to client/server database services in that a client makes a request for some form of processing, and the server performs the raw computing and returns the answer.

A very good example of application services is X-Windows-based applications in the Unix environment. A Unix X client will request an application server to take its raw data from a spreadsheet and compute a resulting graph of the data. The X server will perform the calculations and create the graph itself. It will then forward the resulting graphic answer to the X client.

Servers tend to become specialized in this scenario and can be run on computer hardware processing systems that best meet the requirement. In addition, the hardware can be scalable to grow with increased processing demands.

Other examples of specialized services include communication servers such as modem pools and mainframe access gateways. Before these types of servers were available, each user required individual installation of hardware to perform this function, which tended to be expensive and inefficient. Communication servers allow network clients to share this type of resource based on the concept that not everyone will need access to the modem or mainframe at the same time.

⇨ Workshop

This workshop will help you develop skills in identifying the types of network services and computing environments that are employed in an existing network. This prepares you to assess what network services are needed in particular situations, given end-user requirements.

This workshop and subsequent workshops are based on the case study material for the fictitious company International Technologies. Familiarize yourself with the case study network system diagrams by reading the material in appendix A.

⇨ Exercise

For each network listed in Fig. 1-21, indicate the network services that are employed, the products or protocols that are used to provide the services, and the type of computing—centralized, distributed, or

Figure 1-21

Network	Network services	Product being used	Type of computing
San Jose Building 1 Network B			
San Jose Building 1 Network A			
San Jose Building 2 Network C			
San Jose Building 4 Network A			

Workshop exercise. Learning Tree International

cooperative—that is employed. Also, if a LAN is used, indicate whether the network is file server based or peer to peer.

⇨ Test your understanding

The purpose of this section is to help reinforce the information you have just reviewed. Proceed through the various sections and write down your answers to the questions. The answers are in appendix B. Also see Figs. 1-22, 1-23, and 1-24.

1. Describe:

    Centralized computing: _____

    Distributed computing: _____

    Cooperative computing: _____

2. Describe the characteristics of:

   Local area networks: _____

   Wide area networks: _____

   Metropolitan area networks: _____

3. What are the elements of computer networks?

   _____, _____, _____

4. What is the difference between enterprise networks and global networks? _____

   _____

   _____

5. Describe the characteristics of:

   Servers: _____

   Clients: _____

   Peers: _____

6. What is the difference between file-server-based nets and peer-to-peer nets? _____

   _____

7. What are the popular types of network services and their characteristics?

   a. _____, _____

   b. _____, _____

   c. _____, _____

   d. _____, _____

   e. _____, _____

Figure 1-22

Concept	Description
Prenetwork computing	Room-sized computers, CPU and RAM, early machines used punched-card input. Monolithic. Mini and mainframes endpoints of evolution.
Islands of automation	Use of specialized computers for different parts of an organization. These computer systems could not communicate with each other and needed integration.
Early network development	Connected islands of automation. Monolithic (homogeneous) networks dependent on a vendor's technology. Examples of early networks: Digital DNA and IBM SNA. Later, development of TCP/IP by the ARPAnet technical community crossed manufacturer boundaries with generic protocol solutions. At the same time, personal computers were developed.
Heterogeneous networks	Standards for interoperable protocols. IEEE and ISO. Purpose was to move data between dissimilar computers seamlessly.
Enterprise networks	Connect all parts of an organization together. Includes LANs and WANs.
Global networks	Networks that cross organizational and national boundaries.

History of computer networks. Learning Tree International

Figure 1-23

Concept	Description
Centralized computing	All processing is done on a central computer. Data communications are used to connect I/O devices such as terminals and printers.
Distributed computing	Use of multiple smaller computers to run applications. They may be connected into networks for printing and file sharing.
Cooperative computing	The application or data processing task may be distributed over several computers. May be called *collaborative* computing.
Local area networks	Data communications at high data rates over short distances (within a building or group of buildings in a campus). User owned.
Metropolitan area networks	Data communications within a city. Relatively high data rates, often purchased as a service from a third party.
Wide area networks	Data communication over distances longer than a city, often spanning the globe. Purchased as a service from third-party providers.
Enterprise networks	Connect all parts of an organization. Includes LANs and WANs.
Global networks	Cross organizational and national boundaries.

Elements of computer networks. Learning Tree International

Figure 1-24

Component/service	Characteristic
Servers	Computers that provide network services to other computers. Principally they provide file and print services.
Clients	Computers that consume network services. Typically they run end-user applications.
Peers	Computers with end-user applications that may also provide services.
File services	High-performance file transfer. Centralized file storage and file sharing. Archiving and backup.
Print services	Client printing to shared printers via print queues, typically on servers. Includes shared fax services.
Message services	End-user message passing and routing. Includes E-mail, voice mail, linked-object documents, and directory services.
Application services	Sharing processing power between client and server. Application components run on both client and server machines and process cooperatively.
Database services	Specialized servers that store and retrieve data for clients via queries. Typically use the SQL database language.

Network services and components. Learning Tree International

⇨ **Practice exam questions**

1. Networks that connect virtually all parts of an organization are called:
   A. Enterprise networks
   B. Global networks
   C. Wide area networks
   D. Local area networks

2. Networks that span organizational and geographical boundaries are called:
   A. Enterprise networks
   B. Global networks
   C. Wide area networks
   D. Local area networks

3. Database services provide what additional functionality to networks?
   A. Salability
   B. File transfers
   C. Print queuing
   D. Query processing

4. Which function might not be considered part of printing services of a network?
   A. Fax services
   B. File transfers
   C. Queuing
   D. Printing

5. Which is not a characteristic of a local area network?
   A. A variety of cabling media is used
   B. Data rates are in the range of 1 to 100 Mbits/sec
   C. Distances spanned are short, typically within a building or campus
   D. It uses very few protocols

6. Which of the following is an aspect of database services?
   A. File transfer
   B. Replication
   C. Electronic Mail
   D. Image processing

7. Which of the following is not considered an aspect of message services?
   A. Work flow management
   B. Electronic mail
   C. Directory services
   D. Fax services

8. Print services provide which two of the following features?
   A. Fax services
   B. Queuing
   C. Limited access to specialized printers
   D. Store and forward services

9. File services support mobile (nomadic) computing: True or False?
   A. True
   B. False

10. In peer-to-peer networks:
    A. A computer can be a client or a server, but not both
    B. Security and management of resources is difficult
    C. A centralized server provides services to clients
    D. Is intended to be used by large groups of users

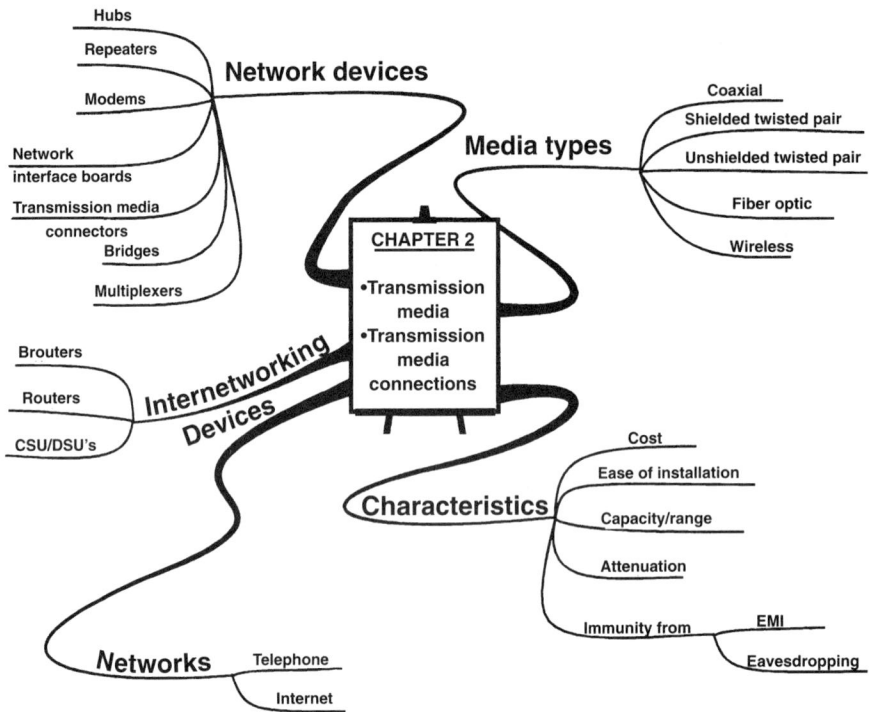

Hubs

Repeaters

Network devices

Modems

Coaxial

Shielded twisted pair

Media types

Unshielded twisted pair

Network
interface boards

Fiber optic

Transmission media
connectors

Wireless

Bridges

Multiplexers

CHAPTER 2

•Transmission
media
•Transmission
media
connections

Brouters

*Internetworking
Devices*

Routers

CSU/DSU's

Cost

Ease of installation

Characteristics

Capacity/range

Attenuation

Immunity from

EMI

Eavesdropping

Networks

Telephone

Internet

2

Transmission media and network hardware

⇨ Introduction

Media and network hardware are the components that bind a network together. Without them, the computers on people's desks would not be able to attach to networks. A wire is not always required. In certain cases the transmission medium is a radio link with no existing wire.

There is a wide variety of media types actively being used to connect local area networks: coaxial, twisted pair, and fiber optics. Some computers today are connected via "wireless networks," of which the radio link is just one form of connection. This chapter explores satellite, infrared, and laser connections and other unbounded media types.

The local area network connectivity solution is just one part of the story. Wide area networks (WANs) are required to connect across town or across the country. An investigation of the telephone system and the services offered by telephone providers is needed to understand WAN technology.

This chapter also describes new approaches to telephone service, such as ISDN. Since the existing telephone system was created and is intended to support voice communications only, we need devices to send out data over voice lines. X.25 is the heart of a class of network services called public switched data networks. This chapter also describes other connectivity devices such as bridges, routers, and repeaters. Keep in mind that the intent of this chapter is to describe the functionality and to help recognize these devices by sight and function, not to learn how they work. The function of these devices is described in depth in later chapters.

This chapter groups the CNE exam objectives that deal with transmission, public networks, and connectivity devices. As in chapter 1, the objectives given by Novell are stated at the beginning of each section to aid in study for the CNE exam.

The material in this chapter will help to identify media types and connectors by sight, describe their functions, and tell where each component fits within a network. The chapter will also help to place complex devices such as routers and bridges within an internetwork.

Knowledge gained is tested with a variety of exercises at the end of the chapter: a workshop for identification of components, a fill-in-the-blanks exercise for concept identification and key facts, memorization, and a sample quiz of multiple-choice questions to practice test-taking skills.

⇨ Transmission media

⇨ CNE exam objectives

➢ Define transmission media as it relates to computer networks.

➢ List and describe common transmission media.

➢ Identify and describe the characteristics of each transmission medium, including cost, ease of installation, capacity, attenuation, and immunity from interference.

➢ Given an organizational scenario, identify the appropriate transmission media that meet the business objectives.

⇨ Media types

There are two categories of network media: guided and unguided. Guided media are also referred to as bounded media. Bounded media describes the situation where a material conduit is present between the communicating computers. The conduit could be a pair of wires or a glass fiber. In bounded media, the signal is constrained to traveling where the medium is present. Engineers strive to design bounded media such that there is very little stray electromagnetic radiation from the cables that would interfere with the operation of electronic devices by others nearby. A good example of a bounded medium is coaxial cable.

Unguided or unbounded media, on the other hand, refers to broadcasting a modulated electromagnetic wave through free space. This type of transmission requires an antenna and does not need a medium for propagation. The electromagnetic waves emitted by the sender can just as easily travel in the vacuum of space as they do through the space between desks in an office. Good examples of unbounded media are point-to-point microwave links such as those between buildings. Other good examples are satellite links and cellular phone connections. Leaving the office environment, unbounded media connections make up "wireless networks."

In both bounded and unbounded media, there is electromagnetic wave propagation. In the first case, bounded, the wave is constrained. In the second case, unbounded, the wave propagates through space without the aid of a medium.

The frequency of the electromagnetic energy is another differentiating factor between the media types. For certain bounded media, such as coaxial and twisted pair, the frequency of the electromagnetic wave is low. In the case of a glass fiber, the frequencies of the propagating electromagnetic wave are in the optical range. Frequencies in the optical range are so high that we don't often refer to the frequency. We refer to its complement, the wavelength of the light. Keep in mind that the product of frequency and wavelength is equal to a constant, the speed of light. So specifying one parameter, either the frequency or wavelength, specifies the other. There are three types of bounded media: twisted pair, coaxial, and fiber optic.

⇨ Twisted pair

Twisted-pair wiring is by far the most popular way to wire a building today. It is easy to use twisted-pair wiring to connect a building in an organized manner and to manage the install-cable plant afterwards. These facts alone account for the popularity of twisted-pair wiring. Twisted-pair wiring of high quality has a broad range of applications. It can be used to wire voice devices, telephones, and computers.

Twisted-pair wiring consists of one or more pairs of copper wires twisted around each other. These pairs are bundled inside an insulating sheath. The most common variety of cable contains four pairs of wires. Twisted-pair wiring is available in two types: shielded and unshielded. Shielded twisted-pair (STP) wiring has a metal protective shield around the cable pairs within the insulating sheath. This type of cable provides better noise immunity than most types of unshielded cables. Noise immunity is achieved only if the shield, which is meant to be grounded, is properly terminated at the connectors. STP wiring is most often found in IBM Token Ring networks.

A more popular variety of twisted-pair cabling is the unshielded type. Unshielded twisted-pair (UTP) wiring is used by phone companies to wire telephone systems within a building. It has recently been adopted for high-speed data communication. UTP is available in many grades or categories of cabling. Table 2-1 describes Category 1 through Category 5 UTP wiring.

Category 3 cabling is the most popular for wiring within a building. It does an excellent job for voice communication and for terminal and Ethernet data networks. For some of the newer, high-speed networks, it is necessary to install Category 5 UTP cabling, which supports data rates up to 100 Mbps. Category 5 cable has better noise immunity than the rest and has a noise characteristic equal to shielded twisted pair.

**Unshielded Twisted-Pair Cables
Classified by Category and Characteristic**

Table 2-1

UTP cable type	Maximum data rate supported	Application
Category 1	1 Mbps	Voice and low-speed data applications
Category 2	4 Mbps	Voice and data, 4 Mbps Token Ring, ARCNET, IBM System/3X, AS/400 over UTP RS-232 and RS-422 applications
Category 3	10 Mbps	10 Base-T networks, voice and data
Category 4	20 Mbps	Voice and data networks, 16-Mbps Token Ring
Category 5	100 Mbps	High-speed desk-to-hub use, 100 Base-X, 10 Base-T, 16-Mbps Token Ring

Figure 2-1 shows examples of shielded and unshielded cable types. Almost every type of network adapter in use today has a way to connect using twisted-pair wiring. Some network types, such as Token Ring, run over twisted-pair wiring since they were created that way. Ethernet, on the other hand, was created to run over coaxial cable,

Figure 2-1

- ## Shielded twisted pair

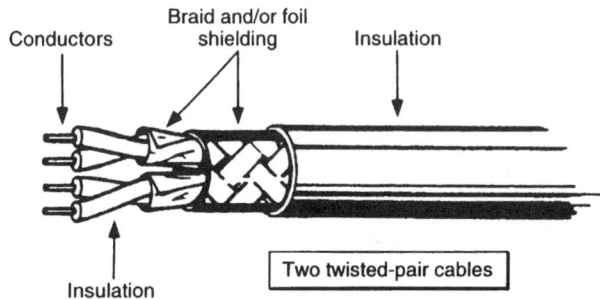

- ## Multiple-pair cables

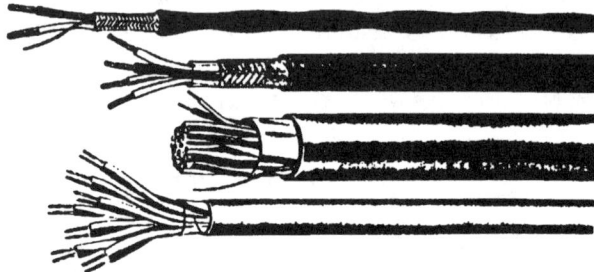

Examples of shielded and unshielded twisted-pair cables. Learning Tree International

but now sports a UTP connection that has become the preferred way of attaching Ethernet adapters to the network. Even FDDI network cards, which were created to run over fiber-optic cabling, have a version of a network card that can be attached to the network via shielded twisted pair. FDDI running over twisted pair is sometimes referred to as CDDI (copper distributed data interface) or TPDDI (twisted-pair distributed data interface). ARCNET, LocalTalk, and synchronous and asynchronous terminals all can be wired with twisted-pair wiring, which demonstrates the universality of the medium.

Category cable classifications

Category 1 cabling is meant to support telephone service and low-speed data transmission, like that found in terminal networks. Category 2 UTP is meant to support ISDN (64-Kbps), 56-Kbps lease lines, and T-1 lease lines running at 1.54 Mbps. Category 3 cabling (UTP cabling) has transmission characteristics up to 60 MHz, which includes support for 10Base-T Ethernet at 10 Mbps. Category 4 UTP wiring has transmission characteristics up to 20 MHz, which allows it to support 16-Mbps Token Ring. The best unshielded twisted-pair wiring is Category 5, which has characteristics up to 100 MHz and supports data rates up to 100 Mbps. It is the preferred type of wiring for the new, fast LANs such as 100Base-T and 100VGAnyLAN. The preferred connector for unshielded twisted-pair wiring is the RJ45 connector.

Twisted-pair wiring has the worst noise immunity of the bounded media types. When compared with coaxial and fiber-optic cables, twisted-pair wiring radiates more, which makes it less secure, and it is more susceptible to noise than the other two types of bounded media. Twisted-pair wiring is certainly much easier to install and relatively inexpensive per foot. It is useful for a wide variety of applications, including telephone and data networks. It might be considered a mature technology from the point of view of both installation and wire construction.

⇨ Coaxial

Coaxial cable is composed of two metal conductors with the center wire completely surrounded by a conductive outer mesh or shield. The inner conductor is most often solid and made of copper. Dielectric insulation separates the inner conductor from the outer shield. The signal is constrained to travel in the space of the dielectric between the inner cable and the inner surface of the shield. In some coaxial cables, there might be more than one shield. The outermost shield is used for noise protection. The inner shield is the signal-carrying component.

Popular types of connectors used with coaxial cable are the N connector and the BNC connector ("baby N connector"). Coaxial cable was very popular in the early days of local area network development. Many of the early adapters connected to the network via coaxial cable. It is a popular type of connection for bus-type networks. It is also popular for direct connection of terminals to hosts. Figure

Figure 2-2

Inner
conductor

Outer conductor
(foil/braid)

Insulating
jacket

Insulation
(dielectric)

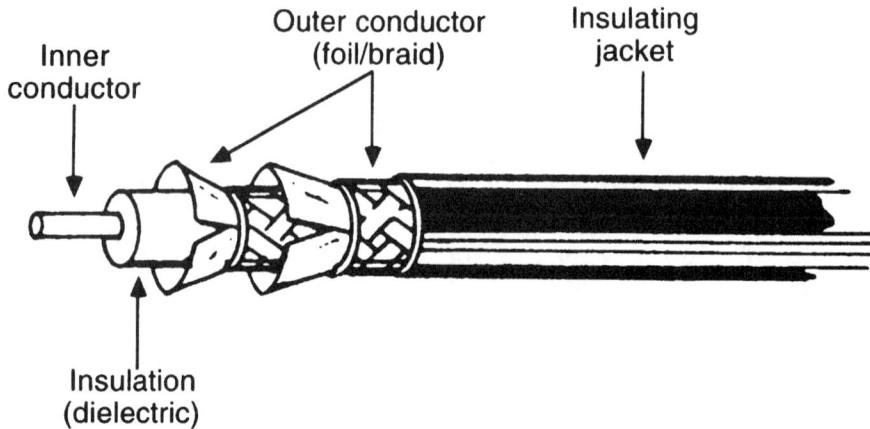

Coaxial cable with multiple shields. Learning Tree International

2-2 shows a coaxial cable with multiple shields. Note the insulating jacket surrounding the outermost shield. Note also that there are foil shields under the mesh.

Coaxial cable comes in three varieties also. The three varieties are classified by the impedance of the cable. The most popular coaxial cable in local area networks is the 50-ohm cable. It is employed in Ethernet and 802.3 networks. It comes in two varieties. The thick kind (RG-8), which is fairly difficult to install and is easily damaged, requires N-type connectors and transceivers for network operation. The thick kind of cable gave rise to the name "Thicknet" for this type of Ethernet wiring. The other type of Ethernet wiring, called "Thinnet," comes from the thin variety of 50-ohm coax. This coax (RG-58) is much easier to install, has a thinner inner conductor, is more flexible, and can only be used for short segments, due to its higher resistance.

Broadband networks that support video and data use 75-ohm coaxial cable. This cable is most often deployed in radio frequency (rf) networks installed in manufacturing plants. It is not very popular in office environments.

The third type of coaxial cable has an impedance of 93 ohms. It is used extensively for IBM 3270 terminal-to-host connections. It later appeared as the preferred wiring for ARCNET networks. This cable has a designation of RG-62.

Coaxial cable is less susceptible to electromagnetic interference than twisted-pair cable, due to the natural shielding cross section of coax. On the other hand, because coax requires metal conductors to guide the electromagnetic wave, it is more susceptible to noise and less secure than fiber optics. As noted previously, some varieties of coax are heavy, difficult to install, and have a high cost per foot.

In general, coaxial cable was the preferred method of connecting computers to each other in the early development of network technology. Today there is a decline in use of coaxial cable in favor of twisted pair. In general, coaxial cables support a higher transmission bandwidth than twisted-pair cables. It is coaxial cable, and not twisted-pair cable, that is used to transmit video programming to the home. Twisted-pair wiring is used for voice telephone services.

⇨ Fiber optic

The installed base of fiber-optic cabling is relatively low compared to twisted-pair, but it is gaining in popularity. As time goes on, more and more networks will be wired with fiber optics. It will become, years hence, the preferred method of network connectivity. Fiber-optic cabling is a marvelous technology. It consists of a very thin glass strand with two components: a very thin inner core of dense glass, surrounded by a cladding of lighter glass. The difference in density of the two glasses can be compared to the light-bending quality of a dense transparent material such as diamond and a lighter transparent material such as window glass.

The inner core is very small, 62.5 micrometers, which is smaller than a human hair. Figure 2-3 shows how a fiber-optic strand supports the propagation of a beam of light. Consider shining light into one end of the fiber-optic cable. The light enters into the inner core and, due to the nature of optical law, is trapped to travel within that core. In other words, those rays of light that penetrate into the core at one end will bounce off the interface between the cladding and the core and bounce their way to the other end with very little attenuation. This low attenuation allows the light to travel long distances and be useful at the other end for signaling.

Figure 2-3

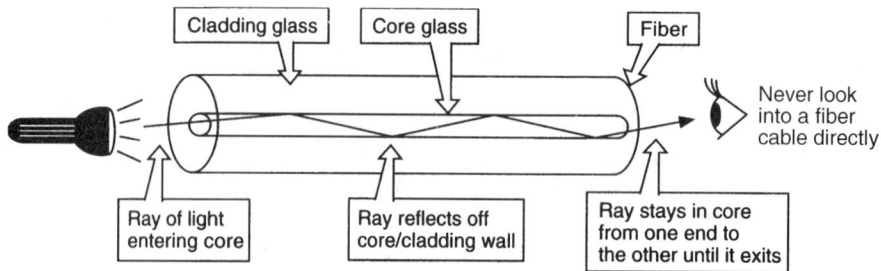

Demonstration of a beam of light propagating in a glass fiber by bouncing off the interface between the core and the cladding. Learning Tree International

The trick is to couple in as much light as possible at the transmitting end and to extract as much light as possible on the receiving end. Great loss of light could occur at the connectors. Connecting fiber-optic cable is expensive and difficult to do in many cases. Light is constrained to travel in one direction in a fiber; in other words, it is used in a simplex mode. Two fibers are required to allow bilateral communications between devices. Each fiber carries a signal in one direction.

Fiber-optic cable comes in two popular varieties. The first variety has a 62.5-micrometer core with 125-micrometer cladding. This type of fiber operates in what is termed "multimode." In multimode operation, the light rays entering in at the transmitting end are not parallel. This causes rays entering at a steeper angle to travel a longer distance than the rays that enter at a shallower angle. The steeper-angle rays travel a longer distance and take longer to appear at the other end, later than the shallower-angle rays. So a very sharp pulse of light with all of the rays emitted at once entering at the transmitting end arrives at the receiver smeared out in time. If the distances are not too long, this smearing of the signal edge is of little consequence. If the distance is long, such as between cities, this could be very detrimental to high-speed signaling. For that reason, 62.5 micron-core fiber is used for LAN connections rather than WAN connections. The main advantage of multimode fibers is that the larger core makes it easier and cheaper to connect and install.

The second variety of fiber, called single mode, has an 8-micrometer core and 125-micrometer cladding. The rays that enter in the core are relatively parallel because of the smaller diameter of the core. They travel the same distance and arrive at the receiver at the same time. This keeps the sharpness of the switched pulse intact from one end of the fiber to the other, a good feature for long-distance transmission. Single-mode fiber-optic type of cable is popular for telephone trunk lines between cities. It is very expensive to connect, since it is difficult to align to an 8-micron core. It is not installed as building wiring.

Of all guided media types, fiber-optic cable is the least susceptible to noise. Fiber-optic cable has the best security characteristics because fiber is very difficult to tap and it is very hard to detect emanations from the cable. Many network types today have a network card that can be connected with fiber. Fiber is not a popular building wiring method due to the expense in installing fiber cable, the high cost of the cable itself and the difficulty in connecting it. For this reason the network cards themselves are not popular, causing them to be expensive. A typical application for fiber-optic cabling is building risers (the vertical runs between floors) and connections between buildings.

Fiber optic is the preferred method for running a connection between buildings. There are two reasons it is so popular for this application. First, the span between buildings is susceptible to electromagnetic interference, especially from lightning. Fiber is completely unaffected by the EMI (electromagnetic interference) effects of lightning. The second reason for its popularity as intrabuilding cabling is that it keeps the two building grounds separate. It often happens that buildings are at different ground potentials with respect to each other. If one were to use a metal-based communication cable—such as coax or twisted pair—between buildings to connect data equipment, the shield or even the data cables themselves could become the signal path for the two grounds to equalize. There will be noise current flowing in a groundloop circuit that includes the copper data cable and the earth return path. This noise signal disturbs data transmission and might even impede communications altogether. Fiber-optic cable does not provide this metal signal path and is immune to this problem.

⇨ How fiber-optic cables are used

Figure 2-4 shows what is required to employ fiber-optic cable as a connection between computers. Network cards generally send out electrical signals that have to be converted to flashes of light for transmission through the fiber. The conversion process takes place in an electrical-to-optical encoder, often called a fiber-optic transceiver. On the receiving end there is an optical-to-electrical decoder that converts the flashes of light back to the electrical signals.

Figure 2-4

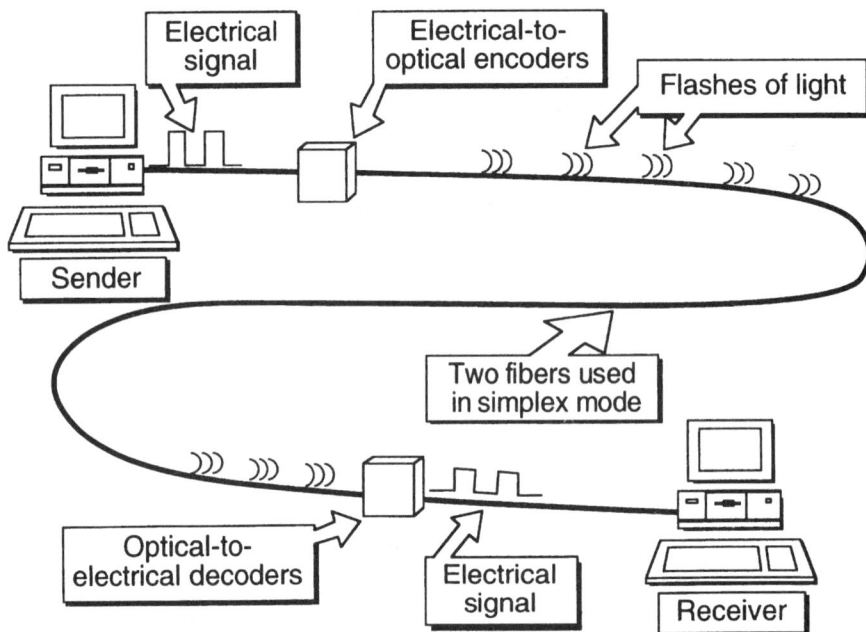

The anatomy of a fiber-optic link showing all needed components. This arrangement uses external transceivers. Learning Tree International

Fiber-optic connections can be deployed in two ways. The network card might already have the optical encoder/decoder on it, in which case the fiber can be brought right to the computer. On the other hand, network cards based on copper wiring might be connected to a fiber-optic wiring scheme using external transceivers. Although Fig. 2-4 shows two computers connected to each other via fiber-optic cable, in general this is not the cabling arrangement. All fiber cables go to fiber-optic wiring hubs that are usually found in a wiring closet. The wiring topology, then, is of the star type. This is similar to the way we install twisted-pair cabling in building wiring.

One last observation should be made concerning fiber-optic cabling. The bandwidth of fiber-optic cable is much higher than either that of twisted-pair or coaxial cabling because electromagnetic signals in the optical range are being used. The wavelength of the signal is very short, and the light can be flashed at a very high rate, in the gigabit-per-second and even higher rates.

The mere fact of installing a fiber-optic cable plant does not guarantee that data will travel faster. A common myth is to think that "to use fiber" automatically means the network will run faster: not so. The data rate depends on the type of network card being used. Consider Ethernet: the data rate is 10 Mbps whether it runs over twisted-pair, coaxial, or fiber-optic cabling. It is true that when a fiber-optic cable plant is installed, a capacity to signal at high data rates is gained. But faster network-card technology, such as FDDI or ATM, must be used to take advantage of this additional capacity.

⇨ Comparison of bounded media types

Figure 2-5 is a chart summarizing the characteristics and uses of the three types of bounded media. The chart should help those studying for the CNE exam and engineers looking for a summary of characteristics of the various bounded media technologies. Figure 2-6 shows additional characteristics of the bounded media: sensitivity to EMI, security, a bandwidth, and typical distances each cable type spans. Figure 2-6 also shows various typical applications of each cable type.

⇨ Structured wiring

Structured wiring (also known as building wiring) refers to the organized cabling of a building for ease of maintenance. As the word "structured" implies, it is a formal method of installing, documenting, and maintaining the cabling in a building. The most economical and

Figure 2-5

Type	Varieties	Specific characteristics	General characteristics	Uses
Twisted pair	Unshielded	4 pairs of 22- or 24-gauge copper cable, no shield Uses RJ-45 connectors 100–150 ohm Available in 5 categories	Poor noise immunity Inexpensive to install Mature technology Star wiring topology Used with concentrators	Voice and data circuits
	Shielded	2 twisted copper pairs inside a wire mesh shield Type 1 and Type 2	Better noise immunity Favored by IBM for Token Ring Used with MAUs	Token Ring installations Also used in some FDDI networks
Coaxial	50 ohm	Coaxial copper conductors May have multiple shields BNC- or N-type connectors	Mesh or solid shield Used with repeaters Medium distances	Bus networks, typically Ethernet
	75 ohm	Coaxial copper conductor BNC- or N-type connectors	Mesh or solid shield Used with amplifiers Long distances	Bus-type broadband networks
	93 ohm	Coaxial copper conductors BNC connectors	Mesh shield Used with hubs	Bus-type network wired as a star ARCNET
Fiber optic	Multimode	62.5-micron core/125-micron cladding	Best noise and security immunity Short distances (campus) Expensive High potential bandwidth	Campus network wiring for all data-link technologies
	Single mode	8-micron core/125-micron cladding	High noise immunity/ security and features Expensive Difficult to connectorize	Long-distance telephone line between cities

Characteristics of bounded media. Learning Tree International

Figure 2-6

Characteristic	Twisted pair	Coaxial	Fiber optic
Access	Baseband	Baseband and broadband	Baseband
Configuration	Two copper conductors twisted	Two concentric metal conductors	A dense glass core surrounded by lighter glass cladding
Types	UTP = 100 ohms STP = 100 ohms	50 ohms 75 ohms 93 ohms	62.5 micron Multimode 8 micron Single mode
Sensitivity to EMI	High	Medium	None
Security	Poor	Poor	Best
Multiplexing	TDM only	FDM broadband TDM baseband	TDM only
Typical LAN uses	802.3 10BASE-T 802.5 Token Ring LocalTalk	Ethernet 802.3 10BASE5 802.4 ARCNET	FDDI Ethernet **Fiber-Optic Inter-repeater Link** (FOIRL)
Bandwidth available	Low	High	Maximum
Typical LAN distances	100 m (10BASE-T) Station to concentrator	500-m (Ethernet) LAN segment	1000 m (FDDI) Station to station

Additional characteristics of bounded media. Learning Tree International simplest way of putting in wiring is to install it as the building is being constructed.

The components of structured wiring are shown in Fig. 2-7. The major components of structured wiring are: wall outlets in the office environment, cables running from the wall outlets to a central point on the office floor, and the wiring closet. In the wiring closet there might be one or more equipment racks. At the top of these racks there is a patch panel. The wiring coming in from the outlets is terminated in a punch block (a typical telephone punch block like a 66 or a 110 block). From there it connects to the back of the patch panel. In the equipment rack there will be a number of connecting devices such as MSAUs for Token Ring or Ethernet 10Base-T concentrators. There will be patch cables from connectors in the patch panel into these connecting devices.

Figure 2-7

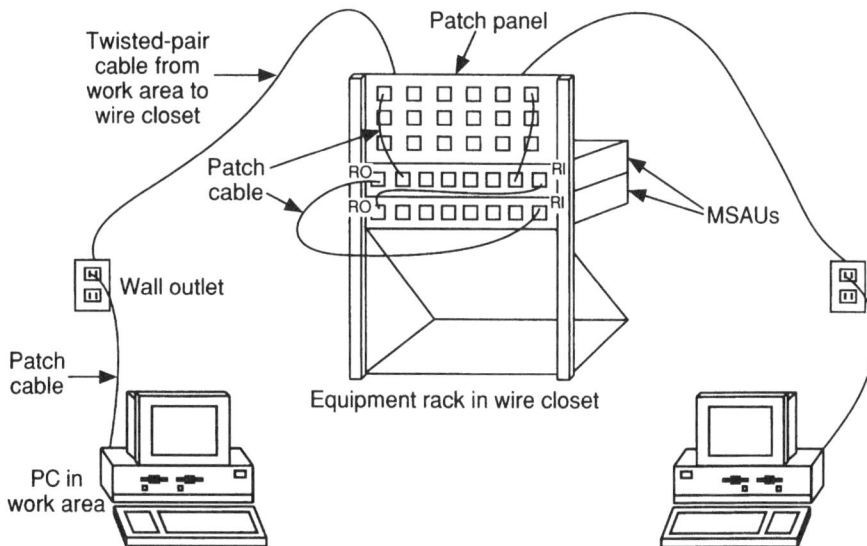

Star configuration wiring for an electrically connected ring

The component parts of a horizontal wiring system that are part of structured wiring. This horizontal wiring system is supporting a Token Ring installation. The cable between the wiring closet and the outlet can be UTP, STP, or fiber-optic cable. Learning Tree International

The power of structured wiring is seen in how simple it is to add new devices to a network. To add a PC to a Token Ring or an Ethernet network, the PC on the desk is connected to a network outlet using a patch cable. The technician doing the installation then goes to the wire closet. Using another patch cable, the socket on the patch panel corresponding to the wall outlet of the PC recently added to the network is connected to the MAU or the Ethernet concentrator in the rack. The procedure is simple; the cost is low.

Contrast this to the cost of adding a PC to a network with unlabeled cables, undocumented wiring, and wiring that has been installed in an unstructured or chaotic manner. The work would be difficult, at best, if not impossible.

An additional component of the building wiring is the riser system. The riser system connects wire closets on separate floors to each other so that the network can be extended throughout the building. The riser system might also allow connections to roof satellite or microwave links or to basement telephone devices such as PBXs and DSU/CSUs. Figure 2-8 shows schematically how a building would be wired using structured wiring. The cable system of Fig. 2-7 applies within a floor. Figure 2-8 demonstrates the riser system with the possible external connections to private WAN links or phone company WAN services.

Unshielded twisted-pair wiring is the preferred method for wiring within a floor. Wiring within a floor is often referred to as horizontal wiring. As the need for higher bandwidth increases in the coming years, the use of unshielded twisted pair in the horizontal system will eventually give way to the use of fiber optics. The riser system between floors could be twisted pair as well. More often it consists of fiber-optic cables.

One important advantage of structured wiring is that the same unshielded twisted-pair wiring that supports data also supports voice. As a matter of fact, it often happens that the need to wire a building for voice—i.e., telephone wiring—pays for the data wiring. In other words, if one is going to wire a building for voice anyway, why not install the appropriate twisted-pair wiring for data? It will carry data and voice. The only requirement is that enough wiring be installed to satisfy the data needs as well. This need to install voice wiring with the data wiring as an afterthought is referred to as "voice pays for data."

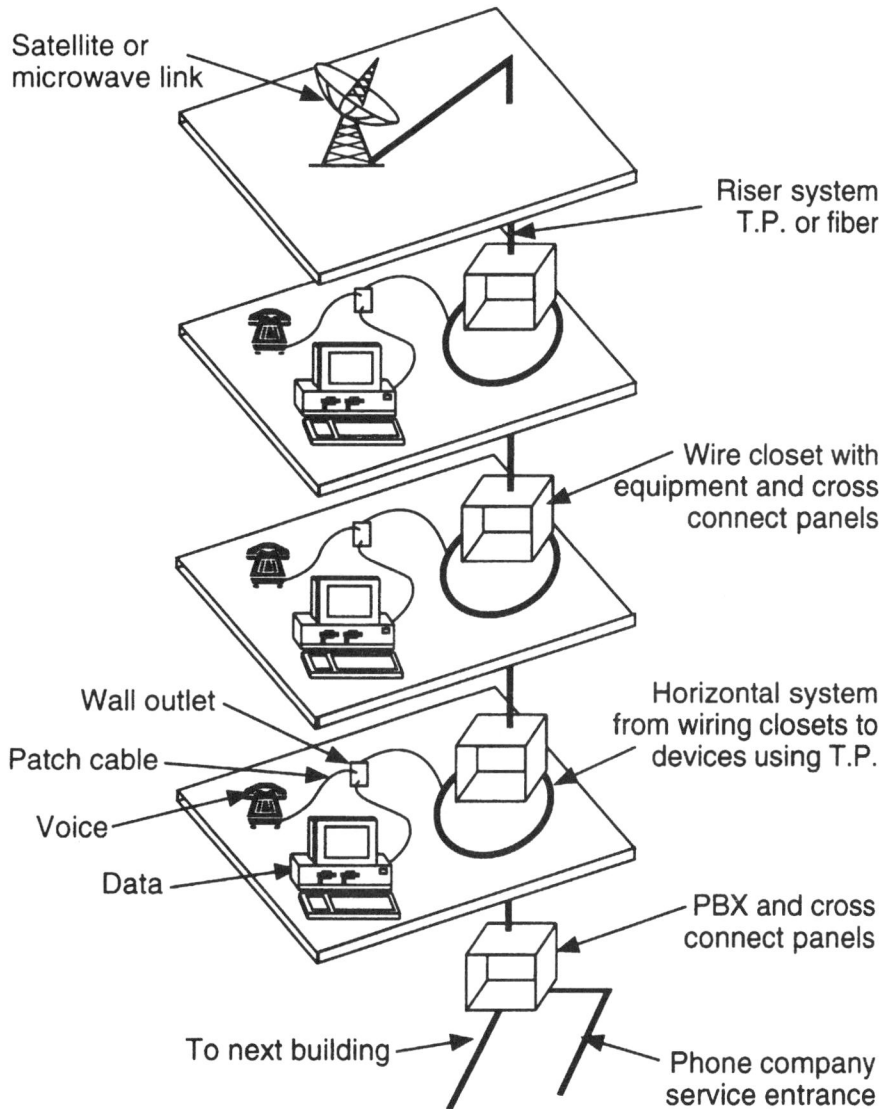

Figure 2-8

Satellite or microwave link

Riser system T.P. or fiber

Wire closet with equipment and cross connect panels

Wall outlet

Patch cable

Voice

Data

Horizontal system from wiring closets to devices using T.P.

PBX and cross connect panels

To next building

Phone company service entrance

Structured wiring showing the horizontal as well as the vertical wiring components. Note the connection to public data networks via equipment in the lower floors and to point-to-point WAN links on the roof. Learning Tree International

Unbounded transmission technologies

Unbounded transmission provides a method of connecting computers without cabling. The field can be broken down into two major areas: the use of radio signals within an office environment in the broadcast mode to replace LAN cabling and the use of point-to-point radio links as a form of WAN cabling. In all these cases, the electromagnetic signal propagates through free space; there is no medium to support its propagation.

We could further subdivide the unbounded transmission technologies by frequency: those in the low end of the electromagnetic spectrum and those in the high end—optical, or near optical. Radio, terrestrial, and satellite microwave fall into the relatively low frequency part of the spectrum. Laser links and infrared links fall into the high-frequency, near optical end, of the spectrum.

Radio links use VHF (very high frequency) and UHF (ultra high frequency) radio channels. The links are relatively inexpensive compared to the other unbounded transmission technologies. Radio links can be used in the broadcast mode as in wireless LANs. Or it might be used point to point as in WAN links. The latter type could be made to span the globe. In the United States, the use of radio links requires FCC licensing. Other countries might also require governmental licensing, since the use of the public airwaves is strictly regulated.

Microwave transmissions also are regulated by government and require approval. Terrestrial microwaves are low-GHz directional beams deployed between buildings. They are often seen in urban areas in use as WAN links between LANs. A higher-frequency microwave beam is used with satellite connections. Laser transmission is employed in point-to-point connection between LANs in a similar manner as terrestrial microwave. One drawback of the use of laser beams is their susceptibility to disturbance by bad weather. An advantage of laser links is that they don't need to be regulated by the government.

Another WAN point-to-point connection technology is the use of infrared beams. These are very useful for short ranges. They are greatly disturbed by bad weather, so they are deployed indoors in connections between computers. Some wireless LANs employ infrared technology. Due to its high frequency and short range, infrared also does not require governmental approval.

Figure 2-9 compares the unbounded media types just discussed, their characteristics, their licensing, some advantages and disadvantages and typical uses. Note that satellite microwave has the one-transmitter-to-many-receivers characteristic, which is not a feature of many of the others. Also, note that satellite and radio both have the one-to-many transmission characteristic, which is not present with the other means.

Figure 2-9

Link type	Characteristic	Need license?	Advantage/ disadvantage	Typical use
Earth microwave	Point-to-point connections with GHz radio links	Yes	Disturbed by weather. High bandwidth.	Private links between remote sites
Satellite microwave	Earth stations to geosynchronous satellite	Yes	Large "footprint" coverage can reach remote sites. Expensive.	One-to-many transmission, CATV
Laser	Point-to-point laser connection	No	Disturbed by weather	Private link between buildings
Infrared	Multipoint transmission using infrared signals	No	Short distances. High bandwidth possible.	Wireless LANs
Radio	Multipoint or point-to-point links via radio transmission	Yes	Need retransmission stations for long distances. Mobile units are available.	Private WANs, wireless LANs

Characteristics of unbounded media. Learning Tree International

⇨ Satellite links

An important characteristic of satellite links is the long signal path, leading to transmission delays. These could be a source of problems in a network. For example, Fig. 2-10 shows a satellite link between a terminal and a mainframe. The terminal is in San Francisco and the mainframe is in New York. They are using multiplexers in between to aggregate the traffic from many terminals onto this one high-speed satellite connection. The microwave signal was retransmitted by a satellite positioned 22,500 miles above the earth. At that height, a satellite traveling at an appropriately high speed will be stationary in one spot over the earth, although it is moving very fast. This particular orbit is called a *geosynchronous orbit*.

Figure 2-10

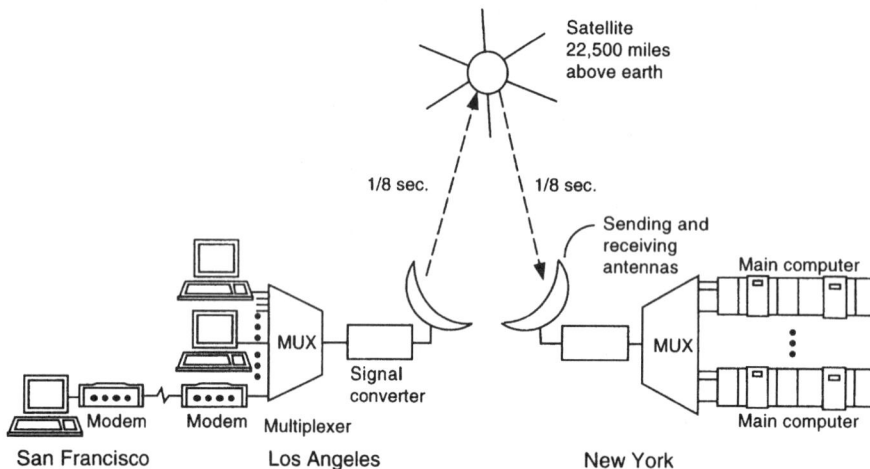

Satellite links help to span long distances, but a long signal path means long delays that must be accounted for in the configuration of sessions.
Learning Tree International

Due to the long distances, the microwave signal will be greatly delayed. Although one thinks of the propagation of electromagnetic signals as instantaneous, in reality their transit time has a finite value. Light travels at 186,000 miles per second. To make the trip from the multiplexer in San Francisco up to the satellite and then down to the multiplexer in New York, the signal has to cover 43,000 miles, which is roughly one-fourth the distance light travels in one second. The entire trip takes one quarter of a second—an eighth of a second to go up to the satellite and an eighth of a second to come back down. This is a fairly long delay that, if not accounted for, might cause processes on the mainframe computer to time out in their reception of data from the terminal. It might result in the loss of a session.

The network administrator must be aware of this long delay when a satellite link is being used as a WAN connection. The configuration parameters for retransmission delay must be appropriately set to maintain session continuity at the workstations. If this is not done, users might see their sessions being disconnected at inappropriate moments.

⇨ Comparison of unbounded media types

Figure 2-11 shows additional unbounded media characteristics and some typical applications. It also notes whether governmental approval is required or not for that type of link. This table is given as a reference for network administrators to have an overview of WAN link characteristics and help them make the appropriate choice of technology.

Type	Characteristic	Application	Approval required
Radio	Use of VHF and UHF radio channels to transmit data	Long-distance data communications. The basis for new wireless LANs.	FCC or governmental licensing
Terrestrial microwave	Point-to-point, low gigahertz links. Bypasses the local loop.	LAN repeater connections	FCC or governmental licensing
Satellite microwave	Geosynchronous satellite connection between earth stations. 250-millisecond delay.	Covers large area. Expensive, high bandwidth.	FCC or governmental licensing
Laser	Point-to-point laser connections. Disturbed by bad weather.	Short-haul links. Bypasses the local loop.	Does not require licensing
Infrared	Point-to-point, short-range infrared links	Wireless LANs. PC-to-PC connection.	Does not require licensing

Figure 2-11

Comparison of unbounded media characteristics, typical applications, and equirements for government approval. Learning Tree International

⇨ Public networks

Network administrators turn to providers of public network services to obtain WAN services. The WAN links are used to interconnect their LANs and span long geographical distances. Refer back to chapter 1, where the differences between LANs and WANs are described. It shows that WAN technology is really the domain of public service providers. The public service providers are often the telephone companies, whose main business is providing voice (phone) services. As the need for data links increases, phone companies have begun to realize that a greater portion of their business will come from the data side, not the voice side, of the market. In general, though, the bulk of the wide area network marketplace is voice. The current WAN economics and technology very much favor voice characteristics rather than data characteristics.

As a consumer of WAN services, the network administrator must understand the characteristics of voice transmission, how voice is digitized, the types of digital voice circuits available today, and how data can be transmitted through a voice network. We refer to a voice/data network as the telephone network. Phone companies also make direct data services available.

⇨ CNE exam objectives

> Identify public network services.

⇨ The telephone network

The smallest component of the public telephone network is the central office switch with a number of local circuits to telephone customers, or subscribers. Figure 2-12 shows this arrangement. The components are fairly basic. There are telephones for voice communication of telephone subscribers or customers. They are connected by a telephone circuit, called the local loop, typically 5 kilometers or less in length. The phone line consists of one 22- to 24-gauge pair of copper wires. All the phone lines terminate at the central office switch. Today that

Figure 2-12

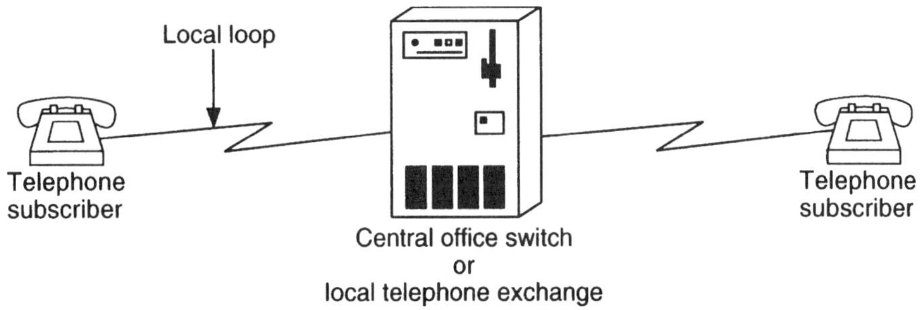

The basic unit of public telephone voice networks: local loops, a central office switch, and subscribers. Learning Tree International

switch is a digital computer that interprets the tones in a phone number dialed by a customer, and the computer makes the proper connection to another subscriber. On the other side of the switch there is another local loop going out to other subscribers, which ends in the other subscribers' telephones.

Typical phone service was designed to support business voice communications only. It has a certain bandwidth and a certain characteristic, which is explored in the next section. This telephone central office and local network are intended for local phone calls. What happens when a subscriber wants to call another part of the country through a long-distance phone call?

Figure 2-13 shows a countrywide telephone system. It includes local central office switches, local exchanges, and local loops to subscribers. Figure 2-13 also shows a private phone switch, called a PBX or private branch exchange, which is installed by a business to support not only connections to the outside phone services, but also for internal intercom communications within the company. All of the internal phone equipment belonging to the customer, including the PBX, is called the customer-premises telephone system. The phone lines between the private branch exchange and the local exchange are often referred to as trunk lines, also called the local loop. The place where the trunk lines connect to the company's internal phone system is designated by the phone company as the demarcation point. The telephone provider's responsibility for phone services ends at the

Figure 2-13

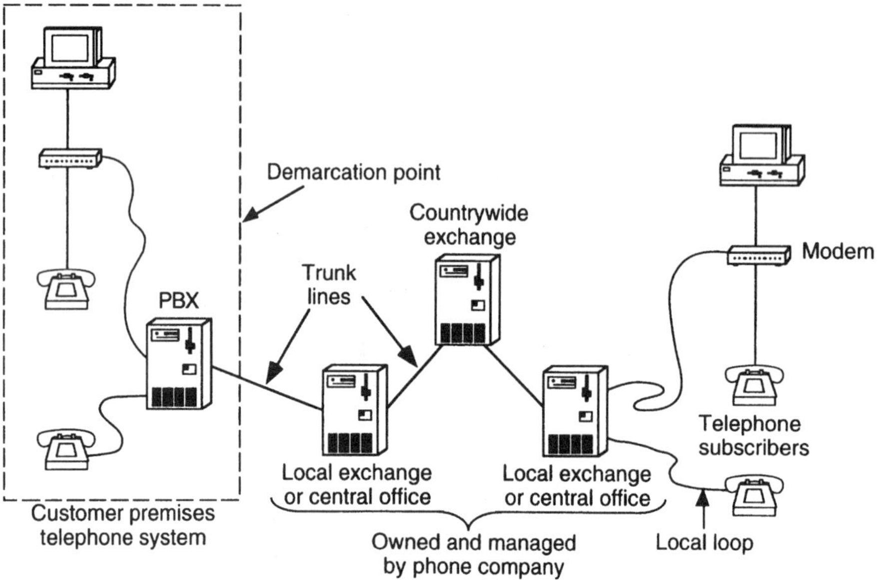

Countrywide telephone network showing the customer premises telephone
system, the demarcation point, the trunk lines to the local loop and
between exchanges, and the local and country-wide exchanges. Learning Tree
International

demarcation point. At that point it is continued by the customer, who
is responsible for the internal phone system.

A customer might have many hundreds of phones as part of the
customer-premises telephone system that uses one or many phone
switches. Although there might be hundreds of internal phones,
hundreds of trunk lines or local loops are not required to connect to
the local exchange. The reason is that not everyone within the
company needs to make an outside phone call. The telephone system
designer within the company has estimated the number of concurrent
external phone calls, both incoming and outgoing, that might be going
on at any one time. With allowances for peak traffic, the telephone
system designer computes how many trunk lines will be needed for the
local telephone company. A company might have 300 phones within
a building but might require only 10 trunk lines for connections to the
outside, for example.

Long-distance phone calls are usually cleared through countrywide exchanges. The trunk lines between central offices and countrywide exchanges are the responsibility of the telephone company. They are high-bandwidth lines to support the transmission of many simultaneous telephone calls. It is the capacity of these interswitch trunk lines that gives us the capability to determine what type of lines are available for our data needs.

Characteristics of voice-grade lines

Voice-grade lines are meant to support business voice communications. This means that the phone company limits the bandwidth of the phone connection between subscribers. Figure 2-14 shows the signal bandwidth allowed by the phone company to support business voice communications. It spans from a low of 300 Hz to a high of 3300 Hz. Ideally, every frequency has the same attenuation. In practice, some frequencies receive greater attenuation than others, due to characteristics of the local loop. This very narrow bandwidth places severe limitations on the data or signaling rate used for data communication.

Figure 2-14

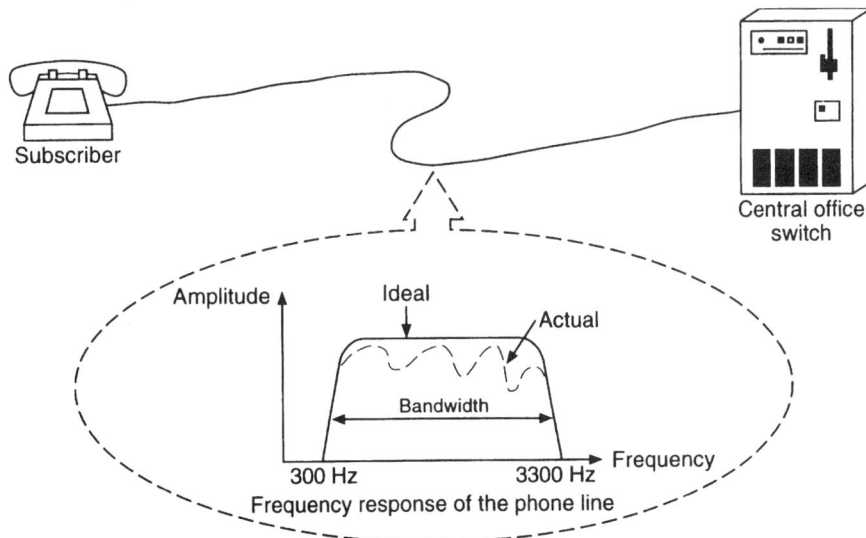

Frequency characteristic of a business voice-grade line. Note the maximum bandwidth of 3000 Hertz. Learning Tree International

The major reason the phone company limits the bandwidth to each subscriber is to be able to aggregate subscriber phone calls on phone company trunk lines between central offices and countrywide exchanges. Limiting the subscribers' available bandwidth allows multiplexing on telephone-company interswitch trunk lines, resulting in the need for fewer trunk lines and the ability to support more customers.

Data transmission over voice-grade lines

Data transmission must emulate the human voice to be sent over voice-grade lines. The required device that converts the digital signals at the computer into analog signals to be sent over the telephone network is called the *modem*. Modem is a contraction for modulator/ demodulator. Essentially, a modem converts digital signals into whistles. Figure 2-15 shows just such a typical arrangement, with computers as senders and receivers and modems to convert the digital signals into analog signals for transmission over the phone network. The modem is acting like a phone in that it can pick up the phone and dial the number for the computing design connection.

Figure 2-15

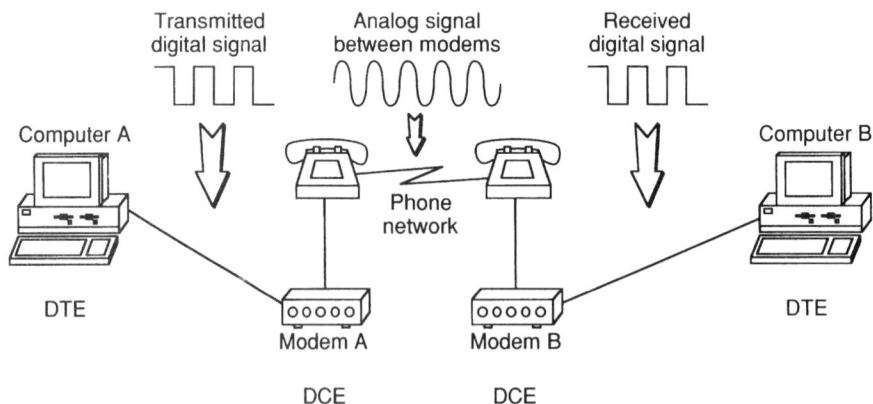

The use of modems to convert digital signals from computers into analog signals sent over a phone network. The phones in the diagram represent the phone network. Learning Tree International

⇨ The modem

A modem matches the data needs of the computer to the characteristics of a telephone system supporting voice transmission. The modem converts one type of signal into the other and back. In the parlance of the telephone business, a modem is considered a DCE. A DCE is data-circuit terminating equipment. The major function of a DCE is to connect the user device, such as a PC, to the communications channel, which is the telephone system. The user's device is considered data terminal equipment, or DTE. It is what the user interfaces with—typically a computer or a terminal. The DTE originates or receives data. DCEs put the data through and match the DTE's characteristics to the telephone network. Other examples of DCEs are an X.25 packet switch, a DSU/CSU (data service unit/channel service unit) and an X.25 PAD. (See Fig. 2-16.)

Figure 2-16

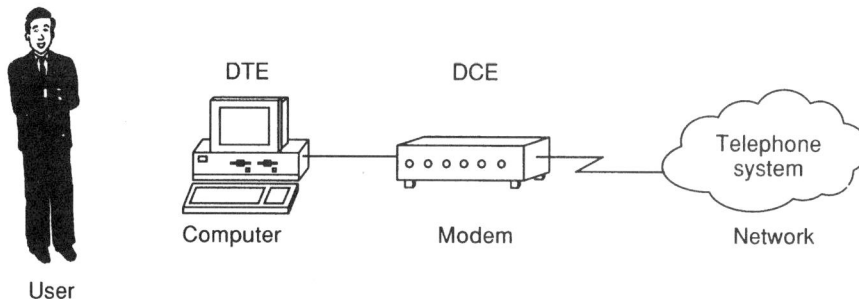

Relationship of user to DTE and DCE equipment. Learning Tree International

✳ How a modem works

The modulator portion of the modem will decode the digital data stream into one of three possible analog signaling schemes. Figure 2-17 shows these three schemes. A popular scheme is amplitude shift keying (ASK). When transmitting a zero, the amplitude of the analog is lower. When transmitting a one, the amplitude is high. The modem shifts back and forth between these two amplitudes to represent the zeros and ones of the digital signal. In other words, an audio frequency tone (a whistle) is modulated in amplitude to represent the digital signal stream.

Figure 2-17

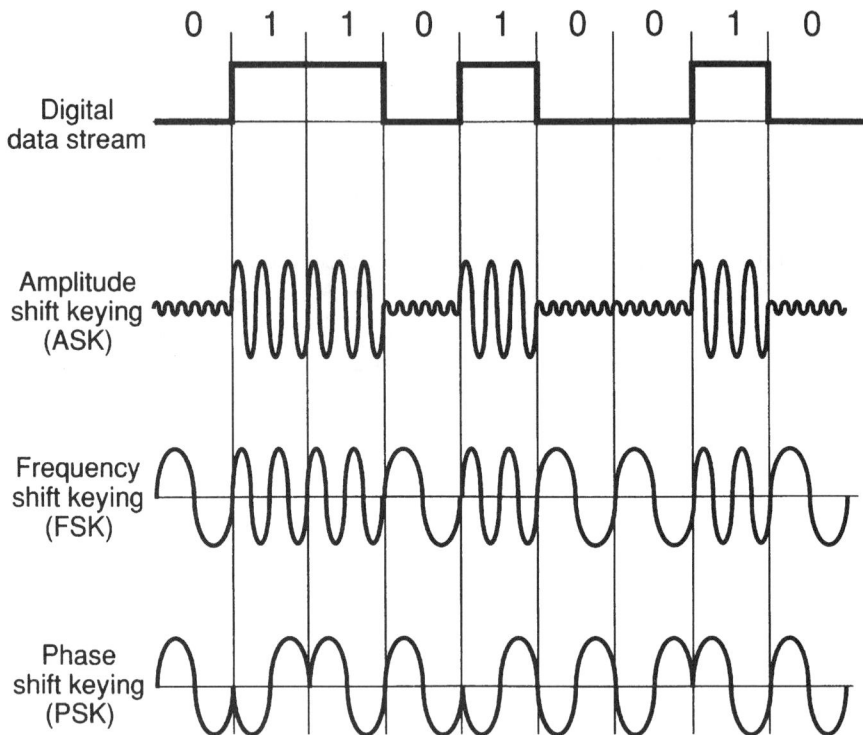

Popular modem modulation schemes. Learning Tree International

Another popular technique is frequency shift keying, or FSK. Here the zeros are represented by low-frequency signals, the ones by high-frequency signals. In other words, the modem whistles at two separate frequencies and hops back and forth between each to represent the zeros and ones.

A third popular scheme is called phase shift keying, or PSK. Here the modem hops between two phases: transmitting a signal with no phase shift for a zero and a signal with 180° phase shift for a one.

There are many popular modem protocols in use today. The Bell modem standards are popular in the United States. Some example modems are: the Bell 103, which is a 300-bps asynchronous; the Bell 212A, a popular 1200-bps asynchronous; and the Bell 219A, which is a 9600-bps synchronous.

The CCITT/ITU modem standards, more popular in Europe, are beginning to become popular in the United States as the market demands for higher and higher-speed modems increases. Popular ones are the V.26, 2400 bps synchronous, and the V.29, 9600 bps synchronous.

The RS-232C protocol The discussion of modems would not be complete without the discussion of this very important interface protocol. The RS-232C protocol, standardized by the EIA (Electronic Industry Association), is a DTE-DCE interface. RS-232C defines mechanical specification (wires, connectors); electrical specifications (voltage levels); functional specifications (pin assignments for specific circuits); and procedural specifications (how the circuits are used in the handshake between the DTE and the DCE).

The RS-232C protocol specifies a 25-wire or 25-pin DB25 connector. Figure 2-18 shows the pin assignments to the various circuits in this 25-pin connector. Keep in mind that these pin assignments are from the point of view of the DTE. This is of particular importance when

Figure 2-18

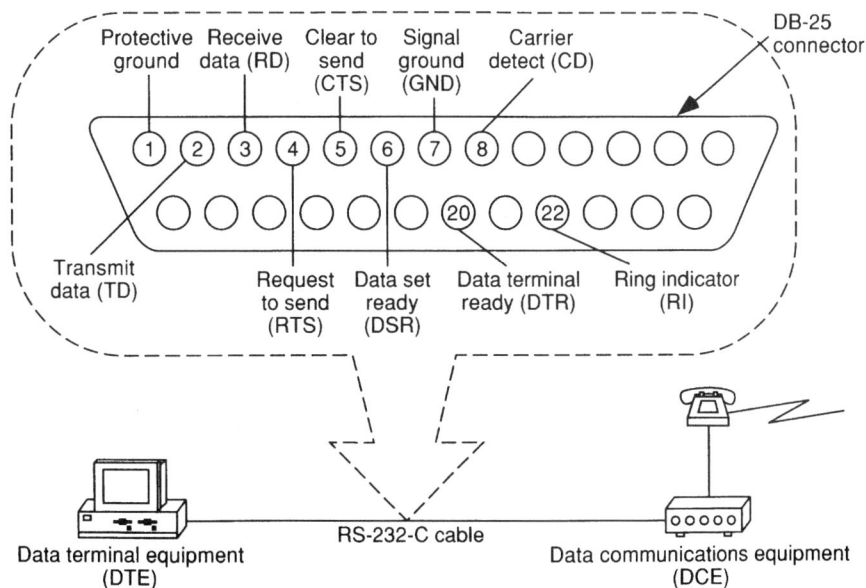

The RS-232C protocol and circuit assignments. Learning Tree International

considering pins 2 and 3 (circuits 2 and 3). Circuit 2 is considered transmit data (TD), but from the point of view of the DTE. The same circuit (circuit 2) is used by the DCE to receive data. Circuit 3, or pin 3, is used to receive data from the point of view of the DTE. The same circuit is used by the DCE to send data. The return wire to complete the circuit for both of these pins is attached to pin 7 (the signal ground).

The RS-232C protocol supports full-duplex transmission. Data can be present on circuits 2 and 3 simultaneously. It is specified for a maximum cable length of 50 feet and a typical maximum data rate of 64 Kbps. A typical application of this protocol is for modem-to-computer connection. It is also used for asynchronous terminal-to-pad connections and the connection between a computer and a serial printer.

✳ Initiating a modem link

Figure 2-19 describes how a modem link between two computers is initialized. It describes how the various RS-232C circuits are used in this "handshaking" process. Circuit 20 (data terminal ready, DTR) is usually brought high, or asserted, when both computers power up. If

Figure 2-19

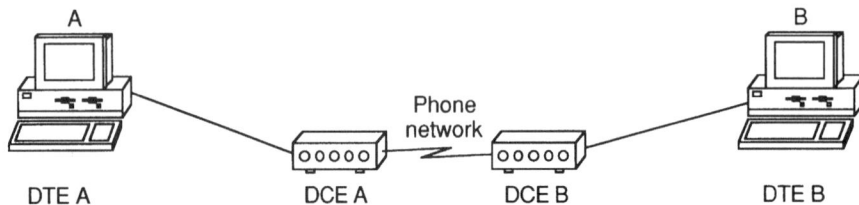

Procedure for initializing a link via modems
1. DTR (pin 20) is asserted when both DTEs power up
2. DSR (pin 6) is asserted when both DCEs power up
3. DTE A starts the process by asserting RTS (pin 4)
4. DCE A asserts CTS (pin 5) in response
5. DCE A also sends a tone over the phone line to DCE B
6. DCE B responds with its own tone and asserts CD (pin 8)
7. DCE A receives response tone and asserts CD (pin 8)
8. DTE A can now transmit data on TD (pin 2)
9. DCE B sends received data out on RD (pin 3) to DTE B
10. The two DTEs can now communicate full duplex

Initiating a computer-to-computer link over a phone line via modems.
Learning Tree International

the modems are powered, then they receive signals indicating that the DTEs are operational. When the modems power up, if they have not been powered up already, they will assert, or bring high, circuit 6 (data set ready, DSR). At this point, both the computer A and modem A are communicating with each other, telling each other they are both powered on. The same occurs on the B side of the connector. Computer B will notify modem B via circuit 20 that it is ready, and the modem will notify computer B of its readiness by asserting circuit 6.

Let's consider computer A the originator of the computer-to-computer link. When computer A is ready to initiate the link, it will bring high circuit 4 (ready to send, RTS). The modem will respond by bringing high circuit 5 in answer. If the phone connection has been made, DCE A (the modem at A) will also send a tone over the phone line to DCE B, letting DCE B know that DTE A is ready to communicate. DCE B responds with its own tone back to A over the phone line. At the same time, computer B brings high circuit 8, the CD circuit. When DCE A (modem A) receives the response tone from DCE B (modem B), it will communicate that to DTE A by asserting its own CD line on circuit 8. At this point, DTE A is in direct communication with DTE B and can begin sending data on circuit 2, the TD (transmit data) circuit.

This data will be sent over the phone line by DCE A with the proper conversion to analog signals. DCE B will then send that data out on its circuit 3, which is receive data, arriving at DTE B on circuit 3, which is the DTE receive data circuit. Simultaneously, DTE B can send out data on its own circuit 2. The transmission of data is full duplex: both DTE A and DTE B can send data to each other simultaneously.

⇨ Summary of telephone network component characteristics

Figure 2-20 summarizes a number of modem and telephone data line protocols.

Figure 2-20

Protocol	Description	Developer	Typical data rate	Characteristics	Typical use
RS-232-C	DTE–DCE interface	EIA	Varies; 9.6 kbits/sec	25-pin interface; 50-foot connection	Connect modems to PCs
RS-449	Similar to RS-232-C. More control circuits. Defines balanced and unbalanced.	EIA	Varies	RS-442 balanced; RS-443 unbalanced	LocalTalk
V.24	DCE–DTE interface	CCITT/ITU	Varies; up to 9.6 kbits/sec	Similar to RS-232	Used with X.25
V.35	DCE–DTE interface	CCITT/ITU	48 kbits/sec	For speeds above 48 kbits/sec	X.25 and modems
X series	Datacomm over telephone systems	CCITT/ITU	Varies, up to 64 kbits/sec	X.25 packet-switched nets	WANs, remote terminal access
T1	Two-channel digital telephone link	AT&T de facto	1.544 Mbits/sec	24x64-kbits/sec channels in a 1.544-Mbits/sec frame	24 digital voice channels, LAN-to-LAN dedicated data link
ISDN	Dialup digitized voice or data link	CCITT/ITU ISO	64 kbits/sec	Basic rate 2B (2x64 kbits/sec) and D (16 kbits/sec)	Voice, data, video dialup
Leased line	Data communication over dedicated voice line	AT&T de facto	56 or 64 kbits/sec	Dedicated digital voice line used for voice or data	LAN to LAN via bridges or routers

Summary of modem and telephone-line protocols. Learning Tree International

⇨ Digitizing an analog voice signal

Digital phone lines are the basis of ISDN networks. To carry analog
signal voice over a digital phone line, the signal must first be digitized.

The process of digitization involves first sampling the signal at prescribed intervals, then converting the samples into a binary sequence corresponding to the height of the sample. Those binary sequences, or pull strings, are then sent out over the digital connection. The reverse process, of course, occurs at the receiver where the received pitch stream is converted into a pulse and the pulse is then integrated, converted by digital analog signal.

The rate at which the analog signal is digitized needs to occur at twice the highest frequency of the analog signal. Since analog voice for business conversations is limited by the phone company to a maximum frequency of 3300 Hz, we typically sample at twice that, or we round up to 8000 samples per second. There will be two samples for every cycle of the highest frequency in that voice signal.

Each sample is then *quantized*, which means it gets approximated to a unique level out of 256 levels. Each level now has been accorded a number from zero to 255, which can then be converted into a binary sequence by the use of 8 bits. Thus we have 8 bits representing the height of a sample, which represents one point in time for an analog signal. If we sample at 8000 cycles per second and we need 8 bits per sample to transmit the information, we therefore have a transmission rate of 64,000 bits per second that is required. This is the basis of the minimum digital voice circuit, one of the ISDN channels.

Figure 2-21 shows such a process from top to bottom, the analog signal at the top being sampled 8000 samples per second, the height of the pulses being approximated to one of 256 levels, each of the pulses then being converted into an 8-bit sequence, and then the 8-bit sequence pulse string being sent out over the digital line.

✳ The CODEC

The digitization process can take place within a phone by a set of circuits called the *CODEC*, which is the reverse of a modem. The word "CODEC" means coder-decoder. Actually, it is an analog-to-digital converter on a transmitter and a digital-to-analog converter on the receiver. The CODEC can also be an external device used to take an analog phone and attach it to a digital phone line. Figure 2-22 shows a CODEC and its use in connecting analog phones through a digital switch.

Figure 2-21

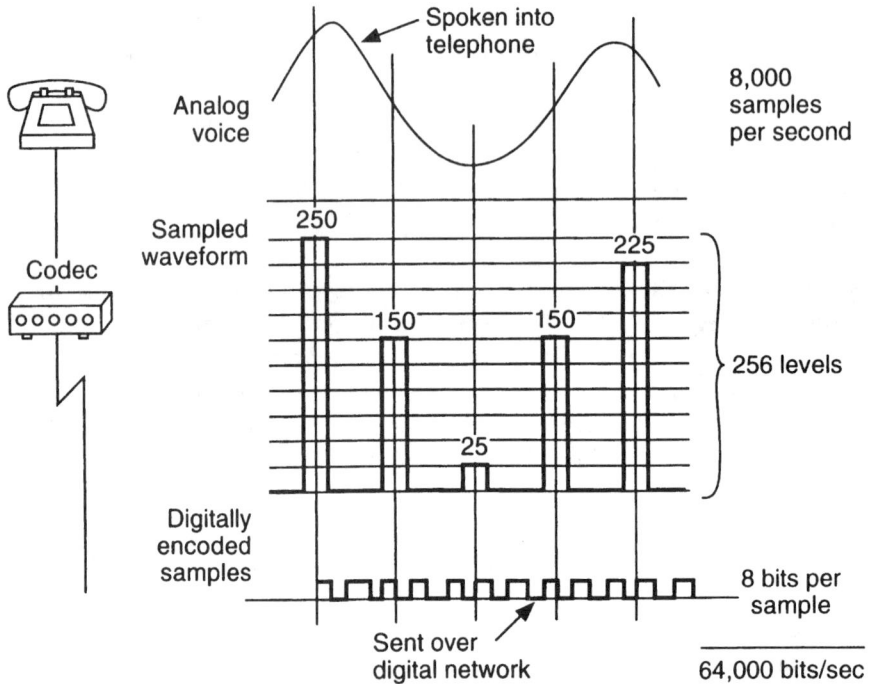

The conversion of an analog voice signal into a digital bit stream for transmission over a digital network. Learning Tree International

Figure 2-22

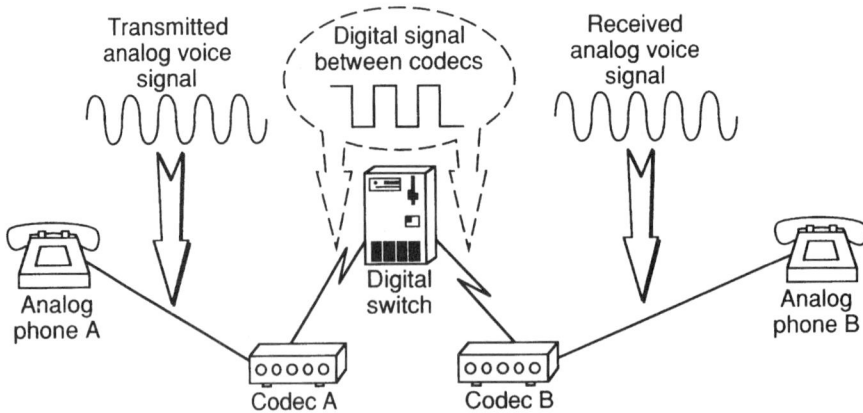

The use of CODECS to connect analog phones to digital switches. Learning Tree International

⇨ Leased lines

A leased line is a phone line dedicated to supporting data transmission. The sender and receiver are both digital devices, sending and receiving digital signals. The phone line in the middle is an analog phone line. To match the characteristics of the sender and the receiver to the phone line, we use devices known as CSU/DSUs. Leased lines are phone lines that the phone company dedicates to a customer 24 hours a day as a continuously available resource. The smallest-capacity line that can be purchased or leased is what is designated as a DS0, which is the use of one voice channel. The data rate is 56 Kbps. When 24 of these voice channels are aggregated, we get the next level, called a DS1, commonly referred to as T1. The DS designators are CCITT/ITU designators. The T designators are the original Bell telephone company designators. The data rate of a T1 is 1.54 Mbps. When you aggregate 28 T1 channels for a total bandwidth equivalent to 672 voice channels, you get 44 Mbps. In Europe a very common high-capacity channel available is called an E1, which is the aggregation of 34 channels giving 2 Mbps. Although there are many other possible lease lines, these four are the most typical and the most readily available today.

Figure 2-23 shows how lease lines are connected via channel-attach units or DSU/CSUs, and Fig. 2-24 shows a chart with the

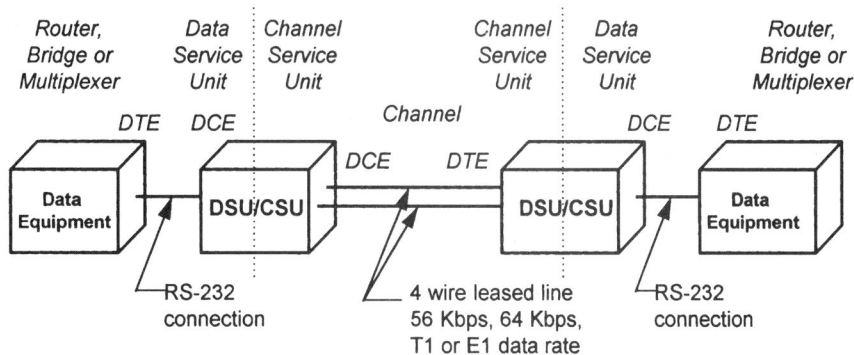

Figure 2-23

The use of digital leased lines for connecting two digital information sources. Note the use of DSU/CSU devices for attaching each computer to the phone line.

Figure 2-24

North America and Japan			International (CCITT/ITU) and Europe		
Digital signal designator	Number of voice channels	Data rate (Mbits/sec)	Level number	Number of voice channels	Data rate (Mbits/sec)
DS0	1	.056			
DS-1 (T1)	24	1.544	1 (E1)	30	2.048
DS-1 C	48	3.152	2	120	8.448
DS-2	96	6.312	3	480	34.368
DS-3 (T3)	672	44.736	4	1920	139.264
DS-4	4,032	274.176	5	7,680	565.148

Characteristics of digital leased lines. Learning Tree International

designators, number of voice channels, and the data rate for many possible digital leased-line services.

⇨ ISDN networks

ISDN networks are digital phone services provided by phone companies. Imagine using digital central office switches rather than analog switches at the central office. The phone line available for connection is digital rather than analog. The traffic carried by the phone company from one point to another is all digital, and the phone company doesn't even know whether it's voice, data, fax, image, or any other form of digital information.

ISDN means Integrated Services Digital Network, and that's the key. First, it is a digital network. Second, it is a service provided by the phone company. It's not something that companies put in for themselves. Third, it provides support for all forms of digital communications. It is true that the basic service of ISDN supports voice communication. But that same basic channel that could support voice can also support transmission of facsimile data, computer-to-computer communication, and even video. Figure 2-25 shows such a network of digital services.

❋ ISDN services
The services provided by ISDN are defined by the CCITT/ITU. It provides for end-to-end digital connectivity that is dial-up. This means

Figure 2-25

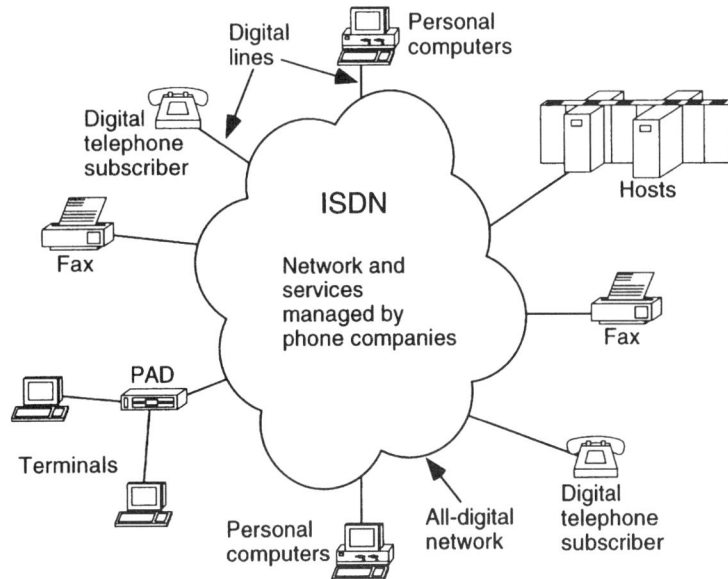

ISDN network and services. Learning Tree International

- ### ISDN: integrated services digital network

that a subscriber normally has the phone on the hook, and when the subscriber desires to connect, he or she picks up the phone, dials the phone number, and makes the connection to a remote subscriber. This is very powerful because now we have digital services that allow computer-to-computer communication directly without necessarily going out and getting a leased line.

The minimum connection to ISDN is provided through what is called the *basic rate*. This service includes two 64-Kbps digital channels plus one 16-Kbps control channel (a 2B+D service). The two digital channels can be aggregated into one 128-Kbps pipe. This type of service is very useful for dial-up high-speed connection into the Internet, for example, for a workstation, or as a connection between remote bridges or routers. Since it is dial up, it is also very useful as a backup line to a T1. A T1 would be continuously connected, giving 1.54-Mbps data-rate service, and if it ever went down, then the ISDN line would take over.

One of the drawbacks of ISDN is its very low data rate compared to LANs. But all WAN services are expensive at very high data rate. And this one is a great improvement over the use of modems over normal voice phone lines.

Another problem, which is quickly being overcome, is that ISDN is not universally available. Most metropolitan areas have some ISDN service. Some countries have extensive ISDN services, such as Japan, but others, such as the United States, do not have as extensive service. So a network administrator often finds that services are available at one point but not at the other. As time goes on, this problem with ISDN will be overcome as the service becomes more and more popular and available.

⇨ Packet-switched networks

Packet-switched networks are worldwide services provided by phone companies to transmit data that has been packetized. Rather than provide the raw telephone line to transmit voice or digital information to customers, phone companies and other providers have set up packet switches in local areas around the country and connected between those areas. The switches are then connected to each other over phone lines on a permanent basis, and subscribers dial into a switch or have a permanent connection to a switch and send packets over this network rather than use a phone line continuously. Probably the most popular form of packet switching is that based on the X.25 family of protocols.

✳ X.25 characteristics

X.25 is a CCITT/ITU recommendation for access by hosts to a packet-switched network. It does not define the protocols within the packet network, but only how a host connects to a packet network. In a sense, it is a well-defined DTE/DCE interface specification where the host is the DTE and the switch takes the place of the DCE. X.25 has been widely adopted since its inception in 1976. The protocol family was updated every four years until 1988. Thereafter it was updated only as required. It is right now a very stable protocol, and it is part of many protocol suites such as the OSI protocol suite, the TCP/IP protocol suite, and the SNA protocol suite.

At the physical layer, X.25 uses standard interfaces. In Europe this interface is called X.21. In the United States it is called RS-232C. X.25 itself is a broad term used for a family of protocols. At the lowest level is the physical layer defined previously. It also calls for a data link layer or frame layer and a packet layer operating at layer 3, the network layer. The layer 3 portion of the X.25 protocol is also referred to as the packet-level protocol (PLP). It defines circuit-switching, connection-oriented technology.

Figure 2-26 shows an X.25 network where an X.25 link is used to connect a host to a PAD (packet assembler and disassembler). The connection between host and PAD is often of the permanent type, called a permanent virtual circuit (PVC). X.25 defines the connection between the host and the packet switch and the connection between the packet switch and the PAD. The packet-level protocol allows for the host to establish a connection to the PAD across the network. This connection is referred to as a circuit.

Figure 2-26

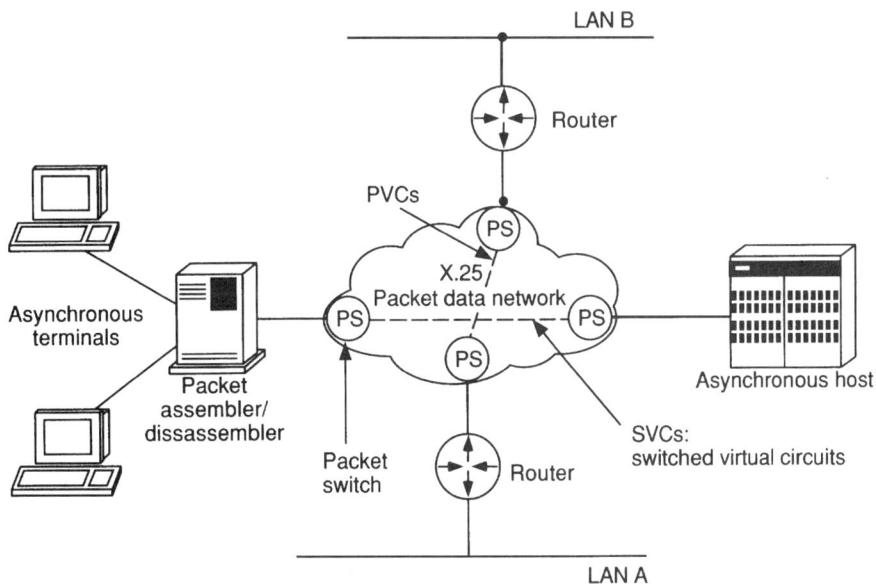

An X.25 packet data network used to connect terminals to a remote host and two remote routers. Learning Tree International

A PAD allows asynchronous or synchronous terminals to use a packet-data network. A PAD literally creates packets and disassembles them, thus its name—packet assembler/disassembler. As a user types on the keyboard and begins sending characters to the host, the characters arrive at the PAD now placed in packets or encapsulated in packets and go across the network to the host. Only packets can exist in the packet-data network. And the encapsulation of the characters from the terminal in packets to send across the network is the function of a PAD.

Figure 2-26 shows a number of terminals all using one PAD. Each terminal will establish a circuit between the terminal and the host. When a user is done with these circuits, the connection is terminated, so we consider these terminal/host connections as switched virtual circuits, or SVCs, which have a nonpermanent nature. Consider two remote routers and the need to connect two local area networks across an X.25 network. The routers will have an X.25 connection to packet switches, but the connection here has a different nature. LAN traffic is steady and heavy between the LANs, so we might want to have a permanent virtual circuit between the two routers. Thus we establish a permanent virtual circuit between the two routers. Those are the two types of virtual circuits available under X.25.

⇨ Summary of public network services

Figure 2-27 shows a summary of various services, leased lines and ISDN classified by their characteristics.

⇨ The worldwide Internet

A worldwide network of computers called the Internet links 35,000 networks and over 20 million users worldwide. It is estimated that more than 2 million of these users use the network every day to do their work. This worldwide network was started by the U.S. government to connect research centers under the auspices of an organization called ARPA (Advanced Research Project Agency). Today the Internet is used by universities for research, by companies for business, and by individuals for pleasure shopping and many more activities.

Figure 2-27

Characteristic	Voice service	Lease data line	ISDN
Bandwidth	300–3300 Hz	Varies 56 kbits/sec (DS0) 1.54 Mbits/sec (T1)	64 kbits/sec
Service	Business voice communication	Point-to-point data links	Digitized voice, data, fax, images
Switched	Dialup	Fixed links	Dialup
Local loop	One pair	Two pairs	One pair
Interface equipment	Voice telephone. Modems for data	DSU/CSU	ISDN device
Availability	Universal	Limited	Limited
Use	Business voice communications. Dialup data connections using modems	Connect bridges and routers over WANs; fixed links, connect multiplexers	Business voice; dialup data connections for terminals, bridges, and routers

Summary of telephone network service characteristics. Learning Tree International

❋ The topology of the Internet

Figure 2-28 shows the topology of the Internet, with the various ways of accessing Internet services broken down. The core of the Internet is Internet sites, computers that act as TCP/IP routers that connect to each other via phone lines, making up a very large worldwide network.

Individuals and organizations connecting to the Internet can do so in one of four general ways. The simplest way is for e-mail access only. Not too long ago, America Online and CompuServe provided only e-mail connection to the Internet. Users on their home PCs or PCs at their office using modems dialed into CompuServe or America Online servers as terminals. From there, users could access a whole range of

Figure 2-28

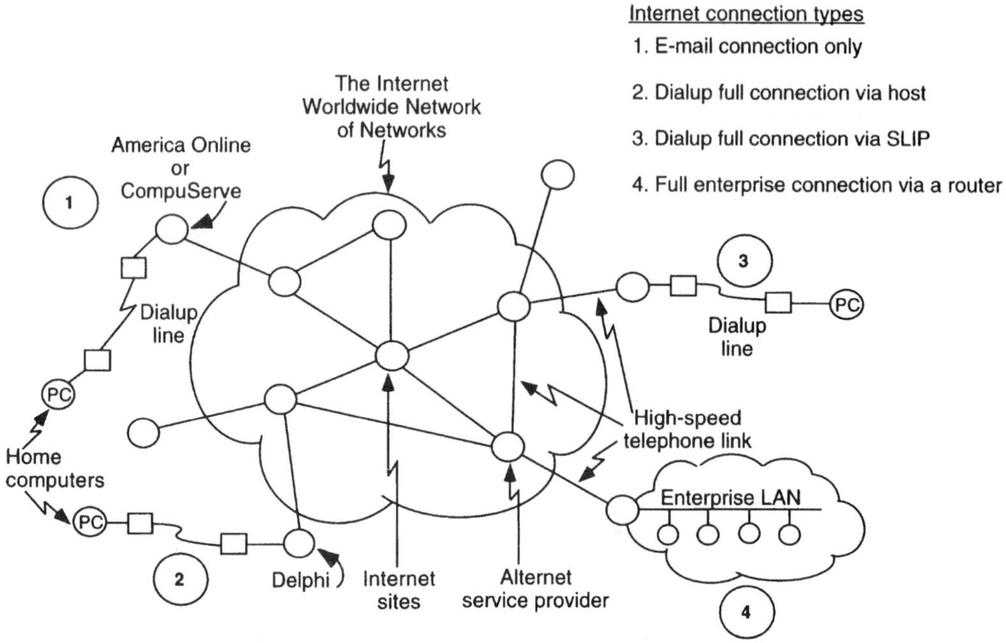

Internet connection types
1. E-mail connection only
2. Dialup full connection via host
3. Dialup full connection via SLIP
4. Full enterprise connection via a router

The topology of the Internet. Learning Tree International

services that these providers had available on their servers. The users had mailboxes where they can send or receive mail to other users of the same service. And eventually, when these services connected to the Internet, the users could send or receive mail to other Internet sites.

Notice that the connection here is via dial-up modems and a terminal into a CompuServe or America Online server. The face of the Internet is changing so quickly that by the time this book makes it to press, America Online and CompuServe will have migrated to more robust services such as those offered by Delphi, Alternet, and other Internet providers.

The second type of connection is also a dial-up connection, but it provides full Internet services such as FTP, Gopher, and remote terminal access via Telnet. In the second case, the user comes in to the Internet provider via a dial-up connection acting as a terminal from its home computer. The Internet provider then runs the client side of the software that provides these services against the server side of the software on the Internet host.

The third type of provider acts directly as a router into the Internet. The user comes into this machine via a point-to-point link over a telephone line using modems. All of the client software for TCP/IP is residing in the user's computer, which issues and makes connections to the Internet servers out on the Internet directly from the home PC. The intervening host that attaches the PC to the Internet acts strictly as an IP router. The connection between the PC and that router host can be done via the SLIP protocol or the PPP protocol, where PPP stands for point-to-point protocol.

Finally, a popular technique for connecting an enterprise network to the Internet is to set up a privately owned router with a point-to-point link to an Internet provider and connect that router to the enterprise network. In Fig. 2-28, this is shown by example number 4. To prevent unauthorized users residing on the Internet from breaking through and gaining unauthorized access to the enterprise LAN, extreme security measures are installed on the enterprise Internet router. Occasionally, that Internet router is actually several computers that provide a buffer between the enterprise network and the Internet. That group of computers is called a fire wall.

✳ Services provided by the Internet

The Internet provides an infrastructure for two-way electronic communication between computers. The most popular service and the very basic service provided by the Internet is electronic mail—the exchange of text messages among users to their computers. This electronic mail system has been enhanced so that today more than just text messages can be exchanged. Some files are binary files containing text, video, spreadsheets, and a variety of other data types.

Another useful service on the Internet is called Anonymous FTP. Under this procedure, companies set up servers connected to the Internet that contain public information of interest and use to a wide Internet audience. These documents can be retrieved from Internet servers via the FTP protocol. Since the information is public and residing on servers for retrieval, it is important that users have an account. That account might be a public account, usually with the user name of anonymous and no password. This type of document database and retrieval is very useful for the posting of press releases, newsletters, catalogs, and technical information for the widest possible dissemination. When FTP server information is indexed, the Gopher service is a useful way to retrieve files from other computers in an organized manner and to keep track of the information that might be on other computers.

Another very important service that's gaining in popularity is the World Wide Web. A certain number of Internet servers have a special program that supports the access of information via a graphical user interface. Using this graphical user interface on a client computer—a PC at home, for example, or one on a desktop at work—pictures, video, text, and audio files can be quickly downloaded and displayed in an almost magazine format. The World Wide Web provides a needed platform for the delivery of multimedia information. It requires much more bandwidth than Anonymous FTP, Gopher, or e-mail, and therefore it requires much higher-speed access lines. But as the price of high-speed modems and high-capacity phone lines drop, the Web will become the standard way of interacting with computers on the Internet.

Network hardware

CNE exam objectives

> Identify the connectivity hardware used to network computers.

> Identify and describe the connectivity hardware used to internetwork computers.

> Briefly describe the functions of connectivity hardware.

> Identify connectivity hardware by sight.

> Given sample network criteria, identify the appropriate connectivity devices.

Network hardware comes in three classifications: connectors (and cables), network interfaces, and connecting devices. Connectors attach cables to network interfaces. Each connector is specific to the type of cable and to the interface being used. Connectors might be considered part of the physical layer of the OSI model. Terminators, splitters, punch blocks, and wire rack termination panels might also be considered in this category.

Ethernet and Token Ring adapters are the first types of devices that come to mind when thinking of network interfaces. But there are many other devices that can be classified in that category. Transceivers and serial port interfaces are two other typical devices that fall in the network interface category.

The connecting device category probably has the greatest variation. Bridges, routers, and repeaters fall into this group. But so do Token Ring MSAUs, modems, FDDI hubs, and CSU/DSUs.

⇨ Connectors

Only the most common types of network hardware connectors are considered here. There are some photographs of the devices in the accompanying figures to assist the reader in identifying the connectors by sight.

✳ RJ-45

This is an eight-pin connector most typically used with unshielded twisted-pair wiring. The most popular application is for 10Base-T 802.3 (Ethernet) and 802.5 (Token Ring) installations. Each of these installations only uses four of the eight wires, and care must be exercised to install the pairs in the connector.

✳ BNC

The connector derives its name from a bulkier predecessor called the "N" connector. Thus the name baby N connector (BNC), since it is a smaller version of it. Actually, the BNC connector has a bayonet twist lock, and the N connector is threaded. BNC connectors are popular with 10Base-2 802.3 and ARCNET installations.

✳ Fiber optic

Fiber-optic connectors come in several varieties. The two most popular are the ST type and the FDDI type of connector, both shown in Fig. 2-29.

✳ DB-25

A 25-pin connector used most commonly with serial interfaces, particularly RS-232 modem connections. Not all 25 circuits are used, as seen earlier in the chapter.

Figure 2-29

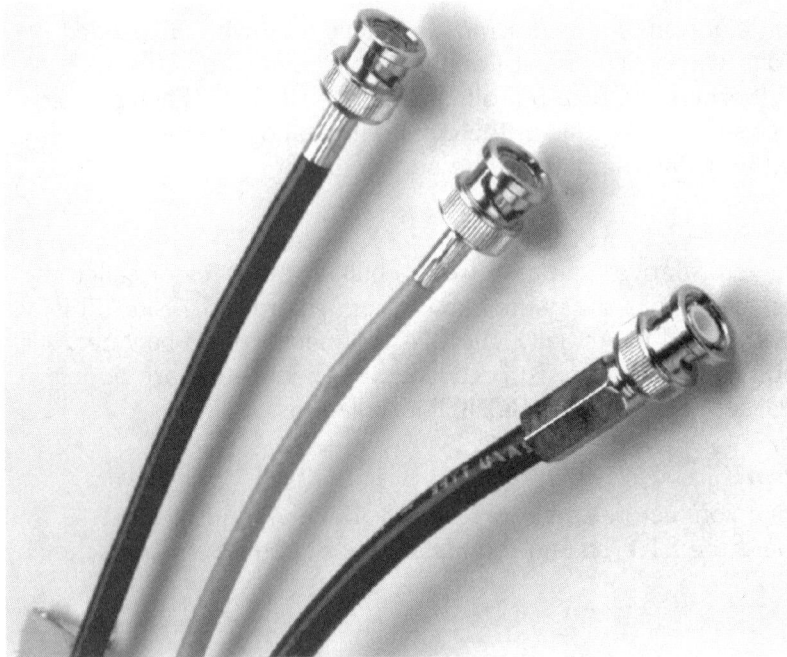

A

B

Network connectors: (a) RJ-45; (b) BNC; (c) Fiber-optic ST connector; (d) FDDI connector; (e) DB-25 25-pin connector used with serial cables; (f) V-35 connector used for high-speed serial cables. South Hill Datacomm

Figure 2-29

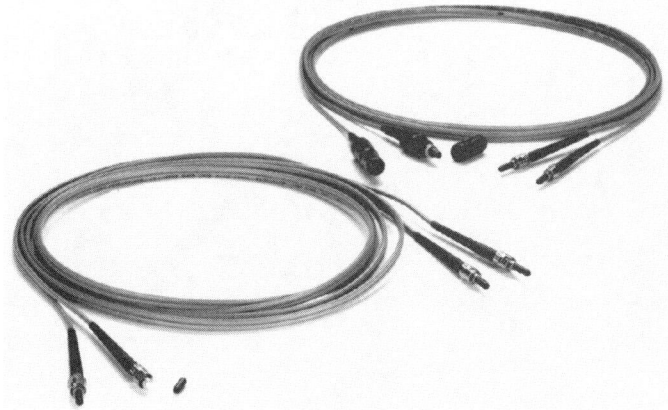

C

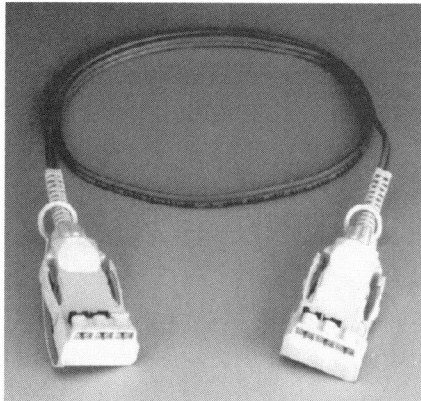

D

E

Continued

F

Continued.

❋ V.35

A 50 connector specified by the CCITT/ITU to work with high-speed data circuits connected to the telephone network. (See Fig. 2-29.)

❋ Summary of connector characteristics

Figure 2-30 summarizes the characteristics of popular connector types.

❋ Network interfaces

The most popular components that fall into this category are network interface cards, transceivers, and transmission media adapters.

❋ Network interface card

This device plugs into the bus of the personal computer. It provides all of the data link and physical-layer functionality for the PC to communicate over the network. The network interface card (or NIC) has many other names: network adapter, network interface unit (NUI), or network card. Most NICs are printed circuits cards, although some are external devices connecting to the PC via a serial or parallel port. Network interfaces are specific to one type of technology. Ethernet cards are different from Token Ring cards, which are different from FDDI cards.

Figure 2-30

Network hardware	Type	Characteristic
Media connectors	RJ-45	8-pin connector used with unshielded twisted-pair data cables
	BNC	Coaxial T-connector used in ThinEthernet (10BASE2) networks for daisy chaining
	DB-25	25-pin connector used with serial interfaces to RS-232 modem connections
	DB-15	15-pin connector used with 15-wire Ethernet transciever cables
	V.35	50-pin connector used with serial interfaces to high-speed modems
Network interfaces	Network card (NIC)	Device that plugs into the motherboard to allow access to the LAN. Examples: Ethernet and Token Ring NICs.
	Transciever	Converts the signals on the media to a digital data stream usable by the NIC. Example: Ethernet transceiver.
	Transmission media adapter	Allows network cards that use one type of media to attach to a network using another type. Example: Coax to UTP adapter.

Summary of popular connector characteristics. Learning Tree International

Transceivers

The transceivers convert the signals on the LAN media to a bit stream suitable for the NIC. The most common transceiver type is the 10Base-5 802.3 transceiver. A special transceiver was created in order to convert existing 10Base-5 networks to 10Base-T cabling. This type of transceiver will connect a 10Base-5 802.3 card to 10Base-T cabling. These special transceivers are sometimes called *transmission media adapters*. (See Fig. 2-31.)

Figure 2-31

A

B

Network interfaces: (a) 802.3 NIC; (b) 802.5 NIC; (c) 10Base5 802.3 transceiver. South Hill Datacomm

Figure 2-31

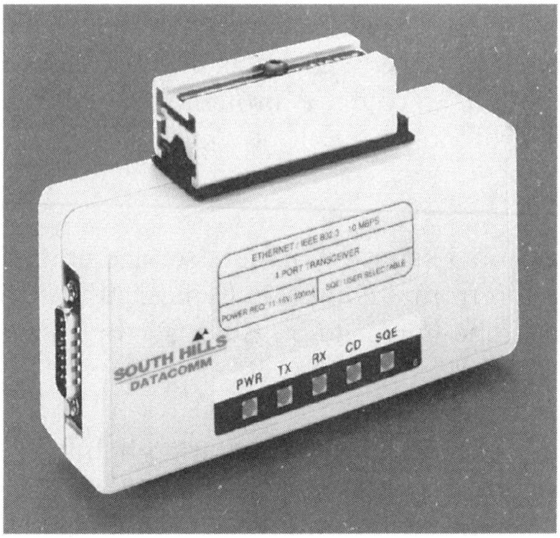

C

Continued.

⇨ Connecting devices

✳ Repeaters

A *repeater* regenerates those digital signals in a LAN that have attenuated after a long transmission path. A repeater extends the LAN to its largest possible geographic coverage, connecting LAN segments. Both 802.3 (Ethernet) and 802.5 (Token Ring) can use repeaters that are unique to each technology.

✳ Bridges

A *bridge* is a device that connects two LANs (typically of the same type) by forwarding frames from one LAN to the other. A bridge creates one larger LAN of the same type as the two LANs. Examples of bridges include Ethernet bridges and Token Ring bridges. Bridges are available in two varieties: local and remote.

✳ Routers

A *router* connects two LANs by forwarding packets or datagrams from one LAN to the other. A router creates an internet, keeps the two LAN segments distinct, and requires the use of a routing protocol (i.e., IP or IPX). A router easily connects LANs via WANs.

✳ Brouter

A *brouter* is a connection device that acts like a router for those protocols it is configured to route. A brouter forwards frames as a bridge for all other protocols.

✳ DSU/CSU

A CSU/DSU is a channel service unit/data service unit. This device adapts the data stream from a computer (typically through a serial port) to a digital telephone line (typically 56 Kbits/sec or T1 leased line).

✳ MSAU

A MSAU (multistation access unit) is the wiring hub that creates the electrical ring in an 802.5 network. This is a passive device. There are electronically passive devices that provide bypass relays for stations removed from the network. Such a device is simply referred to as a "MAU." Don't confuse this name with a MAU in an Ethernet network. In that technology, a MAU (meaning media access unit) is the same as a transceiver.

✳ Modem

The word modem is a contraction of modulator/demodulator. It adapts computer digital signals for transmission over analog telephone lines.

✳ Multiplexer

A multiplexer allows the sharing of a high-speed phone connection for sending traffic from several slower-speed lines. Two devices are needed, one at each end of the phone line. (See Fig. 2-32.)

✳ Summary of connecting device characteristics

Figure 2-33 summarizes the characteristics of popular connecting device types.

⇨ Workshop

For the following exercise, use the case study for the International Technologies enterprise network in appendix A.

Figure 2-32

A

B

C

Connecting devices: (a) modem; (b) bridge; (c) 802.3 repeater; (d) 802.5 MSAU. South Hill Datacomm

Figure 2-32

D

Continued.

Figure 2-33

Device	Types	Characteristic
Modem	—	Adapts computer-transmitted digital signals for transmission over analog telephone lines
Repeater	Ethernet or Token Ring	Regenerates digital signals that have been attenuated to extend a LAN to its maximum limits
Hub	Passive Active Intelligent	A point of connection between media segments
Multiplexers	TDM and stat muxes	Allows the sharing of a high-speed phone line by several slower speed data streams. Used with terminal networks.
CSU/DSU	—	Channel service unit/data service unit: Adapts the digital data stream from a computer to be transmitted over a digital phone connection
Bridge	Ethernet or Token Ring Local or remote	Forwards frames from one LAN to another creating a logically larger LAN
Router	IP or IPX	Routes packets from one network to another. Keeps the LANs distinct. Needs a specific protocol (IPX, IP) to work.
Brouter	—	Combination router and bridge. It bridges those protocols it is not set up to route.

Summary of connecting device types. Learning Tree International

Exercise 2.1—Adding a workstation to an existing network

Consider adding a workstation of the same type to each of the networks noted in Fig. 2-34. Describe the type of cabling, network card, media adapter (if one is needed), and connector, and describe the types of devices and media encountered from that workstation to the file server in the network.

Network	Device type to be added	NIC type	Cable type	Media adapter?	Connector?	Trace route
Building 1 Net B	IBM PC					
Building 2 Net B	Sun workstation					
Paris, France Net B	IBM PC					

Figure 2-34

Worksheet for the workshop.

Exercise 2.2—Determination of connecting device

A customer desires to connect networks B and C in Building 1, networks B and C in Building 2, and networks A, B, and C in Building 3. Determine what type of devices will be needed to connect each network to an Ethernet backbone network. Also determine what cabling choice is appropriate to connect each network to the backbone. You can draw your solution on the network diagrams in appendix E.

Exercise 2.3—Determination of necessary WAN link

A customer desires to connect the engineering network in Hong Kong and the research network in Toronto to the enterprise backbone network in San Jose. Assume that remote router connections will be employed. Determine what type of WAN link is appropriate, and speculate on the bandwidth needed and what devices are needed to connect the routers to the public network.

Test your understanding

To see how much you have learned about the concepts presented in chapter 2, take five minutes to answer the following questions. Some of these will help you survey your system. They will give you an idea of how to think through the questions when you plan configuration management for your own network. Turn to appendix C for typical answers to these questions. (See Figs. 2-35, 2-36, and 2-37.)

Figure 2-35

Media	Types	Characteristic and use	Bound or unbound	Advantage and disadvantage
Twisted pair				
Coax				
Fiber optic				
Satellite				
Radio				

Media worksheet. Fill in the worksheet by writing in the types, characteristics, one advantage, and one disadvantage of the types of media in the chart.

Figure 2-36

Phone link	Data rate	Device needed to attach

Telephone links worksheet. Fill in the worksheet by listing the types of telephone links that can be used for data transmission, the data rate over the link, and the type of device needed to attach the data source to the telephone line.

⇨ Practice exam questions

1. The data rate of a T1 digital transmission link is:
   A. 64 Kbits/sec
   B. 128 Kbits/sec
   C. 1.54 Mbits/sec
   D. 2.048 Mbits/sec

2. Which is an example of a bounded type of media?
   A. Twisted pair
   B. Coaxial
   C. Fiber optic
   D. All of the above

3. Which is not a characteristic of fiber-optic cables?
   A. They are immune to electromagnetic interference
   B. They are much smaller than coaxial cables
   C. Attenuation is much less than that of signals on conductors
   D. They have extremely narrow bandwidths

Figure 2-37

Device	Function	Application
NIC		
Transceiver		
RJ-45		
Concentrator		
Bridge		
MUX		
Router		
CSU/DSU		

Network device worksheet. Describe the function and application of the network devices in the chart.

4. Which unbounded transmission media type does not require FCC or governmental approval before operating?
   A. Terrestrial microwave
   B. Satellite microwave
   C. Laser
   D. Radio

5. The ISDN protocol has been developed and promoted by which standards organization?
   A. IEEE
   B. ISO

C. CCITT/ITU

D. ANSI

6. In local telephone service, the responsibility of the service provider extends to:

A. The central office

B. The local loop

C. The demarcation point

D. The subscriber location

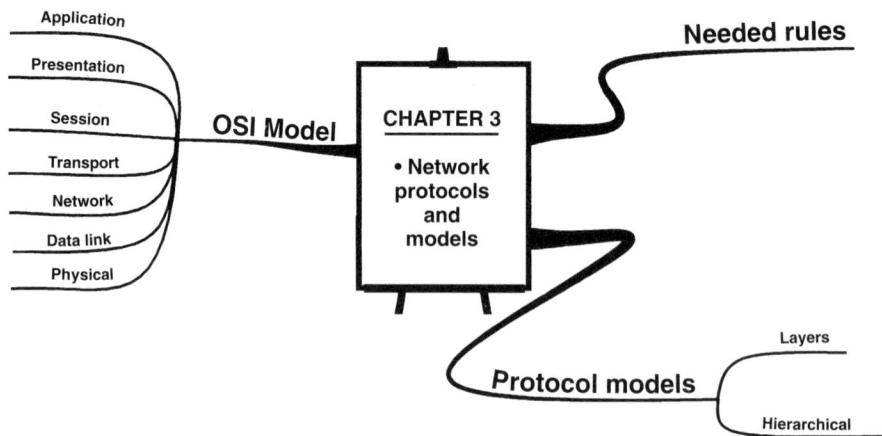

Application
Presentation
Session
Transport
Network
Data link
Physical

OSI Model

CHAPTER 3

• Network
protocols
and
models

Needed rules

Protocol models

Layers

Hierarchical

3

Data communications standards, models, and protocols

C HAPTER 3 covers the concepts associated with network models, protocol specifications, and the organizations (standards bodies) responsible for establishing and maintaining these specifications. Protocols are rules for communication between computers and are one of the three elements of computer networking. Unlike humans, computers must follow exact rules when establishing communication with each other. Both sending and receiving computers must use the same protocols, or communication is not successful.

In this chapter we will review one of the most important aspects of the computer networking industry—the Open Systems Interconnection (OSI) reference model. In subsequent chapters, we detail in greater depth each area of communications specified by the OSI reference model.

⇨ CNE exam objectives

➢ Explain why rules are needed in general networking relationships.

➢ Describe the differences between protocols and models.

➢ List the seven layers of the OSI reference model.

➢ Using the OSI reference model, describe how network protocols interact within their own stack and with peer layers in other stacks.

➢ Define protocol as it relates to computer networks.

➢ Describe the usefulness of the OSI reference model.

⇨ Models and protocols

Confusion often arises on the differences between computer networking models and protocols. In the following section, we review the fundamentals of both models and protocols. A simplistic definition would be that models are the concepts and protocols are the actual procedures for communication.

⇨ Protocol definition

Protocols are the exact rules and conventions by which devices (computers, hosts, bridges, routers, gateways) communicate. Protocols were in use in everyday life long before computers came into the picture. Wedding protocol and military protocol are examples of human beings using protocols. In weddings, the groom and bride have their respective places to stand, and certain events occur at set times throughout the ceremony. The military is an even better example of protocol because it tends to be very strict about its proper application. Soldiers of a lower rank salute soldiers of a higher rank first, and then the higher-ranking soldier returns the salute, for example. The main difference between human and computer implementations of protocols is that while humans can sometimes fudge their way through the process, computers cannot. Communication either works or doesn't.

Multiple protocols are often involved in computer-to-computer communication. We described the three elements of computer networking in the first chapter, and it is important to understand that protocols are in fact used within each element. The protocols employed within each element work together to successfully complete the communication process.

Protocols are arranged according to a layered model. Protocols work on top of or below other protocols within this layered structure. Each communication component is part of a layer that performs a specific task in the communications process. Communication components are software programs and hardware devices that provide a solution to the communications process. As stated earlier, both communicating entities (sender and receiver) must use the same protocols so that communication can take place.

Protocols are used in sets called suites or stacks (multiple protocols). TCP/IP, used on the Internet, and IPX/SPX, used in Novell NetWare networks, are two examples of protocols suites. There are many more. Protocol suites can be compared to languages or dialects. For two people to successfully communicate with each other, they must speak the same language. Alternatively, different languages might be involved in the conversation if there is a go-between or translator. In networking, these translators take the form of gateways.

For example, when a networked computer-workstation client communicates with a Novell NetWare file server, it will use one of the protocol suites supported by the file server. Both the sender and the receiver must use the same protocols so that communication can take place.

Protocols and models are not the same. As stated initially, a model is a concept of how communications should work in a network environment. A protocol is the actual specifications and programs that implement the communication process.

⇨ The OSI reference model

Many network communication models existed before OSI. However, they were mostly proprietary. IBM's SNA and Digital Equipment Corporation's (DEC) DNA are examples of those early protocol families represented by models. The TCP/IP protocol was represented by the Department of Defense (DoD) model and was one of the few exceptions on the public domain. All of these models facilitated one goal—the development of network protocols for end-to-end communication of network applications. Although each model is on paper somewhat different, they all strive to achieve this same objective.

The International Standards Organization in 1977 created a subcommittee of members of other standards organizations, vendors, and end users to develop standards for more open systems that would facilitate multiplatform interconnectivity and interoperability. That committee was charged to come up with a standard data-communications model. Since then, most—if not all—network-related manufacturers build products with functionality that fits the OSI model. (See Fig. 3-1.)

The OSI model has been divided into seven layers or categories of functions. The seven layers divide the enormous task of protocol development into easier, more manageable subtasks. These subtasks can be optimized individually and tailored to specific functions. The

Figure 3-1

7	**Application**
6	**Presentation**
5	**Session**
4	**Transport**
3	**Network**
2	**Data Link**
1	**Physical**

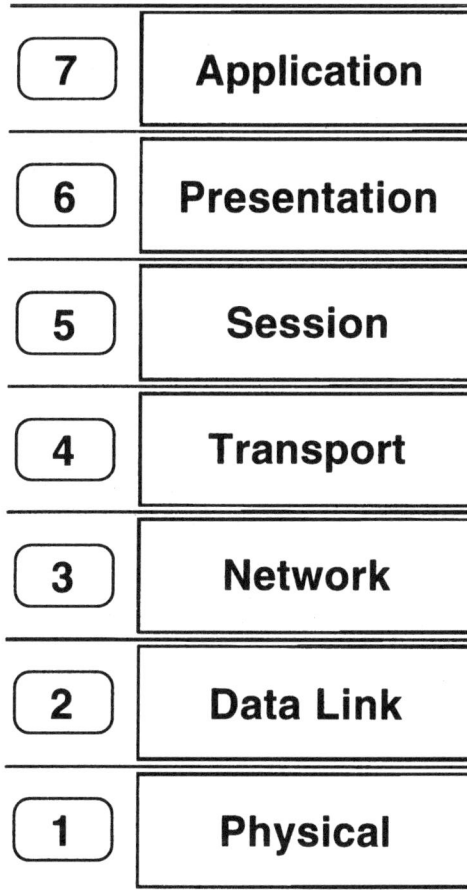

The OSI reference model. Learning Tree International

layers are not protocols, but rather are guidelines of the protocol components to be implemented.

Many people often wonder why seven layers and not more or less? The answer becomes apparent as we look at the functions that each layer is responsible for during the complete communication process, as you will see in the following summary.

Before we move on to a summary review, we would like to point out that for the purposes of the CNE exam, you are expected to have memorized the order of the layers and the responsibilities of each. We have found some of the following key phrases to be helpful in this.

| | **Phrase** | |
Model layers	Top to bottom	Bottom to top*
Application	All	(Arnold or Andres)
Presentation	People	Presented (by)
Session	Seem	Session
Transport	To	Training
Network	Need	Network
Data link	Data	Dynamic
Physical	Processing	Pretty

*Note: Thanks to Mr. Chris Gauthier.

⇨ The physical layer

The physical layer is the lowest common denominator of all network communication. (See Fig. 3-2.) Eventually, all messages transmitted from one host to another will appear in the form of electromagnetic signals over a cable (or through the intervening space as in wireless forms of network communication, discussed in chapter 2). The transmitted electromagnetic signals encode bits of information. Bits are the main element addressed by the physical layer.

Both this layer and the data link layer are predominantly hardware-based standards. The main responsibility of the physical layer is the management of the signal bits through the mechanical and electrical specifications of the transmission medium (cable) and the network interface. Signal patterns for zeros and ones—including voltage levels of the signals, clocking, cable and adapter pin assignments, and types of cables—are all specified by protocols in this layer.

Signal patterns and voltage levels detail how bits of zeros and ones should be interpreted by the network interface of the receiver. Different transmission media support different voltage levels and, as such, the network interface card must be compatible with the medium being used. The timing used to monitor electromagnetic signals on the

Figure 3-2

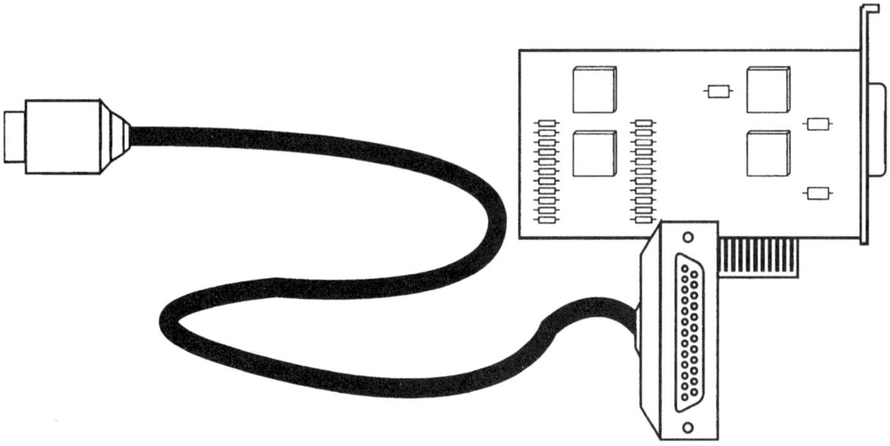

The physical layer. <small>Learning Tree International</small>

cable is called *clocking*. Faster clocking techniques allow for an increase in a transmission medium's potential bandwidth. Coax uses different connectors and correspondingly different pin assignments than UTP. There is a need to establish, given a specific medium, which pin will be responsible for receiving or transmitting information. This assignment is specified by the physical layer protocol. Finally, the physical characteristics of the network interface connector are handled at this layer. This entails the shape of the connector and the location and functions of all pins.

A good example protocol associated with this layer is the RS-232-C serial interface. It is used to connect a modem to a computer. At the computer side, the RS-232-C pin 2 handles bit transfers, and pin 3 handles bit receives. Another example would be a UTP cable with an RJ-45 type connector. RS-449, CCITT/ITU X-, and V-series recommendations are still more example protocols in use at the physical layer.

⇨ The data link layer

The data link layer is responsible for managing frames (groups) of bits. (See Fig. 3-3.) This layer frames bits of data into coherent groupings. In computer communications, this means framing a series of zeros and

Figure 3-3

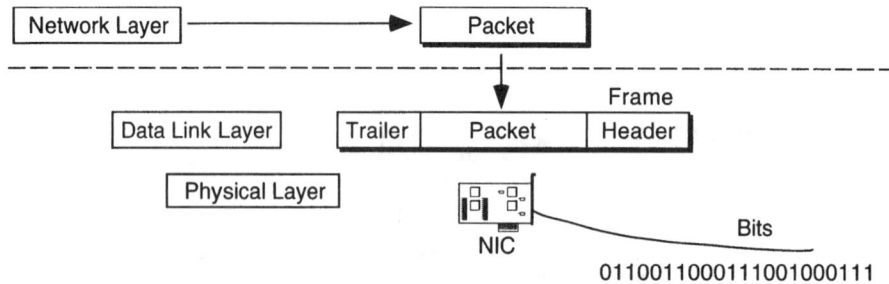

The data link layer. Learning Tree International

ones together at the sender and then interpreting them at the receiver. Since the received train of bits is derived from electromagnetic signals, and because these signals are susceptible to outside interference, the data link layer must also detect errors in transmitted frames. The data link layer is also typically implemented as hardware.

In shared networks, workstations will compete to transmit a frame. Most stations will be waiting in line to take their turns. The manner in which the workstations access the network transmission medium through the network interface card is called the *channel access scheme*. Token passing, polling, and contention are examples of channel access schemes.

Once a workstation begins sending frames, the receiving workstation might not be able to process the frames as quickly as they are being sent. The sending station needs to be able to determine when this is the case and adjust the rate of sending frames. This adjustment process is called *flow control*. Some protocols perform flow control at the data link layer.

When multiple workstations or hosts connect to the same transmission medium, a method is required to uniquely identify each one. Unique physical addresses are embedded in each network interface card for this purpose. The address information of the sender and receiver is included in the transmitted frame.

Finally, the data link layer encapsulates information packets or datagrams from the network layer located directly above it. The packets become the payload or cargo of the frame.

Examples of protocols providing data link layer functionality are Ethernet (802.3), Token Ring (802.5), Attached Resource Computer network (ARCNET), and Fiber Distributed Data Interface (FDDI).

⇨ The network layer

The network layer manages the flow of packets that have been delivered within the frames from the lower layer. (See Fig. 3-4.) As we move to the network layer, software begins to play a dominant role in the communication process. One of the main functions of the network layer is to route packets throughout multiple network segments. This type of service is required because the physical workstation we might want to communicate with might not be on the same physical transmission medium we are connected to. A logical networkwide address scheme is implemented to facilitate the routing process. There are several different routing methods and protocols, which will be discussed in chapter 4.

Figure 3-4

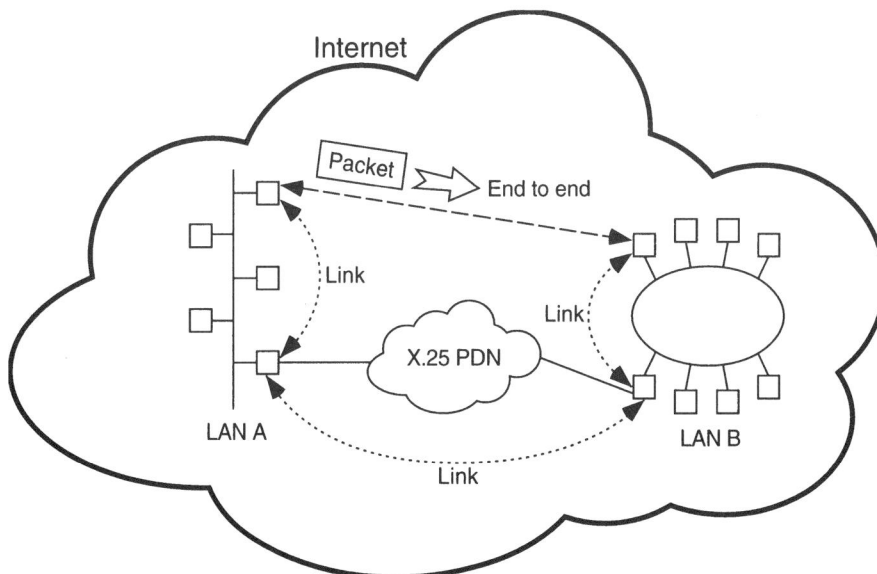

The network and transport layers. Learning Tree International

Packets are created at this layer and are used to carry transport layer segments of information. The network layer protocols are usually unreliable, connectionless oriented in LAN environments (IPX and IP), and connection oriented in the WAN environments (X.25). In connectionless service, no check is made by this layer to ensure that the packet arrives at its destination successfully. We rely on protocols defined by higher layers to perform this function.

Example protocols in use at the network layer are the Internetwork Packet Exchange (IPX), the Internetwork Protocol (IP), the X.25 Packet Level Protocol, and the ConnectionLess Network Protocol (CLNP for OSI protocol suite).

⇨ The transport layer

The transport layer ensures reliable end-to-end delivery of message segments across an internetwork. (See Fig. 3-5.) Segments are the main protocol data unit used here. This layer often compensates for the unreliability of lower layers. Acknowledgments are used to accomplish reliable delivery of segments of information between hosts.

Figure 3-5

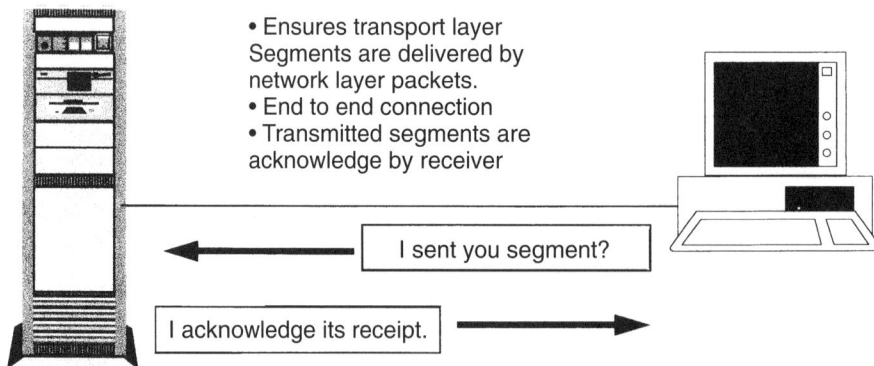

• Ensures transport layer Segments are delivered by network layer packets.
• End to end connection
• Transmitted segments are acknowledge by receiver

I sent you segment?

I acknowledge its receipt.

Transport layer. Infomentat Inc.

An interesting aspect of network layer packet delivery is that packets can take different routes to get to the same destination. As such, transport layer segments can arrive at the receiving workstation in a different order than they were sent. Sequencing of segments assures that the eventual message is reassembled in the proper, intended order, and this is the responsibility of this layer. Flow control might also be implemented at this layer to ensure that information travels on the network at an optimal speed at which the sending and receiving hosts can process the information without flooding the underlying networks.

The session layer

The session layer manages a dialogue between computers, or more correctly, between applications running on two computers. (See Fig. 3-6.) It sets the rules for the beginning and end of segment transmissions. While the network and transport layers provide interconnectivity between the two computers, the session layers provide interoperability services. With these services, we can access applications residing on other hosts.

Figure 3-6

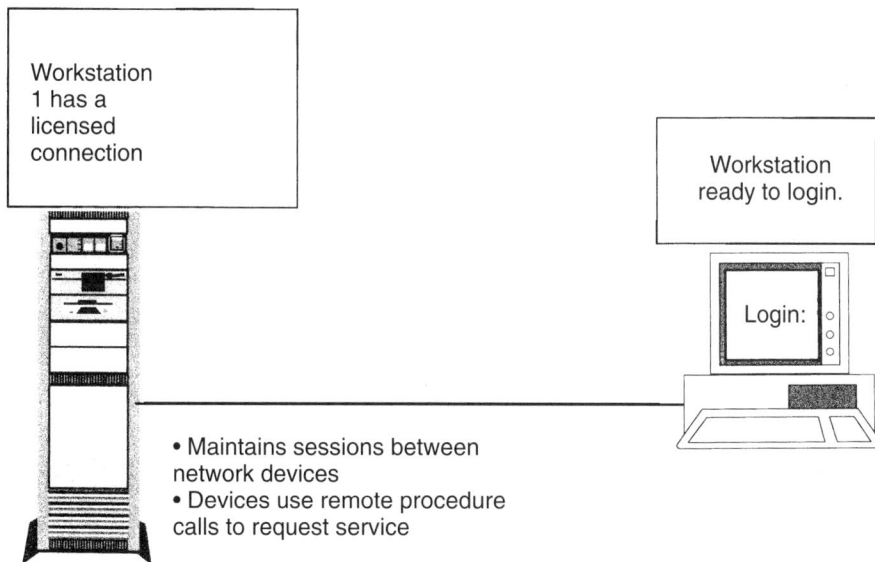

Workstation 1 has a licensed connection

Workstation ready to login.

Login:

• Maintains sessions between network devices
• Devices use remote procedure calls to request service

Session layer. Infomentat Inc.

One form of session layer functionality is the remote procedure calls (RPC). One computer sends an RPC to another requesting some form of service, such as reading of parts of a file on a remote machine. Example protocols implemented at the session layer includes the TCP/IP Remote Procedure Call (RPC) protocol, the NetBIOS protocol, and the ISO 8237 protocol.

⇨ The presentation layer

The presentation layer is responsible for syntax or grammar rules. (See Fig. 3-7.) Up until this point in the stack, we have been dealing with bits or groupings of bits of information. This layer converts a group of zeros and ones into alphanumeric formats that are more easily understood by humans. Character code tables are used to determine the bit patterns to represent alphanumeric characters.

Figure 3-7

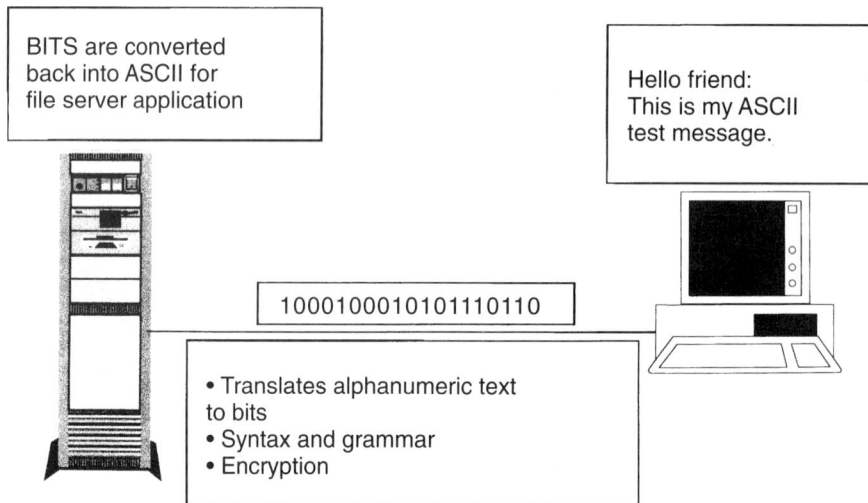

BITS are converted back into ASCII for file server application

Hello friend:
This is my ASCII
test message.

1000100010101110110

• Translates alphanumeric text to bits
• Syntax and grammar
• Encryption

Presentation layer. Infomentat Inc.

Data compression and expansion are presentation layer protocols performed to reduce transmission time. Long patterns of zeros and ones are compressed into shorter representative patterns that are then expanded at the receiving application. Finally, data encryption facilities are provided at this layer. Data encryption scrambles data into incoherent streams of bits that require special keys to decrypt the message.

It is important to note that many gateway services function at this layer to act as translators between computers that are using dissimilar protocol suites or stacks. Example protocols in use at the presentation layer are those that convert ASCII to EBCDIC (or vice versa), Data Encryption Standard (DES), and the eXternal Data Representation (XDR) specifications.

⇨ The application layer

The application layer manages application access and access to network services by users. (See Fig. 3-8.) This layer is often confused with applications that the users run at their client workstations, but it is not the same. The application a user runs uses the services provided by this layer to, for example, copy files to the network file server hard disk drive system.

Figure 3-8

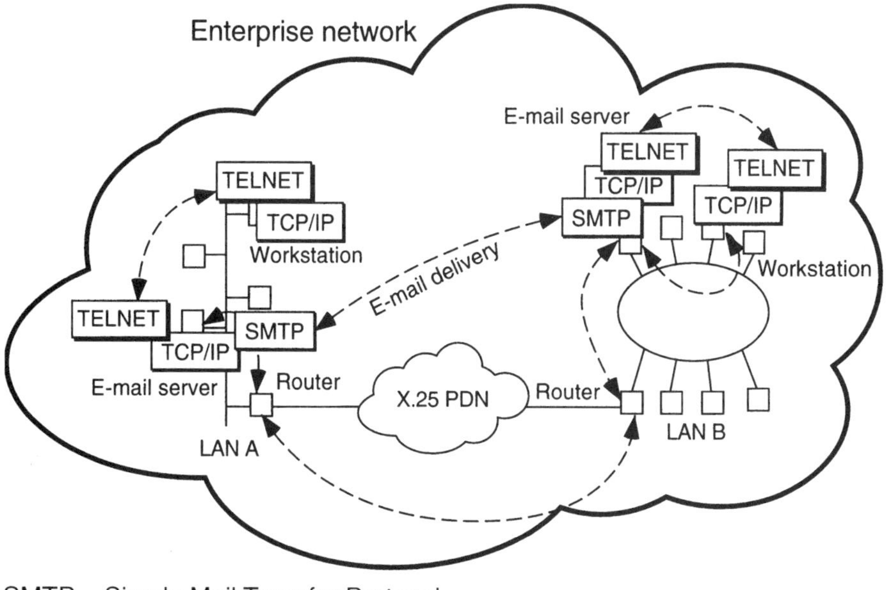

SMTP = Simple Mail Transfer Protocol

The session, presentation, and application layers in action. Learning Tree International

Functions provided by the application layer include file access and transfer, virtual terminal emulation to host computers, directory services, network management, and mail transfer. The main element of this layer is messages in the form of requests and replies for services.

Example protocols providing functionality in this layer include File Transfer Protocol (FTP), File Transfer, Access, and Management (FTAM), NetWare Core Protocol (NCP), X.400 Mail protocol, NetWare Directory Services (NDS), and TELNET for terminal emulation in terminal/host-based computer environments.

⇨ The complete OSI model

The complete OSI model introduces two main components in addition to the seven-layer model: end systems and intermediate systems. (See Fig. 3-9.) *End systems* are the actual clients and hosts or servers. *Intermediate systems* are the devices in between the clients and hosts

Figure 3-9

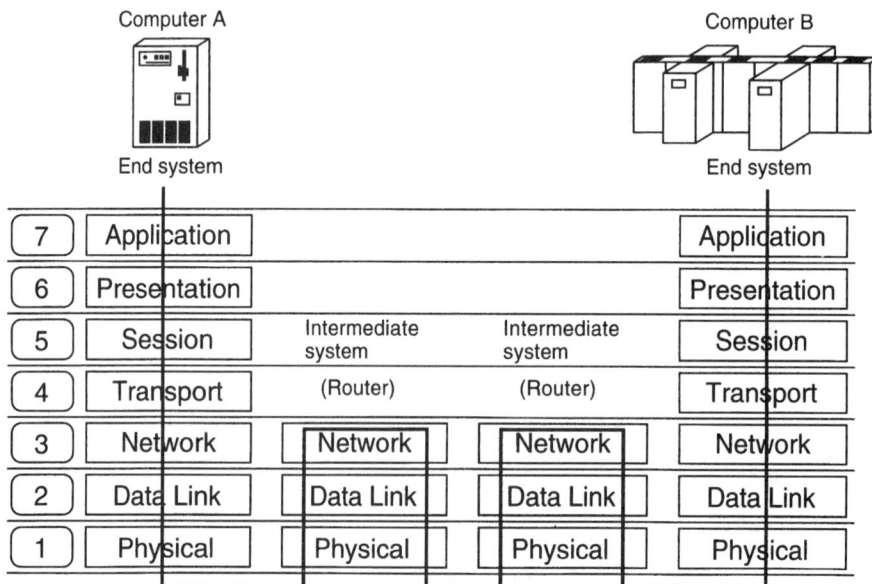

7	Application			Application
6	Presentation			Presentation
5	Session	Intermediate system	Intermediate system	Session
4	Transport	(Router)	(Router)	Transport
3	Network	Network	Network	Network
2	Data Link	Data Link	Data Link	Data Link
1	Physical	Physical	Physical	Physical

The complete OSI model. Learning Tree International

or servers that facilitate the relaying of packets of information between separate, logical networks.

As a system processes user information by its protocols, information flows from a sender's application to the receiver's application in the following manner:

> ➤ Information is processed by the upper layers of the sender.

> ➤ It is passed to the lower layers of the sender (down the stack).

> ➤ It eventually becomes an external signal on the cable.

> ➤ The upper-layer information is assisted toward its destination by a router.

> ➤ It is processed by the receiver's lower layers.

> ➤ The information is handed up through the upper layers to the receiver's application.

The sender and receiver are considered end systems (ES), while routers are considered intermediate systems (IS). The process of passing information from one layer to another is called *protocol layering and encapsulation*.

⇨ Example protocol suites

Figure 3-10 represents two common protocol stacks compared against the OSI model. Each stack has individual protocol software components whose functionality falls into a specific layer or layers of the OSI Model. While we will cover these and other example protocols in more detail in chapter 5, it is interesting to note that the example protocol stacks do not match up exactly with the OSI model. The main reason for this is because the example protocol stacks were created before the OSI model was established, and the functionality of specific protocols within the stack perform the responsibilities of one or more of the layers.

Finally, it is important to remember that the OSI reference model is just a concept and that the layers themselves are not functioning components. It is the communication protocol software and hardware components that implement the functions described by each layer.

Figure 3-10

	OSI Model	NetWare	TCP/IP
7	Application	NCP	
6	Presentation		FTP
5	Session	SPX	
4	Transport		TCP
3	Network	IPX	IP
2	Data Link	Token Ring	Ethernet
1	Physical		

NCP = NetWare Core Protocol

Example protocol suites. Learning Tree International

⇨ Protocol layering and encapsulation

As the protocols within a stack interact, they are layered, so to speak, one on top of the other. (See Fig. 3-11.) Following our explanation of the responsibilities of each layer and starting at the highest one, the message that we type into our electronic mail or word-processing package needs to be converted into a format that each layer of the OSI model can work with. The original text characters are therefore encapsulated into an application layer message element. This encapsulated character text needs then to be converted into a format the presentation layer can work with, such as bits. The bit stream created is then grouped into segments of messages that can be transferred to the lower layers. These segments are encapsulated within a network layer packet that is routed throughout the internetwork. Each packet is further encapsulated by the layer below, the data link layer, into a frame. The data stream of bits is then

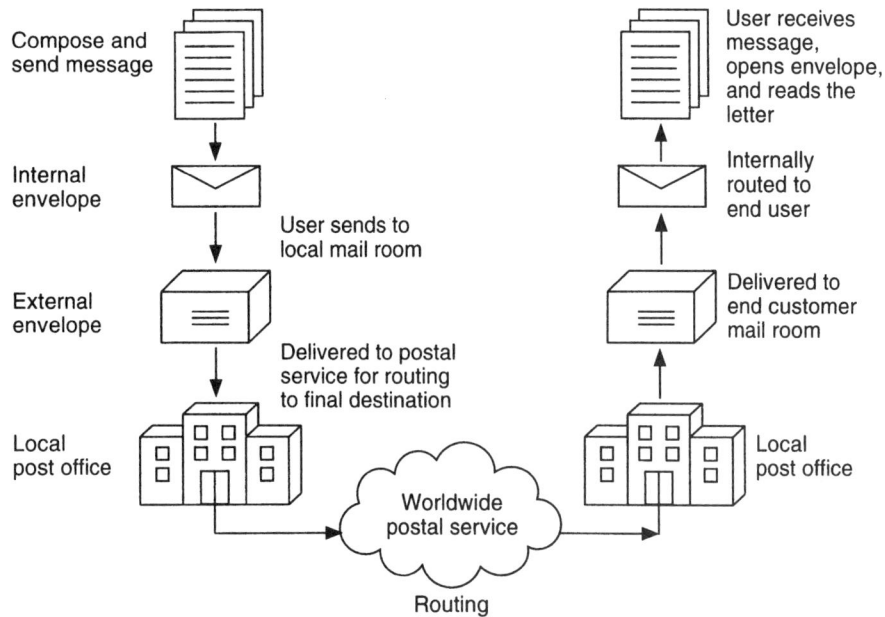

Protocol layering and encapsulation. Learning Tree International

Figure 3-11

transmitted at the physical layer as signals over the cable. The reverse of this process is completed at the end system or partially completed along the way by intermediate systems.

The entire process is similar to the way in which a letter to a friend is initially written and then mailed through the postal system. Your letter is enclosed (encapsulated) in an envelope. Your envelope is then packaged with many other envelopes destined for the same end system (city). The mail is assisted to its final destination by local post offices and the worldwide postal system (intermediate systems). The process reverses itself as the mail arrives closer and closer to your friend's house (end system) until it is finally delivered, opened, and read.

⇨ Layered protocols

Still working from the top of the protocol stack, as each OSI layer element or package is transferred to its immediately lower layer, a header is added to the data to be passed to the lower layer. Figure 3-12 demonstrates this process. The header contains control information that assists the sending and receiving workstations in defining which protocols created the data.

Figure 3-12

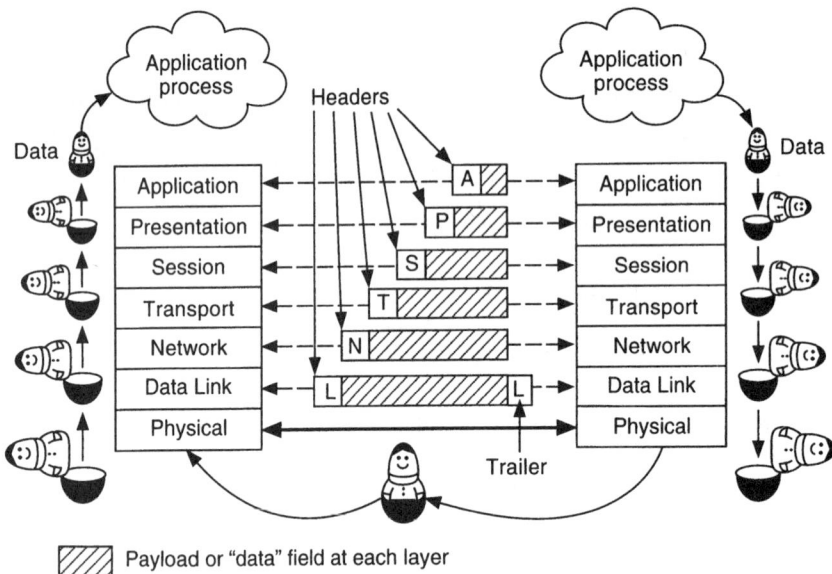

Payload or "data" field at each layer

• **Encapsulation is similar to using "Russian dolls" to transport data**

Layered protocols. Learning Tree International

The application process is actually the data or request being created by an end-user application such as a word processor or database software package. It creates data that is in turn passed to the OSI application layer, where a header is added in front of the data component. The header and the data are then passed to the immediately lower presentation layer, where they become the protocol data unit (PDU) for that layer.

Some protocol families, such as Novell's IPX/SPX, do not have protocols in all of the OSI model layers, as shown in Fig. 3-10. In this example, the Novell application layer protocol message will become a PDU for the network layer protocol directly. No headers will be added by intermediate layers in between the application and the network.

When a protocol is missing for a particular layer, we say that "the layer is null" for that protocol family.

As a receiving station processes the information, it removes the control headers and passes the data component to the upper protocol indicated in the control header.

⇨ Software and hardware protocols components

Figure 3-13 summarizes the hardware and software components in use by a workstation and compares them to the OSI reference model layers. Note that the two lowest layers of the model are hardware based, while the upper layers are software based.

Figure 3-13

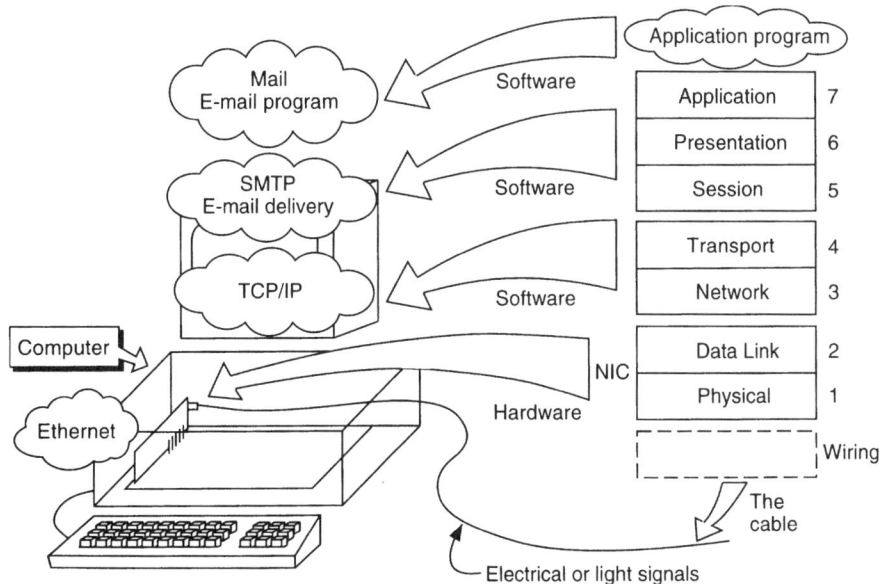

Software and hardware protocol components. Learning Tree International

Protocol data units (PDUs)

Protocols at a sender's specific layer interact with the associated protocols at the same layer on the receiving workstation. In Fig. 3-14, the arrow lines indicate peer communications between adjacent layers on two end systems and intermediate systems. Peer-to-peer communications between end systems further indicate why it is required that both end systems support the same protocol stacks (unless there is a system, such as a gateway, providing translations services in between the two).

Figure 3-14

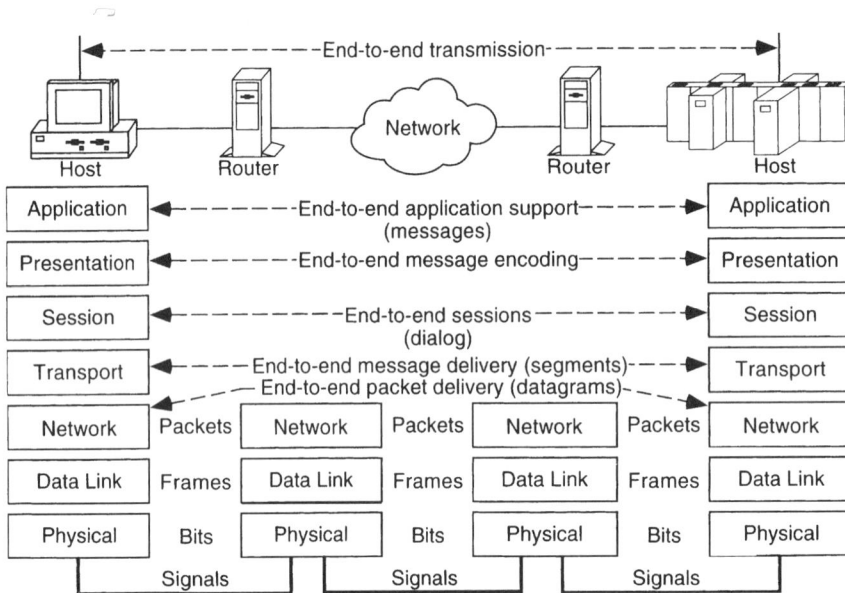

Protocol data units (PDUs). Learning Tree International

What does a packet look like?

One of the most difficult things to conceptualize is the idea of characters being translated to bits, then grouped together in several packages only to be transmitted one bit at a time over the network transmission medium. The resulting transmission, when viewed at the lowest level, looks like one long stream of bits.

Figure 3-15 demonstrates this concept in detail. User data is received by the application layer protocol, and a control header is added describing the application process that created the data. The resulting protocol data unit is passed to the lower layers, where additional control headers are added.

Figure 3-15

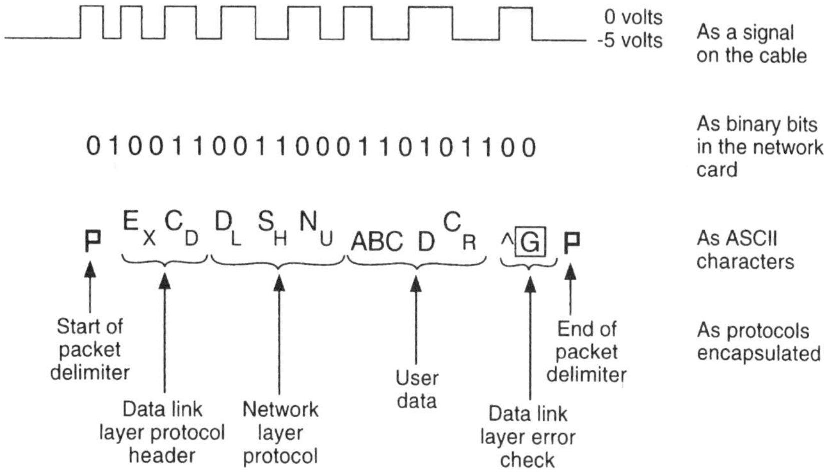

- **Can you tell what is the frame and what is the packet in this transmission?**

What does a "packet" look like? Learning Tree International

In the previous example, the application layer PDU is passed directly to the network layer packet. A data link layer header and trailer (error check) are added to the packet to create a frame. Remember, the process occurring here is called protocol encapsulation. Finally, the resulting stream of bits is sent out as voltage levels on the wire by the network interface card.

⇨ A protocol transaction

We stated at the beginning of this chapter that protocols are used at all layers of the OSI model. We further stated that layered protocols must be able to communicate with their peer layers.

Figure 3-16 demonstrates this further. A protocol is required for electromagnetic signaling and encoding of bits. Both end systems must be able to interpret bits from the signals transmitted on the cable. A protocol is used to establish who starts the conversation (sender) and how the call will be accepted (by the receiver). A protocol is used to create and encapsulate packets of information. A protocol is used to route packets from machine to machine (ES to ES). A protocol is used to encode the language of the user data into machine characters (ASCII or EBCDIC).

Figure 3-16

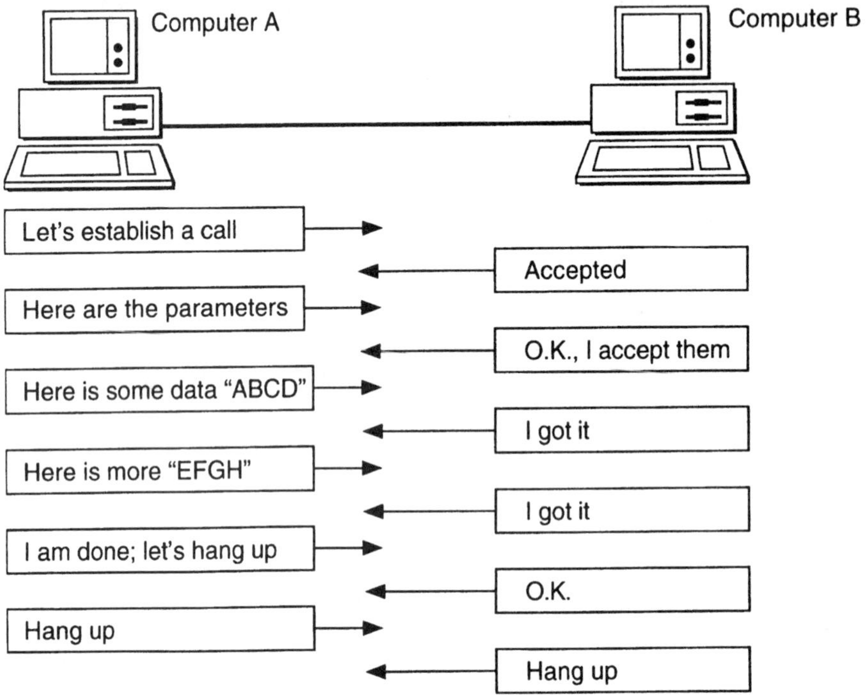

A protocol transaction. Learning Tree International

If even one of these protocols is not available at the peer layer of the receiving-end system, successful communications will not occur. Therefore, a common set of rules is always required.

Standards organizations

CNE exam objects

> Identify which models and protocols are maintained by a particular standards organization.

The standards process

Earlier in this chapter we talked about the need for standards as a primary means of facilitating interconnectivity and interoperability between multiple vendors. Standards evolve based on input from many sources. Sources will include various standards bodies or subcommittees, vendors, manufacturers, and end users. Once established, standards are revised periodically as a way of implementing new technology or satisfying additional requirements.

Figure 3-17 shows the revision process taking place. Using X.25 as an example, the last major review occurred in 1988. Subsequent

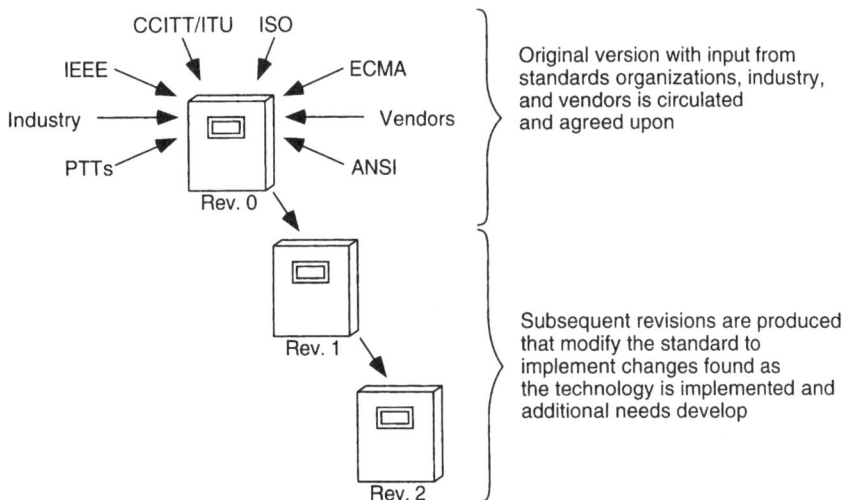

Figure 3-17

CCITT/ITU ISO
IEEE ECMA
Industry Vendors
PTTs ANSI
Rev. 0

Original version with input from standards organizations, industry, and vendors is circulated and agreed upon

Rev. 1

Rev. 2

Subsequent revisions are produced that modify the standard to implement changes found as the technology is implemented and additional needs develop

ECMA = European Computer Manufacturers Association
IEEE = Institute of Electrical and Electronics Engineers

The standards process. Learning Tree International

revisions are made every four years, but there have only been minor revisions since then.

Needless to say that because of the number of parties involved in the standards-making process, it can take a long time for all to agree on the standard and subsequent updates or revisions.

Types of standards

De jure protocols

De jure (by jury) protocols or standards are based on a best-judgment analysis of a standards organization. Usually, these standards are paper based in that the actual protocols do not yet exist. Only a paper description of how the protocol should work is available. However, the protocols in question have been adopted by recognized standards organizations. Many ISO protocols (not to be confused with the ISO model) are still paper based.

De facto protocols (covered next) are subsequently adopted as *de jure* standards. For example, the de jure IEEE 802.3 protocol was derived from the Ethernet *de facto* specification.

De facto protocols

De facto protocols achieve their status through grassroots support (by popular use) throughout the industry. Many *de facto* protocols were originally proprietary protocols that became widely accepted across the industry.

In some instances, the original developers have made the protocol specifications public, thereby encouraging its use. Datapoint's ARCnet, SUN Microsystems' NFS, DIX (Digital-Intel-Xerox) Ethernet, and NetBIOS are examples of these types of protocols. Another term for de facto protocols in nonproprietary protocols.

Proprietary protocols

Proprietary protocols are those developed by a vendor to integrate its computer systems, but the proprietary protocols are not shared with others. Widespread use of proprietary protocols in the early days and the constraints they placed on users led in large part to the development of *de jure* protocol standards.

Some proprietary protocols, like IBM's SNA and Novell's IPX/SPX, have very large installed bases and as such are still in wide use throughout the world. However, end users continue to diminish their use of proprietary protocols as *de jure* protocol standards become more accepted and available.

International Standards Organization

The ISO is an international standards organization that develops standards in many areas, including screws, bearings, lights, and even manufacturing and management processes (ISO 9000, for example). Almost every area of industry is touched by standards set by ISO at some point. In the United States, the American National Standards Institute (ANSI) represents U.S. interests in ISO.

ISO has developed many standards and protocols that apply to networking environments. ISO standards deal with LAN and WAN technologies. A major accomplishment of ISO is the development of the OSI reference model. ISO has also developed OSI protocols, which perform the functions outlined by the OSI model. Example OSI protocols include end system to intermediate systems (ES to IS) routing, and the transport protocols TP0-TP4.

International Consultative Committee for Telegraphy and Telephony— International Telephone Union (CCITT/ITU)

The International Consultative Committee for Telegraphy and Telephony—International Telephone Union (CCITT/ITU) is responsible for public telephone networks. It is the organization that makes recommendations on telephone, telegraph, and data communications interfaces and protocols in use throughout the world.

Example protocols implemented by CCITT/ITU include V modem standards, X.400 electronic mail systems, and X.25 public data networks. The name of the CCITT was recently changed to ITU.

Institute of Electrical and Electronics Engineers (IEEE)

The IEEE promotes the development of communications standards for local area network protocols through its 802 committee. Of all the standards-setting organizations, this one has the greatest impact on our area of interest.

Why are the protocols grouped as 802? The designation 802 is derived from the year 1980, the month of February, when the standard committee was initially established.

Example protocols include the entire 802 series: 802.3 for Ethernet, 802.5 for Token Ring, and 802.6 for metropolitan area networks, and the new 802.12 specification for 100-Mbps networking.

American National Standards Institute (ANSI)

ANSI promotes the development of communication standards and is the U.S. representative to ISO. Example protocols include FDDI and the recently adopted ARCNET proprietary specification.

Electronics Industries Association (EIA)

The EIA is the U.S. industry association that has promoted the standardization of structured wiring. In addition to maintaining the RS-232-C protocol standard, the organization has produced many excellent documents detailing the most effective ways to implement structured wiring installations.

⇨ Internet Activities Board (IAB)

The IAB is a nonprofit organization that promotes the development and acceptance of protocols associated with TCP/IP. It has recently been renamed the Internet Society and is the ultimate regulator of how the Internet functions.

⇨ National Institute for Standards and Technology (NIST)

NIST is also a U.S. government organization responsible for promoting the development of data communications standards for industry. It was formerly called the National Bureau of Standards (NBS). It spearheaded the development of 802.4 (token bus) and the MAP (Manufacturing Automation Protocol) suite.

⇨ The relationship of standards organizations

See Fig. 3-18. Also, a complete list of addresses for the previously discussed standards organizations is available in appendix F.

Figure 3-18

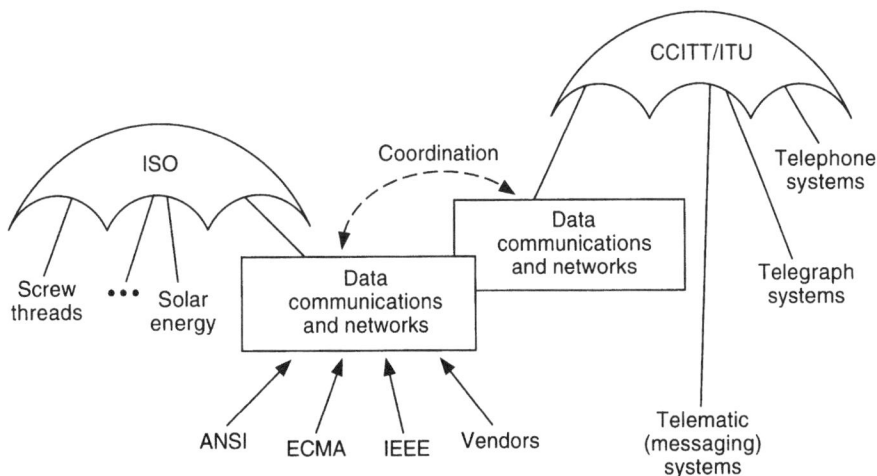

The relationship of standards organizations. Learning Tree International

⇨ Test your understanding

The purpose of this section is to help reinforce the information we have just reviewed. Proceed through the various sections and write down your answers to the questions. The answers are in appendix B.

1. Name each layer of the OSI Model, what it manages, some of its functions, and an example protocol.

	Layer name	What it manages	Functions	Examples
1				
2				
3				
4				
5				
6				
7				

2. The protocol bits added by any layer to the front of the data are called the _____.

3. Name the three types of protocols standards:

_____, _____, _____

4. Name one proprietary, one de jure, and one de facto protocol:

   _____, _____, _____

5. Give the full name, scope, responsibility, and one example protocol for the following standards organizations:

Org.	Scope	Responsibility	Protocol
CCITT/ITU			
ISO			
IEEE			:
ANSI			
NIST			
EIA			
IAB			

(See Figs. 3-19, 3-20, and 3-21.)

Figure 3-19

No.	Layer	What it manages	Functions
7	Application	Messages	Manages user interface to network. File access and transfer, virtual terminal, E-mail delivery, **Application Programming Interfaces** (APIs).
6	Presentation	Format and presentation of data	Format conversion, data encryption, compression, and expansion and data presentation
5	Session	Dialogue between applications	Establishes, maintains, and synchronizes dialogue between communicating applications on remote computers; RPCs.
4	Transport	Segments	Sequencing, acknowledgment, flow control. Ensures reliable end-to-end delivery of messages and data across an internet. Message multiplexing. Fragmentation and reassembly. May be reliable (TCP) or unreliable (UDP).
3	Network	Packets (datagrams)	Creates and route packets (also called datagrams in some nets). Includes definition of networkwide logical addressing scheme for all network devices. May be connection (X.25) or connectionless (IP).
2	Data Link	Frames	Creates frames. Encapsulates packets or user data into a bit-stream organization called frames. Manages access to the media. Uses physical addresses.
1	Physical	Bits	Mechanical and electrical interface specification for connection to the media.

Reference: OSI reference model. Learning Tree International

Figure 3-20

Org.	Scope	Responsibilities	Example protocols
CCITT/ITU	International, government	**Consultative Committee for International Telegraphy and Telephony/International Telephone Union:** Telephone, telegraph, and data communications standards.	X.400 X.25 V.24
ISO	International, government	**International Organization for Standardization:** Adopts, develops, and promotes the use of network protocols for use in heterogeneous networks.	TP0–TP4 FTAM CMIP
IEEE	International, industry	**Institute of Electrical and Electronics Engineers:** Develops and promotes the use of LAN protocols through its 802 committee.	802.1 802.2 802.3 802.5
NIST	U.S. government standards organization	**National Institute for Standards and Technology:** Promotes the development of network protocols for industry. Formerly NBS (National Bureau of Standards).	MAP
ANSI	U.S. standards organization, industry	**American National Standards Institute:** Promotes the development of data communications protocols. It is the U.S. representative to ISO.	ASCII FDDI
DoD	U.S. government agency	**U.S. Department Of Defense:** Promoted the installation of the ARPAnet and early development of the TCP/IP protocol suite.	TCP/IP
EIA	U.S. standards organization, industry	**Electronics Industry Association**	RS-232-C
IAB	International TCP/IP User's Group	**Internet Activities Board:** Nonprofit organization promoting the development of TCP/IP. Took over from DoD ARPAnet.	TCP/IP

Reference: standards organizations. Learning Tree International

Figure 3-21

Standard	Meaning	Example
De jure	"By law." Standards developed, promoted, or adopted by standards organizations such as IEEE, ISO, and CCITT/ITU. Also called nonproprietary.	IEEE 802 ISO TP0–4 CCITT/ITU X.400
De facto	"By use." Standards that become popular when everyone adopts and uses them. Sometimes promoted by one vendor or by technical community user groups. Also called nonproprietary.	Sun NFS ARPAnet TCP/IP ARCNET SNMP Ethernet
Proprietary	Protocols developed by a vendor for use by that vendor's family of computers and devices. Used in vendors' networks only.	IBM SNA DEC DECnet Apple AppleTalk

Reference: standards and protocols. Learning Tree International

⇨ Workshop

See Fig. 3-22.

1. Name the layer of the OSI Model, what it manages, some of its functions, and an example protocol:

Figure 3-22

	Layer name	What it manages	Functions	Examples
7				
6				
5				
4				
3				
2				
1				

2. The protocol bits added by any layer to the front of the data are called the

    _____.

3. Name the three different types of protocols standards:

    _____,_____,_____

4. Name one proprietary, one de jure, and one de facto protocol:

    _____,_____,_____

OSI reference model review.

⇨ Practice exam questions

1. In a peer-to-peer network, the control information inserted into a protocol data unit by a peer layer making a request is called:
    A. Header
    B. Frame
    C. Packet
    D. Message

2. The information units produced by the data link layer of the OSI model are called:
   A. Bits
   B. Frames
   C. Datagrams (Packets)
   D. Segments

3. The information units produced by the network layer of the OSI model are called:
   A. Bits
   B. Frames
   C. Datagrams (packets)
   D. Segments

4. Which best describes the function of the network layer of the OSI model?
   A. It defines the electrical and mechanical specifications for the interface hardware to the network.
   B. It frames the data stream into logical groups of information.
   C. It moves information across a network made up of multiple network segments.
   D. It provides error control and data-flow control between two end points of the network.

5. Which is not an example of the implementation of the application layer of the OSI model?
   A. NFS
   B. FTAM
   C. ES/IS
   D. FTP

6. Which is not a standards-making organization?
   A. CCITT/ITU
   B. ISO
   C. IEEE
   D. ASCII

7. Which organization is most responsible for the production and promotion of the OSI model?
   A. CCITT/ITU
   B. ISO
   C. IEEE
   D. ANSI

8. Models are concepts for communicating, while protocols are actual solutions to a communication process:
   A. True
   B. False

9. Protocols are _____ components:
   A. Hardware
   B. Software
   C. Hardware and software
   D. None of the above

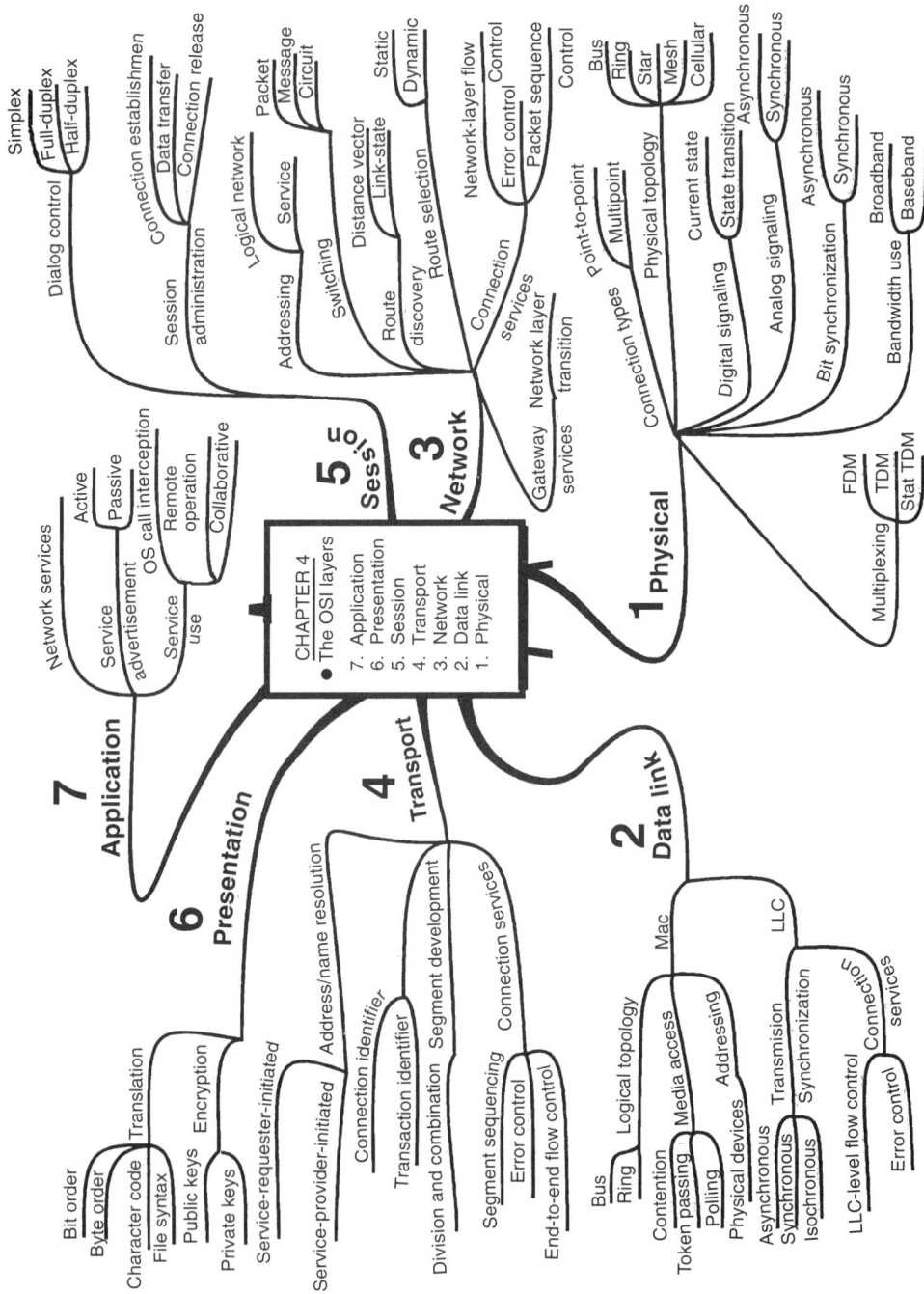

CHAPTER 4
• **The OSI layers**
7. Application
6. Presentation
5. Session
4. Transport
3. Network
2. Data link
1. Physical

7 Application
- Network services
  - Service advertisement
    - Active
    - Passive
  - Service use
    - OS call interception
    - Remote operation
    - Collaborative

6 Presentation
- Translation
  - Bit order
  - Byte order
  - Character code
  - File syntax
- Encryption
  - Public keys
  - Private keys

5 Session
- Dialog control
  - Simplex
  - Full-duplex
  - Half-duplex
- Session administration
  - Connection establishment
  - Data transfer
  - Connection release

4 Transport
- Address/name resolution
  - Service-requester-initiated
  - Service-provider-initiated
- Connection identifier
- Transaction identifier
- Segment development
  - Division and combination
  - Segment sequencing
- Connection services
  - Error control
  - End-to-end flow control

3 Network
- Logical network addressing
- Switching
  - Packet
  - Message
  - Circuit
- Route selection
  - Distance vector
  - Link-state
  - Static
  - Dynamic
- Route discovery
- Connection services
  - Network-layer flow control
  - Error control
  - Packet sequence control
- Gateway services
- Network layer transition

2 Data link
- Logical topology
  - Bus
  - Ring
- Media access
  - Contention
  - Token passing
  - Polling
- Addressing
  - Physical devices
- Transmission synchronization
  - Asynchronous
  - Synchronous
  - Isochronous
- LLC-level flow control
- Connection services
  - Error control

1 Physical
- Connection types
  - Point-to-point
  - Multipoint
- Physical topology
  - Bus
  - Ring
  - Star
  - Mesh
  - Cellular
- Digital signaling
  - Current state
  - State transition
- Analog signaling
  - Asynchronous
  - Synchronous
- Bit synchronization
  - Asynchronous
  - Synchronous
- Bandwidth use
  - Broadband
  - Baseband
- Multiplexing
  - FDM
  - TDM
  - Stat TDM

4

The OSI model layers

⇨ Introduction

The OSI model, with its seven layers, is a very useful tool for analyzing and understanding data communication systems. It is described in detail in chapter 3. In this chapter, each layer is further analyzed by defining its purpose and identifying and describing the technology topics and methods that are associated with that layer.

The words "topic" and "methods" are the Novell designations for characteristics, issues, and techniques involved with each layer. We will make use of that terminology to help you be more successful in passing the CNE exam.

Each of the following seven sections deals with an individual layer. At the beginning of each section, there is a table outlining the topics and the corresponding methods that deal with that topic. After the table there is a detailed description of the topics and the methods.

The OSI model specifies that at each of the communicating entities or end systems, there must be seven protocols or communicating subsystems. The ISO experts have given names to each subsystem: physical layer, data link layer, network layer, transport layer, session layer, presentation layer, and application layer. The physical layer is responsible for the electromechanical interface to the communications media. It is considered the lowest layer in the stack, and it is often called layer one. The data link layer is responsible for transmission framing and error control over a communications link. It interfaces to the physical layer and uses the services of the physical layer and provides services for the layer above it, the network layer. It is considered layer two.

Next comes the network layer, which is responsible for data transfer across the network. This data transfer across the network is considered an end-to-end transmission. The network layer is responsible for the movement of packets from one end of the network to the other. It is independent of the media and the data link in the underlying subnetworks. It is also independent of the underlying topology of those subnetworks. Layers one and two, the physical and data link layers, make up subnetworks, whereas layers three and four, the network and transport layers, make up internets, or concatenated subnetworks. The network layer is considered layer three.

The transport layer works closely with the network layer. The transport layer is responsible for the reliability of the end-to-end transmission and the multiplexing of data across the network. This is above and beyond any services provided by the network layer. It makes use of the routing services of the network layer. It provides services to the three upper layers. The transport layer is considered layer four.

These four layers—physical, data link, network, and transport—are considered the infrastructure of an enterprise network. They are the ones that deliver data transfer across the internet.

The remaining layers—five through seven—provide applications with needed network services to make the network functional. Layer five, the session layer, is responsible for adding control mechanisms to the data exchange. During a session, the session layer manages the establishment and release of session connections and the data transfer.

The presentation layer is considered layer six, and it is responsible for adding structure, encryption, and syntax to the units of data that are exchanged. It is responsible for the formatting of the data in an understandable manner or the conversion of the format so that the receiver will understand the sender. Encryption is a presentation-layer function as well.

The last layer, the seventh in the stack, is called the application layer. It is responsible for managing the communication between the applications. This layer is often confused with the applications themselves. It is sometimes useful to call this layer "application services" so as not to confuse it with the consumer or network services, the applications themselves.

Often, programs that make up the functionality of the application layer are called application programming interfaces or APIs. They belong in this layer, as those APIs assist applications in consuming, or using, the functionality of the network.

This entire protocol stack operating in an end system takes the form of hardware for layers one and two and software programs for the remaining layers. As will be seen in chapter 5, in certain protocol families, some of these layers are null. In other words, there is no program that exists to implement the functionality of that layer. In those protocol families, that works out fine because either that functionality is not needed or it has been included in one of the other layers. So let's see now, layer by layer, what the functionality and the associated characteristics are of this very important protocol model.

⇨ The OSI physical layer

The following network connectivity hardware is considered an implementation of the OSI physical layer: concentrators, hubs, repeaters, any device that generates electrical signal for transmission, amplifiers used in broadband networks, any media connectors that provide connectivity to the media from the physical layer, and other interconnect devices such as modems, Codex, CSU/DSUs. Examples of physical-layer specifications are the EIA RS-232C, the EIA RS-449, the ITU X.21, and V.24 specifications. Figure 4-1 shows a typical network card that is plugged into the personal computer to connect that computer to a network. The card typically embodies both the physical layer and the data link layer specifications. The circuits and

Figure 4-1

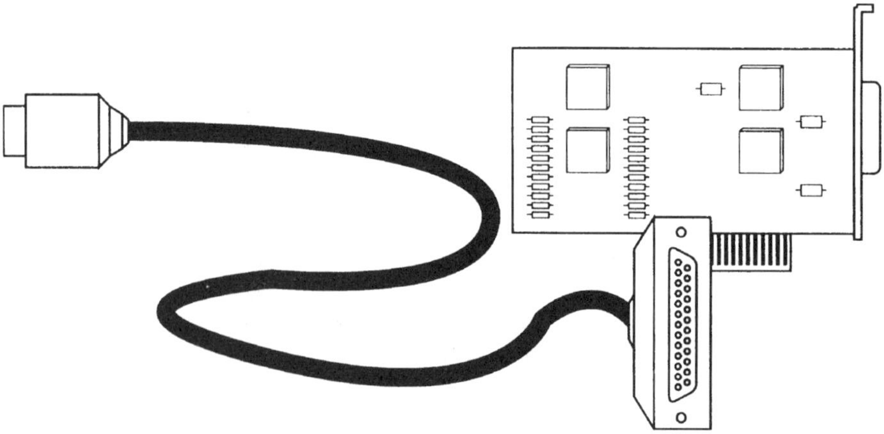

Characteristics of the physical layer. Learning Tree International

chips toward the right side of the card are part of the physical layer signal conditioning and clocking circuits. The connectors shown in the figure on the right side of the network card would be specified by the physical layer standard.

The cable that would connect the network card to the network media is part of the physical-layer specification as well. The pins, the connector, and the definitions for the use of each of the circuits going through that connector are all part of the physical layer.

The physical layer is involved with the type of connectivity between computers, whether a single point or multipoint; the topology of the cabling; the type of signaling that is used, whether it's analog or digital, and the form of signal modulation—amplitude or frequency, for example. Encoding of clocking signals within the transmission for the synchronization of receiver and sender is the responsibility of the physical layer. The form of signal transmission—whether it's broadband or baseband, and the way the bandwidth of the channel is used—is also a responsibility of the physical layer.

Finally, any form of multiplexing that is being done—whether it is sharing the channel in time, such as in time-division multiplexing, or using different frequencies in allocating portions of the bandwidth to different channels—is also in the domain of the physical layer.

⇨ CNE exam objectives

➢ Define the basic purpose of the OSI physical layer.

➢ Identify and describe the networking technology topics associated with the OSI physical layer.

➢ Identify and describe the methods associated with each OSI physical layer topic.

See Table 4-1.

Table 4-1   **Topics and Methods for the Physical Layer**

Physical-layer topics	Physical-layer methods
Connection types	Point-to-point Multipoint
Physical topology	Bus Star Ring Mesh Cellular
Signaling	Analog ASK, PSK, FSK Digital
Synchronization	Bit synchronization
Multiplexing	Time division Frequency division Statistical multiplexing
Bandwidth utilization	Broadband Baseband

⇨ The physical layer

The ITU X.200 document defines the services of the OSI physical layer as:

> The physical layer provides mechanical, electrical, functional and procedural means to activate, maintain, and deactivate physical connections for bit transmission between data-link entities. A physical connection might involve intermediate open systems, each relaying bit transmission within the physical layer. Physical-layer entities are interconnected by means of a physical medium. The mechanical, electromagnetic, and other media-dependent characteristics of physical media connections are defined at the boundary between the physical layer and the physical media.

Note that this definition does not include the physical media itself. That specification is outside the responsibility of the physical layer.

⇨ Connection types

Two types of connections can be identified for the link between sender and receiver. One is point to point, and the other is multipoint.

✳ Point to point

In a point-to-point connection, there is a direct link between the communicating entities. For example, the connection of a computer to a packet switch requires a dedicated link. The connection of a modem to a personal computer is done via a dedicated link. Anytime a link is dedicated for the connection between two machines or two devices, that link is considered a point-to-point connection.

✳ Multipoint

The multipoint connection is established when one cabling plant is shared among many communicating entities. Another term for multipoint is multidrop. Today's LAN environments are almost always of the multipoint connection type. In contrast, most WAN links today are of a point-to-point connection. Multipoint connections, of necessity, require the sharing of the bandwidth of the common cabling plant. The techniques for the sharing of the bandwidth are the responsibility of the next layer, the data link layer.

⇨ Physical topology

Physical topology is involved with the layout of the links between the computers. In cases where there is actual wire between the devices, the topology refers to the way the cabling is installed. In other cases, such as in wireless communications, the topology describes how the links between the computers, the communicating entities, is established.

The discussion that follows on the various types of topologies will focus on comparing and contrasting their characteristics and the description of the topology itself. Points of comparison would be ease of installation of cabling when using one topology versus another, the ease of reconfiguring cabling and troubleshooting a cable plant, and how many units are affected when some portion of the cable plant fails. Different topologies automatically recover from failures; others require technical intervention. The major types of topologies are the star, bus, ring, mesh, and cellular topologies.

✳ Star

Figure 4-2 shows a physical star topology. In this topology, there is a central device that connects all of the communicating entities. That device might be a hub, concentrator, or, in the case of a minicomputer installation, for example, the minicomputer itself. The key is that all communications go through a central point, the center of the star. This particular type of topology makes it much easier to troubleshoot and to isolate network faults. It is reasonably easy to install. The design of the network is fairly simple. In many cases it follows the same topology and design of a voice telephone network within a building. This type of topology for data networks lends itself very well to the use of telephone-circuit installation techniques.

Figure 4-2

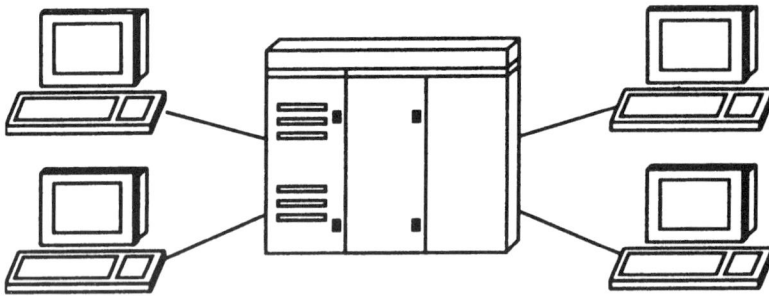

Star topology. Learning Tree International

Today it is the preferred topology in wiring buildings for data and voice. It's very easy to troubleshoot because if there is a failure in a connection between a computer and the central device, only that computer is affected. The central device has provisions for recovering from the loss of that circuit. Most LANs today have some form of star topology as a cabling choice. Ethernet, Token Ring, ARCNET, and even FDDI could all be wired with a physical star topology.

The main flaw of this type of topology is that if the central nerve fails, then, of course, a great number of communicating entities would not be able to exchange data.

✳ Bus

In a bus topology all the devices wishing to communicate are connected to one long cable. There is no central distribution point in this case. It takes a lot less cable to wire this configuration than it does for the star topology. Bus topologies have one major disadvantage: damage to any part of the bus cable disables the entire segment that the computers are connected to. Computers are connected to this bus via taps, which are mechanical devices that allow a parallel connection between a cable coming from the computer onto the segment bus. The segment bus is often called a *backbone bus*. This backbone cable or segment has to be terminated at both ends to prevent signal reflections from the open ends of the cable. Terminators are typically resistors with the same impedance as the cable itself.

In most bus topologies, the propagation of signals is bidirectional. A device connected in parallel to the two conductors and the backbone cable will couple in electromagnetic energy that travels away from that device towards other devices in both directions simultaneously.

Some buses are unidirectional, such as those used in dual-frequency broadband networks where the sending device sends a signal to a device at the end of the cable that retransmits it on another frequency to all of the receivers. In that case, the sender sends at one frequency and the retransmitter converts it to another frequency and resends. All the receivers are tuned to receive at the second frequency.

One of the major problems with a linear-bus topology is that any damage or break to the backbone cable causes the entire network to go down and devices to cease communicating. Early implementations of most data-link technologies were of the linear-bus type. Most of these have since migrated to the more resilient star topology, which has become the standard today.

Figure 4-3 shows such a linear-bus topology. Connecting several of these backbone buses, which are called segments, together via repeaters produces an extension of the bus topology, which is the tree topology. A *tree topology* is a group of linear buses connected in such a manner that there are no closed loops.

Some examples of linear buses are Ethernet and 802.3 LANs, the Token Bus networks used in 802.4, and the LocalTalk network used with AppleTalk in the Macintosh environment.

Figure 4-3

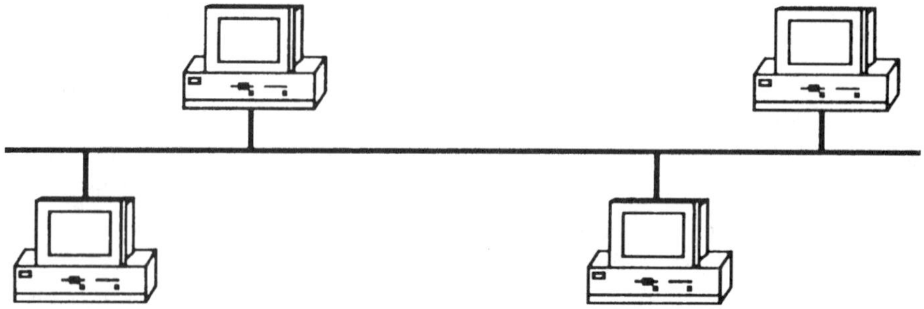

Bus topology. Learning Tree International

✳ Ring

A *ring* is a circular topology composed of a closed loop of point-to-point links. Each device in the ring is connected to two of its nearest neighbors. It receives transmissions from one neighbor and passes that transmission on to its other neighbor. The signals must travel from device to device and be retransmitted by each device for the data to make its way around the ring. Each interface unit contains a receiving circuit and a transmitting circuit. Examples of ring topology are the IBM Token Ring, the 802.5 standardization of that network, and the FDDI token-passing ring.

A major disadvantage of the token ring topology is that some rings cannot recover from damage to any one cable segment. Most ring LANs make provisions for this eventuality and have elaborate schemes to recover from the loss of any one link. Figure 4-4 shows a typical ring topology. In some ring topologies, whenever there is a failure in the cable plant, all units are affected.

✳ Mesh

A *mesh* topology is created by a group of point-to-point links. If every device is connected via a point-to-point link to every other device in the network, it creates what might be called a *total mesh* (that's mesh, not mess). Very few networks can afford to have such a great number of connections, especially as the number of nodes increases. Typically, a mesh topology is composed of point-to-point links between switches or routers in the network, and a mesh topology is often deployed in wide area networks.

Figure 4-4

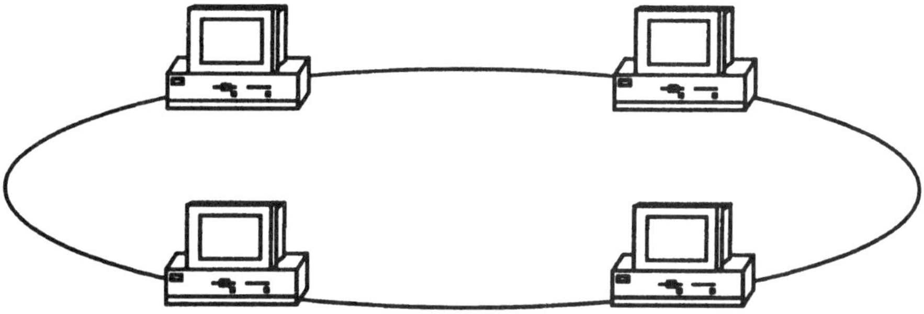

Ring topology. Learning Tree International

Mesh topology is difficult to install and troubleshoot. Sophisticated network management schemes are usually employed to keep track of network outages. It is also hard to reconfigure if the connectivity of the mesh is low—in other words, if there are few redundant paths. On the other hand, whenever a particular link fails, it is relatively easy to identify and theoretically quickly move to repair the outage. A mesh topology is fairly resilient, if it has a high degree of connectivity (i.e., multiple paths from one device to another). It recovers well from failures when there is that redundancy. Mesh topologies are most often seen in WANs, not in LANs.

✳ Cellular

Cellular topology is employed in some wireless networks where there is a retransmitter covering a certain geographic area. The network is made up of strategically located retransmitters with overlapping area of coverage. It creates a transmitting environment where mobile units can be easily connected to any other mobile unit or stationary unit as they move within this area of coverage. The cellular telephone network is an example of cellular topology. It is also the topology for wiring LANs using wireless techniques within a building.

A cellular topology is relatively easy to install within a building and does not require wiring because of its wireless nature. It is much harder to create a cellular technology for a wide area network because of the geographic constraints. It typically requires line-of-sight positioning of retransmitters. Building materials within a building also interfere with wireless transmission, so there will be regions within a building that might not be reached by the retransmitters, causing areas of no coverage. This is by far the most easily reconfigurable network topology. As a matter of fact, it doesn't require any reconfiguration at all for the transmitting stations. They can be as mobile as they need to be within the area of coverage of the cellular topology. It is fairly easy to troubleshoot, since the retransmitters act independently from the devices themselves. But when a particular hub fails, a large portion of the area of coverage is deprived of service, making this topology similar to the star topology in that it has a central point of failure. Figure 4-5 is a chart comparing the characteristics of the major physical topologies.

Figure 4-5

Characteristic	Star	Bus	Ring	Mesh
Point of network connectivity	Hub or concentrator	The cable bus	Each interface	Totally distributed
Connection	To a central point	Each station to the bus	Point-to-point station-to-station in a loop	Many point-to-point connections
Examples	802.3 10BASE-T	802.3 10BASE5 Ethernet	IBM Token Ring FDDI	Wide area networks
Advantage	Easy to troubleshoot	Less cable to install	Each node repeats the signal	Efficient for long-distance connections
Disadvantage	More cable to install	Damage to cable bus disables network	Damage to any part of cable segment may disable network	Many more interfaces to install

Comparison of the characteristics of physical topologies. Learning Tree International

⇨ Signaling

Signaling is a physical-layer topic that refers to the process by which two communicating, geographically separate entities can send information to each other. Consider a basic transmission circuit shown in Fig. 4-6. Here we have a simple car battery, a switch, a pair of wires, and a light bulb. The light bulb is the signaling element at the

Figure 4-6

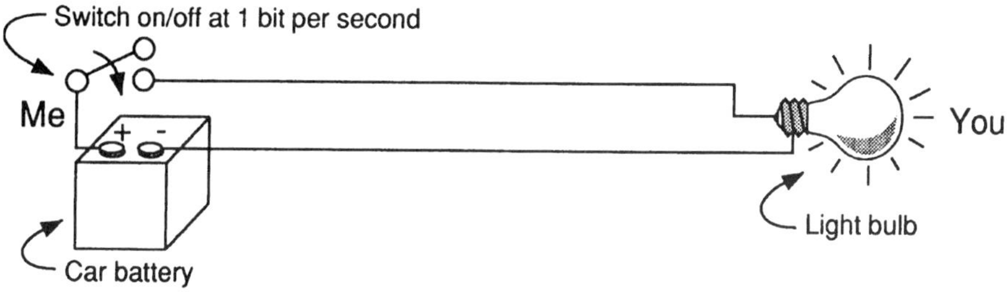

A basic transmission circuit. Learning Tree International

receiver. The switch is the signaling element at the sender. Transmission of information is done electrically. When the switch is closed, current flows, and the light shines. When the switch is open, current doesn't flow and the light is off—a binary information system.

In this case, the on/off state of the light is what contains the information that the sender intended for the receiver to get. This is essentially a digital system, as we will see when we get into the definition of digital signaling later in this section. The encoding of information into this signaling system is the responsibility of additional processes. The actual signaling process itself, its components, the transmission of that signal, and the characteristics of that signal are considered parts of the physical layer.

There are two types of signaling modes: digital and analog. Figure 4-7 shows the main difference between the analog and digital signals. In digital signals, we are working with discreet states or discreet levels similar to the on and off of the switch in our basic transmission circuit. There might be two states, in which case we have a binary transmission circuit or a binary signaling system; there might be more states. The key is that there are states, and the transition from one state to the other is what contains the information. In other words, we encode information into a pattern of states and transmit the states.

In Fig. 4-7 we see the digital signal as being a continuous transition between voltage levels. To represent a binary one, there is a high voltage. To represent a binary zero, there is a low voltage. In signaling, we transition from one state to the other. And we hold that high or low state for a certain period of time. The rate at which the signal changes is called the clocking or data rate.

Figure 4-7

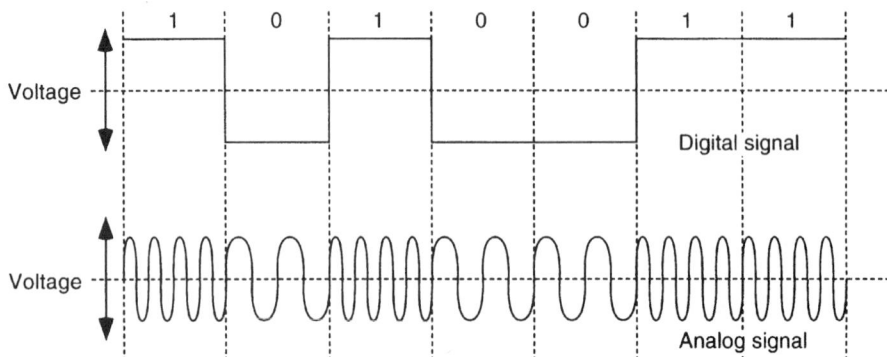

Digital signals: discrete levels

Analog signals: continuously varying

Analog versus digital signals. Learning Tree International

Let's look at analog signals. In contrast to digital signals, analog signals are continuously varying. To convey information, we must modulate some aspect of that continuous signal. We can modulate its amplitude, as is done when we transmit audio information over a high-frequency radio carrier signal in AM radio transmission. We can modulate its frequency, as is done with FM transmission, or we can modulate its phase. Transmission can be done at low frequencies, as with modems that use audio tones or frequencies in the audio range. It could be done with high frequencies, as is done in radio transmission, television transmission, and broadband LANs.

There are two aspects to the analog and digital game. One is a characteristic of the physical layer, a type of signal that is being used for information transmission. The other is the nature of the information itself, which could be digital or analog. These two must not be confused. One form of digital information is the bit stream of data within a computer used to store information in a binary form, and it needs to be transmitted. Analog information is information that is continuously varying, such as voice, music, and television signals.

We could have an analog-signaling scheme carrying either digital or analog information, and a digital-signaling scheme that could also carry either analog or digital information. Figure 4-8 shows various examples of the four possibilities. Radio transmission of music and voice programming is an example of an analog-signaling scheme (the radio-carrier waves) conveying analog information—the voice and music. On the other hand, the same analog signal could be used to carry digital information, as in broadband LANs where an rf wave is modulated with a digital bit stream coming from a computer.

Figure 4-8

	Analog information	Digital information
Analog signaling	• Radio waves carrying music • Telephone voice circuit used for a voice conversation	• Telephone voice circuit used with modems for data transfer • Broadband LAN (e.g.: 802.4)
Digital signaling	• ISDN telephone line used for a voice conversation • A music CD	• ISDN telephone line for a data connection • A CD-ROM containing data files • Most LSNs (e.g.: 802.3, 802.5)

Examples of digital and analog information encoded in digital and analog signals.

A digital-signaling scheme, such as an ISDN circuit, can be used to carry either data, which is digital information from a computer; or voice, which is analog information and has been digitized. There are many other examples of such schemes besides the ones represented in Fig. 4-8.

It's important to understand the differences because in constructing our networks we often use digital- and analog-signaling devices. Each has its place and specific reason for deployment and should not be mistaken for the other. Certain signaling characteristics are better employed for the delivery of certain information types.

❊ **Digital**

Digital signaling can be done by the binary pulsing of electromagnetic signals. They could be low-frequency signals, such as those carried by wires, similar to our basic transmission circuit. It could be the flashing of light signals conveyed by a fiber-optic cable (light is a higher-frequency manifestation of an electromagnetic signal).

There are two ways of manipulating a digital signal stream to convey information. One is the current-state method of signaling. In this method, the binary information is conveyed by the absence or presence of a state. In fiber-optic networks, where light is used for signaling, the presence or absence of light represents the two signal states. There are a number of digital signaling schemes that use this current-state transition method. The unipolar, the polar, the return-to-zero, and biphase-encoding schemes are such schemes. The details of these are described in Figs. 4-9 and 4-10.

The second method of digital transmission is called a *state-transition technique*. In this case, the receiver detects transitions from one state to another to detect the transmission of an information bit. The bipolar alternate mark conversion (AMI) technique, the nonreturn-to-zero (NRZ) technique, the Differential Manchester, and the biphase techniques are all forms of state-transition digital-signaling methods.

One of the problems with digital transmission is its high level of distortion and attenuation that occurs when transmitting the signal over long distances. Analog signals are less disturbed by the attenuation caused by long transmissions. So digital signaling is used for short hops (short networks), and analog transmission is left for the longer distances.

On the other hand, because of the very sharp differences between the states, digital signaling is more immune to noise than analog signaling. Witness the clear and low-noise characteristics of music that has been encoded into a CD, versus the storage of the same analog signal onto an analog medium such as tape, which is far noisier. The same is true of analog voice channels, which are much noisier when compared to a digital voice channel, which appears to the hearer to be much more "quiet." (See Fig. 4-10.)

Figure 4-9

Scheme	Encoding	Self-clocked?	Use	Characteristic
Unipolar	0 = +v 1 = 0 volts	No	Teletype interface	Susceptible to noise
Polar	0 = +v 1 = -v	No	Teletype interface	Less susceptible to noise
Bipolar	Uses Alternate Mark Inversion (AMI) for 1s 0 = 0 volts 1 = AMI	No	Teletype interface	Allows detection of errors by hardware
Non Return to Zero (NRZ)	0 = no transition 1 = transition across bit boundary	No	Terminal-to-modem interface FDDI	Simple and inexpensive scheme
Biphase	0 = -v to +v 1 = -v to +v	Yes	Some LANs implement this type	More difficult to implement
Manchester	0 = -v to +v 1 = -v to +v	Yes	Ethernet LANs	Reliable error detection
Differential Manchester	0 = transition at bit boundary 1 = no transition at bit boundary	Yes	Token Ring LANs	Immunity from polarity reversal

Characteristics of clock-encoding schemes. Learning Tree International

❊ Analog

Analog signals are continuously varying electromagnetic waves. In general, there are three ways of modulating the signals to convey information: varying the amplitude of the analog wave, varying the frequency of the analog wave, or varying its phase. In some cases, even a combination of these is used. Analog waves are often represented as sinusoidal voltage variations. The analog waves might be a single frequency or might be a combination of waves of various frequencies superimposed on each other, making up a periodic wave.

Figure 4-10

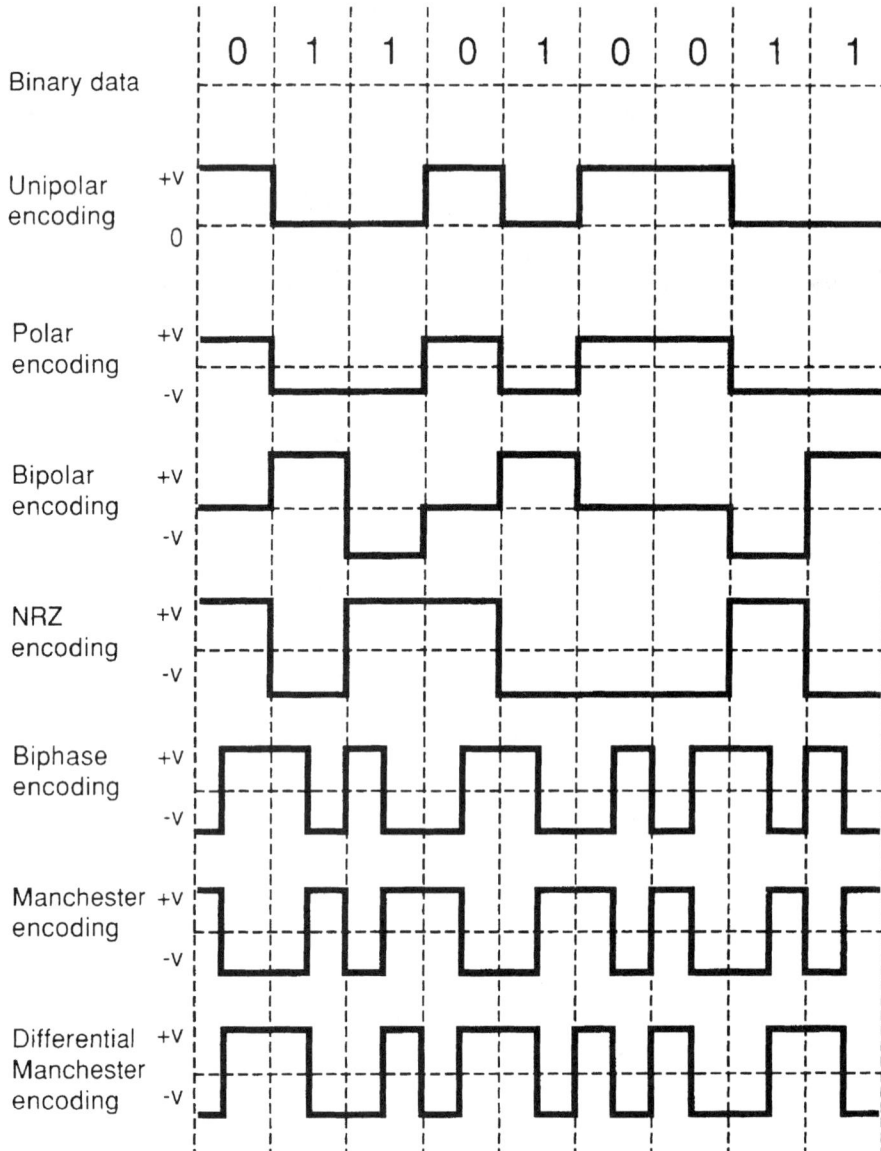

Clock-encoding schemes. Learning Tree International

❋ Amplitude modulation

To convey digital information, the amplitude of the analog sinusoid can be modulated into two amplitude states. A binary zero can be represented by low amplitude and a binary one can be represented by a large amplitude. In conveying binary digital information, this type of modulation is called "amplitude shift keying," or ASK. It can modulate high-frequency carrier waves, such as those used in broadband networks. It also can be used to modulate low-frequency waves in the audio range (0300 kilohertz), as is done in some low-bit rate modems.

The top part of Fig. 4-11 shows the original data stream that will be used to modulate the analog wave in one of three ways. The second signal on the drawing shows how using a digital data stream in an ASK mode would look. Note that in this case a low amplitude is used for the zero digital state, and a high amplitude is used for the one digital state.

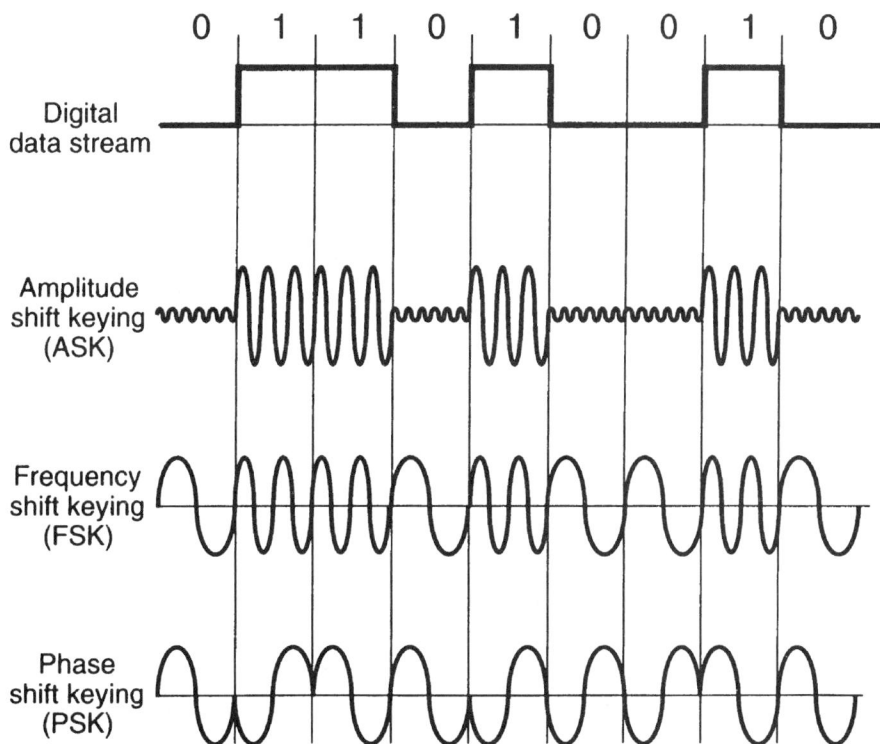

Figure 4-11

Amplitude, frequency, and phase modulation schemes. Learning Tree International

✳ Frequency modulation

The third signal on the drawing in Fig. 4-11 shows how digital information can be conveyed by varying the frequency of the analog wave. The frequency of a sinusoidal signal is the rate at which the pattern of the wave repeats. One complete cycle might take a second. And as that cycle repeats, we say the wave repeats at one cycle per second. Frequency is also measured in hertz where one Hz is equivalent to a cycle per second.

To convey binary information, the analog signal can have its frequency modulated by hopping back and forth between two set frequencies, one frequency representing the binary zero and the other representing the binary one. This is termed frequency shift keying, or FSK. Modems operating at 9600 bps, for example, use this technique for transmission of binary information over a voice-grade telephone channel.

✳ Phase modulation

The last signal on Fig. 4-11 shows phase modulation of an analog signal to convey digital information. We could pick two phases of the signal—the signal and the signal 180° out of phase—as the two binary states to represent the binary zero and the binary one states. The sending circuit would send out for a period of time the signal to represent the binary zero or the signal 180° out of phase to represent a binary one. Hopping back and forth between these two phases, which in this case are 180° apart, is called phase shift keying, or PSK.

We can convey more than one bit of information per signaling interval if we used four different phases—the signal, the signal 90° out of phase, the signal 180° out of phase, and the signal 270° out of phase—and send a burst at the appropriate phase to represent one of four states, or a pair of bits during a signaling interval.

Complex schemes using multiple phases and amplitude shift keying at the same time can pack many bits of information per signaling interval into a voice-grade line. That is how 14.4 Kbps throughput is obtained out of 3.3 kilohertz of bandwidth.

⇨ Synchronization

Synchronization deals with the receiver being able to tell the bit boundaries on the received signal exactly where the sender intended them to be. The alignment of the receiver's clock to the sender's clock at the bit or physical level is called *bit synchronization*. To make sure that the receiver got the message that the sender intended to send—a one—the sender holds the signal for the one on for a period of time. If it's a digital signal, the sender will hold the high state for a period of time. If it is an analog signal, it will hold a high-amplitude modulation for a period of time or the intended frequency for the one for a period of time.

That period of time is called a "signaling interval." These signaling intervals are uniform, or they uniformly divide time into cycles or bits. The sender has an internal clock used for its internal digital purposes. It will use this clock to create the proper signal intervals, or clock rate, to send out information.

There are two ways for the receiver to synchronize its clock with the sender. The first is an asynchronous method. The receiver assumes the sender is using a certain clocking rate. Using its own internal clock, the receiver will generate the proper measure for the signaling intervals and then extract from the receive signal the proper bit sequences. A problem with asynchronous transmission, where the sender uses its clock for clocking and the receiver uses its internal clock to decode the signal, is that if the two clocks are slightly different, then over a period of time, the receiver will get out of synch and begin making errors.

Asynchronous transmission uses two separate clocks, the sender's and the receiver's. It's appropriate only for low data rates when compared to the internal clocks. Internal clock rates in computers are in the order of tens of MHz. Using data rates in the order of kilohertz, then, would allow the receiver's and sender's clock to be slightly off a small fraction of MHz, and the receiver would still be able to decode kilobits-per-second clocked information. For higher transmission rates, the sender must send its clock to the receiver with the signal. It could do this in two ways: on a separate wire, as it is done with modem circuits and the use of RS-232 standard, or it could send it in-line encoded with the signal itself, as is done in some LANs. In either case the type of transmission is called *synchronous transmission*.

For low-data-rate modem communications, in the order of tens of kilobits per second, synchronous transmission by sending the clock on a separate circuit works rather well. In those cases where there isn't a separate circuit for clocking, such as in LANs, where there is only one pair of wires for transmission, the clock must be sent with the signal. This "in-band" type of clock transmission is used for most high-speed LAN technologies today. Figure 4-10 shows various clock-encoding schemes for in-band transmission.

Another useful technique in the area of synchronization is the concept of oversampling. The receiver just doesn't check the state of the receive signal at only one point during the signaling interval. It might check at several points or several times during the signaling interval. For example, sending data out at 1 million bits per second, the signaling interval is 1/1,000,000 of a second. Rather than check the state of the received signal once every one-millionth of a second, the receiver would actually check it 10 or 100 times during that signaling interval—let's say at 10 million times per second or a 100 million times per second. This way it's absolutely sure of what the intended bit state is at each signaling interval.

⇨ Bandwidth use

Bandwidth is best expressed as the "information-carrying capacity" of the link in bits per second for data communication links—in other words, how many bits per second are being transmitted. The use of telephone lines for data transmission allows only low-data-rate transmissions because of the small bandwidth. For example, the bandwidth of a voice-grade channel, shown in Fig. 4-12, is roughly 3000 hertz. This very small bandwidth can only carry low-data-rate signals in the order of tens of thousands of bits per second.

As a rule of thumb, we could use the conversion that one hertz of bandwidth can carry one bit of data. This is a very rough rule of thumb and not to be used literally in all cases, but it is a very useful concept.

Figure 4-12

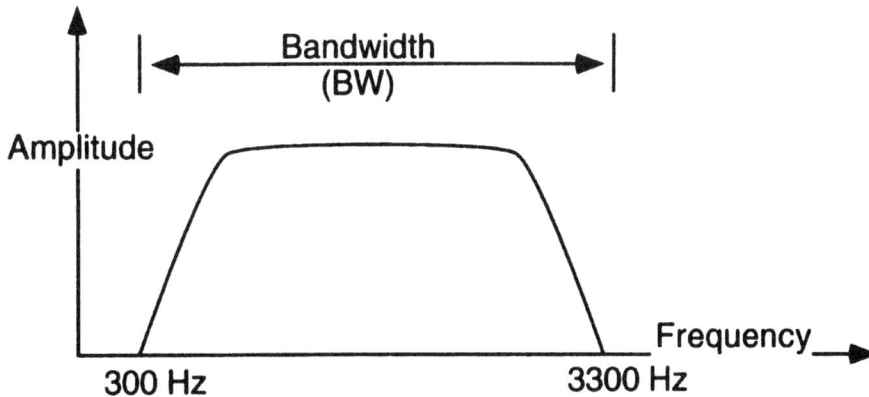

The concept of bandwidth. Learning Tree International

For telephone lines it doesn't seem to match: 3000 hertz of bandwidth can carry a lot more than 3 Kbps of data. That is because very sophisticated schemes can be used to cram more than one bit of data into a signaling interval where it might still be signaling at 3000 signaling intervals per second, but it might be carrying four or even eight times the data rate in that signal. This is accomplished with very sophisticated phase- and amplitude-modulation schemes.

✻ Baseband signaling

In baseband signaling, the digital signal existing within a computer is sent out without further modulation. In other words, the zeros and ones voltage transitions of the internal electrical signals are amplified and sent out onto the wire as is, so the bits are directly applied to the medium as is shown in Fig. 4-13.

One aspect of a baseband signal is that it takes up most of the bandwidth available in the channel, as shown in Fig. 4-14. With networks that use baseband signaling, repeaters must be used to regenerate the signals.

✻ Broadband signaling

In broadband systems, the digital information from each computer must be used to modulate an rf carrier, which is then sent to other computers. This modulated analog signal is decoded by the receiver to extract from it the digital information. Broadband signaling systems

Figure 4-13

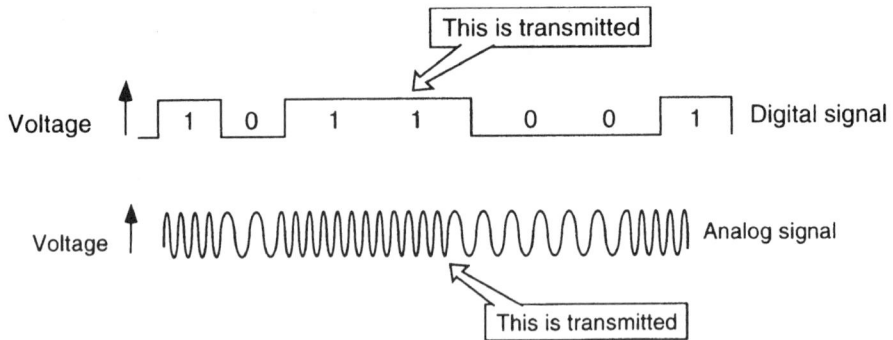

Baseband and broadband signaling schemes. Learning Tree International

Figure 4-14

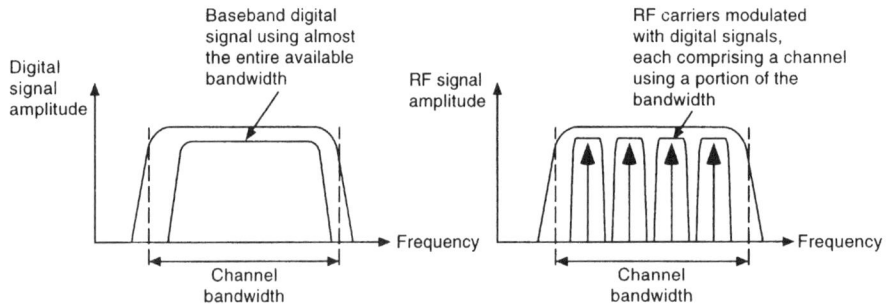

- **Baseband signals**
  - Square-wave voltage levels for the 0's and 1's binary information being conveyed from one computer to another

- **Broadband signals**
  - Using the baseband signal to modulate the amplitude or the frequency of a Radio-Frequency (RF) carrier wave
  - Requires modulation and demodulation

Comparison of broadband and baseband bandwidth utilization schemes.
Learning Tree International

can make use of frequency multiplexing schemes in which multiple carriers at different frequencies can all coexist on the same cable plant, thus allowing many digital streams to be simultaneously present.

Figure 4-14 shows four high-frequency carriers modulated with digital signals, all within the space of the channel bandwidth. One advantage of broadband over baseband is this multiplexing of information not possible with baseband systems. Broadband systems are necessarily more expensive due to the additional hardware for modulation and demodulation, essentially modems, but they are more flexible. Almost all LANs today are of the baseband type, which are simple and less expensive. There are few industrial systems, such as the 802.4 scheme, that rely on broadband signaling.

⇨ Multiplexing

Multiplexing is a technique in which multiple data streams of information might be simultaneously sent over one signal channel. There are three methods of multiplexing: time division multiplexing (abbreviated TDM); frequency division multiplexing (abbreviated FDM); and a form of TDM called statistical multiplexing. The device used for multiplexing the traffic from several low-data-rate terminals across a wide area network link to a minicomputer is called a *multiplexer* or a mux. We will use such a mux as an example in describing the various multiplexing schemes.

✳ Time-division multiplexing

In time-division multiplexing, time on the signaling channel is broken up into time slots. And time on the channel, or a slot, is assigned to data from one of the sending devices. The key to time-division multiplexing is for the sending devices to transmit at a much lower data rate than the link between the multiplexers. That's how the multiplexers are able to keep up with the traffic from many devices and be able to send it across one high-speed link.

Let's take the example shown in Fig. 4-15. Here we have four terminals sending traffic to a minicomputer. There are actually only three terminals in this case, with no traffic from the fourth terminal, which is turned off. Between the multiplexers, there is only one channel, only one high-speed link. The traffic from the terminals arrives at the multiplexer at 2400 bps. The data rate on the link between the muxes must be 9600 bps, at least four times that to keep up with traffic from the maximum of four terminals.

Figure 4-15

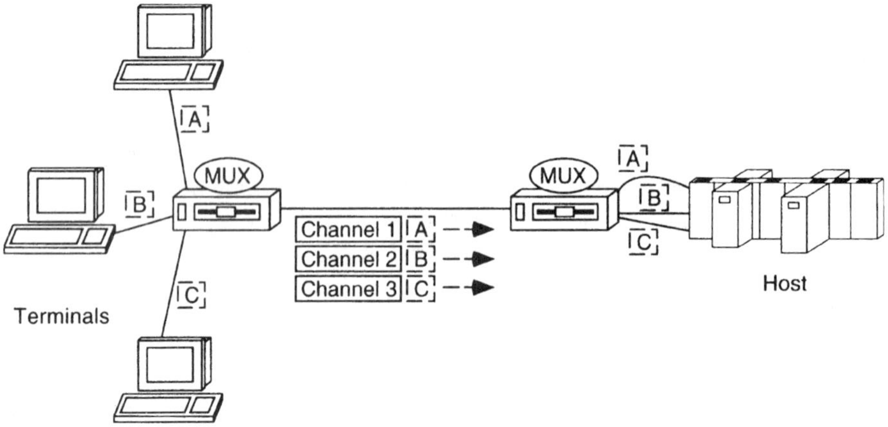

Time division multiplexing. Learning Tree International

The multiplexer at the terminal side combines the traffic from the four terminals by round-robin sampling of the terminal data stream and sending it out over the mux-to-mux link at a high-speed rate. In conventional TDM, time slots are assigned to ports on the multiplexer. If a particular port does not receive traffic from a terminal, that time slot on the high-speed link goes empty, or unused. Conventional TDM, therefore, has wasted bandwidth as one of its drawbacks. As you will see later, there is a technique for getting back that wasted, unused bandwidth. This improved scheme is more complex, but it's more efficient.

TDM is used in terminal networks to aggregate the traffic from multiple terminals onto one wide area network link. It is more cost-effective than buying individual wide area network links for each terminal.

Time-division multiplexing is also used in LANs. As we will see in the next section, schemes to share the cabling plant often use TDM. Basically, when devices connected to a multipoint network take turns in sending information, it is essentially TDM.

✳ Frequency-division multiplexing

In FDM, the muxes use different frequencies for each of the channels. Broadband signaling is done in this case by modulating carriers at different frequencies, one carrier per channel, with the data from each of the sending devices. This is essentially a broadband signaling system. Figure 4-16 shows an FDM scheme with multiplexers.

Figure 4-16

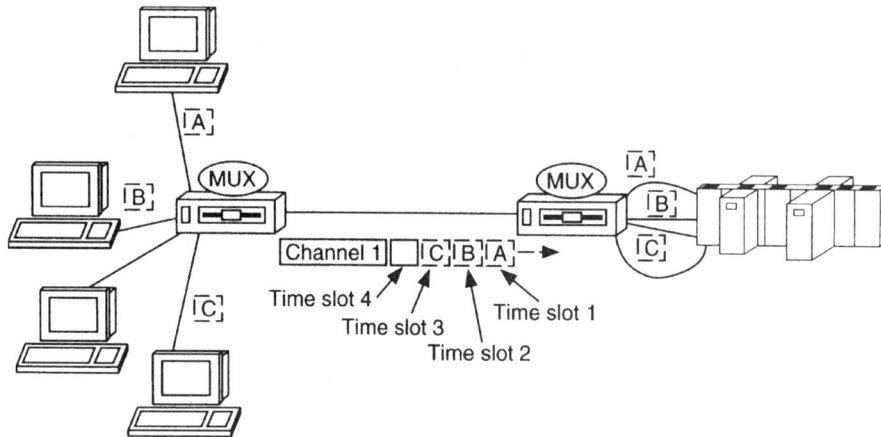

Frequency division multiplexing. Learning Tree International

✳ **Statistical multiplexing**

Statistical multiplexers, or "statmuxes," as they are often called, is a TDM scheme that allows the recovery of unused slots. Consider the statistical time-division multiplexing system in Fig. 4-17. Let's say there is a 9.6 Kbps line between the statistical multiplexers, and there are six 2400-bps terminals attached to one of the muxes. The assumption that makes statistical multiplexers work is that the terminals do not offer to the mux continuous traffic. Although the terminals are set for a maximum data rate of 2400 bps, their data rate—the actual data rate from the terminals—is quite a bit less, so the aggregate from all six terminals is never more than 9.6 Kbps. The terminals still operate at 2400 bps, but the users do not type fast enough to keep the terminal links full. The statmuxes are able to keep up with the traffic from the terminals and be able to send it over the wide area network link.

Instead of assigning a fixed time slot to each terminal, the statistical multiplexer will send traffic from any terminal over the next available slot in a first-come/first-served basis. Since the assignments of the

Figure 4-17

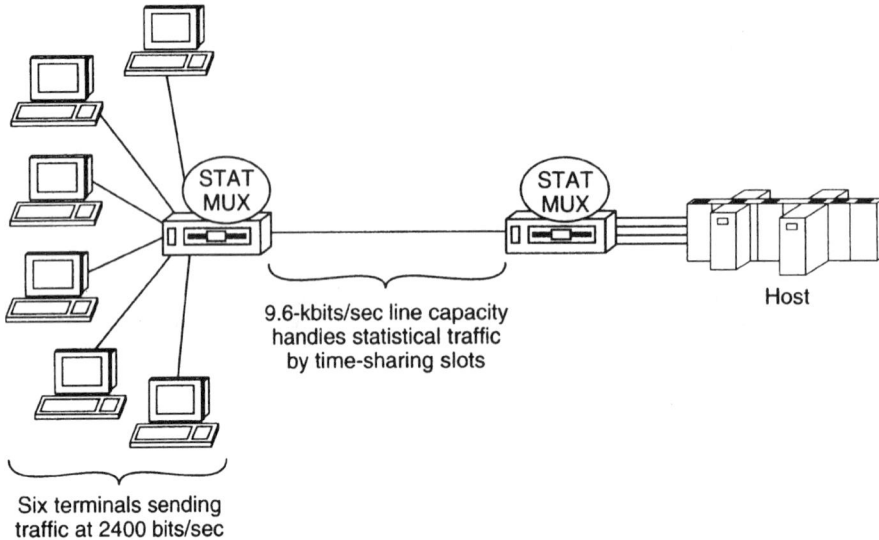

9.6-kbits/sec line capacity
handles statistical traffic
by time-sharing slots

Host

Six terminals sending
traffic at 2400 bits/sec

Statistical time division multiplexing. Learning Tree International

slots are not fixed, the receiving statmux will have to know to which terminal the content slot belongs. For that purpose, the sending statmux must add a little bit of addressing information in each slot to identify the owner of that traffic.

So there is a reduction in the available bandwidth, or, in other words, there is some overhead. But there is the corresponding improvement in efficiency in the use of slots that would otherwise go unused in a normal TDM system. This is how a statmux recovers unused bandwidth over a normal TDM mux. Figure 4-18 gives the characteristics, access methods, types of devices, advantages, and disadvantages of these three multiplexing schemes.

Figure 4-18

Characteristic	FDM	TDM	SDM
Name	**F**requency **D**ivision **M**ultiplexing	**T**ime **D**ivision **M**ultiplexing	**S**tatistical **T**ime **D**ivision **M**ultiplexing
Access	Broadband	Baseband	Baseband
Method	Split bandwidth into channels; use all channels simultaneously	Split time into slots, assign one slot to each communicating entity	Split time into slots, assign slots on a first-come, first-served basis
Devices	RF modems, retransmitters, headend	Multiplexer and DSU/CSU to connect to network	STAT MUX and DSU/CSU to connect to network
Uses	Broadband networks 802.4	Multiplex traffic from many terminals over one phone line	Improved performance over TDM multiplexer
Advantages	One cable plant, many channels, more capacity	One channel shared by many devices. Baseband access makes it simpler.	Recover unused slots. More efficient than TDM.
Disadvantages	Expensive. Hard to install and maintain. Need RF engineers.	Unused slots are wasted bandwidth	More expensive hardware than TDM

Characteristics of TDM, FDM, and Stat TDM. Learning Tree International

The OSI data link layer

CNE exam objectives

> Define the basic purpose of the OSI data link layer.

> Identify and describe the networking technology topics associated with the OSI data link layer.

> Identify and describe the methods associated with each OSI data link layer topic.

See Table 4-2.

Table 4-2   **Topics and Methods for the Data Link Layer**

Data link layer topics	Data link layer methods
Logical topology (MAC)	Bus Ring
Media access (MAC)	Contention Token passing Polling
Addressing (MAC)	MAC addresses
Framing (MAC)	Address Control Data Error check
Synchronization (LLC)	Asynchronous Synchronous Isochronous
Services (LLC)	Flow control Windowing Logical link control Error checking

⇨ The data link layer

The ISO defines the services of the data link layer as:

> The data link layer provides functional and procedural means to establish, maintain, and release data-link connections among network entities and to transfer data-link-service data units. A data-link connection is built upon one or several physical connections.
>
> The data link layer detects and possibly corrects errors that might occur in the physical layer.
>
> In addition, the data link layer enables the network layer to control the interconnection of data circuits within the physical layer. (ITU X.200 standard definition.)

As seen in the definition just given, the major task of the data link layer is to organize the data stream into frames. Framing is a major task of the data link layer. Another important task is the management of the establishment of the link between computers. This involves error detection, flow control, and the access mechanism in a multipoint environment. The data link layer provides these services to the layer above it, the network layer. The data link layer encapsulates the packet in a frame and provides link services to the network layer. The data link layer consumes the services of the physical layer—the clocking, synchronization, and encoding services seen in the previous section. Figure 4-19 shows the data link layer creating a frame for a packet and consuming physical-layer services.

Figure 4-19

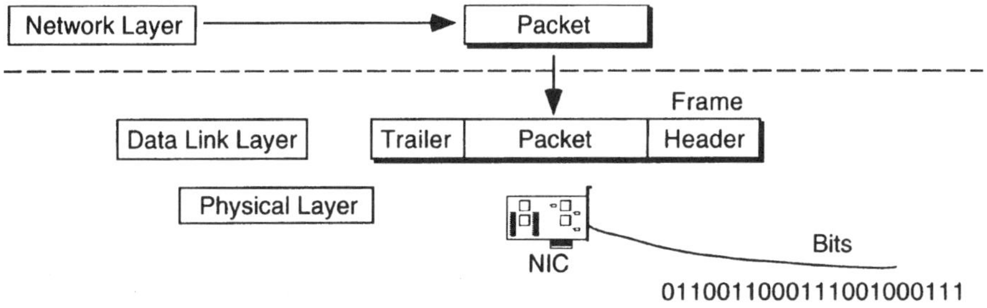

How the data link layer is used. Learning Tree International

The topics associated with this layer are the logical topology (which is different from the physical wiring topology), media access techniques, and frame addressing. Data link topics also include frame composition, frame synchronization, and services provided by the data link layer. Table 4-2 summarizes the topics with the associated methods in this important area.

The devices that are normally associated with this layer are bridges and network interface cards. The technique of the data link layer is described by the IEEE as the media access control sublayer (MAC). The acronym MAC is associated with LANs. Another responsibility of the data link layer is the guarantee of delivery of frames at the link level. This is a service that the data link layer provides for the network layer. The methods and techniques for frame delivery assurance are called *logical link control*.

⇨ Logical topology

In an earlier section we learned that cabling topologies might take the form of a star, bus, or ring. That is not necessarily how stations might be taking turns in using that cable plant. When we learn in a later portion of this section about media access techniques, we'll find that there are different approaches for sharing the cable plant. The way computers share a multipoint network is termed the *logical topology*. The way the cable plant is installed is termed the *physical topology*. And the two might be quite different.

Look at the example network in Fig. 4-20. It has a 10Base-T concentrator, which is a hub used on Ethernet networks when they are wired with twisted-pair cabling. There are six computers connected to that concentrator via cables that contain two twisted pairs each. The physical topology, the way the cabling is installed, is a star, as we learned in the last section. The logical topology, the way the computers communicate, is a bus. In other words, when one computer

Figure 4-20

10BASE-T concentrator

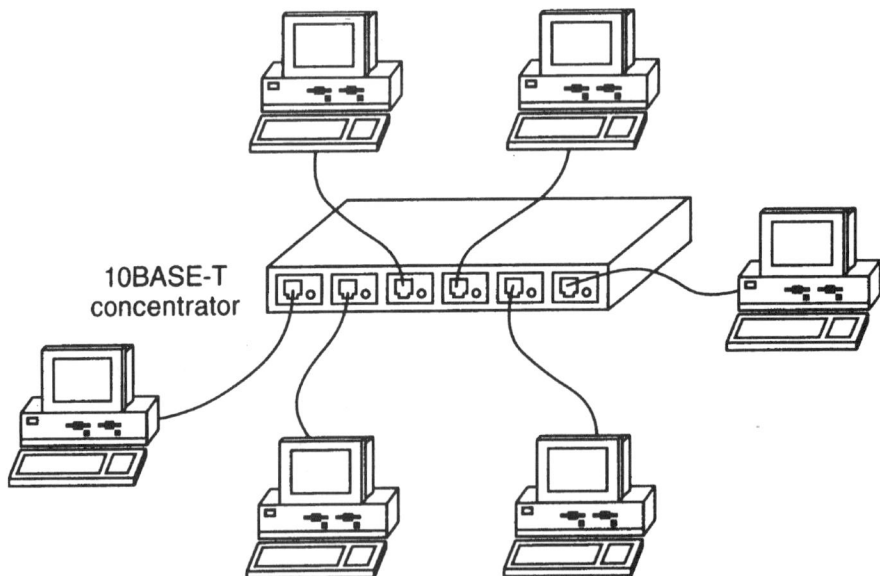

Example of logical versus physical topologies—802.3 wired with twisted-pair cabling. There is a physical star wiring topology supporting an electrical bus logical topology. Learning Tree International

transmits, the signal from that computer reaches all the others almost simultaneously. The concentrator is used as a retransmitter of that signal. This acts like an electrical bus. So the logical topology in this case would be a bus—physical star topology supporting a logical bus operation.

A similar situation occurs with Token Ring networks. Imagine the same network with the same physical layout as the one just discussed, but instead of a 10Base-T concentrator, substitute a MSAU—same wiring, different network cards, and different type of hub. The physical topology is still a star. In this case, the MSAU creates an electrical ring by taking one of the pairs from each machine and connecting it to a pair from another machine going around from port to port creating a ring out of all the pairs.

In this case, the logical topology would be a ring because the signal goes from machine to machine to machine in an electrical ring rather than all machines receiving the transmission simultaneously, as in the bus discussed previously. The key thing to note here is that there is a difference between the way a network is wired (the physical topology) and the way computers access the network, the access scheme, and the electrical transmission of signals (the logical topology).

⇨ Media access techniques

It is the responsibility of the media access control (MAC) portion of the data link layer to allow stations to use, or share, the bandwidth in a multipoint network. And there are essentially three techniques, as shown in Fig. 4-21: contention-based access, token-passing-based access, and polling-based access. The key issue is that the cable plant is not dedicated for point-to-point connections between computers but is shared among all the computers. There has to be some scheme by which a device designed to send gets access to a portion of "time on the network." These are bandwidth-sharing schemes.

Each of the LAN protocols in use today uses one of these three forms of access. Each of these access techniques has different characteristics. The choice of network type must be dictated by

Figure 4-21

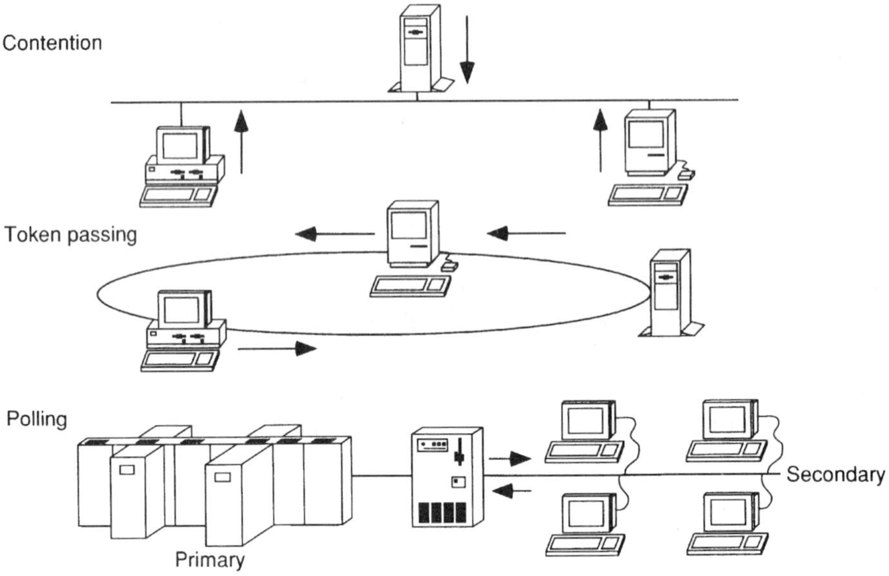

How the three principal media access techniques work. Learning Tree International

matching the characteristics of the access method to the data communication needs.

There are four major issues, or factors, to differentiate these access methods. One is whether the nature of the transmissions is bursty or steady. Another is the amount of data to be sent, the third is the sensitivity of the data, and the fourth is how many devices make up the network. These factors will be considered as we compare the various access methods in the following sections.

✳ Contention

In contention-based access networks, a sending device must listen before using the network. If it finds the network free, then it can begin sending a frame. The frame in this case is sent out to all other devices. They receive it almost simultaneously, due to the nature of the bus-type propagation. The IEEE has termed this scheme carrier-sense multiple access to denote the multipoint nature of the network and the fact that stations are listening for a "carrier" before they begin sending.

There could possibly be two stations waiting for the bus to be free before sending and they will both begin transmitting when they sense the bus is clear. In that case, when the two signals cross, they will interfere with each other, causing an error in reception for all of the devices in the network. This is called a collision.

There are two ways of resolving problems with collisions. One is to detect collisions and stop transmitting, then use an algorithm to resolve who's going to go next, and retransmit the frame. That's called collision detect (or CD). This is the scheme used by Ethernet and 802.3 LANs.

The second scheme, implemented by the Apple LocalTalk network, is a form of collision avoidance (CSMA/CA). In that case, computers reserve the use of the bus before committing to sending a frame. This scheme is discussed in greater detail in chapter 5.

Contention schemes are relatively simple, and they have little overhead. CSMA networks are considered nondeterministic, or not predictable (probabilistic, if you will). This nondeterministic characteristic is of concern for certain user groups, such as manufacturing, where they have very tight time tolerances for controlling processes over a network. Contention schemes are not acceptable, and these users prefer more predictable or deterministic schemes. They have chosen token passing over the CSMA scheme for that reason.

Another consideration with this type of scheme is that priorities are very difficult to implement. Also, as the number of devices on the network increases, there is a consequential increase in collisions, or conversely, as the amount of traffic on the network for the same number of devices increases, there is also a consequential increase in the number of collisions. Contention schemes do not allow for orderly allocation of bandwidth, either on a priority basis or to individual stations. On the other hand, it is a very popular scheme. It is the basis for Ethernet and 802.3 LANs, which are very useful in most business situations.

✳ Token passing

In token-passing systems there are two types of network frames. There is a permission frame called the token and there is an information frame to carry data. Token-passing LANs have computers that are connected point to point, either logically or physically, and pass the token around in a ring for access. When a device finishes transmitting an information frame, the device will subsequently send out a token frame to notify all other devices on the ring that the network is free for anyone else to use. That token frame is a short transmission giving permission to any other device that wishes to transmit.

Typically, in token-passing LANs, each device that wishes to transmit will capture the token and send out one data frame before relinquishing the use of the network by sending out the token again. There are some token-passing LANs in which the station wishing to transmit will hold onto the token for a period of time and send out as many data frames as it can during that period of time. These schemes use a "token-holding" method. The FDDI LAN uses such a scheme.

There are two ways of creating a token-passing topology. One in which the devices are physically connected by point-to-point links, making a ring. The IBM Token Ring, the FDDI LAN, and the 802.5 LANs are examples of this type of topology. There is one scheme that implements token passing on a linear bus. It is called a token-bus scheme—the IEEE 802.4 LAN. In that case, a multipoint network is employed where all stations are connected to a bus. When a station relinquishes control of the network, it will send out a token to another station that's been logically identified on a ring. The token is broadcast along the bus, and all stations will receive it. It will be captured and used by the next station in the logical ring.

The next chapter we will go into the details of the implementation of various token-passing schemes. One of the major benefits of token-passing schemes is the predictable loading and delay that they exhibit. These networks are considered deterministic because there is a known maximum delay that stations observe in getting on the ring.

It's also much easier to implement priority schemes in token-passing LANs. There are no collisions, since no one can put a frame on the network unless they have possession of the token. Thus, there is no wasted bandwidth due to collisions. On the other hand, there is a certain amount of bandwidth usage in passing the token around, which is overhead. Because of the physical ring implementation, many of these schemes have the additional requirement of implementing a complex network recovery procedure in the event of a link outage. This might be considered a disadvantage of these schemes.

When comparing contention to token passing, we see that contention schemes have lower overhead and are more efficient in lightly loaded situations. As the load increases, contention schemes begin to see degradation in performance due to the increased number of collisions. Token-passing schemes, on the other hand, exhibit much better characteristics under heavy load and perform much better than contention schemes under those circumstances. But they do have the additional overhead of managing the controlled access.

✳ Polling

Figure 4-21 shows a polling-type network. In this case, there is a central controlling device that gives permission to communicating entities to transmit. The central controlling device is called the *primary*, or master, device. It gives permission to communicating entities by querying them in a round-robin fashion. The communicating entities are referred to as *secondaries*.

The function of polling can be embedded or can be performed by one of the communicating devices itself. This type of access technique is very popular with mainframe computing environments. It is easy to control the minimum and maximum access times. It is also relatively easy to implement priority schemes on a software or hardware basis, due to the centralized control of the network.

Polling schemes are not used in LANs but are used mostly in terminal networks between mini or mainframe computers and their terminals. It has a great deal more overhead than techniques previously listed, due to the polling or querying process and a great deal more bandwidth usage in acknowledgments or in querying stations that have nothing to transmit. But the polling scheme is popular in the environment of large hosts.

Figure 4-22 shows a table comparing and contrasting the characteristics of the three channel-access techniques just discussed.

Figure 4-22

Characteristic	Contention	Token passing	Polling
Description	Multiple access Listen before send Broadcast transmissions	Pass token Capture token and send a frame	Primary sends to or polls secondary, secondary sends when polled
Types	CSMA CSMA/CD CSMA/CA	Token Ring Token bus	Primary/secondary
Examples	Ethernet LocalTalk 802.3	802.5 FDDI 802.4	LAPB SDLC
Where used	PC LANS Enterprise networks	IBM mainframe networks PC LANs Backbones Industrial networks	X.25 WANs IBM mainframe networks
Advantages	Low overhead, simpler	Deterministic, performs well under load	Deterministic, efficient for terminal traffic
Disadvantages	Nondeterministic, degraded performance under heavy load	Added overhead due to token passing	High overhead

Media access techniques compared. Learning Tree International

⇨ Addressing

Devices on a network are assigned unique identifiable addresses. These addresses are used to identify stations on an individual link. They are managed by the details of the data link layer. The device address identifying a particular station on a link is called a MAC address or a physical device address. They are typically embedded in the network hardware in the form of an address assigned by the manufacturer and burnt in a read-only memory chip.

The address scheme used in most LANs is universally administered by the IEEE organization. Vendors wishing to produce network cards adhering to IEEE specifications or even ANSII specifications, such as

FDDI, apply for a block of addresses to be uniquely assigned to them by the IEEE. There are some networks, such as ARCNET, where the addresses are administered locally by a network administrator. They are set on the board by DIP switches.

The format of the addresses is discussed in great detail in chapter 5. These addresses are used by the data link hardware to identify the sender and the receiver of the frame, and they are encoded into the frame structure. Physical addresses in the frame are used by bridges in determining whether to forward or filter a particular frame.

⇨ Framing

The frame is the basic unit of information created and transmitted by the data link protocol. Figure 4-23 shows a typical frame. Most frames are composed of four basic components: an address field, a control field, a data field, and an error-check field. In some networks, there might be a group of bits in the front of the frame called the *preamble* to allow synchronization between sender and receiver. And there might be an end-delimiter set of bits at the end of the frame to indicate frame conclusion. Neither the preamble nor the end delimiter are considered part of the frame but are external to the frame. These two groups of bits are often added onto the frame as the frame goes through the physical-layer set of circuits on its way out onto the wire. Some data link protocols reverse the order of some of the fields. In Token Ring networks, for example, the control field comes before the address field.

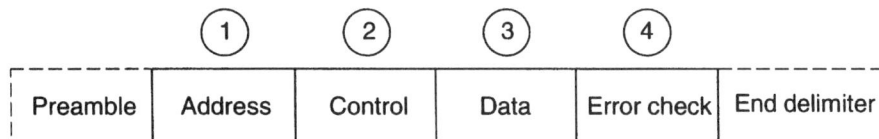

Figure 4-23

| Preamble | Address | Control | Data | Error check | End delimiter |

A generic frame showing the typical basic components. Learning Tree International

✳ Address
The address field contains the physical, or MAC, addresses of the sender and the receiver devices.

181

✳ Control

The control field is used for many different purposes and it depends on which LAN is being studied as to what the field is used for. In Token Ring LANs, the control field might contain an indication of whether this is a data frame or a token frame. In Ethernet LANs it is used to identify the type of network protocol using the frame for transport, whether it's IP, IPX, or NetBIOS. In wide area network protocols such as X.25, the control field is used for acknowledgment and sequencing of frames.

✳ Data

The data portion of the frame contains the packet that the data link protocol is required to transmit over the link. It is the aggregation of all of the protocol overhead from all the upper layers 3 through 7, plus the actual user data, if any. At the start of this field, there might be additional data link protocol information used for sequencing and flow control called *logical link control* (LLC).

✳ Error check

The error-check portion of the frame contains a bit sequence generated by a special algorithm. Those bits are checked by the receiver to assure the integrity of the received frame. Two very popular error-checking schemes are the 16-bit cyclic-redundancy check (CRC) used with ARCNET, X.25, and LocalTalk networks, and the 32-bit CRC scheme used by 802.3, 802.4, 802.5, and FDDI data link protocols.

⇨ Synchronization

There must be some way for the receiver to know that it has received the entire frame intended to be sent by the sender. This is done by the data link layer with a technique called *synchronization*. We saw bits of synchronization at the physical level. A technique called clocking was used to accomplish synchronization.

At the data link level, there are three methods by which a sender will indicate to the receiver that the transmission of a frame is complete. Data is organized by senders into characters or frames. Character transmission is popular in terminal networks where the data to be sent is a keystroke that has been encoded into a 7- or 8-bit sequence. That sequence is sent individually with no coordination with any other subsequent 8-bit sequence. That is termed asynchronous communication. The other two techniques, synchronous and isochronous, are used when characters are grouped into frames.

✳ **Asynchronous**

In asynchronous transmissions, the characters are sent independently of each other. They are typically enveloped with a certain protocol overhead—a bit at the beginning to indicate the start of the character, followed by the data, then typically 7-bit ASCII-encoded data, a parity bit, and, finally, a bit to indicate the end of transmission, called the *stop bit*. This is a 10-bit group used to send 7 data bits. The overhead is 30% (7 data bits, 3 protocol bits).

It is a popular synchronization scheme in terminal networks. The main advantages are simplicity and universality. The main disadvantage is that it is inefficient due to the sizable overhead. Bit synchronization with this scheme is also asynchronous, for sender and receiver use their own clocks, which causes problems for this scheme. Asynchronous transmission is popular with minicomputer terminal networks. (See Fig. 4-24.)

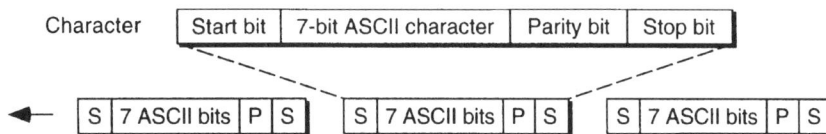

Figure 4-24

- **Asynchronous protocol**
    - Characters are sent independently of each other
    - 10-bit characters: start bit, 7-bit data ASCII encoded, parity bit, stop bit
    - Used to connect terminals directly to hosts or for PC-to-PC file transfers
    - Low-data-rate applications: 2,400 bits/sec, 9,600 bits/sec
    - Uses ASCII encoding
    - Advantages: simple technology, universally used
    - Disadvantage: inefficient use of channel bandwidth

Asynchronous encoding of the bit stream. Learning Tree International

✳ Synchronous

Synchronous transmission techniques require the sender to include clocking information with the transmission. This can be done in one of two ways. In low-speed terminal networks, the sender is continuously sending a special 8-bit character called a *SYN character* whenever not transmitting any data. The SYN character keeps the receiver constantly synchronized to the sender. A second method is to send a separate clocking signal via separate circuit to the receiver.

The major difference between synchronous and asynchronous transmission is that characters are synchronized on a character-by-character basis under asynchronous transmission, and they do not have to be under synchronous transmission. In synchronous transmission the characters are sent one after the other without start or stop bits, and they are sent as a block. An entire block of characters is a frame that might contain an error check at the end of the frame, and they will contain an end delimiter as well.

Figure 4-25 shows synchronous encoding of a bit stream. The error check is normally a 16-bit CRC and the characters are 8-bit encoded data characters without parity.

Figure 4-25

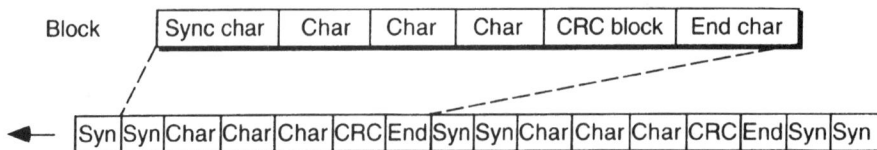

Synchronous encoding of the bit stream. Learning Tree International

A major benefit of synchronous transmission for terminal traffic is that it is more efficient than asynchronous transmission; there is less overhead. Also, since there is synchronization of the receiver's clock to the sender's clock, this scheme allows for higher data rates and better use of channel bandwidth. It also has improved error detection (CRC versus a parity bit), but the penalty paid is the increased complexity of the required circuits. Synchronous schemes are very popular with IBM mini and mainframe terminal networks. The character encoding is uses the EBCDIC character set.

✳ **Isochronous**

The isochronous technique is a third method of synchronizing devices on a network. In this technique a clock signal generated by a designated network device is sent onto all other devices on the network. Each device is allocated a certain time slot or length of time that it is allowed to put data on the network. At the end of that time slot, the device must relinquish control and pass on the control of the network to another device.

While the transmitting device, the sender, has control of the network, it may send as many frames as it wishes. Using this method, a clock signal is sent with every frame. Clocking is provided by the single designated device on the network. The FDDI LAN employs the isochronous transmission technique. This synchronization method guarantees a minimum bandwidth to each device, and consequently it is considered a deterministic method. It requires very little overhead to run. A major drawback of this scheme is that an external clocking mechanism is required for operation, making this scheme fairly complicated to implement. Figure 4-26 compares the asynchronous and synchronous transmission techniques.

⇨ Connection services

Transmission of information from one computer to another over links external to the computers is inherently error prone. All forms of noise might interfere with the transmission, causing the received signal to be in error and requiring the receiver to reject the frame.

Techniques to recover from lost transmissions fall in the area of connection services. At the very least, a data link protocol will do error detection (not correction). This protocol might also recover from loss of a frame in the event of an error by retransmission. The process of transmitting and recovering lost frames is called a *positive acknowledge-retransmit protocol* (PAR). In the PAR protocol scheme, the sender will send a frame and will include in that frame an error-check sequence. It will number the frame and will start a timer when the frame leaves the sending machine.

Figure 4-26

Characteristic	Asynchronous	Synchronous
Transmission	Each character separately	Blocks of characters
Error check	Parity bit in each character	CRC at end of block
Framing	10 bits per character—start bit, 7 bits of data (ASCII encoded), parity bit and stop bit	Block SYN character, data characters, CRC character
Encoding scheme	Typically ASCII (7-bit)	Typically EBCDIC (8-bit)
Access scheme	I/O connection to host	SDLC, polling
Typical application	Terminal traffic PC-to-PC file transfer VT100 terminal connected to a VAX	IBM SNA networks 3270 terminal connected to an IBM mainframe
Synchronization	Derived from signal stream	Separate clock signal
Typical data rates	2400 bps, 9600 bps	19.2 Kbps
Advantages	Mature technology Universally employed Inexpensive hardware	More efficient Better error detection
Disadvantages	Poor error detection Inefficient use of channel bandwidth	More complex hardware

Comparison of synchronization schemes. Learning Tree International

The receiver will receive the frame sometime later, perform its error-check procedure, discover that the frame has been properly received, and send a frame in return to acknowledge the receipt of the transmitted frame. This must occur before the sender's time runs out. It must be done within a certain limit. If the receiver, upon checking the frame, finds that an error has occurred, its task is to discard the received transmission and do no more. At the sender's end, the timer eventually will reach the limit of its allotted time span, at which point the sender assumes that the sent frame had an error and will send the frame again. Hopefully this time the frame arrives without errors. This process goes on until the frame is acknowledged and properly received. This process produces an error-free communication link from an error-prone channel. A protocol might provide two kinds of connection services. One is considered connectionless and the other is connection oriented.

✳ Connection-oriented versus connectionless

In a connectionless network, the protocol is not responsible for recovery from lost transmissions. Applying this to the data link level, we see that if frames are lost it is not the responsibility of the data link protocol to recover those frames. So how does complete transmission take place? If we are sending a file in small transmissions via frames and a frame is lost, how do we assure that the entire file arrives? Who is responsible for retransmitting those frames that are lost? In the case of a connectionless protocol, that protocol would have to work in conjunction with another protocol, usually an upper-layer protocol, that retransmits and assures delivery. The responsibility of the connectionless data link protocol is only for framing, access control, error check, and delivery across the link, not recovery from lost frames.

Connection-oriented protocols, on the other hand, do take on the responsibility to recovery from lost frames. To that end, they require several additional techniques. One is flow control and the other is sequencing, which are discussed later in this chapter. Connection-oriented protocols guarantee delivery. They also guarantee sequencing of the data so that they keep track of each frame, or each transmission, by number. They have one drawback in that they require the opening of the connection at the start of a transaction before data must be sent, and then they must gracefully close the connection, or close the link, at the end of the transaction. This creates the additional overhead of link establishment and close, which is not present in connectionless protocols. Figure 4-27 compares the services of connectionless versus connection-oriented protocols.

Applying this to the data link layer, we see that there are three types of connection services that the data link layer can provide. One is considered unacknowledged, connectionless services—essentially a

Figure 4-27

Connectionless	Connection-oriented
Best efforts delivery	Guaranteed delivery
No call setup before transmitting data	Must do a call setup before transmitting and a close afterward
No acknowledgments or retransmissions	Acknowledged, sequenced delivery
Datagram service	Virtual circuit service

Characteristics of connection-oriented and connectionless lines. Learning Tree International

connectionless type of service where framing, access, and error check are all that is provided by the data link protocol and nothing else. This is typical of most LAN protocols today, such as 802.3, 802.5, and FDDI.

Functionality is added to the data link layer to provide connection-oriented services with the addition of another protocol called *logical link control* (LLC). This protocol will provide basic connection-oriented services—flow control, sequencing, and error checking—besides access and framing.

✳ Flow control

The most basic form of transmission is a stop-and-wait protocol. In that case, the sender sends out one frame and waits until the receiver acknowledges that frame. When the sender receives acknowledgment, it will send out the next frame and wait for acknowledgment, then send out the next frame and wait for acknowledgment. Only one frame at a time is being sent by the sender. In this stop-and-wait protocol, there is an acknowledgment for every frame, which is a good deal of overhead.

✳ Windowing

To improve performance, some networks allow the sender to transmit a number of frames before stopping and waiting to receive an acknowledgment. The acknowledgment is for the group of frames that have been sent. The receiver doesn't acknowledge each frame but acknowledges the group of frames. The number of frames allowed for the sender to send out before stopping and waiting is called the *window*.

This is termed *windowing flow control* because essentially the sender is stopped from sending any additional frames until the receiver has acknowledged any outstanding frames. The receiver might need to wait a period of time to send an acknowledgment, due to many factors. This is a form of controlling the flow of frames to allow the receiver to match the speed at which the sender sends frames to the receiver's ability to process them.

The size of the window (the number of outstanding frames at any one time) can be negotiated between sender and receiver in two ways. It could be a fixed parameter that is set at the beginning of the transaction, with no possibility of negotiation during a call in progress. Or it is a parameter that is set at the beginning of the transaction by the sender negotiating with the receiver a mutually agreeable value. If, for example, the sender is a minicomputer, with the ability to send many frames per second, and the receiver is a personal computer with only the ability to receive one frame per second, when the sender suggests three frames per second, the receiver will respond with, "No, I can only do one frame per second." Then they both agree to the lower number of one frame per second. Figure 4-28 shows the window flow-control protocol in action with a window of 3.

Error checking/error recovery

The logical link control portion of the data link layer can perform error control via its acknowledgment capability.

Bridging

Bridges are used to link LANs. They do this by transferring frames from one LAN to another based upon the addresses in the frame. In general, there are two types of bridges: transparent bridges that are used to link Ethernet (802.3) LANs, and Token-Ring bridges that are used to link two 802.5 LANs. The two types of bridges work quite differently.

Figure 4-28

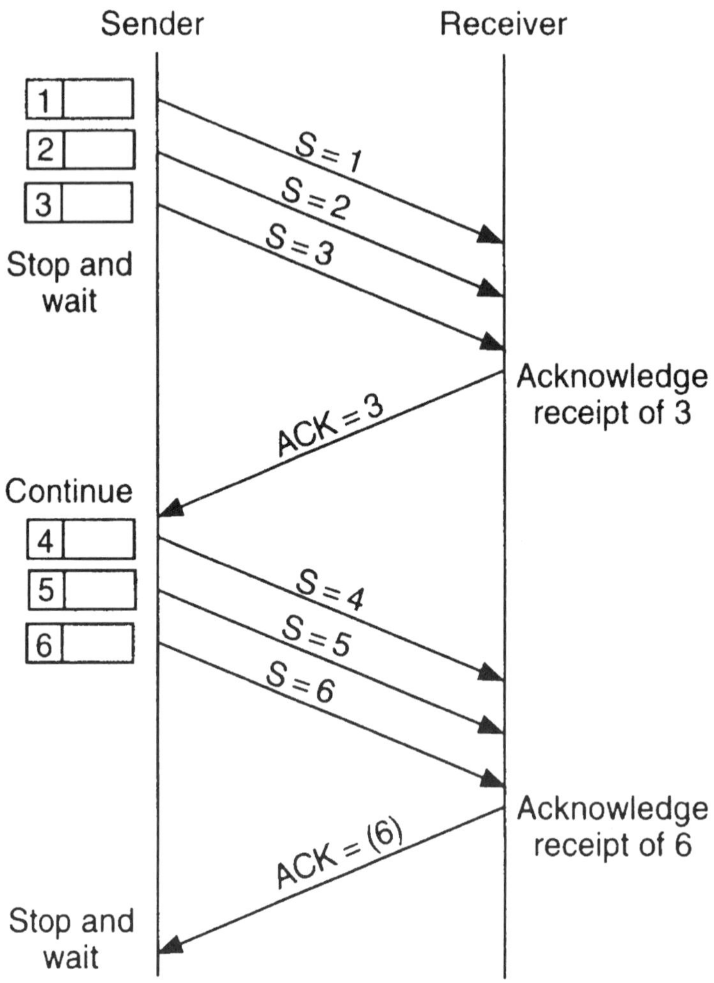

How windowing flow control works. Learning Tree International

Ethernet bridges forward frames from one network to the other based on a forwarding table in the bridge. The forwarding table might have been entered by hand by a network administrator, or the table might have been created dynamically by the bridge. To create the forwarding table dynamically, a bridge would have observed the source address on all frames on all LANs. With a device in one LAN used to transmit a frame to a device on another LAN, it places that other device's address in the destination portion of the frame and launches that frame onto the LAN that it is attached to.

The bridge automatically picks up the frame, reads the content of the address field, notes the source address, and uses that to update its forwarding table. The bridge uses the destination address to make a decision as to what to do with that frame.

If the receiving device is on another LAN, as in this case, the bridge will forward that frame onto that other LAN through the bridge connection to that LAN. If the intended receiver is on the same LAN as the sender, the bridge will ignore the transmission. (This action is called *filtering*.) For that reason, Ethernet bridges are considered filter-forward devices. (See Fig. 4-29.)

⇨ The OSI network layer

⇨ CNE exam objectives

➢ Define the basic purpose of the OSI network layer.

➢ Identify and describe the networking technology topics associated with the OSI network layer.

➢ Identify and describe the methods associated with each OSI network layer topic.

See Table 4-3.

Topics and Methods for the Network Layer   Table 4-3

Network-layer topics	Network-layer methods
Addressing	Logical Service
Switching	Circuit Packet Message
Route discovery	Vector distance Link-state
Route selection	Static routing Dynamic routing
Services	Packet sequencing Error recovery Flow control

Figure 4-29

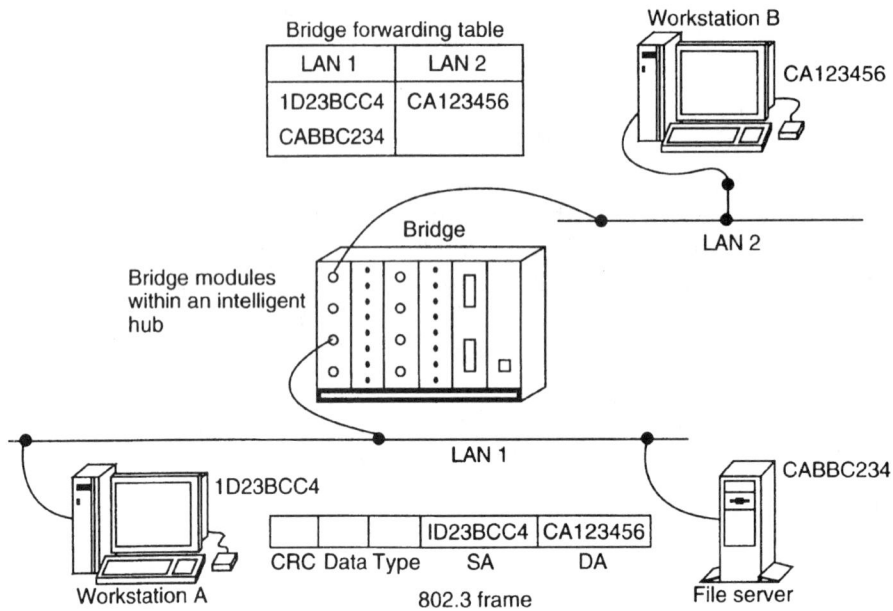

An Ethernet bridge in action. Learning Tree International

⇨ The network layer

The ITU X.200 document defines the services of the OSI network layer as:

> The basic service of the network layer is to provide the transparent transfer of data between transport entities. This service allows the structure and detailed content of submitted data to be determined exclusively by layers above the network layer.

> The network layer contains functions necessary to provide the transport layer with a firm network/transport layer boundary which is independent of the underlying communications media in all things other than quality of service. Thus the network layer contains functions necessary to mask the differences in the characteristics of different transmission and subnetwork technologies into a consistent network service.

The service provided at each end of a network connection is the same even when a network-connection spans several subnetworks, each offering dissimilar services.

Note—It is important to distinguish the specialized use of the term "service" within the OSI reference model from its common use by suppliers of private networks and carriers.

The quality of service is negotiated between the transport entities and the network service at the time of establishment of a network connection. While this quality of service might vary from one network connection to another, it will be agreed for a given network-connection and be the same at both network-connection endpoints. (See Fig. 4-30.)

Figure 4-30

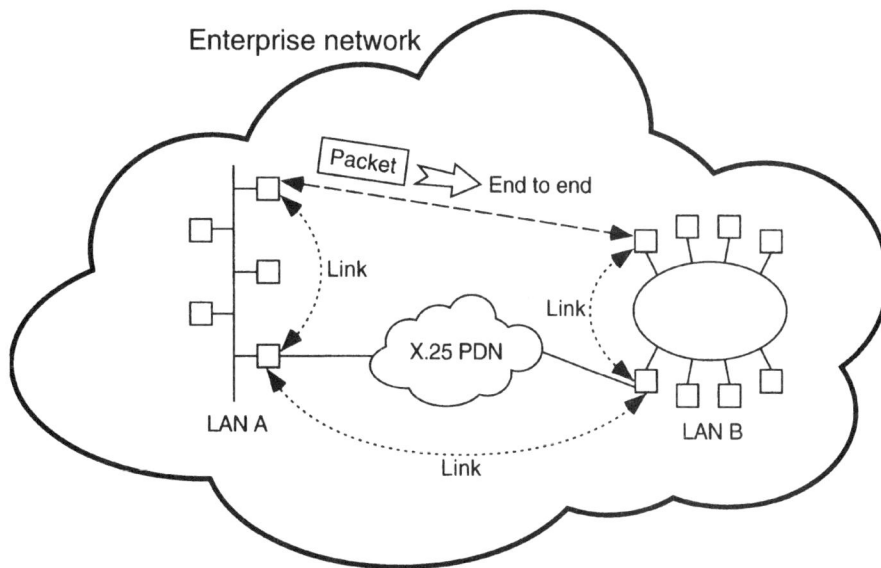

End-to-end transmission requiring the services of layers above the data link layer. Learning Tree International

Similarities can be drawn between the data link and network layers. Both have as a primary responsibility moving protocol data units between network devices using addressing techniques. The data link layer addressing is restricted to a single physical network segment (the device address must be on the same cable segment). Network-layer addressing, however, groups devices on a cable segment into one logical entity or address and then moves protocol data units between multiple network segments or internetworks. These individual network segments can be composed of different underlying data link layer protocols (and often are).

Network layer characteristics

> Moves information across the network using routing techniques.

> Creates packets (datagrams) to carry upper-layer protocol data units called *messages*.

> Implements a logical, networkwide address scheme (i.e., IP or IPX).

> Typically unreliable, connectionless functionality in LANs (i.e., IP or IPX), and reliable, connection-oriented functionality in WANs (i.e., X.25).

Addressing

Addressing is a feature used at all layers of the OSI reference model in order to uniquely identify entities, devices, and processes. At the network layer, addressing uniquely identifies logical networks throughout an internetwork. It further identifies the lower-layer individual hardware devices on a specific network and the upper-layer services. As demonstrated in the next chapter, different network protocols implement network addressing differently, however they still provide the same basic functionality as defined by this layer.

The postal system is a very good example of this addressing scheme. In simplistic terms, a complete postal address is made up of the person the letter is destined for (service or process), the house the person lives in (network device), and finally the street the person lives on (logical network address).

Network communities likewise need to get packets or datagrams transferred among themselves and finally to the service or process running on a specific device on the destination network. The complete network address is composed of the logical network address, the network interface card MAC address on the device (see data link layer in this chapter), and the address of the higher-layer service or process running on the device or workstation. The OSI reference model identifies the following two network layer addressing techniques: Logical network address and Service address.

⇨ Logical

At the data link layer, we introduced the concept of having a unique address for each and every network interface card (NIC) installed in a network device or workstation/host. This address is hard coded or burnt in to each network interface card; no two NICs have the same address. This address is sufficient when trying to deliver information to a workstation or host device attached to the same physical network segment as the sender. However, to deliver information to workstations on other network segments, a logical network number or address is used.

The address for the NIC is specified by the manufacturer and is the same regardless of the data link layer frame type used. The logical network address number, however, is specified by the network administrator. The network address is specified at the time that the network layer protocol is bound to the NIC. The process of binding is used to indicate which data link layer frame type will be responsible for transporting or encapsulating the network layer protocol (i.e., IPX encapsulated within an Ethernet frame). The format for network layer logical addresses varies for different protocols. For example, the IPX network address format is not the same as IP, and they are not interchangeable.

Routers are very dependent on the network layer address in order to perform their function of moving packets (datagrams) between different logical networks. The router reads the packet network address (discussed in chapter 5 for protocol) to determine how to forward the packet. Routers use route discovery and route selection techniques to facilitate the packet forwarding process.

⇨ Service

As recounted previously, the logical network and physical device address are not enough to complete the communications process. The examples of postal delivery of a letter where several people live at the same house is similar to several application processes running on the same workstation or host computer (i.e., file and print services). Service addressing specifies the many different and unique higher-layer processes that can be running concurrently on one workstation or host. Service addresses are referred to as "port" or "socket" in various protocol implementations (see chapter 5).

As two higher-level applications communicate in a peer-to-peer relationship, the addresses in question must be defined or "well known" and not change from one vendor's implementation to another's. The "port" or "socket" addresses, therefore, are predefined and usually not changed in order to ensure compatibility over different hardware and software platforms.

It is important to note that as we review individual protocol suites in chapter 5, some protocols do not have network-layer functionality. As such, these protocols are not routable, and they require that the destination station they are communicating with is either on the same physical network segment or that a bridge device is forwarding frames carrying its protocol data unit.

⇨ Example routable protocols

Protocol	Routable
NetWare IPX	Yes
Internet IP	Yes
Apple AppleTalk DDP	Yes

Example nonroutable protocols:

NetBIOS	No
DEC LAT	No

⇨ Switching

In order to route or forward packets throughout an internetwork, the concept of switching is introduced as a mechanism to accomplish this function. There are three switching techniques in use: circuit, packet, and message. The following section will explore their differences. (See Fig. 4-31.)

Figure 4-31

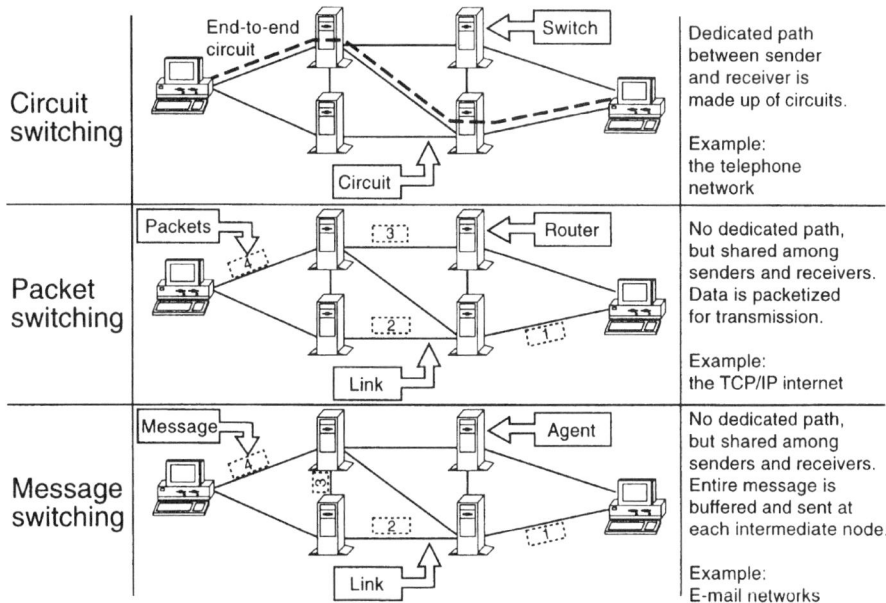

Circuit switching	End-to-end circuit ... Switch ... Circuit	Dedicated path between sender and receiver is made up of circuits. Example: the telephone network
Packet switching	Packets ... 3 ... Router ... 2 ... 1 ... Link	No dedicated path, but shared among senders and receivers. Data is packetized for transmission. Example: the TCP/IP internet
Message switching	Message ... Agent ... 3 ... 2 ... 1 ... Link	No dedicated path, but shared among senders and receivers. Entire message is buffered and sent at each intermediate node. Example: E-mail networks

Switching technologies: circuit, packet, and message. <small>Learning Tree International</small>

❈ Circuit

Circuit switching is similar to the telephone system. When you telephone someone, a complete circuit composing of a pair of wires (transmit and receive) is established between your telephone and that of the person you are calling. The circuit remains in place until the telephone conversation is completed. The dedicated path or connection is terminated at the end of the telephone call when both parties hang up the phone.

Circuit switching in a computer network environment functions in a similar way. A dedicated, end-to-end connection must be established before successful communication can occur. The destination network device must acknowledge a connection from the source network device before communication can take place. In doing so, a dedicated path between the two networks is established. However, in the case of computer network devices, this might only be a logical connection and not necessarily done with physical pairs of wires.

Circuit switching has some advantages and disadvantages. While a dedicated communication path provides better data transmission capability, it is also usually more expensive to maintain. Additionally, dedicated links tend to make very inefficient use of the underlying transmission medium.

❋ Packet

Packet switching can be considered the next level up from circuit switching. Packet switching can use multiple circuits to forward packets to their final destination. No dedicated path needs to be established before packets are forwarded between a sender and receiver. Packet switching makes use of intermediate routers to forward individual packets to their destination. Packet switching provides a lot of flexibility in the sense that packets composing the entire message can be directed to more favorable (faster) routes as network traffic changes. The Internet Internetwork Protocol (IP) is an example of a protocol that uses a packet switching technique to forward packets over different networks in order to reach their final destination. Packet (datagram) and virtual circuit are two packet switching techniques that have been implemented.

Packet (datagram) switching does not rely on a specific path being established between the sender and receiver beforehand. Instead, it relies on a higher-layer protocol to provide sequencing of the protocol data units encapsulated in the packet to ensure that the entire message arrives at its destination, even though all message packets might not take the same route. Packet switching relies on the intermediate points or routers to determine if the packets need to be further encapsulated or changed in size. As such, it is generally considered a connectionless-oriented type of network communication. The switching technique is commonly used in multipoint configured networks.

Virtual circuit switching establishes a logical link or connection between the sender and receiver. The connection is established before any transmission of data packets takes place. Agreement is reached between the communicating devices as to the nature of the conversation, such as packet size and the intermediate paths to be taken. In this manner, virtual circuit switching sets up a connection-oriented form of network communication. The connection can be temporary and remain in place for as long as two specific devices communicate. Or it can be permanent and used by several communicating network devices over a period of time.

The main difference between the two forms of packet switching is their use of connectionless or connection-oriented communications. In the first case, the intermediate devices (routers) select the paths to be taken between two devices. In the latter case, the path is established before communication occurs.

✳ Message

With message switching, an entire message or file is transferred between two network devices using the same internetwork path for the duration of the transfer. The best example of message switching is electronic mail. For an electronic mail message to move from the source to the destination through intermediate systems (router-based host), the entire message or file must be transferred to each intermediate host before being transferred onto the next host and eventually to its final destination. Message switching is a "store-and-forward" technique used in electronic mail, work-flow processing of forms, calendaring and scheduling, and work-group applications.

Message switching provides many benefits over other switching techniques, but it also has a few disadvantages. On the down side, it does not provide real-time application services and requires a fair amount of resources of intermediate hosts. On the up side, more devices can make use of the network. Traffic loads can be reduced through selective message processing times and priorities. Also, the type of network traffic is different. Because it is an entire message, it can be broadcast to many network locations simultaneously. Additionally, the communications process is not time sensitive and can accommodate messages crossing different time zones very easily.

⇨ Routing

See Fig. 4-32.

The routing of network-layer protocol data units (packets or datagrams) can be accomplished on hosts, dedicated computers acting as routers, or file servers with routing capability. The purpose of the router is to forward packets over an internetwork of LANs or WANs. As stated earlier, routing requires a routing-based protocol and a logical networkwide addressing scheme. Example routing protocols are IP and IPX.

Figure 4-32

	Host A				Host B
7	Application				Application
6	Presentation				Presentation
5	Session				Session
4	Transport		Router		Transport
3	Network		Network		Network
2	Data Link		Data Link		Data Link
1	Physical		Physical		Physical

Network A   Network B

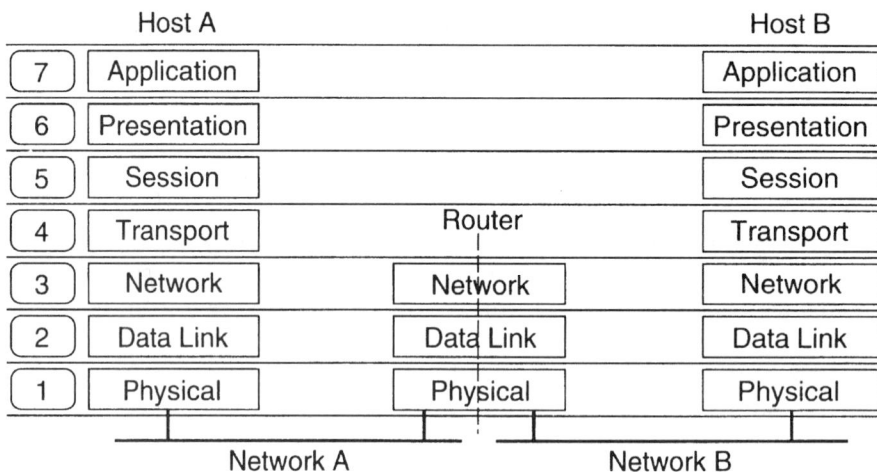

End-to-end transmission requiring the services of layers above the data link layer. Learning Tree International

⇨ How a router works

See Fig. 4-33.

A simple synopsis of the routing process is as follows:

1 The source host determines the destination network address for the packet by looking at its routing table to find an appropriate intermediate router to forward the packet to.

Figure 4-33

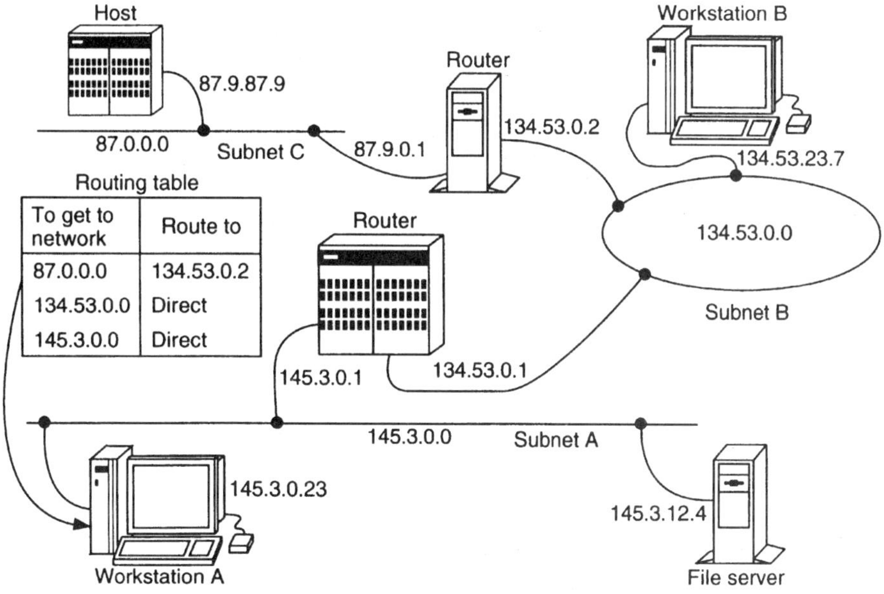

To get to network	Route to
87.0.0.0	134.53.0.2
134.53.0.0	Direct
145.3.0.0	Direct

The process of routing a packet through an internet using routers. Learning Tree International

2 The receiving router, which receives the frame, removes the packet from the frame and discards the frame-related information (NIC physical addresses, frame type, etc.).

3 The router obtains the destination network address number information from the packet destination address field.

4 The router checks the address against its own routing table to find the next router to forward the packet to.

5 The network-layer protocol data unit packet is then encapsulated in a frame (could be different from the original frame type the packet arrived in because it is using a different NIC) and forwards it to the next router.

6 Steps 2–5 repeat until the packet arrives at the next router.

7 The last router delivers the packet in a frame to the destination network device (workstation/host).

Routers notify other routers about the networks they can access. To do so, they broadcast their routing tables to other network routers. Broadcasts inform other routers and hosts of network addresses, IP addresses of routers, and the number of hops (routers) required to transmit packets to those networks. Hops are also referred to as a metric that measures how far a particular network might be from the current router. Routers choose or select paths to a network based on hop counts. In the following two sections, we will look at methods used by routers to discover and select internetwork routes.

✳ Route discovery

The forwarding of packets between connected networks requires that the routers (host based, dedicated, or file server based) discover not only the existence of other networks and routers, but also the path to them through intermediate routes. This learning process is called *route discovery*. In order for a packet to be routed throughout an internetwork of networks, the route the packet is to initially take to its final destination must be discovered.

Routing tables are used to maintain information regarding the availability and cost associated with taking a particular route. The information tracked by routing tables includes logical network addresses, the next router address required for a data path, and a cost or hop count associated with taking a particular path. Routing algorithms are used to determine the cost associated with taking one route over another.

Some of the routing table parameters are:

1 Hop count is associated with the number of routers that a data packet must take to reach its final network destination.

2 Tick count is the time needed in $\frac{1}{18}$ of a second to reach the destination network.

3 Relative expense is a number assigned based on optional variables to use as route selection criteria. For example, two logical networks might be interconnected by two physical links. However, one link might be slower than the other and is used only as a backup link. Both links are still only one hop away in terms of hop count, even though one is clearly much faster to use. The second link can be assigned a much higher relative expense so that it is only used when the primary link fails. Two route-discovery techniques are implemented at the network layer: distance vector and link state.

⇨ Distance vector-based route discovery

Distance vector-based protocols form the main route discovery technique in use today. This method requires each router to maintain its own routing table of networks. To update these tables, routers broadcast their complete routing table to each other over the network. Although the frequency of broadcasts varies for different routing protocol types, it usually occurs very often within short periods of time. The process of updating all routers throughout a network can take a considerable amount of time because routers can only broadcast the new routing table configuration as they learn about them. The amount of overhead traffic associated with broadcasting router information can be considerable in large networks, especially those with slow WAN links.

Routing table information includes network address numbers, the number of hops to reach a particular network address, the number of ticks ($\frac{1}{18}$ of a second) it takes to get there, and relative cost information. As a router learns of new networks from other routers, it increments the hop count by one. For example, if Router 1 indicates to Router 2 that the network with address 5000 can be reached in 2 hops, Router 2 would add the network number to its own routing table with a hop value of 3.

In summary, the distance vector-route discovery method gets the job done but requires a router device to broadcast its entire routing table on a very frequent basis, even if changes in the table do not occur. The Routing Information Protocol (RIP) is an example of a distance vector-routing information protocol. NetWare's IPX and the Internet's IP protocols are examples of protocols that use a form of RIP for route discovery.

❋ Link-state-based route discovery

Using the link-state-route-discovery method to update routers on a network, each router on the network first gets a copy of the entire routing table from a local "designated" router. Thereafter, routers keep each other updated of changes to the status of the network by forwarding only the information that changes, not the entire routing table. As routing changes are broadcast, each device in turn updates its own table. Periodically, entire routing tables are sent out across the network to ensure that every router has a complete, synchronized copy.

The advantage of link state over distance vector is a reduction in the size and broadcast frequency of network routing status information. Examples of link-state-route-discovery-based protocols include NetWare's NetWare Link State Protocol (NLSP) and the Internet's Open Shortest Path First (OSPF).

⇨ Route selection

Route selection is the process the router uses to determine which is the best path for a packet to take over the internetwork. The status of routes can change frequently, and as such a router needs to adjust to the changes. However, there might be cases where we want packets destined to a particular network to always use a specific route. Routers can use two methods of route selection: static or dynamic.

✳ Static routing

Static route selection requires routes to be essentially hard coded into the routing table. In this method, a network administrator must manually enter the routing information into the routing table so that each time the router starts up, it will force packets to choose this route even if a shorter or faster route exists. Computers or devices can also force static route selections on routers connected to an internetwork.

✳ Dynamic routing

Internetworks generally provide several paths for packets to take to a destination network. The status of these routes can change frequently as new, faster routes are brought online or existing routes are shut down. Dynamic route selection is an algorithm or process used to ensure that routers are advised of the new route status. As such, they dynamically update their routing tables. Dynamic routing updates are also facilitated through route-discovery-based protocols.

⇨ Services

Networked devices establish connections at various levels or layers of the OSI reference model as they communicate with each other. Similar to the data link layer, the network layer offers connection services. Connection services ensure that packets transmitted on the network are accounted for, and connections services also regulate the flow of packets. As indicated in the previous section on the data link layer, there are three connection services implemented:

1 Unacknowledged connectionless services.

2 Connection-oriented services.

3 Acknowledged connectionless services.

Some protocol families use connectionless routing services. Novell's IPX and the Internet's IP are examples of unacknowledged connectionless network-layer protocols.

Other protocol families, most notably those based on the X.25 specification, use connection-oriented network services. The network layer in that case uses connection services with acknowledgments. These acknowledgments maintain three crucial aspects of network traffic on the internetwork: packet sequencing, error control, and network-layer flow control.

⇨ Packet sequencing

All of the packets associated with a complete message can take many routes on an internetwork in order to arrive at their final destination. Some routes will be faster than others, and some packets might be lost along the way and require retransmission. As a result, packets can arrive at the destination network device (host) in a different order than they were originally transmitted. Packet sequencing ensures that packets are put back in the original order before they are processed at the receiving host. For connectionless network protocols, packet sequencing is implemented in upper-layer protocols rather than at the network layer.

✳ Error recovery

As described previously, packets can be lost along the way to their final destination. Packet loss or damage can occur as route links fail or data link layer collisions occur. Another problem is when a network device repeats a packet before a receiving device has an opportunity to acknowledge the original's receipt.

Cyclic redundancy check (CRC) is the process used to determine if packets have been damaged (bits within the packet have been altered by noise in the process of transmission). CRC checking is often performed at the frame level by the data link protocol. Some network layer protocols implement error checking for the packet header. A checksum method is used for that purpose. Each intermediary device recalculates the checksum value to ensure the packet does not have errors. Along the way, the checksum is also changed as each router changes the hop count value to indicate the number of routers the packet has traversed (hop count is a parameter carried in the packet header).

⇨ Flow control

Traffic on a single physical network segment is regulated by the flow control of the data link layer. In an internetwork, we are also concerned about the flow of traffic between network segments, and the network layer can provide this functionality.

Route discovery and selection aid the flow control process as internetwork routes are added or removed and transmission speed support varies. As the cost of using an internetwork links change (increase in the number of ticks to reach the network) due to overuse, flow control deals with the change by attempting to find a more efficient route. Flow control is sometimes referred to as *congestion control*.

⇨ Gateways

See Fig. 4-34.

	Host A	Gateway	Host B	
7	Application	Application	Application	
6	Presentation	Presentation	Presentation	
5	Session	Session	Session	
4	Transport	Transport	Transport	
3	Network	Network	Network	
2	Data Link	Data Link	Data Link	
1	Physical	Physical	Physical	

Network A   Network B

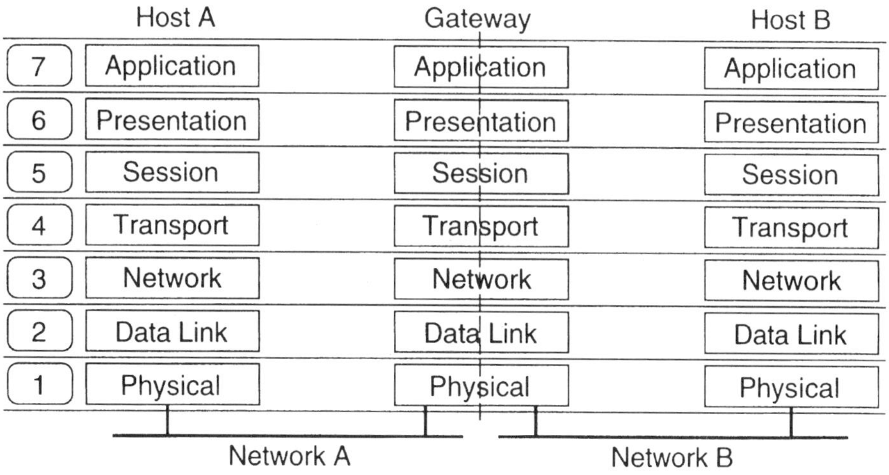

Gateways referenced to the OSI model. Learning Tree International

Internetworking devices allow us to connect networks that differ at the data link level. Routers help in this connection if the network-layer protocol is the same throughout the internetwork. When an internetwork supports several kinds of protocol families and there is a need for these protocols to interoperate, the needed device is a gateway.

Gateways are used to translate the required services from one protocol family to another. A common example is when going between two networks that support different packet sizes. Before the large packet can be placed onto the network segment that supports a smaller packet size, the gateway must intelligently split the packet in half or more, depending on the difference. Another example is when one protocol needs to be entirely converted into a different format (i.e., NetWare IPX to Internet IP).

Finally, gateways are implemented at various layers of the OSI reference model, depending on the type of information that needs to be transferred and the format required. Examples of gateways include e-mail gateway services (i.e., CCITT/ITU X.400 mail to TCP/IP SMTP mail format), asynchronous gateways (i.e., local area network protocols to public telephone networks data), and gateways that link distributed processing LANs to centralized-processing-based mainframes. (See Figs. 4-35 and 4-36A.)

Figure 4-34

Figure 4-35

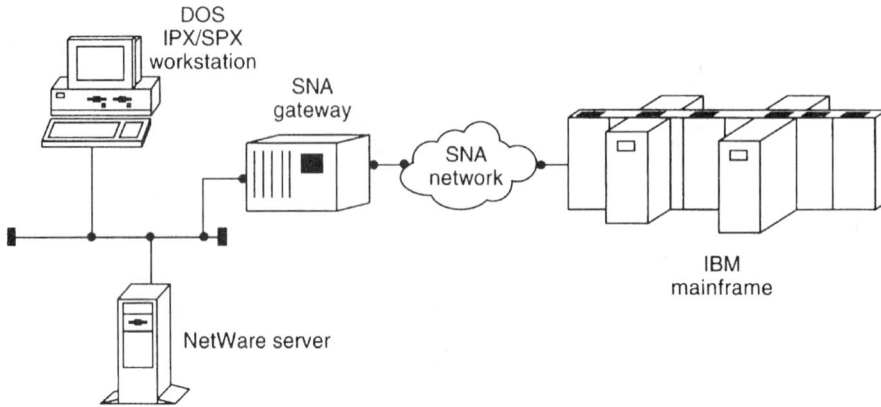

Typical gateways. Learning Tree International

⇨ The OSI transport layer

⇨ CNE exam objectives

➤ Define the basic purpose of the OSI transport layer.

➤ Identify and describe the networking technology topics associated with the OSI transport layer.

➤ Identify and describe the methods associated with each OSI transport layer topic.

See Table 4-4.

Table 4-4

Topics and Methods for the Transport Layer

Transport-layer topics	Transport-layer methods
Address/name resolution	Client requested Server requested
Addressing	Connection identification Transaction identification
Segmentation	Segmentation Reassembly
Services	Flow control Sequencing of segments Error recovery

Figure 4-36A

Device	Layer	Transfers	Address	Characteristics
Repeater	Physical	Bits	None	Regenerates bits. Extends LAN to maximum topological limits. Example: Ethernet repeaters.
Bridge	Data Link	Frames	Physical	802.3: Filters and forwards frames based on destination frame addresses. Remote and local bridges available. 802.5: Source routed frame delivery; discovery process finds route using the routing indicator field. Remote and local bridges available. Independent of Network Layer protocols.
Router	Network	Datagrams or packets	Network	Routing of packets based on Network Layer logical address. Requires network-wide logical addressing scheme established by network administrator. Routers are protocol specific. Routable protocols: IP, IPX, AppleTalk, DECnet Nonroutable protocols: LAT, NetBIOS
Brouter	Network Data Link	Packets and frames	Network and physical	Combined device. Routes whatever packets it can and bridges the rest as frames.
Gateways	Above Network	Data	As necessary	Translates between incompatible protocols suites. Examples: SNA-X.25, DECnet-TCP/IP, NetWare IPX/SPX-SNA

Reference table of internetworking devices. Learning Tree International

⇨ The transport layer

The ITU X.200 document defines the services of the OSI transport layer as:

> The transport service provides transparent transfer of data between session entities and relieves them from any concern with the detailed way in which reliable and cost-effective transfer of data is achieved.

The transport layer optimizes the use of the available network service to provide the performance required by each session entity at minimum cost. This optimization is achieved within the constraints imposed by the overall demands of all concurrent session entities and the overall quality and capacity of the network service available to the transport layer.

The transport layer is relieved of any concern with routing and relaying since the network service provides network connections from any transport entity to any other.

The transport layer uniquely identifies each session entity by its transport address. The transport service provides the means to establish, maintain, and release transport connections.

The following services [are] provided by the transport layer . . .:

a. transport-connection establishment;

b. data transfer; and

c. transport-connection release.

The transport layer's responsibility, as seen from the previous definition, is to hide the details of networking performed by the lowest three layers from the rest of the upper layers. The transport layer also provides connection services to those upper layers. Transport programs add functionality to the lower layers by providing these two most important and needed services.

The transport layer protocol data unit (PDU) is typically called a segment. And the upper layers are identified usually to the lower layers by protocol ID.

In most protocol families, it is the responsibility of the transport layer to provide reliable data transfer. For that purpose, connection-oriented versions of transfer protocols have been created. For example, in the TCP/IP protocol suite, the very popular connection-oriented transport protocol called Transmission Control Protocol (TCP) was created. Alternatively, the TCP/IP protocol family has a connectionless version of transport called UDP (User Datagram Protocol).

One of the major responsibilities of the transport layer is to identify upper-level protocols by some form of logical address scheme. This way, any received data is delivered to the appropriate and rightful owner expecting that data. In connection-oriented protocols, the identification is done on a connection basis, each connection having its own address. Connections are started, maintained, and closed as part of the maintenance of the connection-oriented service.

Another important responsibility of the transport layer is to break up large transmissions into the appropriate-size data units to fit in the packets or frames in the appropriate technology being used for the lower layers. In other words, if a large file—say, 2 megabytes—is being transferred using a file-transfer protocol such as FTP and it will be sent over a packet-oriented protocol such as IP, it is the responsibility of the transport layer, TCP, to segment the large 2-megabyte file into small enough pieces to fit in the packet. Furthermore, it will be the responsibility of the transport layer in the receiving machine to reassemble all the pieces into the original file.

The transport layer is responsible for sequencing of the segments and the recovery of any segments that are lost. To do so, it must keep track of the segments in some manner. This recovery process makes the connection-oriented service of the transport layer reliable. The transport layer also manages flow control.

⇨ Address/name resolution

Upper layers and services in computers are often referred to by a name that is easily recognizable by human operators. Computer addresses of computers and other nodes on a network are typically expressed in numbers. One of the functions of the transport layer is to associate specific name addresses of upper-level functions and applications with machine addresses assigned by network administrators. A typical service associated with this function is "directory services." Address/name resolution is classified into two methods: those initiated by the requester of a service and those initiated by the providers of a service.

❊ **Client requested**

If a client process in the machine needs the services of another machine on the network, the client becomes the requester. The requester in this case sends out a special request packet with an identification of the service needed. An example of this is a request by an FTP client on a workstation to create an FTP session with an FTP server on a UNIX host. The transport layer mediates this process and is able to provide the connection and the name resolution between the client and server FTP processes and the IP addresses involved.

❊ **Server requested**

In some cases, the server processes themselves initiate connections. They do this by announcing their availability via broadcast transmissions. For example, Novell servers will send out SAP broadcasts to announce the availability of a server to provide file and print services on the network. Directory servers collect information from these broadcasts to update their directory information.

⇨ Addressing

Figure 4-36B shows the layers of addressing used in a TCP/IP network by the form of multiplexing connections. It also shows the encapsulation performed by the successive layers within the transmitted frame. Let's take, for example, an Ethernet network as a connection between the sender and receiver. The computers use the IP protocol, which in turn supports two transport protocols, TCP and UDP. They in turn support a number of application services such as FTP, TELNET, NFS, and SMTP.

At the lowest layers there is an Ethernet address that resides in the network card, as we saw in the data link section. The received transmission comes in an Ethernet frame. The Ethernet frame carries in the control field a number corresponding to the EtherType that identifies the type of network protocol of the packet. So EtherType is the address of the multiple network protocols that might be waiting for a packet. The network protocol that will receive the packet, in this case, will be IP. Within the network packet, there is an identifier that allows the IP program to deliver the contents of the packet to the

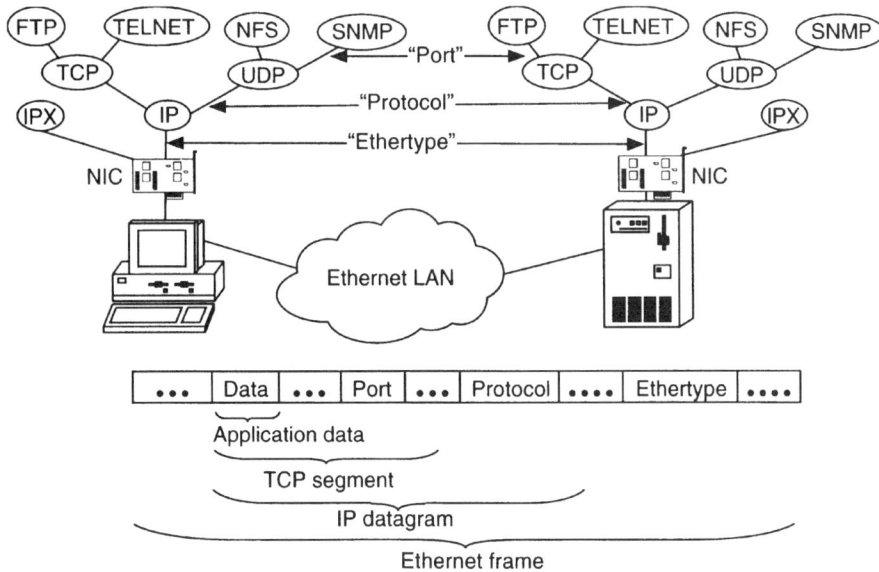

Figure 4-36B

The use of multiplexing addresses. Learning Tree International

appropriate transport protocol. That identifier is called the protocol ID. In this case IP will either deliver it to TCP or UDP.

Let's say in the current case that TCP is the receiver of the content of the packet. TCP itself will be able to identify which service protocol, FTP or TELNET, is meant to receive the contents of the segment. The type of address used to identify the waiting service protocol in the case of a TCP/IP network is the identifier "port." FTP has a well-known port address. TELNET also has its own different and unique port address. So do many other service protocols that might be waiting to receive the contents of a segment.

There are two ways by which the transport protocol identifies the address of the program that it is servicing: one is via a connection identifier, the port; the other is via a transaction identifier.

✳ Connection identification

A connection identifier is a form of identification assigned to a conversation. It could be a permanently assigned identifier to that particular server or service, or it could be assigned dynamically when the service is requested. In the TCP/IP protocol family, for example, there are a well-known set of ports that are connection identifiers for the major service protocols, such as FTP and TELNET. In other cases, port IDs are issued on a connection-by-connection basis as the connections are being requested.

✳ Transaction identification

Transaction identifiers deal with connections that are used to support conversations. And the conversation pieces are small segments, each a request or a reply to a request being exchanged by a client and a server. Typically, the server provider keeps track of the conversation pieces or the transactions themselves. The transport layer is there just for address resolution, to correctly send a received segment onto the appropriate server or requester. The conversation itself is managed by the session layer.

⇨ Segmentation and reassembly

One of the services provided by the transport program is breaking up a large transmission into pieces that are small enough to fit into the protocol data units of the lower layers. The transmission must be reassembled on the other end, which is the responsibility of the transport layer on the receiver.

✳ Segmentation

Let's say a large 2-megabyte file is to be sent from a FTP server through a TCP/IP network to an FTP client on another machine. Let's say we are using an Ethernet network that has a maximum frame size of 1518 bytes, the largest data portion of that frame being 1500 bytes. When one subtracts the IP overhead, typically 20 bytes, and the TCP overhead, typically another 20 bytes, we are left with 1460 bytes of data-carrying capacity per frame. The 2-megabyte file is $2 \times 1024 \times 1024$ bytes = 2,097,152 bytes. If we divide this many bytes by the largest carrying capacity of the Ethernet frame, 1460 bytes, we determine that we will need 1437 frames. This translates into 1437 packets and 1437 segments.

Both the data link layer (Ethernet) and the network layer (the IP protocol) are connectionless protocols in this case. They do not recover from lost frames. They also have no idea which segment is which. In other words, they don't keep track of the segments, and they don't number them to reassemble them in order. It is the responsibility of the transport layer to break up the 2-megabyte file into 1460-byte segments to match the capacity of the lower layer and to number (sequence) and keep track of each segment in case any are lost. The recovery is done by retransmission. Of course, the transport layer in this case (TCP) will not be able to recover if a major catastrophe occurs to the network, such as a cable break or when the receiving machine is turned off. But if the underlying network (physical, data link, and network layers) is operational, the transport layer will be able to recover from any segments lost due to transmission errors.

✳ Reassembly

These 1437 segments arriving at the FTP client will have to be put in the proper order and assembled into the original file that the sender meant to transmit. That is the job of the transport layer—the function of reassembly of the segments.

When transmitting information across an enterprise network, or from one enterprise network to another, there might be a mismatch in frame sizes of the two networks to be accounted for. Suppose one network is a Token Ring at the data link level with a maximum frame size of 4000 bytes, and it is connected to an Ethernet network with a maximum frame size of 1518 bytes. The sending station will create large segments that fit into the Token Ring frame fairly easily. But what occurs to that segment at the router connecting the Token Ring to the Ethernet network? That router certainly cannot take the 4000-byte segment and directly put it into a 1518-byte frame. Thus, that router will perform the job of fragmenting the segment. This fragmentation is done by a layer-three process in the case of TCP/IP. The reassembly of these fragments take places at the receiving station.

⇨ Services

The transport protocol provides three services for connection-oriented transactions. The first is flow control; it allows the sender and receiver to match their transmission speeds. The second is the sequencing of segments to preparation for recovery from loss and for the reassembly of segments at the receiver. The third is recovery—some form of acknowledgment and retransmission to recover from lost segments.

✳ Flow control

Frequently the two communicating entities across an internet have different speeds at which they can process information. On one end there might be a personal computer and on the other end there might be a large UNIX host. Certainly the UNIX host can process transactions much faster than the personal computer. If a file is being transferred from the UNIX host to the personal computer and the segments are being transmitted at a very high rate by the UNIX host, but the personal computer is not able to receive them at that rate, there has to be a mechanism to adjust the flow to allow the PC to receive it at its own speed. That mechanism is called flow control.

The transport protocol usually embodies such a service by the use of a special ON/OFF control process. For example, if the PC receive buffers are full and it cannot receive any more (if it were to receive another, it would be ignored and there would be a lost segment that would need to be retransmitted), then it would send to the UNIX host a transmission to be interpreted by the transport protocol on the host to ask the host to hold the flow for a while. This would be an OFF signal. As the personal computer's buffers are cleared of transactions and it is able to receive more segments, it would then send an ON transmission to the UNIX host for the flow to start again.

Different protocol families implement flow control functionality in different ways. It is a very useful tool whether dealing with a transport-level connection-oriented service or a connectionless service.

✳ Sequencing of segments

As we saw in the preceding segmentation section, to accurately transmit a large file in small pieces, each segment must be numbered with a sequence, must be accounted for by the receiver segments, and are usually acknowledged on a segment-by-segment basis.

�֍ **Error recovery**

Transport protocols typically rely on the error detection properties of the data link layer. They themselves do not provide error detection. Most data link layers do not recover from transmissions that have an error, since they are typically connectionless. The same is true with network protocols. It is the transport layer in most protocol families that provides error recovery. The error recovery is done with a positive-acknowledged retransmit protocol, where the sending station (the transmitter) will start a clock once it has sent a numbered segment. If it has not received a positive acknowledgment of the accurate transmission of that segment within a certain time, it will retransmit that segment. The sender does not have to wait for an indication that the segment was not received because in general we don't expect the receiver to know bad segments. Typically, the transport protocol on the receiver does not even see a bad segment. It is discarded at the level of the data link layer by the error-check mechanism of that layer.

It is the responsibility of the transport protocol at the receiver to then send positive acknowledgments on a segment-by-segment basis for properly received transmissions.

⇨ The OSI session layer

⇨ CNE exam objectives

➢ Define the basic purpose of the OSI session layer.

➢ Identify and describe the networking technology topics associated with the OSI session layer.

➢ Identify and describe the methods associated with each OSI session layer topic.

See Table 4-5.

Table 4-5 | **Topics and Methods for the Session Layer**

Session-layer topics	Session-layer methods
Dialog types	Simplex Half duplex Full duplex
Dialog Administration	Connection establishment Data transfer Connection release

⇨ The session layer

The ITU X.200 document defines the services of the OSI session layer as:

> The purpose of the session layer is to provide the means necessary for cooperating presentation entities to organize and synchronize their dialogue and to manage their data exchange. To do this, the session layer provides services to establish a session connection between two presentation entities, and to support orderly data exchange interactions.
>
> The following services [are] provided by the session layer . . .:
>
> a. session-connection establishment;
>
> b. session-connection release;
>
> c. normal data exchange;
>
> d. quarantine service;
>
> e. expedited data exchange;
>
> f. interaction management;
>
> g. session-connection synchronization; and
>
> h. exception reporting.

Consider the session layer as a service of establishing, maintaining, and closing a connection between a server and a client. A good example of how the session layer works is what happens when you go to a restaurant to order a meal. You, as the restaurant's guest, are the client. The chef in the kitchen cooking your food is the server.

Between you and the server is the session layer, the waiter. The waiter, by means of a meal ticket, establishes the conversation between you and the chef. This conversation might have a number of pieces. When you arrive at your table, the waiter assists you in talking to the chef by opening the conversation, acknowledging that you're there, and creating an open ticket to begin receiving your order; the waiter takes your order and brings it back to the chef, who begins filling your order. When the food is ready, the chef will deliver it to the waiter, who will deliver it to your table.

You continue the conversation with the chef by ordering more food, perhaps dessert, which the waiter also sends to the chef; the waiter returns with your order filled. And at the end, there is a closing of the transaction by the waiter writing a bill, your paying it, and leaving the restaurant. In a similar manner, the session layer facilitates the communication between clients and servers.

There are two topics in this area. The first is the subject of dialog control. There are three methods of managing a dialog, and there are three dialog types: simplex, full duplex, and half duplex. The second topic under the session layer is the administration of a session—how a connection is established, how it is maintained for data transfer, and the eventual release of the connection through a session close.

Dialog types

In general, there are three types of information flow: simplex, half duplex, and full duplex. Figure 4-37 shows the three types, their characteristics, and some simple examples.

✳ Simplex

In the simplex dialog type, there is information flow in only one direction. A good example of that is any type of broadcasting, such as a television station to television receivers. The key element here is that the television receivers cannot and do not talk back. There is no flow of information back to the sender. It works very well in networks for servers to advertise their services. Many protocols work in this manner, such as the Service Advertising Protocol (SAP), which is a good example of a simplex-type dialog.

Figure 4-37

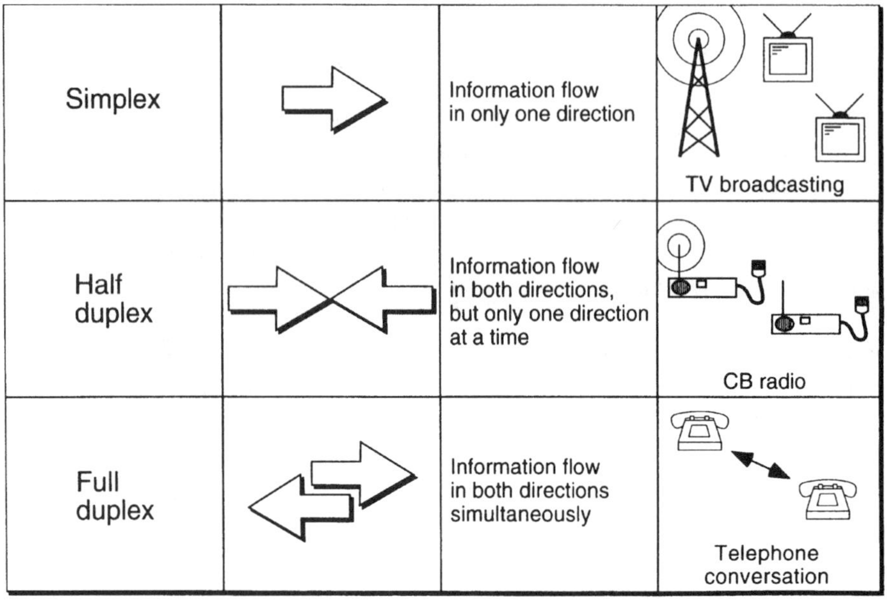

Characteristics of dialog types: simplex, half duplex, and full duplex. Learning Tree International

❋ **Half duplex**

In a half-duplex system, there is information flow in both directions but the key element is that it is in one direction at a time only. The two parties wishing to communicate take turns in communicating. A CB radio system, for example, is a good example of the half-duplex type. Anyone wishing to send has to wait until the channel is clear before taking a turn. So a conversation between two communicating entities would require control to bounce back and forth between them as they send each other transmissions.

Figure 4-38 describes the operation of a typical session protocol, the remote procedure call, or RPC, part of the TCP/IP protocol suite. In this case we have two computers: computer A, the RPC client; and computer B, the RPC server. There's a client process in A, and there is a remote process, a server process, in B.

The session protocol (RPC) supports the half-duplex interaction between the two application processes. A client will send off a request.

Figure 4-38

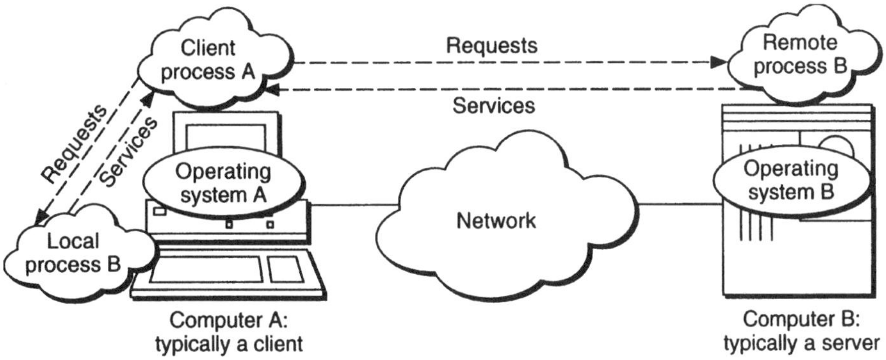

The TCP/IP remote procedure call as an example of a session protocol.
Learning Tree International

The server processes the request and sends back a reply in the form of services. In the RPC protocol, only one service at a time from a client is supported. And the client waits to receive the response to the service before the next request. So the system is operating half duplex in that only one entity at a time is communicating.

✳ **Full duplex**

The full-duplex system supports information flow in both directions simultaneously. This requires the use of two channels so information can go on in both directions at the same time.

An example that is an accurate description of a full-duplex transmission system is a modem. It uses audio tones to create two separate transmission channels to send and receive, over one phone line, the transmitted zeros and ones.

⇨ **Dialog administration**

Dialog, or session, administration has three phases. The first is the establishment of the connection, sometimes expressed as the "call." After the call is accepted by the remote machine and a session is established, there is a data-transfer phase. The session layer is needed to maintain orderly data transfer and recovery from possible loss of connection during this session. The last phase is when data transfer is complete and the connection must be released. This last phase is sometimes called the "close."

Figure 4-39 shows a typical session between two communicating entities with call, data transfer, and close phases of the session clearly depicted. Notice that either one of the two communicating entities could begin the transaction in this case. It happens to be computer A that establishes the call, but a connection is not made until computer B acknowledges and accepts that call. There might be a transfer of parameters about the session, e.g., name of the file needed to be transferred, or encryption details, or handshaking on segment sizes. These can be accepted as is or adjusted by the receiving computer in reply to the call request.

Figure 4-39

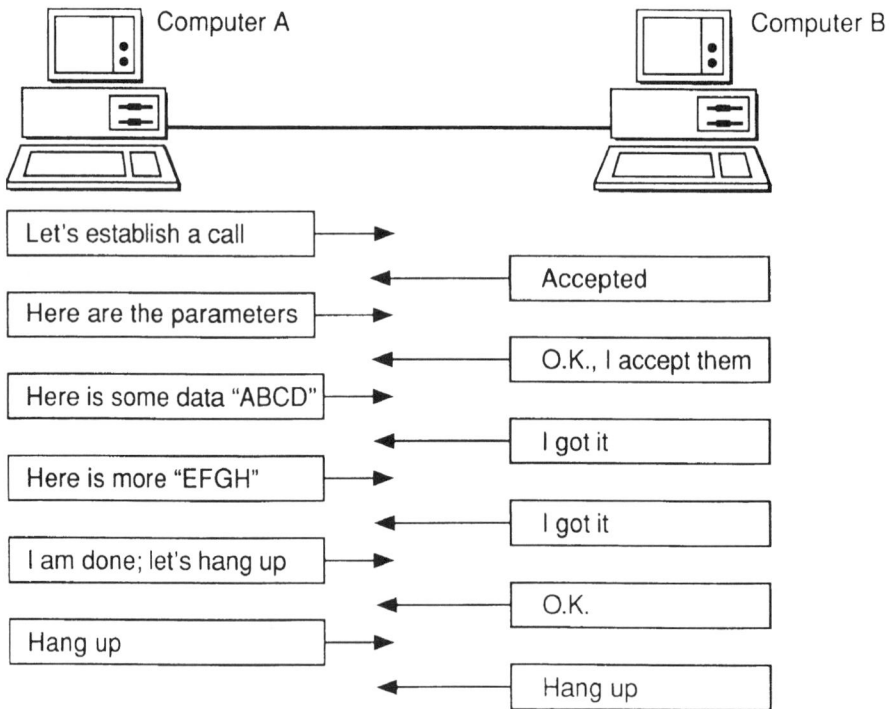

A typical protocol session showing call, data transfer, and close phases of a connection. Learning Tree International

And then they enter into the data-transfer phase. Note that acknowledgment of each of the received segments occurs until the end of data transfer. It is common for the computer that initiated the connection to also close the connection. In this case, computer A will initiate the connection clearing by requesting a hanging up of the connection. It has to be acknowledged by computer B for a successful close.

✳ Connection establishment

This phase of a session not only begins the connection by a request from one of the two communicating entities but also is used to transfer session parameters. Some of these parameters might be user login passwords. User authentication is part of the connection-establishment phase. Required services and length of requirements are also sent and acknowledged. Negotiation of who will be doing the data transmission and the establishment of procedures for acknowledging and retransmitting also are part of the connection-establishment phase

✳ Data transfer

Once the connection is established, data will begin flowing from one computer to the other. The major task here is the actual transfer of the data. A subtask would be acknowledgment of the receipt of data. Some protocols only use positive acknowledge (ACK); others make use of the negative-acknowledge (NAK) interactions. An important element of the data-transfer phase is the recovery from interrupted communications. Many session protocols allow a session to remain active even though the underlying network might be unavailable for a short period of time.

✳ Connection release

Once data transfer has taken place and there is no further need for the connection, the session protocol closes the connection gracefully. Connection-oriented protocols must account for the graceful close of connections. There is a very well worked out procedure to close the connection. Typically, this is initiated by the connection requester, but the close could be requested by the receiving station, although that is not commonly done.

The OSI presentation layer

CNE exam objectives

➤ Define the basic purpose of the OSI presentation layer.

➤ Identify and describe the networking technology topics associated with the OSI presentation layer.

➤ Identify and describe the methods associated with each OSI presentation layer topic.

See Table 4-6.

Table 4-6   **Topics and Methods for the Presentation Layer**

Presentation-layer topics	Presentation-layer methods
Translation services	Bit order
	Byte order
	Character codes
	ASCII
	EBCDIC
	File syntax
Encryption	Private key
	Public key

The presentation layer

The ITU X.200 document defines the services of the OSI presentation layer as:

> The presentation layer provides for the representation of information that application entities either communicate or refer to in their communication.

> The presentation layer covers two complementary aspects of this representation of information:

a. the representation of data to be transferred between application entities; and

b. the representation of the data structure which application entities refer to in their communication, along with the representations of the set of actions which might be performed on this data structure.

The presentation layer is concerned only with the syntax, (i.e., the representation of the data) and not with its semantics, (i.e., their meaning to the application layer), which is known only by the application entities.

The presentation layer provides for a common representation to be used between application entities. This relieves application entities of any concern with the problem of "common" representation of information, i.e., it provides them with syntax independence.

The presentation layer works between the application and the session layers. It provides services of data translation and encryption to the application layer, and it makes use of the connection services.

One of the services of the presentation layer is to encode information that is in a natural language into a form representable within a computer. Figure 4-40 shows the translation of natural-language information that is in characters into a digital representation using ASCII character code. These characters are then sent out as a single stream that propagates on the wire as a series of voltage levels, the latter service being provided by the lower layers. The service of encoding the natural language into digital information is one of the responsibilities of the presentation layer.

⇨ Translation services

Different machines with different operating systems represent data internally in different forms. Natural-language characters are encoded digitally into byte blocks of information. How the bits are arranged within the byte, the actual bit pattern to represent a character, how the bytes are arranged into a file, and how various file control

Figure 4-40

Information in natural language   "A B C"   Characters

Digital representation   1000001 1000010 1000011   ASCII codes
                                    A   B   C

Signal stream propagating on wires   +12
                                        0   A   B   C   RS-232-C signals
                                      -12v

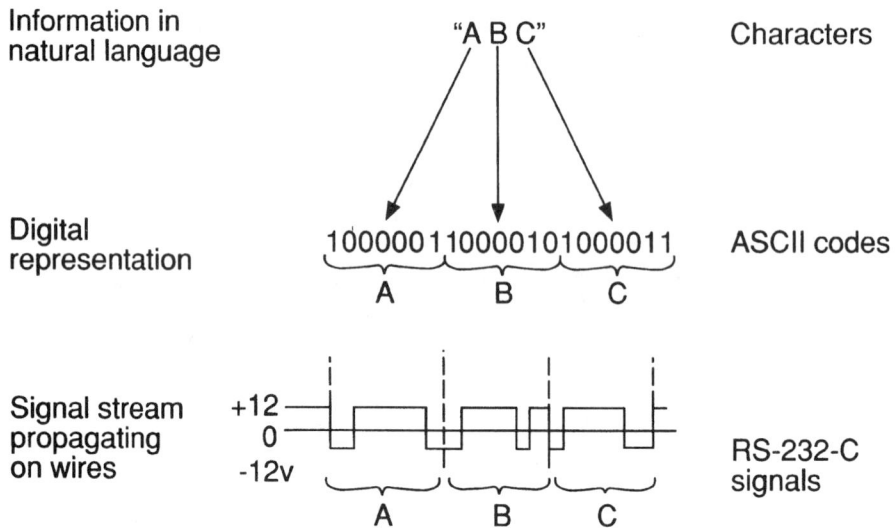

The conversion of natural language characters into digital character representations. Learning Tree International

characters are represented might differ from machine to machine. It is the responsibility of the presentation layer to make these differences transparent to application programs wishing to use network services. So the translation services provided by the presentation layer might be classified as data-order translation, byte-order translation, character-code representations, and file-syntax translation.

✳ Bit-order translation

Character codes encode natural language information into digital form. The actual codes are treated in a later section. The number of bits representing each character is a much more basic issue. Some codes use four bits; some use seven bits. Others use eight bits. When a transmission is received, it is the responsibility of the presentation layer to sort through the strings of zeros and ones and pick out the appropriate groups of bits that represent each character. In some cases, the receiving application being supported by the presentation-layer protocol requires the data to be presented to it in 8-bit-encoded characters; but the data coming in might be in 7-bit-encoded characters. It is the responsibility of the presentation layer to appropriately convert a received character pattern into that required by the application layer.

❊ Byte-order translation

Within each character there is a higher-order bit. Bits must be arranged in a certain order to be properly interpreted. In some machines, the most significant bit is sent first, and the least significant bit in the character is sent last. This type of ordering is called "big-endian." It is typically used by Motorola microprocessor-based machines (such as the Macintosh).

Other machines, such as those based on the Intel microprocessors (486, Pentium), use the "little-endian" method of ordering the bits within a character. In this method, the least significant bit is sent first. So for a Macintosh to talk to an Intel-based machine, some program must take charge of reversing the data order within each character so the two machines are able to communicate. This bit-order reversal is the responsibility of the presentation layer.

❊ Character codes

The encoding of natural-language information into digital representation is done via a character-code template. Two popular character codes are the ASCII and the EBCDIC character codes. The ASCII code (American Standard Code for Information Interchange) is the more popular of the two and is used with all machines other than the IBM line of computers. The EBCDIC (Extended Binary-Coded Decimal Interchange Code) is a popular digital representation in the IBM mainframe family of computers. IBM mainframes and other computers often have to exchange information. To do so, a translation from one character code to another has to take place. It is the presentation layer in the two machines that handles this character-code translation.

Figure 4-41 shows examples of ASCII-code encoding of typical characters. The second half of the figure shows the ASCII representation of control characters such as the bell line-feed and the delete characters. The ASCII character code is a 7-bit code, and the standard form of it is called the International Alphabet Number 5 (AI5). Figure 4-42 shows the representation of the English alphabet numbers and character codes as 7-bit characters.

Figure 4-41
- **A protocol for encoding the English alphabet into binary signals of 7 bits**

- **Example of ASCII encoding of characters:**

A	1000001	a	1100001
B	1000010	b	1100010
C	1000011	c	1100011
1	0110001	2	0110010
+	0101011	%	0100101

- **Example encoding of control characters:**

  <u>Some uses for control characters</u>

DEL	1111111	Delete previous character
BEL	0000111	Ring the bell at the terminal
LF	0001010	Go to the next line on the terminal

Example ASCII character representations. <small>Learning Tree International</small>

Figure 4-42

Bit positions			7	0	0	0	0	1	1	1	1
			6	0	0	1	1	0	0	1	1
			5	0	1	0	1	0	1	0	1
4	3	2	1								
0	0	0	0	NUL	DLE	SP	0	@	P	\	p
0	0	0	1	SOH	DC1	!	1	A	Q	a	q
0	0	1	0	STX	DC2	"	2	B	R	b	r
0	0	1	1	ETX	DC3	#	3	C	S	c	s
0	1	0	0	EOT	DC4	$	4	D	T	d	t
0	1	0	1	ENQ	NAK	%	5	E	U	e	u
0	1	1	0	ACK	SYN	&	6	F	V	f	v
0	1	1	1	BEL	ETB	'	7	G	W	g	w
1	0	0	0	BS	CAN	(	8	H	X	h	x
1	0	0	1	HT	EM	)	9	I	Y	i	y
1	0	1	0	LF	SUB	*	:	J	Z	j	z
1	0	1	1	VT	ESC	+	;	K	[	k	{
1	1	0	0	FF	FS	,	<	L	\	l	l
1	1	0	1	CR	GS	–	=	M	]	m	}
1	1	1	0	SO	RS	.	>	N	^	n	~
1	1	1	1	SI	US	/	?	O	_	o	DEL

The 7-bit ASCII character set, also known as the International Alphabet 5, or IA5. <small>Learning Tree International</small>

Figure 4-43

Bit positions			4	0	0	0	0	0	0	0	0	1	1	1	1	1	1	1	1
			3	0	0	0	0	1	1	1	1	0	0	0	0	1	1	1	1
			2	0	0	1	1	0	0	1	1	0	0	1	1	0	0	1	1
			1	0	1	0	1	0	1	0	1	0	1	0	1	0	1	0	1
8	7	6	5																
0	0	0	0	NUL	SOH	STX	ETX	PF	HT	LC	DEL			SMM	VT	FF	CR	SO	SI
0	0	0	1	DLE	DC1	DC2	DC3	RES	NL	BS	IL	CAN	EM	CC		IFS	IGS	IRS	IUS
0	0	1	0	DS	SOS	FS		BYP	LF	EOB	PRE			SM			ENQ	ACK	BEL
0	0	1	1			SYN		PN	RS	UC	EOT					DC4	NAK		SUB
0	1	0	0	SP										¢	.	<	(	+	|
0	1	0	1	&										!	$	*	)	;	¬
0	1	1	0	−	/										'	%	-	>	?
0	1	1	1											:	#	@	,	=	"
1	0	0	0		a	b	c	d	e	f	g	h	i						
1	0	0	1		j	k	l	m	n	o	p	q	r						
1	0	1	0			s	t	u	v	w	x	y	z						
1	0	1	1																
1	1	0	0		A	B	C	D	E	F	G	H	I						
1	1	0	1		J	K	L	M	N	O	P	Q	R						
1	1	1	0			S	T	U	V	W	X	Y	Z						
1	1	1	1	0	1	2	3	4	5	6	7	8	9						□

The IBM 8-bit EBCDIC character set. Learning Tree International

Figure 4-43 shows the 8-bit representation of the same English character set plus a number of other control characters. The latter figure is the IBM 8-bit EBCDIC character set.

✳ File syntax

Files are stored in different computers in different formats. For example, on a DOS computer at the end of each line in the text file there would be a carriage return and a line feed, whereas in a UNIX machine, the same file would not have the line feed following the carriage return. When translating or transferring a text file from a UNIX machine to a DOS machine, a program is needed to either insert the line feeds or delete them, depending on the direction of the file transfer. The translation program used to match the file syntax in both machines is classified as a presentation-layer program. File syntax conversion is a presentation-layer service. Files stored on one machine also carry with them certain attributes under the local operating system. Those attributes would be different or perhaps more or less extensive under another operating system. So as the file is transferred, copied, or moved to another machine, some program will have to create, delete, or translate file attributes from one operating system to the other. Again, this is one of the services performed by presentation-layer programs.

The control characters used to indicate the beginning and end of files are different under different operating systems and different storage methods. Again, the presentation-layer program would have to do the translation as that file is transferred so that the local operating system characteristics are matched and the file is properly stored on the receiving machine.

⇨ Encryption

Communication security is enhanced by the process of encryption. This is a method of protecting information from unauthorized use by anyone intercepting the information as it is being transmitted. The encryption of data can be done by a hardware device just before the data is sent out over the wire, or it can be done by a program as a service to the application-layer program. If it is done in software by the program as a service to the application layer, then it is a function being performed by the presentation layer. This is a very common way to enhance security. The hardware method is considered part of the physical layer.

✳ Private key

Encryption is the process by which data is converted from a human-understandable form to one that is unintelligible to anyone but the sender and receiver. To recover the intelligible form of the data, one requires a procedure and a key used to scramble the data. That key is a particular bit sequence or pattern employed by the encryption algorithm to render the data unintelligible. The encryptor must use the key to scramble the information, and the receiver must have the key to decode it. It is of paramount importance that the key be kept secure. There are two methods by which key-type encryption is performed: private key encryption and public key encryption.

✳ Private key encryption

Figure 4-44 shows the private key encryption technique process. Let's say a client program requires encryption of data before sending. The

Figure 4-44

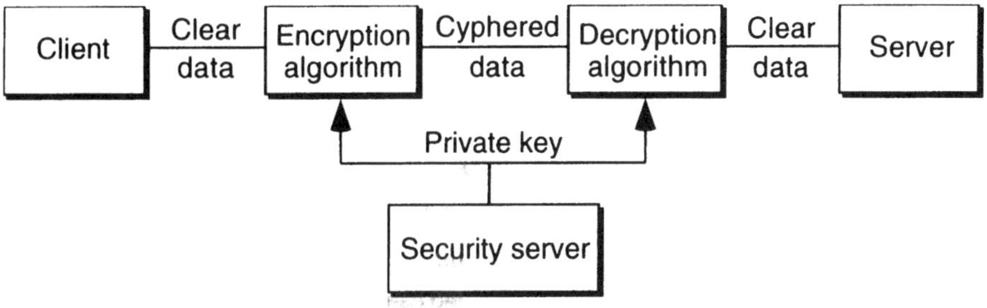

Private key encryption system. Learning Tree International

encryption algorithm (part of the presentation layer) has a private key that it uses to encrypt the information (cyphered data) that is sent over the network to the receiver. The receiver has a decryption algorithm and also possesses the private key by which it can decode the reception and create a clear message, which it then delivers to the server process on the receiving machine.

This method is private key encryption because the key must be kept private, must be secured. The same key is used by the encoder and the decoder. If anyone else possesses the key and has copied the transmitted cyphered data, that person would be able to decode the message. Private key encryption relies on protection of the key. Keys are usually issued by security persons, often by a different method than that used to transmit the data. In other words, private keys are not sent over the network but are distributed by a secured physical mechanism.

❊ Public key encryption

The major drawback of a private key encryption is that if the key ever becomes compromised, the whole system is no longer secure. A key is issued for continuous use in encryption. And there have to be alternative methods of delivering keys other than the network used for data transmission. This makes it inconvenient and a source of possible security breaches.

A much more popular and more robust method is the public key encryption technique. Figure 4-45 shows the flow of information and keys in such a system. Again, let's say there is a client needing encryption services. It sends the data in the clear to the encryption

Figure 4-45

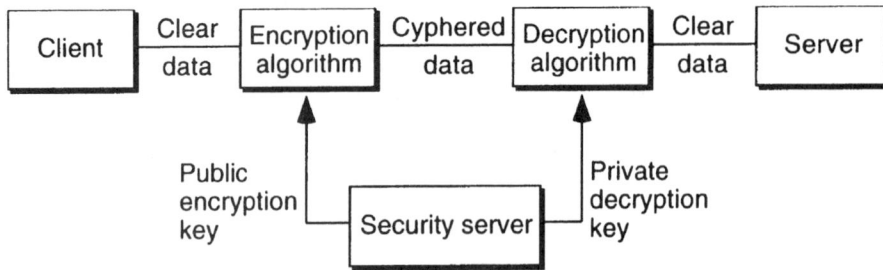

Public key encryption system. <small>Learning Tree International</small>

algorithm. Both the client process and encryption algorithm are in the same machine. This is very secure because the transfer process occurs within the same machine. The encryption algorithm (also part of the presentation layer here) will encrypt the data, and does so with a public key.

The data is sent over the network encrypted, or cyphered. The receiving machine decrypts the data using a private key and delivers the translated, decrypted information to the waiting program on the receiver.

Now there seems to be two keys here, and that is true; there is a public key and a private key. This system requires two keys. And both keys are created with a certain algorithm by the receiver, not the sender. They could be created on a session-by-session basis, or they could be created as a permanent set of keys. The important thing is that the public key is created by the use of the private key. And only one device—the receiver—has the private key on the system. Whenever a device needs to send information, let's say a password, to another device, the sender queries the receiver to receive a public key. This public key could be sent over the network for everyone to see. Or it might be issued by a security server and sent over the network. The sender, the client in this case, uses the public key that it receives from the receiver to encode the transmission. (Let's say in this case it is the password.) It sends that password encrypted. The encryption is done within the sending machine using the public key.

The encrypted transmission might be seen by everyone else, including intruders. But the important thing is that no one is able to decrypt it except the one holding the private key. Public keys are only used to encrypt, not to decrypt. So public keys can be seen by everyone. And the encrypted information can be seen by everyone but no one can decrypt the encrypted information except the one holding the private key, in this case the receiver.

Novell uses this method to encrypt user passwords employed in the user-authentication process. A user wanting to log in to a file server will send out a request for a public key. The file server will create a public key with a private key. No one sees the private key except the server. It will send the public key to the client, to the user, over the network in the clear, able to be seen by everyone. The user will encrypt the password with that public key and send that encrypted password over the network. It can be seen by everyone, but it cannot be decrypted by anyone because no one holds that private key except the server. The encrypted password arrives at the server. The server uses its private key to decrypt the message and obtain the original password transmitted by the client.

⇨ The OSI application layer

⇨ CNE exam objectives

➢ Define the basic purpose of the OSI application layer.

➢ Identify and describe the networking technology topics associated with the OSI application layer.

➢ Identify and describe the methods associated with each OSI application layer topic.

See Table 4-7.

Table 4-7   **Topics and Methods for the Application Layer**

Application-layer topics	Application-layer methods
Network services	File services
	Print services
	Message services
	Application services
	Database services
Service advertising	Active
	Passive
Service use	OS call interception
	Remote operation
	Collaborative

⇨ The application layer

The ITU X.200 document defines the services of the OSI application layer as:

> The application layer contains all functions which imply communication between open systems and are not already performed by the lower layers. These include functions performed by programs and functions performed by human beings.

> As the highest layer in the reference model of Open Systems Interconnection, the application layer provides a means for the application-processes to access the OSI environment. Hence the application layer does not interface with a higher layer. The application layer is the sole means for the application processes to access the OSI environment.

> The purpose of the application layer is to serve as the window between correspondent application processes which are using the OSI to exchange meaningful information. The application services differ from services provided by other layers in neither being provided to an upper layer nor being associated with a service access point.

> In addition to information transfer, such services might include, but are not limited to the following:

> a. identification of intended communications partners (e.g., by name, by address, by definite description, by generic description);

  b. determination of the current availability of the intended communication partners;

  c. establishment of the authority to communicate;

  d. agreement on privacy mechanisms;

  e. authentication of intended communication partners;

  f. determination of cost allocation methodology;

  g. determination of the adequacy of resources;

  h. determination of the acceptable quality of service (e.g., response time, tolerable error rate, cost vis-à-vis the previous considerations);

  i. synchronization of cooperating applications;

  j. selection of the dialogue discipline including the initiation and release procedures;

  k. agreement on the responsibility for error recovery;

  l. agreement on procedures for control of data integrity; and

  m. identification of constraints on data syntax (character sets, data structure).

Application layer programs typically perform their work between end-user applications and the network services provided by the lower six layers. Please be careful not to confuse end-user applications with application layer protocols. Programs such as WordPerfect, Microsoft Excel, QuatroPro, dBase, inventory control, and accounting programs are all forms of end-user programs that are not part of the application layer but use application-layer services. The application-layer protocols are sometimes described as application services rather than applications. Such services were described in detail in chapter 1 under the heading of "File and print services," "Message and application services," and "Database services." In this section we will complement that discussion by covering service-advertisement services and how these services of the application layer are used.

⇨ Service advertisement

The function of a server in advertising its available services to clients over the network falls in the application layer. Such services might include all of the network services described in chapter 1—file, print, message, database, and application services. There are two forms by which a server advertises the services that it suggests: active advertisement and passive advertisement.

※ **Active advertisement**

In active advertising, a server will periodically send out broadcasts to notify all possible clients of the services that it can perform. It also will advertise that it is available to receive requests for these services. Typically, network clients will receive these broadcasts and use the information to build tables of service-provider availability and functionality.

※ **Passive advertisement**

Rather than broadcast its services on a periodic basis, servers that use passive advertisement will register the services they provide with a directory server. In this case, clients will go to that directory server and query it for available servers that could perform the desired function. Servers then are waiting to receive requests from clients without having to notify clients of their available services directly.

⇨ Service use

Network services must work hand in hand with the local operating system to provide their functionality to applications running on a particular computer. There are three methods by which network services work with operating systems.

One of these is called *interception*. In this case, the local operating system is not aware of the existence of the network services. There is a program running on the host that intercepts calls made by the application to services, and this program decides from the nature of the request whether to invoke network services and use the services at servers across the network or pass on to a local operating system.

For example, a workstation might have a local drive and be connected to a network that might be using the services of a file server that maps the file server drives as a local logical drive. To the application, both local and logical drives look like local drives being managed by the local operating system. The application itself can make direct calls to use any one of the three drives. Those calls are intercepted by this application-layer program, sometimes called the shell, or redirector. If the call is to a local drive, it gets passed on to the local operating system. If it is to the logical drive, remote drive, it passes the request on to the network programs to implement.

This is a popular technique employed by PC network operating systems on the client side. The Novell shell and the Microsoft redirector are examples of these programs.

The next category of application service that provides this functionality is remote operation. In this case, the local operating system is aware of the network services, and it is directly responsible to submit requests for network services. An example of this might be the UNIX operating system and its close integration with the TCP/IP protocol family. As a matter of fact, the TCP/IP protocols themselves are considered part of the UNIX operating system. Client requests are first handled by the operating system, which in turn invokes the appropriate network service directly.

Finally, there is a form of network awareness by an operating system called *cooperative computing*. In this case, not only are the network services visible to the operating system but so is the remote server itself and the application-layer program on the remote machine that provides services to the local client. This is very popular in peer-to-peer collaborative computing situations used in PC networks such as Microsoft Windows for Workgroups.

⇨ Workshop

For the following exercise, use the case study for the International Technologies enterprise network in appendix E. Consider each of the following networks using the system diagrams and the information given in appendix A. For each network types listed in Fig. 4-46, determine the wiring and logical topology employed, the format of the data (ASCII or EBCDIC), the type of signaling employed (baseband or broadband), and channel access mechanism employed (contention, token passing or polling).

Figure 4-46

Characteristic	San Jose Building 1 Network A	San Jose Building 2 Network B	San Jose Building 4 Network C
Wiring topology			
Logical topology			
Data format			
Baseband or broadband			
Channel access technology			

Worksheet for the workshop.

Test your understanding

To see how much you have learned about the concepts presented in chapter 4, take five minutes to answer the following questions. Turn to appendix C for typical answers to these questions.

The Physical Layer

Network topologies: _____, _____, _____

Switching modes: _____, _____, _____

Encoding protocols: _____, _____

Transmission modes: _____, _____, _____

Signal types: _____, _____

Signaling technologies: _____, _____

Multiplexing techniques: _____, _____, _____

Modulation types: _____, _____, _____

An analog device used to send digital information over analog phone lines: _____

Popular modem protocols: _____, _____

The Data Link Layer

The services provided by the data link layer are:

_____, _____, _____

Three types of data communications transmissions are:

_____, _____, _____

IBM computers employ what types of data link protocols?

_____ and _____

What are the three popular types of channel access technologies?

_____, _____, _____

Internetworking Devices

In what layer of the OSI Model do the following internetworking devices operate?

Gateways _____

Routers _____

Bridges _____

Repeaters _____

How does a bridge accomplish its function?

_____

What addess does a bridge use to perform frame forwarding?

_____

What address must a router use to perform packet forwarding?

_____

How does a router accomplish its function?

_____

What is the key feature of using bridges?

_____

What is the most important decision to be made in using routers?

_____

When should you use a router over a bridge?

_____

Name some popular types of gateways:

_____, _____, _____

When should you use a gateway?

_____

⇨ Practice CNE exam questions

1. Which factor contributes to the attenuation of electrical signals as they propagate over copper wires?
   A. Capacitance of the wires
   B. Resistance of the wires

C. Both A and B

D. None of the above

2. The difference between analog and digital data is:

A. Analog data can take any value in a range; digital data is discrete and can have only a limited number of values.

B. Analog data is discrete and can have only a limited number of values, whereas digital data can take any value within a range.

C. Both A and B

D. None of the above

3. Which is an example of analog signals carrying analog data?

A. The use of modems and voice-grade lines

B. Music transmitted by commercial radio stations

C. A terminal directly connected to a host computer

D. Music encoded in compact disks (CDs)

4. Which digital encoding scheme is not self-clocking?

A. Bipolar

B. Biphase

C. Manchester

D. Differential Manchester

5. A voice telephone switch employs which type of switching technology?

A. Packet switching

B. Message switching

C. Circuit switching

D. Both packet switching and circuit switching

6. Which technique is used to recover unused bandwidth in conventional TDM systems?

A. Signal regeneration

B. Statistical multiplexing

C. Broadband signaling

D. None of the above

7. Which network type employs twisted-pair cabling?

A. Token Ring networks

B. Ethernet networks

C. ARCNET networks

D. All of the above

8. The RS-232-C interface was standardized by which standards organization?
   A. ANSI
   B. CCITT/ITU
   C. EIA
   D. IEEE

9. Which is not a characteristic of a DCE?
   A. It connects a DTE to a communication channel.
   B. Its function is to convert a DTE's data format to a signal suitable for the media.
   C. A modem is an example of it.
   D. The user interfaces with it.

10. Which statement about modems is not true?
    A. A modem modulates an analog signal with digital data for transmission.
    B. A modem on the receiving end demodulates the analog signal, extracting digital data for the destination DTE.
    C. A modem is used for transmitting digital voice.
    D. A null modem is a cable that connects the transmit circuit of one DTE to the receive circuit of another DTE.

11. Which is not specified by the RS-232 standard?
    A. The mechanical characteristics of the interface
    B. The electrical characteristics of the interface
    C. The functional characteristics of the interface
    D. The framing characteristics of the interface

12. In which communication mode is the transmission two-way simultaneous?
    A. Simplex
    B. Half duplex
    C. Full duplex
    D. Both half duplex and full duplex

13. Which statement is not true of asynchronous transmissions?
    A. Each character being sent is transmitted separately.
    B. There is a random interval between transmissions.
    C. The transmitter and receiver clocks are continually synchronized.
    D. A bit might be added at the end of the character to detect errors in transmission.

241

14. Which protocol employs a token-passing method of sharing a common channel?
    A. 802.4
    B. 802.5
    C. FDDI
    D. All of the above

15. Which protocol employs a collision-detection mechanism?
    A. 802.3
    B. 802.4
    C. 802.5
    D. LocalTalk

16. What technique is employed in block transmissions to ensure that the frame does not contain the unique pattern of bits representing a flag?
    A. Manchester encoding
    B. Zero-bit stuffing
    C. Nonreturn to zero (NRZ) encoding
    D. None of the above

17. A repeater operates at which layer of the OSI Model?
    A. Physical
    B. Data Link
    C. Network
    D. All layers

18. A bridge operates at which layer of the OSI model?
    A. Physical
    B. Data link
    C. Network
    D. Transport

19. A router operates at which layer of the OSI model?
    A. Physical
    B. Data link
    C. Network
    D. Transport

20. Which device reconstructs and retransmits a signal from one part of a network to another as an exact duplicate of the originally transmitted signal?
    A. Repeater
    B. Bridge

C. Router

D. Gateway

21. What address does a bridge use in forwarding frames in a linked network?

A. Node logical address

B. Station network address

⇒ C. Station physical address

D. All of the above

22. Which device uses filtering/forwarding as a technique for linking two networks?

⇒ A. Bridge

B. Repeater

C. Router

D. Gateway

23. Which is not a type of bridge?

A. Transparent

B. Source routing

C. Remote

⇒ D. Asynchronous

24. In a network that uses routers for linking subnetworks, the logical network addresses of nodes are assigned by:

A. The router manufacturer

B. The network card manufacturer

⇒ C. The network administrator

D. They are automatically configured by the routers.

25. Which is not an example of a routing algorithm used by routers to forward packets on an internet?

A. DDP

B. IP

C. ICMP

D. ES/IS

26. Which statement best describes the function of a gateway?

⇒ A. It translates between incompatible protocol implementations.

B. It acts as a router for various protocols implemented in the gateway.

C. It connects two different types of networks.

D. None of the above.

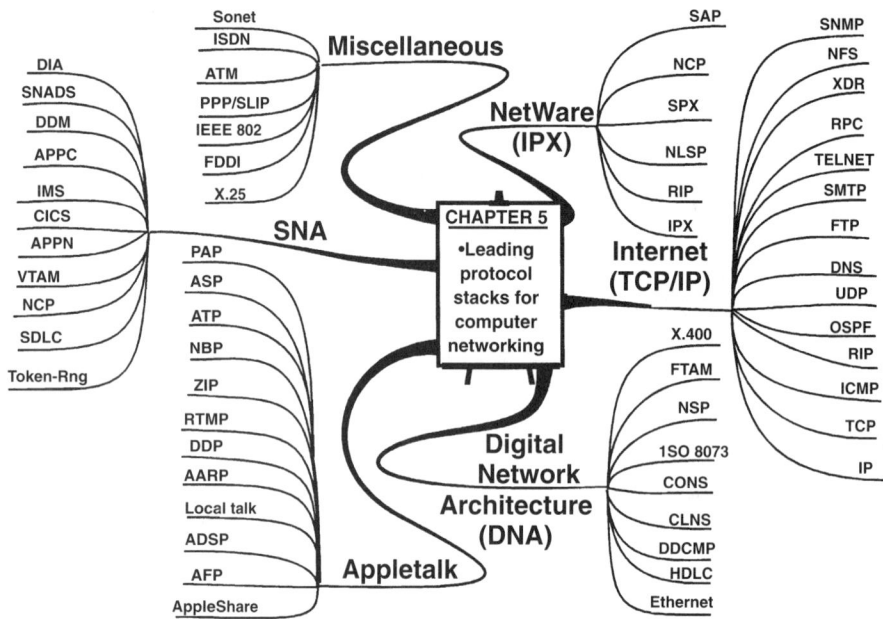

5

Popular protocol
suites

THIS chapter covers the most popular protocol stacks or suites (family of protocols) within the networking industry. In previous chapters we talked about the methods that are used throughout the networking industry. In this chapter, we explore the most popular protocol solutions that facilitate the network communications process. As we proceed through this chapter, we will relate each of the topics or methods to the associated protocols within the stack or suite so that we can better understand their purpose and function. Finally, we will review some of the less used but equally important protocols implemented throughout the industry.

At the beginning of this chapter we review the need for rules and the relationship between models and protocols. The first protocol reviewed will be the IEEE Project 802 because most popular network protocols function on top of the IEEE 802 series of protocols. The chapter then covered the most popular networking protocol stacks in use today. Finally, a review of several miscellaneous but equally important communication protocols is undertaken at the end of the chapter.

⇨ Chapter outline

> ➤ CNE exam objectives

> ➤ Rule, model, and protocol relationships

> ➤ The IEEE Project 802

> ➤ The TCP/IP protocols

> ➤ Novell's NetWare protocols

> ➤ IBM's SNA protocol

> ➤ DEC's DNA protocol

> ➤ Apple's AppleTalk protocol

> ➤ Industry Standards Organization's OSI protocols

> ➤ Additional protocols and standards: FDDI, ARCNET, ATM, CCITT/ITU X.25, PPP/SLIP, ISDN and B-ISDN, SONET/SDH, SMDS

⇨ CNE exam objectives

> ➤ Given a protocol stack displayed with the OSI reference model, identify the purpose of the protocol.

> ➤ Given a protocol stack displayed with the OSI reference model, identify and describe the topics addressed by each protocol.

> ➤ Given a protocol and networking technology topic, identify the methods the protocol uses.

> ➤ Explain the practical limitations of applying models to protocol stacks.

> ➤ Given a network scenario, determine which protocol should be evaluated.

> ➤ Given a product description or other industry literature, identify the protocols, topics, and/or methods addressed.

⇨ Rule, model, and protocol relationships

In chapter 3, we discussed the need for rules and adherence to these rules in order to achieve successful computer-to-computer communications. In this same chapter, we reviewed in summary one of the most important aspects of computer communications, The OSI reference model. This model is not a communication protocol or family of protocols in and of itself. It is a conceptual model only of the topics and methods employed for computer network communications.

We saw that the OSI reference model was divided into seven sections, each section with a description of the functionality that is to be provided at each layer. The specification of this functionality is commonly referred to as a protocol.

Protocols are the solutions to a communication task. They provide the functionality described by the layers of the OSI reference model. They are a set of rules, conventions, and standards and must be adhered to by both communicating entities. In this chapter, we will review many protocols and their relationship with the OSI reference model. A protocol stack is usually referred to as a family of protocols because it is ordered (stacked up) logically, starting from the lowest layer on up. The protocol suite usually refers to a group of protocols that are meant to function together.

While the Industry Standards Organization (ISO) created the OSI reference model, standards organizations and vendors create protocols. The protocols are then implemented in products or remain paper based (defined but not implemented). As protocols evolve, they go through revisions, and not all revisions are backward compatible. Implementing protocol stacks or suites, therefore, requires attention not only to the family of protocols themselves, but also to the revisions of individual protocols in order to ensure complete interoperability.

As we work through this chapter, you will notice that despite having a very complete conceptual model to reference the popular protocols against, not all protocols match up exactly with the OSI reference model as defined by ISO. The main reason for this is the time of creation for the OSI reference model itself and the various protocols in question. The main observation here is that some "vendor protocols" perform the functionality of several of the OSI reference model layers. However, the end result is still the same; the model's functions are still performed.

Because many early protocols were vendor based, we have seen the industry move towards and demand open-systems-based protocols. Most vendors have moved to support open systems protocols based on the OSI reference model, but much work is still taking place in this area.

Finally, in order to promote open systems throughout the world, the ISO has developed its own set of protocols based on the OSI reference model, and it hopes most vendors and users will adopt them. Most of the OSI protocols already existed and have simply been pulled into the protocol stack. Others have been defined by various committees and are still somewhat paper based in that, although well defined, they have not been widely adopted or implemented. (See Fig. 5-1.)

Figure 5-1

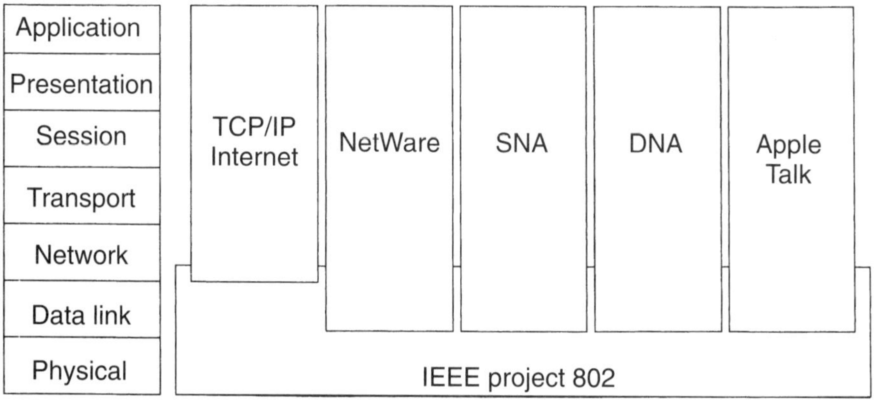

Protocol suites mapped to the OSI reference model. <small>Learning Tree International</small>

The IEEE Project 802

A special subcommittee of the Institute of Electrical and Electronics Engineers (IEEE) began defining LAN standards in February 1980. The standards this committee defined all start with 802 based on the year and month the committee came into existence. The standards were published in 1985 and defined the physical and data link layers of the OSI reference model. Twelve technical subcommittees are developing specific IEEE 802 standards and a thirteenth might soon be added to evaluate and develop 100Base-X standards for 100 Mbits/sec Ethernet. The standards were first adopted by the American Standards Institute (ANSI) and later by ISO as part of the OSI protocol stack and are referred to as ISO 8802 protocols (more on ISO protocols later in this chapter). Since 1985, several new standards have also been added to reflect new and changing technology, such as optical fiber cable and routing in bridged networks. (See Fig. 5-2.)

While adopting the IEEE Project 802 standards, it should be noted that "the wheel was not reinvented." In fact, IEEE Project 802 protocol standards were based on existing standards available at the time, with some slight modifications. As you will see, IEEE 802.2 and 802.3 protocols were based on the Digital-Intel-Xerox (DIX) Ethernet protocol, IEEE 802.4 was based on the Datapoint Corporation, and IEEE 802.5 was based on IBM's Token-Ring standard. Although there

Figure 5-2

Application			802.10

(The diagram shows the OSI seven-layer model on the left: Application, Presentation, Session, Transport, Network, Data link, Physical. The IEEE 802 protocols are mapped across the Data link and Physical layers.)

802.1 Internetwork

802.2 Logical link control

MAC	MAC	MAC	MAC	MAC		
802.3	802.4	802.5	802.6	802.9	802.11	802.12

802.7 & 802.8

The IEEE 802 protocols. Learning Tree International

is some resemblance between the new IEEE standards and the protocols upon which they were based, they are not compatible or interoperable. (See Fig. 5-3.)

⇨ The four basic standards as defined in 1985 by the IEEE Project 802 committee.

> ➢ IEEE 802.2—Logical link control.

> ➢ IEEE 802.3—CSMA/CD contention network.

> ➢ IEEE 802.4—Token-passing bus network.

> ➢ IEEE 802.5—Token-passing ring network.

- **Typical fields in frames for bit-oriented protocols:**

Figure 5-3

Preamble	Address	Control	Data	Error check	End delimiter

Generic frame structure. Infomentat Inc.

802.1 Internetworking (Higher Layer Interface)

The 802.1 Internetworking (also referred to as the Higher Layer Interface) protocol is a more recent standard that is still under development and is used for network architecture, internetworking, and network management for LANs. One of the main protocols to emerge from the 802.1 specification is the Spanning-Tree Algorithm for transparent bridges. The Spanning-Tree Algorithm is also commonly referred to as routing in a bridged network (please refer to chapter 2 for a description of bridges and routers). In a Spanning-Tree-based network, one bridge is selected as the "root" bridge. Although initially selected as the bridge with the lowest physical network interface card address, the "tree" can also be configured based on the network layout and equipment in use. All other bridges in the network then calculate the shortest path to the "root" based on the number of hops between their segment and the "root." Finally, the Spanning-Tree Algorithm is dynamically configurable in that it notifies other bridges of its location in the "tree" and its status on a periodic or as-needed basis. These updates take place very quickly, and in some instances allow the client to continue to work unaware of a breakdown in one segment of the network.

IEEE 802.2 is a protocol that is common to all other IEEE Project 802 protocols. IEEE 802.3 and 802.5 are the predominant protocols within the industry and are found in most offices today. IEEE 802.4 is predominantly used within the manufacturing industry, although it is being replaced by higher-speed systems. IEEE 802.6 remains a fairly paper-based protocol in that it has not been widely adopted by vendors or implemented by users. Several other protocols are currently being developed by the IEEE Project 802 and will be reviewed at the end of this section.

Additional IEEE Project 802 protocols:

> 802.6—Metropolitan Area Network (MAN).

> 802.7—Broadband Technical Advisory Group.

> 802.8—Fiber Optic Technical Advisory Group.

> 802.9—Integrated Voice and Data LAN Interface.

> 802.10—Standard for Interoperable LAN Security.

> 802.11—Wireless LAN.

> 802.12—Demand Priority.

See Fig. 5-4.

The IEEE Project 802's original mandate was to deal the two lowest layers of the OSI model: physical and data link. The physical and data link layer functions are well defined in chapter 4. However, at this stage the data link layer can be divided into two categories or components: media access control (MAC) and logical link control (LLC).

Media access control (MAC) is the method the network interface card (NIC) uses to access the physical medium (usually cable). The process is also referred to as the channel access methodology. While the physical layer describes aspects such as signal voltage levels, clocking techniques, and pinouts, the data link layer MAC function is more concerned with issues like how the workstation accesses the physical medium itself. It is the MAC component of the data link layer that determines how and when a workstation or computing host accesses or is allowed to access lower-layer physical medium and how it interprets and groups (frames), the bits of signals that it receives on the cable. MAC functionality is provided by the latter four protocols: 802.3, 802.4, 802.5, and 802.6.

Logical link control (LLC) is the method used for allowing many higher-level protocols to share and use the same data link MAC

Figure 5-4

Protocol	OSI Layer	Topics	Methods
802.1	Network	Routing in a Bridge Network Environment	Identification of MAC Addressing and Frame Format
802.2	Data Link Logical Link Control	Protocol Specific	Identification of upper layer protocols
802.3 (exept as noted)	Physical	Connection Types	Multipoint
		Digital Signaling	State Transition
		Bit Synchronization	Synchronous
		Bandwidth Use	Baseband (except for 10Broad36)
	Data Link MAC	Logical Topology	Bus
		Media Access	Contention
		Addressing	Physical Device
802.3 1BASE5	Physical	Physical Topology	Star
802.3 10BASE2	Physical	Physical Topology	Bus
802.3 10BASE5	Physical	Physical Topology	Bus
802.3 10BASE-T	Physical	Physical Topology	Star
802.3 10BASE-F	Physical	Physical Topology	Star
802.3 10BROAD36	Physical	Physical Topology	Bus
		Bandwidth Used	Broadband
802.4	Physical	Connection Types	Multipoint
		Physical Topology	Bus
		Digital Signaling	State Transition
		Bit Synchronization	Synchronous
		Bandwidth Used	Baseband
	Data Link MAC	Logical Topology	Ring
		Media Access	Token Passing
		Addressing	Physical Device
802.5	Physical	Connection Types	Point-to-Point
		Physical Topology	Star Ring
		Digital Signaling	State Transition
		Bit Synchronization	Synchronous
		Bandwidth Used	Baseband
	Data Link MAC	Logical Topology	Ring
		Media Access	Token Passing
		Addressing	Physical Device

IEEE 802 protocol topics and methods. Learning Tree International

Figure 5-4

802.6	Physical	Connection Types	Point-to-Point
		Physical Topology	Ring
		Bandwidth Used	Baseband
	Data Link MAC	Logical Topology	Ring
802.11 (proposed)	Data Link MAC	Media Access	Contention
802.12 (proposed)	Physcial	Connection Types	Multipoint
		Physical Topology	Star
		Bandwidth Used	Baseband
	Data Link MAC	Logical Topology	Bus
		Media Access	Contention

Continued.

component. It has also been referred to as a protocol multiplexer. In other words, several higher-level protocols like IP and IPX (discussed later in this chapter) can both use the same MAC access method and frame type. LLC is modeled after the High-Level Data Link Control protocol, (HDLC) although the functions of the frame formats have been altered somewhat. Because the LLC is common to the main LAN-based 802.x protocol standards, we will begin our discussion by explaining LLC functionality and then cover the individual media access control formats and characteristics.

As we review the data link layer frame formats, remember that the purpose of the frame is to encapsulate the network layer packet. The network layer packet therefore is the protocol data unit (PDU) or payload off the frame. To review the concepts of protocol encapsulation and layering techniques, please review chapter 3.

⇨ Data link layer: logical link control

⇨ IEEE 802.2 logical link control

To support multiple protocols from the network layer within the same frame format, the LLC uses service access points (SAPs—although not to be confused with Service Advertising Protocol SAPs found at the application layer in the NetWare protocol stack). The service access points are internal software addresses that describe which higher-level network layer protocol is being carried by the frame assembled by the

Figure 5-5

IEEE Service Access Points (SAP)		
00	0	Null SAP
02	2	LLC Sublayer Management / Individual
03	3	LLC Sublayer Management / Group
06	6	IP (DoD Internet Protocol)
0E	14	PROWAY Network Management, Maintenance and Installation
42	66	BPDU (Bridge PDU / Spanning Tree)
4E	78	MMS (Manufacturing Message Service) EIA-RS 511
5E	94	ISI IP
7E	126	X.25 PLP ISO 8208
8E	142	Proway Active Station List Maintenance
AA	170	SNAP Subnetwork Access Protocol
E0	224	IPX/SPX Novell NetWare
FE	254	ISO Network Layer Protocols
FF	255	Global DSAP
IBM Service Access Points (SAP)		
04	4	SNA Path Control / Individual
05	5	SNA Path Control / Group
D4	212	Resource Management
DC	220	Dynamic Address Resolution (Name Management)
F0	240	NetBIOS
F4	244	LAN Management / Individual
F5	245	LAN Management / Group
F8	248	IRPL (IBM Remote Program Load)
FC	252	Discovery

Example service access point table. Learning Tree International

MAC component of the data link layer. A detailed list of service access points is included in Fig. 5-5.

The SAP is composed of a destination service access point (DSAP) and source service access point (SSAP). The DSAP is the logical address of the network layer process within the target station for which this frame is directed. The SSAP is the logical address of the network layer within the source station that is sending out the frame.

The information stored in the SAP fields also determines what type of 802.2 network services are required. One or two control bytes specify this information.

Type 1. Unacknowledged connectionless.

Type 2. Connection-oriented service.

Type 3. Acknowledged connectionless service.

Additionally, LLC provides for flow control and error recovery during frame transmissions. This additional functionality is facilitated through positive acknowledgment and retransmission protocol techniques. Sliding-windows full-duplex protocols are used for flow control. Finally, LLC is able to logically connect and recover from loss of connectivity at the link level, depending on the type of service specified in the control byte.

In earlier versions of DIX Ethernet, and the Ethernet_II frame format in particular (described latter in this section), the SAP is referred to as the Ethertype field. The Ethertype field lists which type of network-layer protocol is being encapsulated within the frame.

One of the interesting things to note about 802.2 Logical Link Control is that it is common to all other 802.x MAC-based protocols (like 802.3, 803.4, 802.5) found in most LANs. All of these protocols will carry 802.2 information in one way or another within their frame format. In fact, it has often been stated that there is no real 802.2 frame format, but simply 802.3 with 802.2 information within it. These frame formats are often referred to as "802.3 with 802.2" and "802.3 with 802.2 SNAP" (Ethernet_802.2 and Ethernet_SNAP in Novell NetWare environments).

While this issue might be debated in a purely technical forum, the way in which bits from the physical level are grouped together does demonstrate that 802.3 and 802.2 frame formats are indeed different. What is similar about them is their use of the 802.3 media access control method for accessing the physical layer, and as such they are often grouped together. The issue is also true of 802.5 frame formats used in Token-Ring environments to support multiple network layer protocols. These frame formats are referred to as Token-Ring_SNAP or IEEE 802.5 with SNAP (see IEEE 802.5 later in this section).

The second 802.2-based frame format is referred to as 802.2 with a Subnet Access Protocol or SNAP. Figure 5-6 highlights this frame format. The main purpose of the 802.2 with SNAP frame format is to support the extended addressing capability of the AppleTalk and TCP/IP protocols stacks. (See Fig. 5-7.)

- **Service Access Points (SAPs) are internal software addresses**
- **Example SAPs include**
  - 06 Hex = Internet Protocol
  - E0 Hex = Novell NetWare
  - F0 Hex = IBM NetBIOS

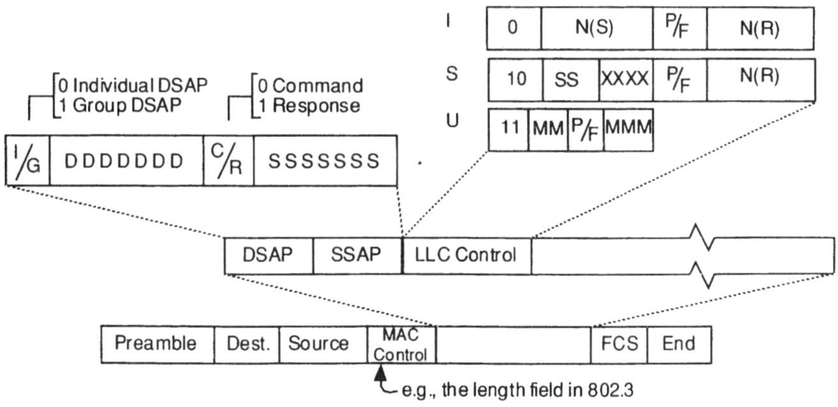

Figure 5-6

IEEE 802.3 with 802.2 logical link control frame format. Learning Tree International

- **A special 802.2 SAP has been set aside to indicate that the software address is in the data field**
  - The Ethernet type field is utilized

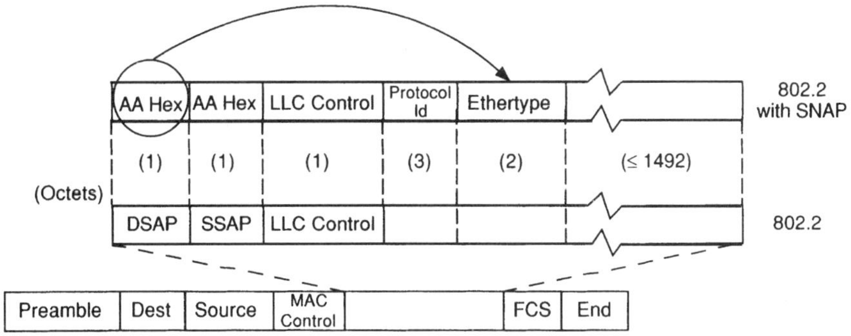

Figure 5-7

IEEE 802.3 with 802.2 SNAP frame format. Learning Tree International

IEEE 802.2 LLC field definitions

Destination service access point: A 1-byte field, the destination SAP is the network layer process that is to receive the process being delivered.

Source service access point: A 1-byte field, the source SAP is the network layer process that created the process being transmitted.

Control: One of three LLC services. Length of field is either 1 or 2 bytes, depending on the type of service being requested or supplied. It is the higher-layer protocols that determine the type of service in this field.

Information or data: A variable-length field that is the actual network layer packet protocol data unit (i.e., IPX or IP).

Novell's 802.3 RAW frame format

Novell NetWare also supports an 802.3 frame format without 802.2 information and is referred to as 802.3 RAW. This frame format was the older standard for Novell NetWare networks that predate NetWare 3.12 and NetWare 4.0, and 802.3 RAW is not supported by IEEE. NetWare's 802.3 RAW protocol supported only one network layer protocol, namely Internetwork Packet Exchange (IPX). As all frames will be carrying the same network-layer protocol, there is no need for an Ethertype or SAP field. There is a Length field instead of an Ethertype field. (See Fig. 5-8.)

NetWare's IPX header is located at the start of the data portion of the 802.3 RAW packet or frame. The IPX header is hard coded as FF-FF to denote that the frame is carrying an IPX network-layer packet. In networks that use multiple frame types on the same physical cable segments, the receiving stations must identify if the value in the length field is smaller than 1518 bytes to determine whether or not it is an Ethernet_II frame type. If the receiving station determines that the length field is less than 1518 bytes, it checks the value in the next two bytes for FF-FF. As stated previously, a value of FF-FF in the beginning

Figure 5-8

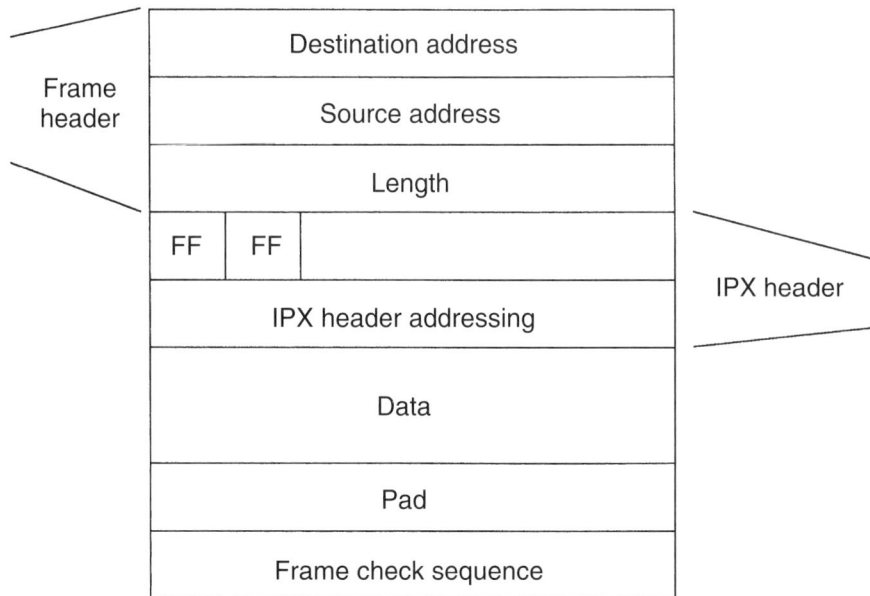

Novell NetWare 802.3 RAW frame format. Novell Inc.

of the data component of the frame denotes that the frame is carrying IPX network layer packets. FF-FF is not a value supported by IEEE 802.2 DSAP and SSAP fields.

You now have an understanding of how the LLC component of the data link layer acts as a higher-layer protocol multiplexer to facilitate the support of multiple network-layer protocols within the same frame format. The LLC is also used to assist the receiving station in identifying the type of frame it has just received and subsequently how to identify the fields and their byte start and end locations within the frame. We will now look at the MAC component of the data link layer and explore how it is responsible for managing access by the network interface card to the physical cable medium.

⇨ Data link layer: media access control

⇨ IEEE 802.3—CSMA/CD contention network

IEEE 802.3 is known as a contention bus access-based channel access methodology and is very similar to the original 10-Mbits/sec Ethernet.

CSMA/CD stands for carrier sense multiple access, collision detection. Although long, the name is actually very descriptive of the process that is taking place. When the device is ready to transmit a signal, or rather series of signals, is listens to see if another station is already transmitting on the cable (carrier sense). Each network device is connected to a common logical bus (multiple access). Because network devices transmit on the same logical bus (see chapter 4, data link layer section for a description of logical versus physical topologies) there is the opportunity for collisions. (See Fig. 5-9.)

Figure 5-9

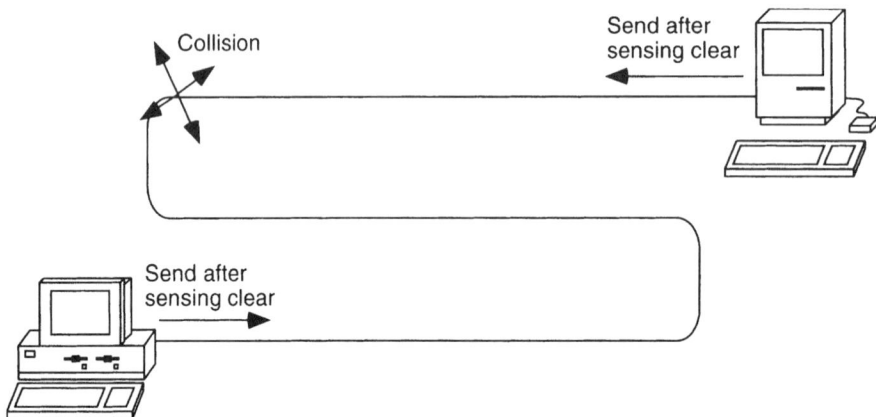

802.3 contention bus access. Learning Tree International

As you can appreciate, the process of transmitting and receiving electrical signals on the cable occurs very rapidly. The electrical signal itself travels at approximately three meters per nanosecond. Despite the speed of signal creation and propagation, Fig. 5-7 demonstrates that collisions are indeed possible. This is where collision detection (CD) circuitry comes into play. All Ethernet, or more appropriately IEEE 802.3-based network interface cards, have special hardware circuitry designed to determine when a series of signals composing a complete frame is not fully transmitted without encountering a series of signals transmitted by another device on the network.

When a collision occurs, the device transmitting the signal invokes a back-off algorithm before trying to retransmit. The back-off algorithm is in fact a random count timer that activates while waiting to retransmit. When the count is completed, the transmitting device starts the process over again. Should another collision be detected, then transmitting devices repeat the back-off algorithm process, only this time they count a little longer than the last time. The process will be repeated until a higher-level protocol (such as NetWare Core Protocol or Telnet, discussed later in this chapter) breaks off the communications process.

One of the common issues associated with contention bus networks is use of the underlying bus. The term use is sometimes confused as an indicator of the number of collisions on the network. A network use percentage is actually arrived at by calculating the number of times the network device went to the bus and was not able to transmit because it sensed that another device was currently transmitting a signal (carrier). If there is no traffic on the network bus, it is said to have a 0% utilization. If 30% of the time, there is traffic on the network bus, it is said to have 30% utilization. The number of devices connected to a network segment (bus) and the type of traffic they are trying to transmit (DOS or Windows-based programs) will affect network segment use. While network traffic analysis is beyond the scope of this book, we believe that it is important to point out the correlation between the often-used term "network use" and collisions on an 802.3 contention bus-based system.

As a result of the potential for collisions on the network of transmitting devices, CSMA/CD networks are considered *nondeterministic*. Essentially, nondeterministic means that we cannot predict or accurately determine how long it will take for a device to successfully transmit its signal to a receiving station. As a result of the nondeterministic characteristic nature of CSMA/CD networks, this technology has not been implemented very much in manufacturing environments that require very time sensitive transmission of information and commands to robotics devices within the plant. However, the typical office does not require that information or commands be delivered within such tight time frames, and the CSMA/CD network has been implemented in most such environments. It will be important to remember the definition of nondeterministic when we compare CSMA/CD to token-passing or IEEE 802.4 and 802.5 networks.

In addition to the channel access methodology, the IEEE 802.3 standard also determines the frame format or the way in which a series of bits are interpreted. Previously under the "Logical link control" section, we displayed several Ethernet and 802.3 (with and without 802.2 and SNAP) formats. However, Fig. 5-10 displays the original Ethernet_II with the IEEE 802.3 frame format for comparison.

Figure 5-10

IEEE 802.3

Preamble	Start of frame delimiter	Destination address	Source address	Length	802.2 LLC header, data, and padding	CRC
7 bytes	1 bytes	6 bytes	6 bytes	2 bytes	46–1500 bytes	4 bytes
		48 bits	48 bits			32 bits

———————————————Frame———————————————

Ethernet

Preamble	Destination address	Source address	Type	Data and padding	CRC
8 bytes	6 bytes	6 bytes	2 bytes	46–1500 bytes	4 bytes

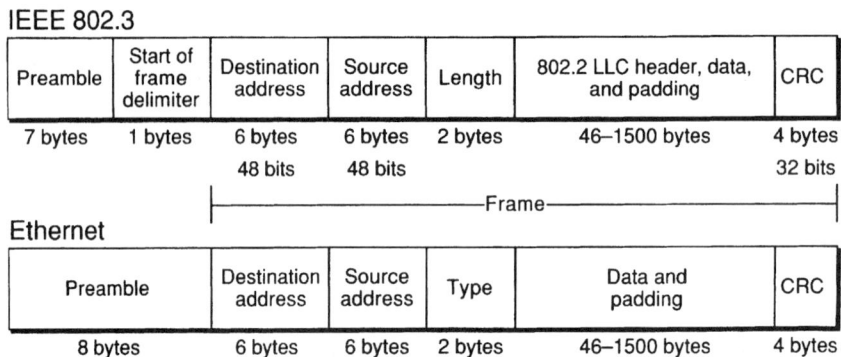

- **Minimum frame size (with CRC and without preamble) = 64 bytes**
- **Maximum frame size (with CRC and without preamble) = 1518 bytes**
- **Frame overhead = 18 bytes (not including preamble)**

Length is always ≤ 1500 dec
Type is always > 1500 dec

Comparison of Ethernet_II and IEEE 802.3 frame. Learning Tree International

Field definitions for Ethernet_II and IEEE 802.3 frame formats

The preceding frame formats share many of the same fields, and the following describes the functionality of each one.

Preamble and start of frame delimiters: A review of the two frame formats shows that the first 8 bytes are used either for a frame preamble (Ethernet_II) or a combination of preamble and start of frame delimiter. However, both achieve the same result, which is to identify to the network interface card that this is the beginning of the frame. The Ethernet_II frame preamble is denoted by 8 bytes of alternating zeros and ones, while the IEEE 802.3 preamble is denoted by 7 bytes of alternating zeros and ones, followed by two ones to indicate the start of a frame.

Destination address: A 6-byte address follows the preamble/start of frame delimiter and represents the hardware address that has been "burnt in" to the network interface card by the manufacturer. The destination address identifies which station(s) receive and act upon the frame. The address can be directed to one specific station (unicast or single host), several selected hosts (multicast or multiple hosts), or broadcast addresses (all hosts).

Source address: A 6-byte address that is the "burnt-in" address of the network interface card, but this one is of the network device sending or transmitting the frame. The address of the source that is "burnt in" or hard coded into the network interface card is not randomly generated. IEEE provides or designates each network interface card manufacturer with a 3-byte value that is assigned to the first three bytes of the 6-byte address. The manufacturer then selects a unique 3-byte address value for the last three bytes of the 6-byte address in order to ensure that each and every network interface card has a unique address throughout not only the manufacturer's own cards, but also across the industry as a whole.

Length and type fields: Ethernet_II uses a type field to identify which higher-layer protocol the frame in question is transporting. IEEE

802.3 uses a length field to denote the length of the higher-layer protocol data unit encapsulated in the frame. The original 802.3 frame format was only capable of supporting one network layer protocol within a frame so that a type identifier was not required.

Data and/or padding: This field contains the protocol data unit packet of the network layer itself. In some instances, this field will be smaller than the minimum size required, and additional padding will be added to ensure that a subsequent minimum-size frame is created.

Frame check sequence: (Cyclical redundancy check). The value in this field is the total sum of the number of bytes of the frame. It is used as a way of verifying that the frame was received correctly in its entirety. This aspect of frame transmission is particularly important when you consider the issue nature of CSMA/CD networks.

Signal quality error

Another feature of Ethernet_II and IEEE 802.3 networks is called signal quality error or SQE. Depending on how it is implemented, this can be viewed as a feature or a major problem if the equipment is installed incorrectly. The main responsibility of SQE is to ensure that devices that connect the network interface card to the physical cabling segment are able to properly establish attachment to the network. The devices include external transceivers, or more appropriately termed medium attachment units (MAUs). SQE performs its function by sending a heartbeat signal from the network interface card to the transceiver or MAU to test the network connection. The problem occurs in some network environments using older network interface cards that are based on Ethernet Version I standards. The SQE signal creates an electrical signal on the network segment that is not an actual frame. This signal then tends to "jam" the network segment and increases the potential for collisions.

IEEE 802.3 addressing method

Each network interface card has its own unique address. The address is composed of 6 bytes (48 bits). The address is embedded into the read only memory (ROM) chip on the card itself. Although the address is essentially hard coded into the network interface card, there is an option for a 2-byte (16-bit) user-definable address.

The embedded address is composed of two parts. The IEEE assigns the network interface card manufacture the first 3 bytes (24 bits). The first 1 byte (8 bits) is reserved for broadcast and multicast addressing. The next 2 bytes (16 bits) are the manufacturer identification portion of the address. The last 3 bytes are uniquely assigned by the manufacturer to each network interface card. The end result is that each and every address on a network interface card is unique throughout the universe. The entire address is usually expressed as 12 hex characters. (See Fig. 5-11A.)

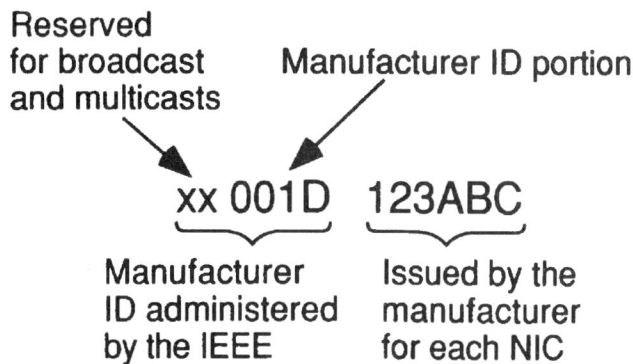

Figure 5-11A

Reserved
for broadcast
and multicasts

Manufacturer ID portion

xx 001D 123ABC

Manufacturer
ID administered
by the IEEE

Issued by the
manufacturer
for each NIC

Sample IEEE 802.3 NIC address. Learning Tree International

The following is a list of some IEEE-issued manufacturer IDs for some of the more popular network interface cards.

Ethernet hex value	Manufacturer IDS	Manufacturer
00 00 03	SMC	Standard Microsystems Corp.
00 00 0C	CISCO	Cisco.
00 00 1B	NOVELL	Novell/Eagle
00 00 1D	CBLTRN	Cabletron
00 00 21	D-LINK	D-Link/Surecom/Others

Ethernet hex value	Manufacturer IDS	Manufacturer
00 00 93	PRTEON	Proteon (bit reversal from Token Ring address)
00 00 C0	WD	Western Digital (jetzt zu: SMC)
00 00 C6	HP_EON	Hewlett-Packard/EON Systems
00 1C 84	TMSCRD	Thomas Conrad
00 60 C5	3COM	3Com
00 80 C7	XIRCOM	Xircom
00 80 C8	D-LINK	D-Link
00 AA 00	INTEL	Intel
00 C0 8C	3COM	3Com
08 00 07	APPLE	Apple
08 00 09	HP	Hewlett Packard
08 00 1E	APOLLO	Hewlett Packard/Apollo
08 00 2B	DEC	Digital Equipment Corp., UNIBUS, QBUS, VAX
08 00 5A	IBM	IBM (bit reversal from Token Ring address)
10 00 5A	IBM	IBM
AA 00 03	DEC	Digital Equipment Corp. (global)

Having stated earlier in this chapter that IEEE 802.3 was based on existing implementations of Ethernet, several new naming conventions were created to differentiate between the various potential configurations. For example, the older Ethernet networks used thick coax cabling and were sometimes referred to as Thick Ethernet or DIX specification (Digital-Intel-Xerox). This implementation of Ethernet supported 10-Mbits/sec CSMA/CD access using baseband signaling (see chapter 2 for a definition of baseband). The IEEE implementation of Thick Ethernet is designated as 10Base-5. Figure 5-11B describes the general format for IEEE specifications of LAN protocol standards.

Figure 5-11B

Standard 802.3 designations

Baseband or
broadband

10BASE5

Data rate
in Mbits/sec

Segment length in
100-m multiples or
technology type

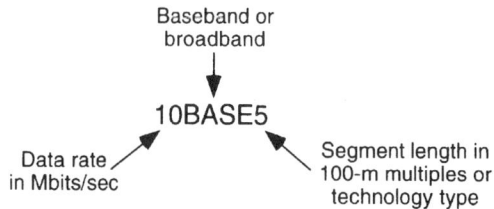

IEEE 802.3 specifications naming format. Learning Tree
International

⇨ 10Base-5 has the following specifications

➢ 10-Mbits/sec CSMA/CD access methodology, baseband signal.

➢ Uses 10-mm thick 50-ohm coaxial cable (ThickNet or Thick Ethernet).

➢ 500 meters per segment on a physical bus topology.

➢ Requires the use of transceivers called attachment unit interfaces (AUIs) and MAUs to connect the transceiver to the network interface card.

➢ Bus cabling topology and access.

➢ Uses repeaters between segments.

Note that Thick Ethernet was the precursor to 802.3 and is still used in many older network environments. It is also important to remember that IEEE 802.3 frame structure differs from Ethernet_II. Many other standards have also been defined by IEEE for Ethernet-based networks.

⇨ 10Base-2 has the following specifications

> ➤ 10-Mbits/sec CSMA/CD access methodology, baseband signal.

> ➤ Uses 5-mm thin 50-ohm coaxial cable (also-called ThinNet, Thin Ethernet, or Cheapernet).

> ➤ 185 meters per segment on a physical bus topology.

> ➤ Bus topology.

> ➤ Transceiver functions added to network card directly.

> ➤ Uses BNC T-type connectors and daisy-chain wiring configuration.

> ➤ Uses repeaters to connect segments.

⇨ 10Base-T has the following specifications

> ➤ 10-Mbits/sec CSMA/CD access methodology, baseband signal.

> ➤ Uses two pairs of 24-AWG UTP wiring.

> ➤ Deployed as a physical star wiring cable topology with an active center hub or concentrator.

> ➤ 100 meters distance limitation from the network interface card to the hub or concentrator.

> ➤ Hubs or concentrators are connected in a spanning-tree network configuration (not to be confused with Spanning Tree Algorithm, although it is used in this type of network).

> ➤ Hubs or concentrators act as repeaters working at the physical layer and are unaware of the frame structure.

Special note: Hubs and concentrators are two terms used throughout the industry for equipment that performs essentially the same function. Vendors often create terminology in order to distinguish their products from the competition. The standard name for the device that is used throughout the industry today is hub.

10Base-F has the following specifications

> ➤ 10-Mbits/sec CSMA/CD access methodology, baseband signal.

> ➤ Signal distance up to 4 kilometers on a physical star topology.

> ➤ Three types of implementation:
>   • 10BASE-FL for fiber-optic link.
>   • 10BASE-FB for fiber backbone.
>   • 10BASE-FP for fiber passive.

100Base-X specification is currently being reviewed by the 802.3 subcommittee. Similar in nature to 10Base-T, it will increase the data rate from 10 Mbits/sec to 100 Mbits/sec. It is intended that the higher data rate will be achieved by increasing the timing rates of the original 10Base-T technology. The IEEE 802.12 committee is currently charged with evolving this standard.

1Base-5 has the following specifications

> ➤ 1-Mbit/sec CSMA/CD access methodology, baseband signal.

> ➤ Uses 24-gauge UTP wiring with hubs.

> ➤ Signal distance up to 500 meters (250 meters between station and hub) on a physical star topology.

> ➤ Hubs cascade in hierarchical tree structure.

> ➤ Usually referred to as AT&T Starlan.

> ➤ Not in use that much today.

⇨ 10Broad-36 has the following specifications

> ➤ 10-Mbits/sec CSMA/CD access methodology, broadband signals.

> ➤ Uses 75-ohm coaxial cable with CATV components (similar to what the average household television uses).

> ➤ Broadband access with rf modems.

> ➤ Modems integrated into MAU.

> ➤ 1800 meters in distance per segment on a physical bus topology.

> ➤ 3600 meters using dual cables.

> ➤ Segments are connected to a retransmission device called a "headend."

This concludes the IEEE 802.3-based standards. We will now proceed to cover the other IEEE Project 802-based protocol standards.

⇨ IEEE 802.4— Token-passing bus network

IEEE 802.4 was developed mainly to address the requirement for implementing LAN based technology in the factory and manufacturing environment. It uses a token-passing channel access methodology. The electrical and cabling topology are bus based. Typically, this standard is implemented on a broadband network using several channels on an FDM frequency-allocated rf spectrum, although baseband signaling is also supported. Other available channels in the broadband spectrum are then used for data, voice, fax, and video.

The network uses 75-ohm coaxial cable with components from the CATV industry. Given the very high magnetic interference of some manufacturing environments, this protocol standard was also designed to work with fiber-optic cabling systems. It was originally developed for and deployed in industrial automation and factories. A component of the standard is the Manufacturing Automation Protocol (MAP) suite of protocols used for NIST. Finally, the token bus network offers controlled, low-delay access to the network for every participating host. In this regard, it is considered a deterministic network environment, which means that we can accurately calculate how long it will take before a network device has an opportunity to transmit its signal to a receiving station.

The latter feature is a very important one when you look at a manufacturing environment. For example, if we were to take a car manufacturing production line, the network must be able to guarantee that a specific robotics device on the production line will be able to receive and process a command to place the tire on the chassis at the appropriate time, or one can only begin to imagine what the consequences will be. Timing is one of the main reasons that manufacturing environments require deterministic network protocol standards, whereas office environments can function with nondeterministic protocol standards. The subcommittee responsible for the IEEE 802.4 protocol standard was very active during 1984 until 1988.

⇨ IEEE 802.5—Token-passing ring network

In the same manner that IEEE created the 802.3 protocol standard based on DIX Ethernet, the IEEE 802.5 protocol was based on IBM's proprietary Token Ring protocol. Once again, some modifications were made, and as a result Token Ring and IEEE 802.5 are not compatible. Figure 5-12 displays the format of the IEEE 802.5 Token and Information (data or command) frame structure.

Three types of frames are used in a Token Ring environment. Information frames or data/command frames provide the main functionality of moving data around the ring to ensure that the ring is performing properly (maintenance). Command frames operate at the MAC component level only and carry ring maintenance information. Unlike Ethernet, Token Ring technology has a built-in ability to

Figure 5-12   IEEE 802.5 information (data or command) frame

Start of frame delimiter	Access control	Frame control	Destination address	Source address	Data	CRC	End delimiter	Frame status
1 byte	1 byte	1 byte	6 bytes 48 bits	6 bytes 48 bits	>0 bytes	4 bytes 32 bits	1 byte	1 byte

Token frame

Start of frame delimiter	Access control	End delimiter
1 byte	1 byte	1 byte

The access-control byte

P	P	P	T	M	R	R	R

Priority bits   Reservation bits

Token bit   Monitor bit

Token bit:
0 = free, token frame
1 = busy, data frame

IEEE 802.5 token and information frame formats. Learning Tree International

monitor the status of the ring and take corrective action in the event of a breakdown. Data frames carry LLC information and the upper layer protocol data unit and user data. Information frames can be between 21 bytes and 4096 bytes in size, just over two and a half times greater than the largest Ethernet frame size.

Token frames are 3 bytes long. The main purpose of the token frame is to act as a permission control monitor. A network device can only transmit information frames when it is in receipt of the token frame. It then holds the token frame and transmits its information frame. When the information frame completes the ring and returns to the original station, the token is then put back onto the ring for the next downstream device to access. The fourth most significant bit of the middle byte (field) is the token bit, and it is used by network devices to identify whether the frame it is assembling is an information frame or a token frame. Note in Fig. 5-12 that the token bit is a 1-bit value representing 0 for a token frame and 1 for an information frame. If the token bit is a value of 1, the device knows that it possesses an information frame and begins to process it to determine if the frame is destined for it. If the token bit is a value of 0, then the device knows it has free access to the ring and can begin to transmit its own information frame.

The last frame is the abort sequence frame (not really a frame, but more like a special signal to tell all stations to stop transmissions). It is a 2-byte frame with a start and end delimiter. This frame is used to purge the ring of any frame whenever a problem occurs. Frame transmission is stopped, and then a new token frame is released on the ring.

⇨ Field definitions for IEEE 802.5 frames

Start delimiter: Indicates the start of the token or information frame. The start delimiter is made unique by violating the Differential Manchester encoding rules (see chapter 2).

Access control byte: Priority and reservation bits are used in a priority scheme. The token bit indicates whether the frame is information or token and is used to determine if the station can access the frame as a token frame. The monitor bit is used by the monitor station to clear (purge) unused or endlessly repeated frames from the network.

Frame control byte: Differentiates information (data/command) frames from token frames. Certain patterns in command frames are used for ring maintenance activities.

Destination and source addresses: A 6-byte (48-bit) address used to uniquely identify each network interface card. The address method is the same as that used in IEEE 802.3 address scheme and is administered by IEEE in the same manner. The destination address denotes which network device is to receive and process the frame. The source address denotes which network device created the frame for transmission. As with 802.3 addressing, there is an option for the user to select an address.

Data information: The length of this field depends on the ring length and token holding time. Typically, PC ring frames might have up to 4096 bytes of data.

CRC: A 32-bit cyclical redundancy check sequence used to detect errors in the frame. Calculated by the sending station on the frame control, destination and source addresses, and data fields. The receiver calculates its own CRC value based on the same fields described previously for the frame and compares it with the CRC sent. It they fail to match, the frame is discarded.

End delimiter: Denotes the end of the token or information frame. As with the start of the frame, it is made unique by violation of the Differential Manchester encoding rules.

Frame status byte: A way for the receiving station to indicate to the sending station that the frame sent was received and processed successfully. The field is also sometimes referred to as the hardware acknowledge field. Two fields in the byte—A (address resolution) and C (frame copied)—are both set to 0 by the original sender. The receiver sets both fields to 1 if it is responding (A) and has correctly copied or processed the frame (C). If no change is detected to the A field, then the original sending station is alerted to the fact that the destination device is not on the local ring.

The original IBM Token Ring has the following specifications:

> ➤ Baseband signal, logical token-passing ring topology.

> ➤ Star-wired ring (physical topology) with two twisted pairs connected to a multistation access unit (MSAU).

> ➤ The original ring speed was 4 Mbits/sec and was later increased to 16 Mbits/sec.

> ➤ Each Token Ring network interface card acts as a repeater of the original signal.

> ➤ IBM promoted two cabling schemes.
>   • Unmovable: 260 stations per ring using shielded twisted pair.
>   • Movable: 72 stations per ring using unshielded twisted pair.

IEEE 802.5 has the following specifications:

> ➤ Token Ring was adopted by IEEE 802 as 802.5.

> ➤ IBM Token Ring and 802.5 have slight differences.

> ➤ Baseband signal, token passing ring logical topology.

> ➤ Physical topology was note specified but in practice uses physical star topology.

> ➤ 4-Mbits/sec and 16-Mbits/sec versions were adopted.

> ➤ Each Token Ring network interface card acts as a repeater of the original signal.

> ➤ 250 stations per ring on unspecified wiring and different from the IBM Token Ring specification.

Multistation access units (MSAUs) were originally 8-port connector units or wiring centers. MSAUs are usually located in a wiring closet, and the cabling runs from each office back to the wiring center MSAUs. The MSAU creates a ring by connecting the two pairs of wires coming from all network devices. In order to support more than 8 devices per ring, multiple MSAUs are connected or concatenated. When connecting multiple MSAUs, however, the logical ring topology is still maintained by connecting a ring out (RO) port of one MSAU to the ring in (RI) port of the next MSAU. Finally, the last MSAU's Ring Out port is connected to the Ring In port of the first MSAU, preserving the ring. Figure 5-13 demonstrates the concept of the wiring closet with multiple MSAUs concatenated together.

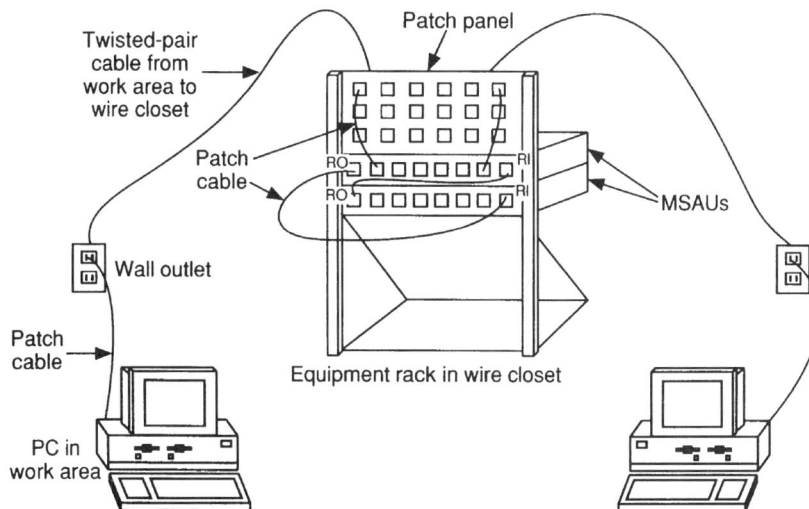

Figure 5-13

- **Star configuration wiring for an electrically connected ring**

Token Ring components. Learning Tree International

We have previously described both the structure of the Token Ring frames and the specifications of IEEE 802.5. In the next section we will review how the IEEE 802.5 functions as a token-passing channel access methodology.

⇨ IEEE 802.5 channel access methodology

A Token-Ring-passing network is similar in nature to a relay race. Each runner waits for its turn to run. However, in order to start running the runner must have possession of the relay baton. Once in possession of the relay baton, the runner completes his or her part of the race and passes the baton on to the next individual. The process repeats itself in an endless loop around the oval racetrack. While the race is being run, monitors watch to ensure that all the rules are being followed.

A Token-Ring passing starts with an initial station releasing a token frame (relay baton) on the network. Another station on the ring can then grab the token and send out an information or data frame. The intended destination station copies the frame into its own memory and resends the frame back onto the ring (remember, every Token Ring NIC acts as a repeater). The original sending station looks at the information frames, determines that it actually sent the frame (source address), removes the frame from the ring, and releases the token frame back onto the ring. Part of the IEEE 802.5 specification rules state that even if the station currently holding the token (permission) frame has more data to transmit, it must release the token and wait for it to come around on the ring again before transmitting another information (data/command) frame. In this sense, Token Ring is considered a deterministic type of channel access methodology. The time it will take before a given station has an opportunity to transmit can be fairly accurately calculated. (See Fig. 5-14.)

During the transmissions on the ring, a designated monitor station checks for duplicate or lost tokens. The monitor station provides timing for all devices on the ring. It is also the monitor that releases the initial token on the ring for access by all ring devices. If it does not

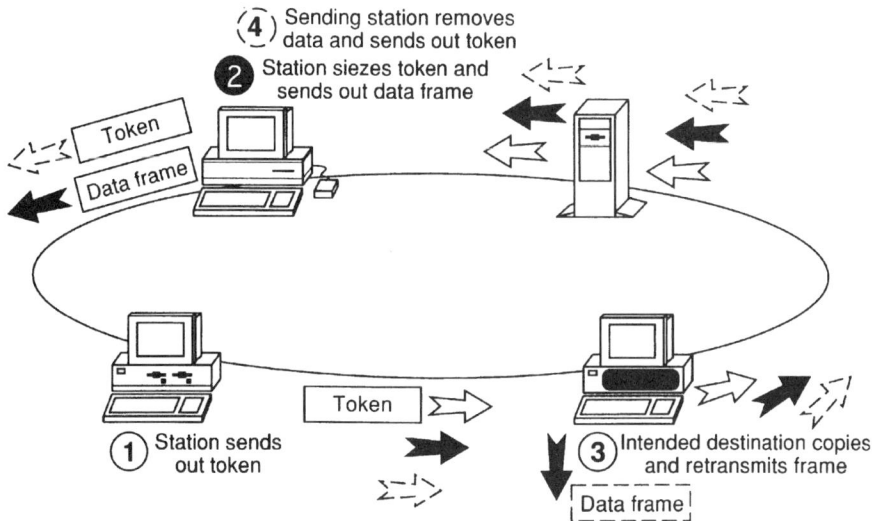

Figure 5-14

IEEE 802.5 Token Ring access. Learning Tree International

see a token frame within a predefined amount of time, it activates automatic recovery procedures. (See Fig. 5-15.)

When implementing a new network, many people are often faced with the decision of selecting between 802.3- and 802.5-based technology. Both implementations have their advantages and disadvantages.

We have reviewed above in some detail the main IEEE 802.x protocol standards in use in LAN environments today. In the following sections, we will review in summary additional IEEE protocols that are defined.

⇨ IEEE 802.6 metropolitan area network

The IEEE 802.6 subcommittee created and standardized a metropolitan area network specification named Distributed Queue Dual Bus (DQDB). DQDB uses fiber-optic technology in a dual bus topology that provides very good fault tolerance. Each bus functions in a unidirectional mode. The DQDB specification calls to dynamically allocate bandwidth through a time division multiplexing. Transmissions can be either synchronous or asynchronous, and as a result, data,

Figure 5-15

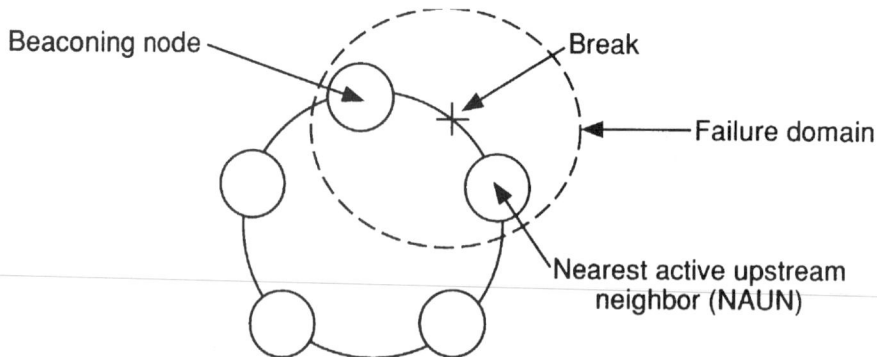

Recovery from breaks in ring. Learning Tree International

video, and voice formats are supported. The specification still remains a fairly paper-based one due to lack of vendor support and user demand. The main reason for its lack of implementation is because other technologies are more prevalent throughout the industry.

⇨ IEEE 802.7—Broadband technical advisory group

The IEEE 802.7 specification is still under development. The main goal of the subcommittee is to amalgamate the existing standards for broadband technology for use in existing networks. A key emphasis of the specification will be for the installation, maintenance, and management of broadband networks. There is a lot of activity in this area now, as cable TV companies promote using their existing broadband cable infrastructure to support computers and telephones in addition to televisions.

⇨ 802.8—Fiber-optic technical advisory group

Also still in the initial stages of development, the IEEE 802.8 goal is to review fiber-optic cable standards for 802.3, 802.4, and 802.5 networks. A standards for fiber-optic installation and training documentation is also one of this subcommittee's main objectives.

IEEE 802.9—Integrated voice and data LAN interface

IEEE 802.9 provides for integrated voice and data LAN integration for the networked workstation desktop. The main objective is to make the standard compatible with ISDN technology. Also referred to as Isochronous Ethernet or IsoEnet, it provides for a 16-Mbits/sec data rate by joining one asynchronous 10-Mbits/sec channel with one 6-Mbits/sec dedicated channel on UTP cabling. The desired end result is to have a technology standard that is designed to support both bursty and time-sensitive traffic.

IEEE 802.10—Standard for interoperable LAN security

The IEEE 802.10 subcommittee is currently developing security standards for local area networks. The main areas of emphasis are on OSI compliance for security, data transfer security, network management security, and encryption and authentication encoding methods.

IEEE 802.11—Wireless LAN

The IEEE 802.11 subcommittee is developing standards for the fast-changing wireless LAN technologies. While the CSMA/CA (collision avoidance) method for accessing the transmission medium (air) has been approved, a final specification has not been adopted.

IEEE 802.12—Demand priority

The IEEE 802.12 subcommittee is currently reviewing proposed 100-Mbits/sec standards developed by AT&T, IBM, and Hewlett-Packard known as 100VG-AnyLAN. The new standard uses a physical star topology contention-based network. However, it is different from other contention based channel access methods in that network devices will need to signal the hub before accessing the media. This scheme for media access will allow the hub to determine which transmission has the highest level of priority during occasions when multiple, simultaneous requests occur. The hub then provides the network device with the highest "demand priority" with control of the media for transmission. A very interesting aspect of the IEEE 802.12 proposal is that it will support both IEEE 802.3 (Ethernet) and IEEE 802.5 (Token Ring) frame formats.

Summary of IEEE Project 802 protocol standards

In the second section of this chapter, we have covered the range of IEEE Project 802 protocol standards. Particular emphasis and detail was given to those standards that are used and deployed throughout most office environments today. All of the popular higher layers (network layer through to application layer) use the IEEE 802.x protocol standards, which will be the focus of the following section.

Popular high-level protocol stacks

The goal of this section is to review the high-level protocol stacks or suites that are in use throughout the industry today. As we review each protocol suite, remember that each protocol within a family carries out a specific function according to the OSI reference model. While the OSI reference model defines layered functionality, the protocol stacks provide the solution to the communication problem. They facilitate the communication process according to what the OSI reference model layers state a protocol within each layer should do. It will be important to compare the OSI reference model layer functionality with the implemented protocol solution being reviewed to analyze how the protocol in question provides its services.

Finally, each major protocol stack has its own reference model that the individual protocols fit into. The reference models for some protocols do not match up nicely with the OSI reference model. The main reason for this is that some of these protocols were created in advance of the OSI reference model itself. However, the Apple Protocol stack does match up very well with the OSI reference model. Apple's protocol stack was created after the OSI reference model's draft standard had been published.

The TCP/IP protocols

The Transmission Control Protocol (TCP) and Internet Protocol (IP) are arguably the most widely used protocols throughout the world. A public-domain protocol suite, it continues to surpass proprietary vendor protocols and ISO-defined OSI protocols. TCP/IP offers true internetworking and interoperability between disparate network operating systems and host platforms. In one way or another, every major operating system supports an implementation of TCP/IP. See Fig. 5-16.

The TCP/IP suite of protocols is also very tightly integrated with the UNIX operating system. TCP/IP packet driver software has been written for almost all network interface cards (if not all of them). And finally, TCP/IP supports all major lower-layer wide area network protocols and services (i.e., X.25).

On the right-hand side of Fig. 5-17, you will notice the TCP/IP model (sometimes referred to as the Department of Defense DOD model). The TCP/IP model, when lined up with the OSI reference model, does not match the seven layers. However, the protocols that fit within each of the four TPC/IP model layers perform the functions described in each layer of the OSI reference model.

TCP/IP model

Layer 1: SubNet

The SubNet Layer protocols provide the same functionality as the OSI Physical and data link layers. Protocols in use at this layer include Ethernet, X.25 and Token Ring to name a few. The SubNet protocols were covered in the IEEE Project 802 section earlier and additional

Figure 5-16

Protocol	OSI Layer	Topics	Methods
IP Internet Protocol	Network	Addressing	Logical NetWork
		Switching	Packet
		Route Selection	Dynamic
		Connection Services	Error Control
ICMP Internet Control Message Protocol	Network	Connectoin Services	Error Control
			Network Layer Flow Control
RIP Routing Information Protocol	Network	Route Discovery	Distance Vector
OSPF Open Shortest Path First	Network	Route Discovery	Link State
TCP Transmission Control Protocol	Network	Addressing	Service
	Transport	Addressing	Connection Identifier
		Segment Development	Division and Combination
		Connection Services	Segment Sequencing
			Error Control
			End-to-end Flow Control
UDP User Datagram Protocol	Transport	Addressing	Connection Identifier
		Segment Development	Combination
		Connection Services	Connectionless
ARP Address Resolution Protocol	Network	Address Resolution	Protocol specific resolution method that is similar to Logical and Physical Addresses
DNS	Transport	Address to Name	Initiated by Service

TCP/IP Internet protocol topics and methods. Learning Tree International

Domain Name System		Resolution	Provider
FTP File Transfer Protocol	Session	Session Administration	Connection Establishment
			File Transfer
			Connection Release
	Presentation	Translation	File Syntax
	Application	Network Services	File Services
		Service Used	Collaborative
SMTP Simple Mail Transfer Protocol	Application	Network Services	Message Services
TELNET Remote Terminal Emumation Protocol	Session	Dialog Control	Half Duplex
		Session Administration	Connection Establishment
			File Transfer
			Connection Release
	Presentation	Translation	Byte Order
			Character Code
	Application	Service Used	Remote Operation
RPC Remote Procedure Call	Session	Session Administration	Connection Establishment
			File Transfer
			Connection Release
XDR External Data Representation	Presentation	Translation	Byte Order
			Character Code
			File Syntax
NFS Network File System	Application	Network Services	File Services
		Service Used	Remote Operation

Figure 5-16

Continued.

Figure 5-17

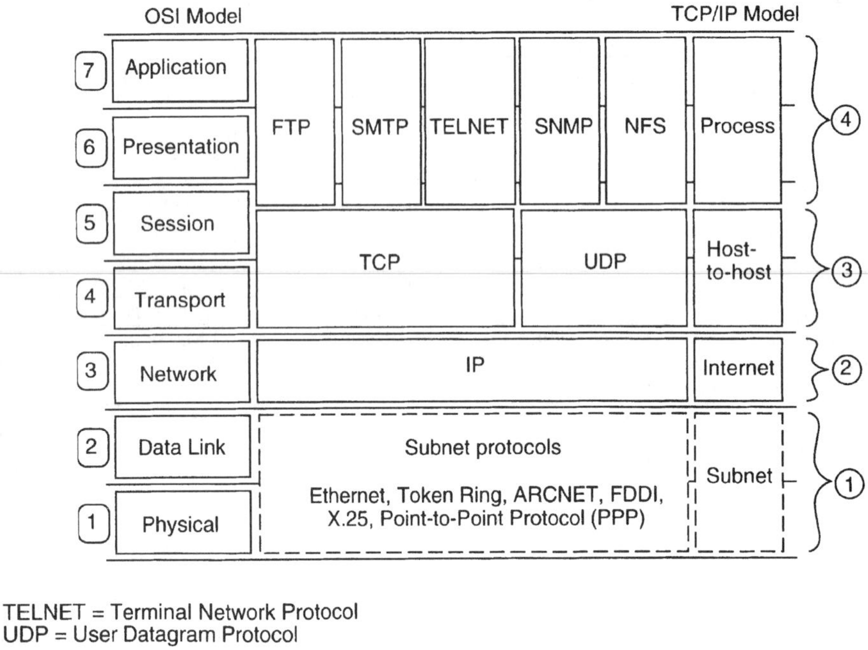

OSI Model / TCP/IP Model

TELNET = Terminal Network Protocol
UDP = User Datagram Protocol

TCP/IP protocol suite. Learning Tree International

protocols like X.25 that TCP/IP supports will be covered at the end of this chapter.

⇨ Layer 2: Internet

The Internet Layer protocols provide the same functionality as the OSI network layer. Implementation of IP, ICMP, RIP, OSPF, and ARP occur at this layer.

⇨ Layer 3: Host-to-host

The Host-to-Host Layer protocols provide the same functions as the OSI transport layer and some functions of the session layer. TCP, UDP and DNS are the main protocols implemented at this layer.

⇨ Layer 4: Process/application

The process/application layer provides the same functions as some of the session layer, and predominantly those functions at the presentation and application layers. Protocols implemented at the process/application layer include FTP, NFS, SMTP, Telnet, SNMP, and NFS.

TCP and IP are regarded as protocols that provide Internetwork functionality. IP has become the *de facto* standard for routing of packets in network environments both large and small, but IP excels in large networks. IP defines the composition of the network layer packet, services, and networkwide addressing. The IP packet's protocol data unit is TCP or UDP.

TCP provides for reliable, connection-oriented communications between networking devices. IP packets, once sent, do not check to verify that the packet reached its intended destination. It's the responsibility of the TCP protocol to provide for more reliable transmission over IP networks. Some communication services, however, do not require reliable end-to-end transmissions because the higher-level information is not crucial in nature, or it can always be retransmitted at a later time. User Datagram Protocol (UDP) provides connectionless transmission of data. Domain Name Service (DNS) is a distributed database service that provides IP address to host name resolution for client applications.

Additional higher-level protocols provide application-based services. The application-based services allow for interoperability between network devices. Briefly, the upper-layer protocols providing interoperability between network devices include File Transfer Protocol (FTP, Simple Mail Transfer Protocol (SMTP), Telnet, Simple Network Management Protocol, Network File System (NFS), External Data Representation (XDR), and Remote Procedure Call (RPC). These protocols will be individually reviewed later in this chapter.

⇨ TCP/IP Protocol suite definitions

⇨ Network layer protocols

✳ Internet Protocol (IP)

The IP protocol works at the network layer and, as such, defines the composition or structure of the packet (or commonly referred to as datagram in the UNIX environment). The Internet Protocol provides connectionless delivery of packets in that the protocol does not establish a connection with the destination network device before transmitting packets to it. The connectionless delivery of packets or datagrams is sometimes referred to as a "best-efforts" service, or it is compared to the postal system for delivering the mail. The routing function uses packet switching to route packets throughout the Internetwork. IP packets can also be fragmented into smaller portions and reassembled at the remote destination host. Every IP packet has a header and is the protocol data unit of the data link layer frame.

As highlighted in Fig. 5-18, the IP packet is composed of a number of fields. The Version field identifies the revision of IP protocol being used. The Type of Service field designates how a datagram is to be handled (slow, fast, high reliability). The Length field value is the entire length of the packet including IP header information. Flags are used to indicate whether the packet can be fragmented or not. The Time to Live counter ensures that packets do not travel endlessly around the Internetwork. The Protocol field indicates what transport-layer protocol process (port or socket) is to receive the protocol data unit (TCP or UDP). The Header Checksum is an error check for the IP header only and is recomputed after each hop, since it might change. Source and Destination Addresses are the 32-bit IP network address fields. Finally, Options is a variable-sized field to support additional capabilities like source routing.

Several routes are potentially available for the packet to be routed or switched through. IP will always try to choose the best route or available path. In order to facilitate this process, IP routers make

Figure 5-18

```
            Frame
        Ethernet
         header                                        Packet
                            ──32 bits──
   ┌──────────┬──────┬──────────────┬──────────────────────────┐
   │ Version  │ IHL  │ Type of service │      Total length        │
   ├──────────┴──────┴──────────┬────┬────┬────────────────────┤
   │       Identification        │ D  │ M  │  Fragment offset    │
   │                             │ F  │ F  │                     │
   ├─────────────────┬───────────┴────┴────┴────────────────────┤
   │   Time to live  │  Protocol   │      Header checksum         │
   ├─────────────────┴────────────────────────────────────────┤
   │                      Source address                        │
   ├────────────────────────────────────────────────────────────┤
   │                    Destination address                     │
   ├────────────────────────────────────────────────────────────┤
   │                    Options and padding                     │
   ├────────────────────────────────────────────────────────────┤
   │                    Data (variable field)                   │
   └────────────────────────────────────────────────────────────┘

        Ethernet
          CRC
```

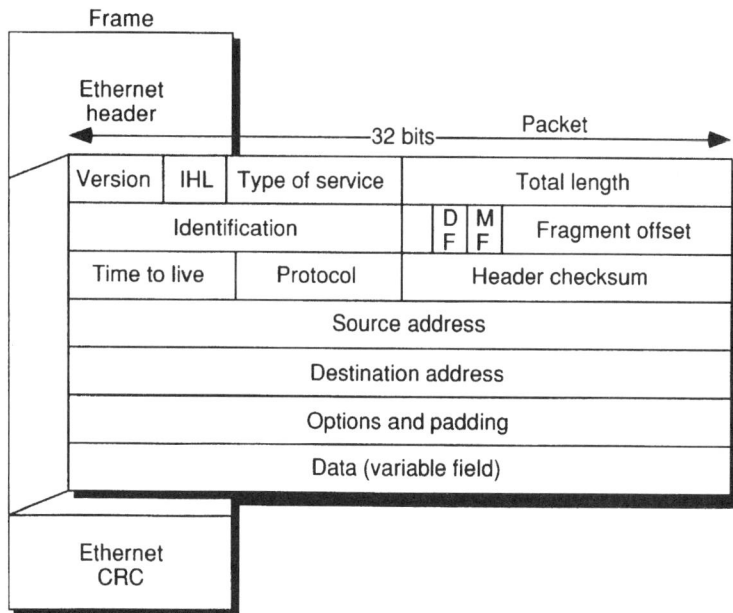

IHL = Internet header length

IP packet structure. Learning Tree International

independent routing decisions. Using additional network layer protocols, the routers keep each other informed of the status of each connected logical network and the number of hops required to reach them. Routing tables are continually updated to ensure that available paths are kept current.

Finally, IP defines a networkwide logical addressing scheme. The network address numbers are maintained by the network administrator. This logical address uniquely identifies the host network device and the network that the device resides on. An isolated network might use any range of network and host device addresses that the network administrator chooses. However, when a network or host is connected to the worldwide Internet, specifically assigned network addresses must be used. Internet addresses are assigned by the Internet Activities Board. (See Fig. 5-19.)

Figure 5-19

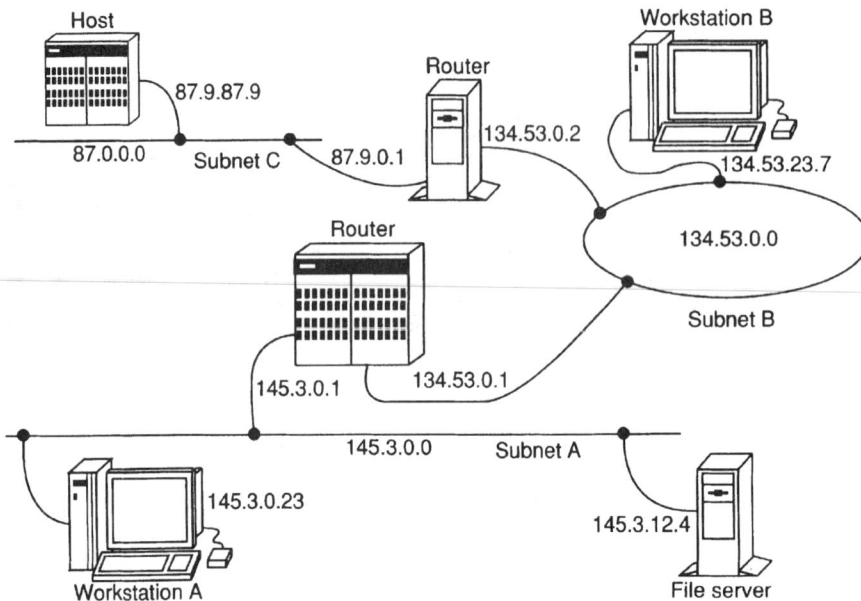

IP addressing assignment example. Learning Tree International

IP uses three main classes of addressing, Class A, Class B, and Class C. A Class D and Class E are also available but are reserved by IAB for future use. IP addresses can also be subnetted for even further network addressing flexibility. (See Fig. 5-20.)

Additional Internet protocols implemented at the network layer are Routing Information Protocol (RIP) or Open Shortest Path First (OSPF), Internet Control Message Protocol (ICMP), and Address Resolution Protocol (ARP).

✳ Routing Information Protocol (RIP)

RIP is a distance vector route discovery protocol used to advertise what networks can be reached by a router and at what cost. RIP broadcasts are periodically sent out to advertise their routing tables throughout the network. The broadcast routing tables include information on the destination networks and their distances from the transmitting router in terms of the number of routers (hops) that must

Figure 5-20

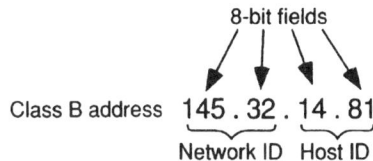

0   31

Class A | 0 | Network ID | Host ID
                7 bits   24 bits

Class B | 1 | 0 | Network ID | Host ID
                    14 bits   16 bits

Class C | 1 | 1 | 0 | Network ID | Host ID
                        21 bits   8 bits

Example dotted decimal notation:

8-bit fields

Class B address 145 . 32 . 14 . 81
                 Network ID   Host ID

IP addressing. Learning Tree International

be crossed. While it performs its job sufficiently, RIP has a number of setbacks, in particular in large, complex internetworks.

✳ Open Shortest Path First (OSPF)

OSPF is a link-state route discovery protocol that was designed to address some of the weaknesses or limitations of RIP. One of the major benefits of OSPF over RIP is that routing table updates do not need to occur as frequently, reducing the overhead traffic created to maintain network routing information. With a link-state discovery protocol, routing information is only transmitted on an as-needed basis or at a preconfigured interval of time, usually every two hours. Additional OSPF features include load balancing and class-of-service-based routing. Load balancing allows multiple network interface cards to be directly connected to the same hub service devices on the same logical network. Class-of-service-based routing allows routing decisions to be made depending on the type of network service required. There is no doubt that OSPF will eventually replace RIP as the routing protocol of choice.

※ **Internet Control Message Protocol (ICMP)**

ICMP is used by routers to provide error and flow control information. One very common use of ICMP is the "ping" protocol, which employs an "echo request" ICMP message. Although ICMP does not make IP more reliable as a protocol, it does make it more efficient by making better paths available for routing of packets.

⇨ Host-to-host layer protocols

※ **Transmission Control Protocol (TCP)**

The TCP protocol is a connection-oriented protocol. Unlike IP, in order for TCP protocol data units to be delivered to a remote network device, a connection must first be established between it and the transmitting device. As such, TCP compensates for the connectionless unreliability of the lower-layer IP protocol. It uses full-duplex communications, acknowledgments and flow control to accomplish this. TCP also is responsible for accepting messages for the upper process/application-layer protocols (Telnet, SMTP, FTP) and can support numerous simultaneous conversations between these processes (see Fig. 5-21). TCP protocol data units are sent as a continuous, unstructured byte stream.

The TCP protocol data unit also has many fields like IP. The Source Port is a 16-bit field designating which process (FTP, Telnet, etc.,) in the host device initiated the message. Each of these processes have well-known port numbers. If you have access to a UNIX host, these numbers are displayed in the SERVICES file located in the ETC directory. The Destination Port is the port number of the communicating process on the receiving device. The Sequence Number is used by TCP for fragmentation and reassembly of the byte stream. Acknowledgment Number is the sequence number of the next TCP message the sender expects to receive. Data Offset is the length of the TCP header in 32-bit words. Flags are used by TCP for control messages and indicate, like IP's Type of Service, the type of

Frame

Figure 5-21

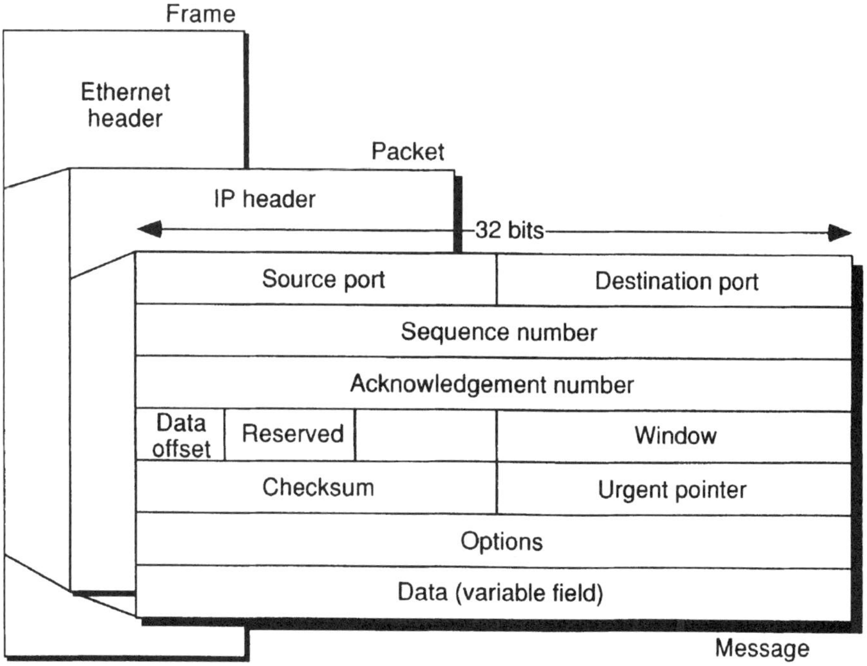

TCP protocol data unit structure. Learning Tree International

processing the TCP protocol data unit requires. The Windows field is used for TCP's sliding flow control protocol data unit transmission service. Options provide for the capability to support special functions such as the maximum TCP segment size. The Data field contains the upper-layer protocol data unit.

✳ User Datagram Protocol (UDP)

Some process/application-layer protocols do not require the reliability that TCP provides and can be handled by a host-to-host protocol that has less connectivity overhead associated with it. User Datagram Protocol (UDP) provides this service. It is a connectionless-oriented protocol (it does not require a connection to the remote host before transmitting) and does not acknowledge receipt of protocol data units sent. The protocol, while functioning on a network device, simply sends and receives packets as required. Rather than establishing a virtual circuit connection between two network devices, a port is set up as a pointer to a local running process. Because UDP does not require the overhead associated with establishing remote connections before transmission, and ensuring reliable delivery, it is usually faster than TCP.

❋ Domain Name Service (DNS)

The last host-to-host layer protocol is Domain Name Service. DNS servers on the network maintain a hierarchical naming convention and structure through a distributed database system. DNS allows IP network addresses that computers understand to be mapped to host names that humans understand.

⇨ Process/application layer protocols

❋ File Transfer Protocol (FTP)

File Transfer Protocol is a process protocol that enables users on one host to copy (move) a file to another host. The really neat aspect of FTP is that it provides for transparent interoperability between different host operating environments. FTP, when implemented, looks the same to all users, regardless of the workstation operating system they are using. The same FTP command set is available to each user.

To access the remote file system, the user must have established a user login account on the remote system and be provided with the account's password. The account determines which areas of the file system the user can see and whether the user can upload files to the remote system. A low level of remote system access is also provided through the Trivial File Transfer Protocol (TFTP). TFTP is like a read-only access level to the remote file system so that users can copy files to their own local file systems.

❋ Simple Mail Transfer Protocol (SMTP)

Simple Mail Transfer Protocol is probably the most widely used protocol in the world, given the daily electronic mail traffic that takes place each day on the Internet. SMTP is the electronic mail workhorse used between network hosts. Although users access an electronic mail front-end application, it is SMTP that shuttles (routes) the mail around the Internet from host to host until it reaches its final destination. Despite what most people think, SMTP requires the reliability and connection-oriented TCP protocol to deliver the mail. A review of message switching in chapter 2 will highlight why this is the case. Essentially, a connection is established between intermediate hosts as mail is routed to its final destination, which could be several hosts away. However, for the period of time that mail is transferred from one host to another during its journey, a reliable connection is established to ensure that the mail message is delivered successfully, in its entirety to that host. This host in turn establishes a reliable end-to-end connection to the next host that mail must be routed to.

✳ Remote terminal emulation (Telnet)

Remote Terminal Emulation allows users to access terminal/host centralized computing system applications on the network. The original terminals were "dumb" in that they did not have any local centralized processing unit (CPU) and relied on the host to provide all application computer processing. Today, personal computers emulate terminals to connect to centralized host computers. Telnet provides connectivity to host systems by allowing the user to login to and run applications. In this sense, Telnet provides some degree of interoperability. However, the personal computer must emulate the terminal type that the host supports, and the session does not appear simply as an extension of the native operating system. As such, a Telnet session to a DEC VAX system is not the same as a Telnet session to an IBM mainframe system.

✳ Simple Network Management Protocol (SNMP)

Simple Network Management Protocol specifies the communications between network listening agents and network management systems. *Agents* are devices that sit out on a network and collect information on the health of the network. *Network management stations* collect information from agents and allow network management staff to better maintain network operations and availability. While SNMP is the protocol used to communicate between agents and network management stations, information statistics are collected in a management information base (MIB) on the agent for forwarding to the network station.

✳ Network File System (NFS)

The Network File System was developed by SUN Microsystems. NFS is most often associated with SUN's suite of protocols that make up Open Network Computing (ONC). Although the protocol was originally developed by SUN, it was released into the public domain, an event that helped promote and solidify its position in the computing industry. The three ONC protocols that are used most often are NFS, XDR, and RPC. All three protocols work together to provide true interoperability between dissimilar host operating and file systems. Once the system is set up, the local user sees the remote file system as an extension of itself. For example, a DOS-based personal computer with NFS would see a UNIX host file system as just another DOS drive letter to be accessed.

Having stated that NFS provides great interoperability features, one must be aware that it does not automatically convert the underlying file formats to that of the local operating system. If the same DOS user described previously copies a text file created by a UNIX user down to his or her local file system, the DOS user will still need to run a conversion utility to put the file into a format that the user can work with locally.

✳ External Data Representation (XDR)

External Data Representation is a group of "C" programming language routines that allow for machine-independent description and encoding (formatting) of data. The "C" programming routines allow a programmer to describe various data structures. TCP's XDR is similar to OSI's ASN.1 protocol (see OSI protocol suite later in this chapter).

✳ Remote Procedure Call (RPC)

A Remote Procedure Call allows a programmer to request services regardless of the type of underlying operating and file system. This simplifies the process of sending and receiving files from dissimilar host machines. A redirector or shell filters calls made by a host process. Local calls are passed on to the local operating system for execution. Remote calls are forwarded via TCP/IP for remote execution.

Many network operating systems use RPCs. Novell NetWare, Banyan Vines, Microsoft's LAN Manager, and Windows NT Server all use a form of RPC. However, not all RPCs are compatible with each other.

✳ TCP/IP protocol suite multiplexing

Earlier we stated that TCP receives messages from upper-layer protocols like Telnet, FTP, and SMTP. TCP can also process multiple, simultaneous conversations with these upper-layer protocols as it encapsulates their requests with a TCP header into an IP packet. Figure 5-22 demonstrates this process quite well. In it you can see multiple process/application-layer processes interfacing with the host-to-host TCP and UDP protocols, and finally, how these protocols are placed inside an IP packet.

⇨ Novell's NetWare protocols

Novell is currently the market leader in the local area network field. Since the early 1980s, NetWare's network operating systems have been the backbone for interconnecting personal computer workstations in many office environments. Although the market share number varies greatly depending on which NOS competitor you talk to, it is generally agreed that NetWare has over 50%. Its success in the market has also created a very extensive, installed base of compatible third-party software and hardware products and a large force of trained technical people. The first popular version of NetWare started

Figure 5-22

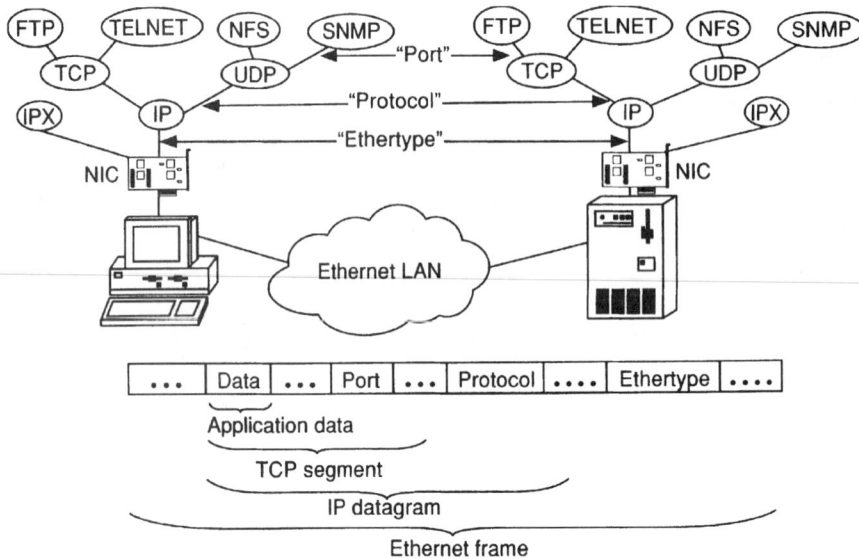

TCP/IP multiplexing. Learning Tree International

with NetWare v2.0 and has since moved on through versions v3.x and v4.x. And Novell has a reputation for improving on the core NOS with each new revision or upgrade. NetWare supports large disk drive storage capacities into the gigabyte range. NetWare Directory Services, a distributed network database management directory based on X.500, was implemented with NetWare 4. Figure 5-23 links the topics and methods implemented through the NetWare protocols suite.

The NetWare Operating System is a client/server implementation (see chapter 1). NetWare is also commonly referred to as a file-server-based system because the main service it provides is remote file system support. (Novell also has a peer-to-peer NOS called Personal NetWare.) The two core services the NOS provides are file and printer sharing. Novell has long stated that its main goal is for NetWare to be the backbone of an organization's networking environment, gluing together all the dissimilar platforms. Through its NOS's communication services, it provides connectivity to other types of networks and host operating systems, including DOS, UNIX, Windows NT, MacIntosh, OS/2, and more. Given Novell's market dominance, as new host operating systems are created (Windows 95), LAN driver software is created to facilitate access to the NetWare services.

Figure 5-23

Protocol	OSI Layer	Topics	Methods
MLID Multiple Link Interface Driver	Data Link MAC	Media Access	Contention Token Passing Polling
LSL Link Support Layer	Data Link LLC	Protocol Specific	Interface between MLID and upper layer protocols
IPX Internetwork Packet Exchange Protocol	Network	Addressing	Logical Network Service
		Route Selection	Dynamic
		Connection Services	Connectionless
RIP Routing Information Protocol	Network	Route Discovery	Distance Vector
NLSP NetWare Link Services Protocol	Network	Route Discovery	Link State
SPX Sequenced Packet Exchange Protocol	Transport	Addressing	Connection Identifier
		Segment Development	Division and Combination
		Connection Services	Segment Sequencing Error Control End-to-end Flow Control
NCP NetWare Core Protocols	Transport	Connection Services	Segment Sequencing Error Control End-to-end Flow Control
	Session	Session Administration	Data Transfer
	Presentation	Translation	Character Code File Syntax

NetWare protocol topics and methods. Learning Tree International

Figure 5-23

	Application	Service Used	OS Redirector Collaborative (depends on client redirector or requestor)
SAP Service Advertising Protocol	Session	Session Administration	File Transfer
	Application	Service Advertisement	Active

Continued.

The NetWare suite of protocols is based on the Xerox Network System (XNS) protocols that were developed in the 1960s at its Palo Alto Research Center (PARC). Banyan Vines, 3Com Open, and Ungermann-Bass are examples of other networking operating systems that use XNS as a basis for their development. As with the TCP/IP protocol stack, NetWare's protocols do not match up exactly beside the seven-layer OSI reference model. Figure 5-24 details NetWare's various protocols and their mapping to the OSI reference model layers based on the functionality that each protocol provides. However, even though protocols like NetWare's don't link up directly with each layer, the task that the protocols must accomplish is similar to all networking systems—access to file and print services on a remote host.

The main protocols NetWare implements are Internet Packet Exchange (IPX), Sequenced Packet Exchange (SPX), and NetWare Core Protocol (NCP). IPX and SPX provide the internetworking capabilities for NetWare network devices and function at the Network and transport layers respectively. The session-, presentation-, and application-layer functionality is provided by the NCP protocol. Through NCP, client network devices access NetWare NOS file and print services. A protocol that emulates the Network Basic Input Output System (NetBIOS) protocol is also provided but is not required for core communications between the NetWare servers and clients. NetBIOS provides similar services to NCP.

Figure 5-24

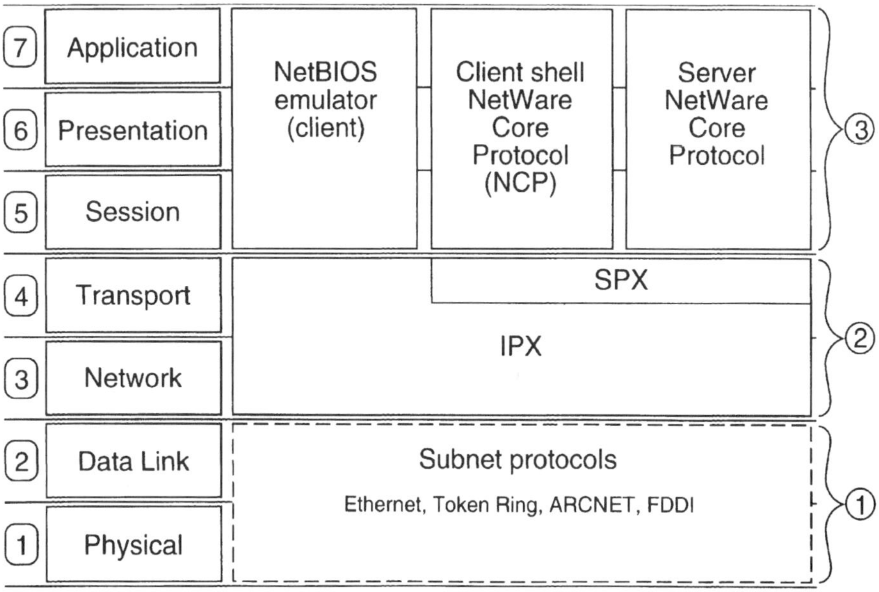

The NetWare protocols. Learning Tree International

NetWare protocol suite definitions

Multiple Link Interface Driver (MLID)

MLID is the software component that Novell defines as a component of the Open Data Link Interface (ODI) specification. This piece of software is a link between the client workstation operating system and the workstation network interface card. It tells the workstation operating system that the network interface card is located at a specific hardware location. The MLID driver also specifies which frame structures the MAC component of the data link layer the client workstation will support. The OSI reference model defined what the functionality is for the data link layer MAC component. The MLID software driver implements, or is the solution to, that functionality.

While it is not part of the actual protocol stack, the MLID software driver plays an important role in moving the bit stream up and down the NetWare protocol stack. Novell has made the ODI specification open to all manufacturers of network interface cards, and it is the manufacturer's responsibility to create the MLID driver software for its network interface card hardware.

The main purpose of the ODI specification is to allow one network interface card to support multiple data link layer frame structures— (IEEE 802.2, 802.3)—and upper layer protocols—(IPX/SPX, TCP/IP)—simultaneously.

⇨ Link support layer (LSL)

LSL also works at the data link layer and performs the functionality described under the LSL component of the data link layer of the OSI reference model. The LSL software is a link or interface between the MLID and the NetWare protocol stack. The main function of LSL is defined under the IEEE 802.2 protocol standard and provides upper-layer protocol multiplexing. Novell's LSL is responsible for receiving the packet protocol data unit from the frame and forwarding it up to the appropriate upper-layer protocol stack.

⇨ Main NetWare protocols

❊ Internetwork Packet eXchange Protocol (IPX)

Functioning at the network layer of the OSI reference model, IPX is a connectionless network protocol. It is proprietary to Novell and is a subset of the Xerox XNS specification. IPX performs routing of packets based on routing table information maintained via the Router Information Protocol (RIP) (see below). IPX also provides a networkwide addressing scheme. The IPX packet is the protocol data unit of the data link layer frame, and the IPX header immediately follows the frame header information. An IPX packet contains 10 control fields, plus 1 data field for a total of 11 fields. (See Fig. 5-25.)

The first field is always a 16-bit field with each bit value being a 1. This translates to a hex value of FFFF and is called a check sum. The

Frame

Figure 5-25

	IPX packet

Checksum (2 bytes)	FF FF
Length (2 bytes)	00 28
Transport control (1 byte)	00
Packet type (1 byte)	01
Destination network address (4 bytes)	00 00 00 00
Destination node address (6 bytes)	FF FF FF FF FF FF
Destination socket (2 bytes)	04 03
Source network address (4 bytes)	AB 01 01 01
Source node address (6 bytes)	00 00 1B 09 08 07
Source socket (2 bytes)	40 03

Ethernet header

Data

Ethernet CRC

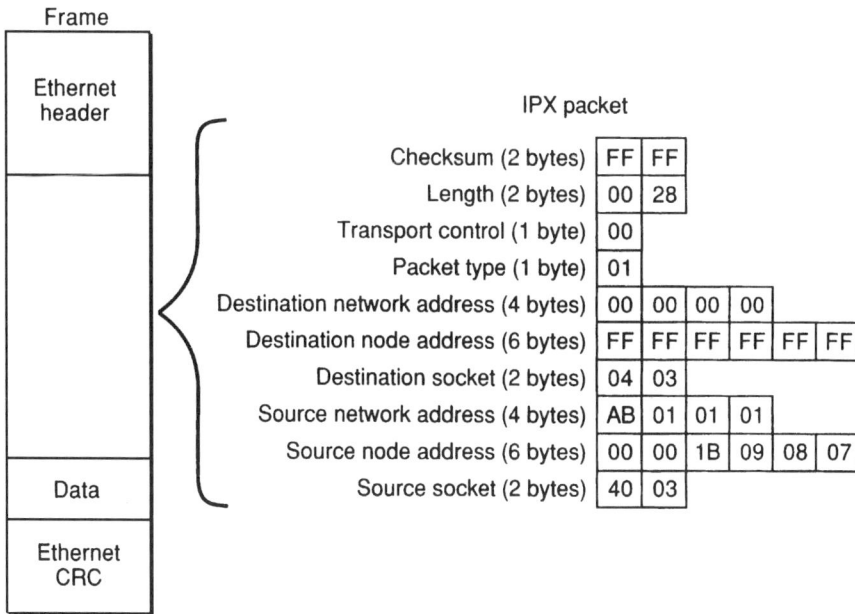

IPX packet protocol structure. Learning Tree International

Length field denotes the entire length of the IPX packet. The minimum field length is 30, and the maximum is determined by the link support layer (1518 bytes for IEEE 802.2 and 4096 bytes for IEEE 802.5). The Transport Control field value is incremented each time a packet is processed by a router. The Packet Type field is a 1-byte field giving the type of upper-layer protocol that the packet is carrying. Example upper-layer protocols include SPX and NCP. Destination and Source Network Address fields are each 32 bits in length (8-character hex fields) and assigned by the network administrator (similar to IP addressing but using a different format). The IPX address is the logical network address assigned to a cabling segment. The destination and source host addresses are the actual network interface card physical addresses burnt into the ROM. Destination and source sockets are similar to TCP/IP's port addressing scheme. The sockets denote which upper-layer process should receive the protocol data unit. Novell assigns socket numbers, and example sockets are 0452h for Service Advertising Protocol (SAP) and 0452h for NetWare Router Information Protocol (RIP). The data field is the protocol data unit of the upper-layer protocol.

※ **Sequenced Packet eXchange (SPX)**

SPX is Novell's proprietary transport layer protocol. It is a connection oriented packet delivery service and functions similar to TCP. SPX was derived from the Xerox Sequenced Packet (XSP) protocol. The protocol performs flow control, sequencing, and acknowledgment of packets. Not all client/server services provided by a NetWare server require SPX, and this is why it does not cross the entire stack, as highlighted in Fig. 5-26. Two main applications that require the reliability of SPX communications are Rconsole for remote file server console support, Rprinter for remote network printers connected to workstations, and SNA Gateway services for mainframe host communications.

Figure 5-26

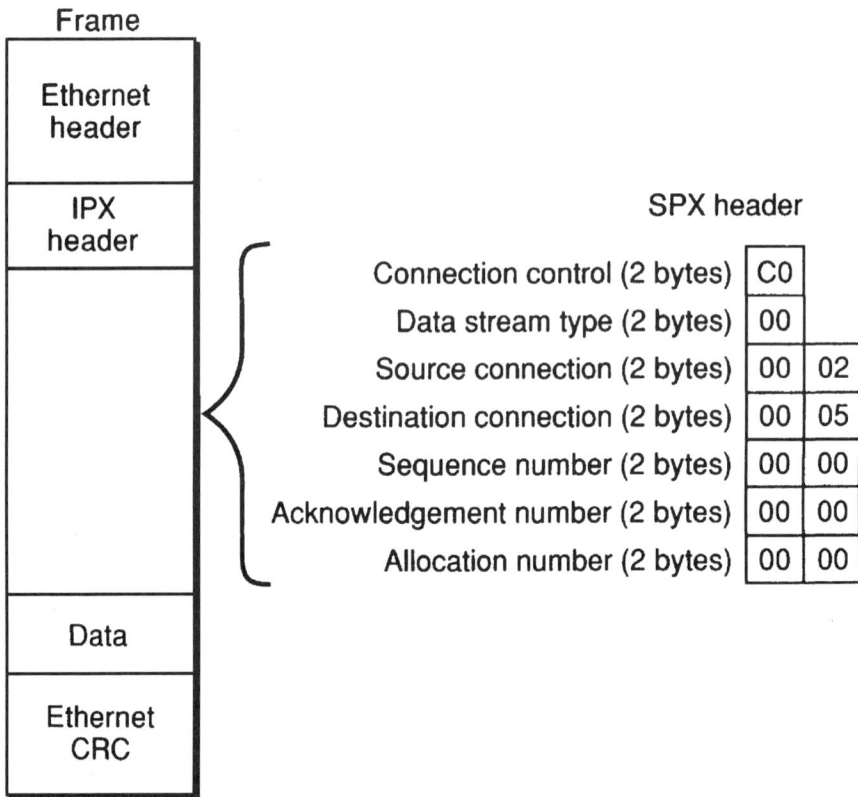

SPX protocol header structure. Learning Tree International

✳ **NetWare Core Protocol (NCP)**

NCP is the protocol that provides the interoperability within a NetWare network. The main function of NCP is to provide file and print service access by client workstations. In addition to this, it also manages file and record locking, security, and network file server access. Workstation or network devices use redirector or requester (shell) software that make the file server services appear as a transparent extension of the local operating system. NCP calls are made by the NetWare (shell). NCP calls are proprietary to Novell. (See Fig. 5-27.)

Figure 5-27

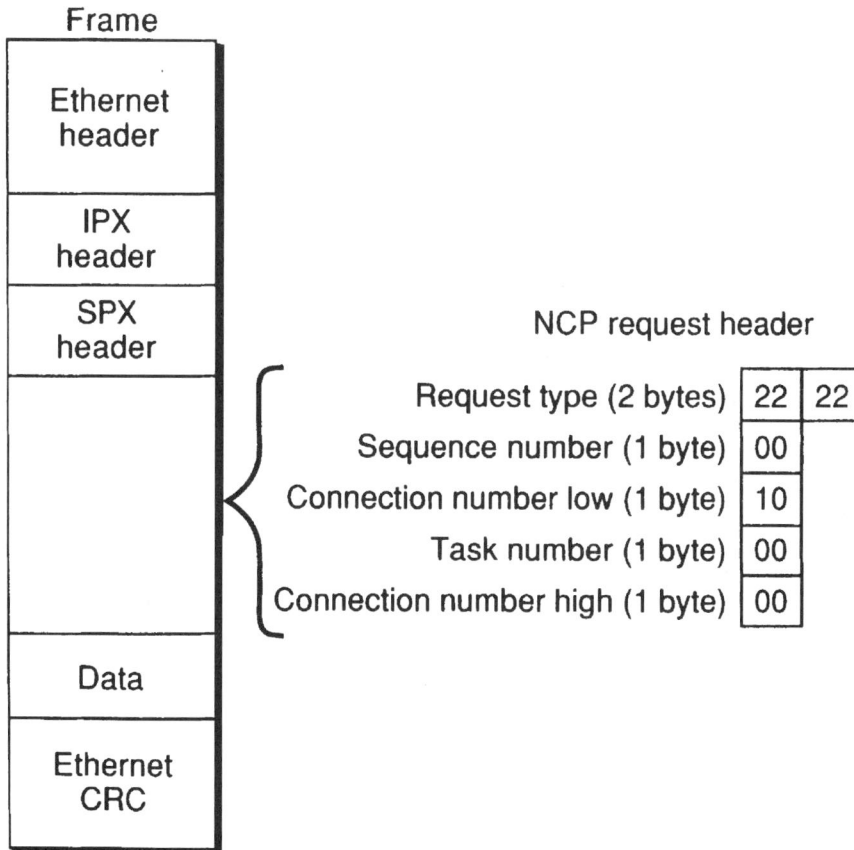

NCP header structure. Learning Tree International

⇨ Additional NetWare protocols

❋ Router Information Protocol (RIP)

Similar to TCP/IP's RIP, NetWare RIP was derived from XNS's Internetwork Datagram Protocol (IDP). RIP is a distance vector based routing protocol that uses hop counts to assign a cost to network routes. The protocol functions at the network layer and is assigned its own unique socket number.

❋ NetWare Link Services Protocol (NLSP)

NLSP is a link-state route discovery protocol and is based on the ISO's Intermediate System to Intermediate System (IS-IS) protocol standard. NLSP provides better router information update processes and supports the more reliable mesh and hybrid mesh network topologies. NLSP will no doubt replace NetWare's RIP as the router information protocol of choice.

❋ Service Advertising Protocol (SAP)

SAPs are the services that network servers provide. Although the main services are file and print, many other server services are available, such as database, communication, and mail delivery. SAP is used to advertise the services available on servers to other servers, and sometimes clients, on the network. Services information is maintained in SAP tables on each server. SAPs are broadcast every 60 seconds and can, in large networks with many services, cause a lot of traffic on the network. NLSP also incorporates SAP information and reduces the frequency of these broadcasts.

❋ Network Basic Input Output System (NetBIOS)

NetBIOS is a protocol that emulates the standard NetBIOS and provides some, but not all, of the specifications services. The main benefit of using Novell's NetBIOS in a NetWare environment is that the NetBIOS messages can be encapsulated inside IPX packets. The disadvantage is that NetWare does not support all of the NetBIOS functions.

⁕ **International Business Machines' System Network Architecture (SNA) protocol**

SNA is IBM's proprietary networking architecture. Introduced in 1974, it is one of the most widely used commercial networking architecture schemes. The main purpose of SNA is to provide 3270-type terminals with access to IBM's family of mainframe systems. The terminals allow users to access applications, files, and printing services running on the centralized host. These sessions are referred to as 3270 data streams. Terminal traffic is synchronous and employs the Synchronous Data Link Control protocol. Figure 5-28 highlights the SNA topics and methods.

⇨ SNA protocols topics and methods

While initially a terminal/host-based architecture, recent advances in the protocol have implemented host-to-host and peer-to-peer application development. The new version, released in 1984, supports internetworking, distributed processing, and network management capability. In 1987, IBM produced the Systems Application Architecture (SAA) as its future networking platform. Although SAA has many sought-after features, IBM's large base of clients and SNA installations will be around for some time to come. Figure 5-29 compares the OSI reference model with IBM's SNA reference model.

Physical and data link layers specify the electrical, cabling, and framing characteristics of the network. SNA uses two types of data link layer protocols—SDLC and 802.5 with 802.2 LLC. Some older system might still be using IBM's original Token Ring frame structure, so it is important to be aware of this when integrating newer PC-based systems on the same network.

Figure 5-28

Protocols	OSI Layer	Topics	Methods
Token Ring	Physical	Connection Types	Point-to-Point
		Physical Topology	Star
		Digital Signaling	State Transition
		Bit Synchronization	Synchronous
		Bandwidth Used	Baseband
	Data Link MAC	Logical Topology	Ring
		Media Access	Token Passing
		Addressing	Physical Device
SDLC Synchronous Data Link Control	Data Link MAC	Media Access	Polling
		Addressing	Physical Device
	Data Link LLC	Transmission Synchronization	Synchronous
		Connection Services	Flow Control
			Error Control
NCP Network Control Program	Data Link MAC	Media Access	Polling
		Addressing	Physical Device
	Data Link LLC	Connection Services	Flow Control
	Network	Addressing	Logical Network
		Route Selection	Static
		Gateway services	Network Layer Translation
VTAM Virtual Telecommunications Access Method	Transport	Addressing	Connection Identifier
		Segment Development	Division and Combination
		Connection Services	End-to-End Flow Control
	Session	Dialog Control	Half Duplex
		Session Administration	Connection Establishment
			Data Transfer
			Connection Release
APPN (PU 2.1) Advanced Peer-to-Peer Networking	Network	Addressing	Logical Network
		Route Discovery	Dynamic
	Transport	Connection Services	Segment Sequencing

SNA protocol topics and methods. Learning Tree International

Figure 5-28

			End-to-End Flow Control
CICS - Customer Information Control System	Session	Dialog Control	Half Duplex
		Session Administration	Connection Establishment
			Data Transfer
			Connection Release
	Presentation	Translation	File Syntax
IMS - Information Management System	Session	Dialog Control	Half Duplex
		Session Administration	Connection Establishment
			Data Transfer
			Connection Release
	Presentation	Translation	File Syntax
APPC (LU 6.2)	Transport	Addressing	Connection Identifier
Advanced Program-to-Program Communications		Connection Services	Segment Sequencing
			End-to-End Flow Control
	Session	Dialog Control	Half Duplex
		Session Administration	Connection Establishment
			Data Transfer
			Connection Release
DDM Distributed Data Management	Application	Network Services	File
		Services Used	OS Call Interception
SNADS - SNA Distribution Services	Application	Network Services	File Message
DIA - Document Interchange Architecture	Application	Network Services	File

Continued.

Figure 5-28

Network Virtual Terminal Service			(commands)
	Application	Network Service	Terminal Service
		Service Used	Remote Operation
MAILbus and X.400	Application	Network Service	Message Service
Naming Service and X.500	Transport	Address and Name Resolution	Service Provider Initiated
	Application	Network Service	Directory Service

Continued.

Figure 5-29

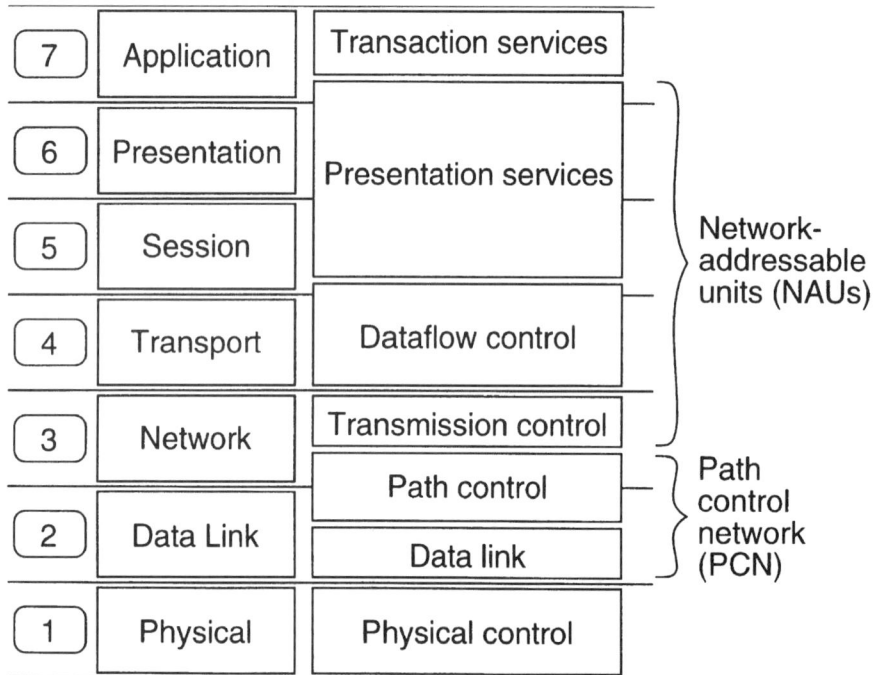

7	Application	Transaction services	
6	Presentation	Presentation services	Network-addressable units (NAUs)
5	Session		
4	Transport	Dataflow control	
3	Network	Transmission control	
		Path control	Path control network (PCN)
2	Data Link	Data link	
1	Physical	Physical control	

SNA reference model. Learning Tree International

The data link and path control layers formulate what is referred to as the Path Control Network (PCN). The upper layers make up actual network addressable units (NAUs).

The path control layer also includes some functions from the data link layer and is responsible for creating a hierarchical network layout. Path control provides routing, segmentation, and data link control. All of these functions are embodied in the network control program, which runs on a front-end processor (FEP) or possibly on the host itself.

Network addressable units (NAUs) are endpoints of sessions and the services supporting the sessions. Each communicating entity at the endpoints of a session must have a unique address. The presentation, data flow control, and transmission control functions support session communications. These functions are embodied in the Virtual Telecommunications Access Method (VTAM) program and typically reside or run on the host.

Transmission control ensures reliable end-to-end connection services like the transport layer. This layer also provides data encryption and decryption functions, a service normally provided by presentation-layer protocols.

The data flow control layer maps to the OSI session layer and controls request and response processing, groups messages together, assigns priority for data transmissions, and stops data flow when required.

Presentation services specify data translation algorithms, which is the main function provided by the OSI presentation layer. However, presentation services also manage resources sharing and synchronize operations.

Transaction services perform similar functions to OSI's application layer. Application services are provided to implement distributed processing, network management, and application access. SNA distribution services (SNADS) is an example of this type of service. SNADS provides distribution services for application use.

⇨ SNA components

SNA networks are set up hierarchically in a tree structure. Three main components make up the network: systems services control point (SSCP), physical units (PUs), and logical units (LUs). All of these components are NAUs.

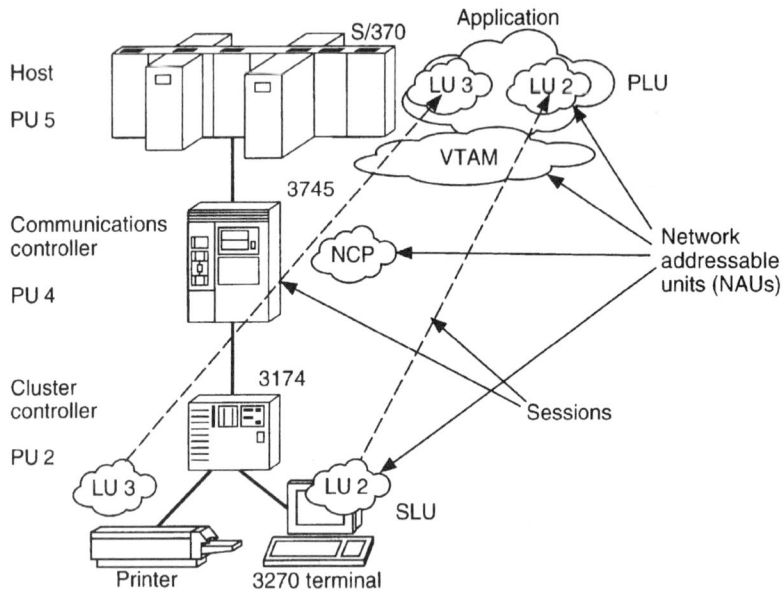

SNA network. Learning Tree International

SNA networks can be made up of several domains. Each domain originates from a systems services control point. The SSCP controls the flow of all network traffic and requests. The SSCP also keeps track of all the network addressable units in an SNA network. SSCP is also often referred to as a control point. SSCP manages the routing and activation of sessions. Session types include SSCP-SSCP, SSCP-PU, and SSCP to LU.

The physical unit is a combination of software and hardware that manage node resources. A PU can be a host (PU5), a communications controller (PU4), or a cluster controller (PU2) that manages the physical terminal or node hardware. The following list highlights PU types.

PU type	Comment
1.0	terminal nodes
2.0	terminals, printers, cluster controllers
2.1	minicomputers, cluster controllers, gateway devices that communicate with a host of other PU Type 2.1 devices
4.0	communication controllers that link hosts and cluster controllers with other PU Type 2 devices
5.0	host computers

The logical unit is a logical network connection, and sessions are established between LUs. Figure 5-30 demonstrates the LU-to-LU connection session between the terminal and the application running on the host. The following list highlights the many LU types.

LU type	Communication	Comment
0	Program to program	general-purpose LUs
1	Program to slave	batch-type terminals, card readers, printer
2	Program to device	terminals
3	Program to device	batch-type terminals, card readers, printers
4	Program to program	older peer-to-peer connections

There is no LU5 type.

6.0 & 6.1	Program to program	peer-to-peer interprogram communications CICS-CICS, IMS-IMS, CICS-IMS
6.2	Program to program	new peer-to-peer communications
7	Program to device	advanced 5270 terminals

⇨ SNA protocols

Please note that some of the following protocols have also been adopted by some standards organizations and will be covered in more detail in other areas of this chapter.

Token Ring is IBM's LAN protocol upon which IEEE 802.5 was originally founded (refer to IEEE Project 802 section at the beginning of this chapter).

Synchronous Data Link Control (SDLC) is a protocol generally used in point-to-point or multipoint connections. The connection uses either dedicated leased or dial-up lines from the telephone company. Transmission mode can be half or full duplex. SDLC is reviewed in more detail later in this chapter.

Virtual Telecommunications Access Method (VTAM) is an IBM offering that functions on a communications controller managing end nodes. VTAM and NCP function together to manage network resources.

Advanced Peer-to-Peer Networking (APPN) is used for peer-to-peer computing, as its name denotes. It is used in network environments with only PU Type 2.1 devices and no mainframe hosts. Similar to other network- and transport-layer protocols, APPN provides for route discovery, directory services, and flow control.

Customer Information Control Systems (CICS) is the heart of many business systems today. Transaction-processing-based applications make use of CICS. The protocol is used by application developers to provide distributed processing on local and remote hosts. CICS services include terminal-to-application communication, transaction tracking and recovery (very important in large database systems), transaction reversal, distributed file access, security services, disk storage and management, multitasking, and system restart facilities.

Information Management System (IMS) is composed of two IBM products: IMS Transaction Manager and the IMS Database Manager. IMS is similar in functionality and service offering to CICS.

Advanced Program-to-Program Communications (APPC) provides LU 6.2 capability to SNA and allows peer-to-peer communication sessions on LUs without using a mainframe host.

Distributed Data Management (DDM) provides seamless remote file access to SNA devices. Similar in nature to services provided by the application layer of the OSI reference model, DDM provides file access services.

SNA Distribution Services (SNADS) provides store-and-forward transfers of messages and documents.

Document Interchange Architecture (DIA) is a multiplatform document exchange facility. The product manages the movement of documents and file transfer services.

⇨ Digital Equipment Corporation's Digital Network Architecture (DNA) Protocols

DNA is DEC's proprietary networking architecture and protocol suite. Introduced in 1974, it has evolved through five revisions. The DNA architecture is commonly called DECnet, although this title also refers to a family of products produced by DEC. The most recent revision is DECnet Phase V. However, most systems implemented today still use the proprietary DECnet Phase IV. DECnet Phase V is fully OSI compliant. It supports all OSI protocols in addition to DNA protocols to remain backward compatible with older DNA application interfaces using OSI transport services. DNA also uses many industry-standard physical and data link layer protocols. Some of these protocols are described in other sections of this and other chapters.

⇨ DNA protocols topics and methods

See Fig. 5-31.

Figure 5-31

Protocols	OSI Layer	Topics	Methods
Ethernet V.2	Physical	Connection Types	Multipoint
		Physical Topology	Bus
		Digital Signaling	State Transition
		Bit Synchronization	Synchronous
		Bandwidth Used	Baseband
	Data Link MAC	Logical Topology	Bus
		Media Access	Contention
		Addressing	Physical Device
HDLC (ISO 3309, 4334, 7809, and 8885) High Level Data Link Control	Physical	Connection Types	Point-to-Point
	Data Link LLC	Transmission Synchronization	Asynchronous
			Synchronous
		Connection Services	LLC - Level Flow Control
DDCMP Digital Data Communications Message Protocol	Physical	Connection Types	Point-to-Point
			Multipoint
	Data Link LLC	Transmission Synchronization	Asynchronous
			Synchronous
		Connection Services	LLC Level Flow Control
			Error Control
			Message Sequencing
CLNS (ISO 8473, 9542, and 10589) Connectionless Mode Network Service	Network	Addressing	Logical Network
		Route Discovery	Link State
		Route Selection	Dynamic
CONS (ISO 8878, 8208) Connection Mode Network Services	Network	Addressing	Logical Network
		Route Discovery	Link Sate
		Route Selection	Dynamic
		Connection Services	Network Layer Flow Control
			Error Control
			Packet Sequence

DNA protocol topics and methods. Learning Tree International

Figure 5-31

			Control
ISO 8073	Transport	Addressing	Connection Identifier
Connection Oriented Transport Protocol Specificiation		Connection Services	Segment Sequencing
			Error Control
			End-to-end Flow Control
NSP Network Services Protocol	Transport	Addressing	Connection Identifier
		Connection Services	Segment Sequencing
			Error Control
			End-to-end Flow Control
Session Control	Transport	Address / Name Resolution	Service Request or Initiated
		Addressing	Connection Identifier
	Session	Session Administration	Connection Establishment
			Data Transfer
			Connection Release
ISO 8327, Session Protocol Specification	Session	Dialog Control	Half-Duplex
		Session Administration	Connection Establishment
			Data Transfer
			Connection Release
ASN.1 with BER Abstract Syntax Notation	Presentation	Translation	Character Code
FTAM and DAP File Transfer, Access, and Management	Application	Network Service	File Services
NVTS	Presentation	Translation	Character Code

Continued.

Figure 5-31

Network Virtual Terminal Service			(commands)
	Application	Network Service	Terminal Service
		Service Used	Remote Operation
MAILbus and X.400	Application	Network Service	Message Service
Naming Service and X.500	Transport	Address and Name Resolution	Service Provider Initiated
	Application	Network Service	Directory Service

Continued.

⇨ Summary of DNA-specific protocols

See Fig. 5-32.

Ethernet Version 2 was originally developed by DEC, Intel, and Xerox in the DIX Ethernet Version 1 Specification. Initially a 10-Mbits/sec physical and data link layer protocol, it was based on an earlier

Figure 5-32

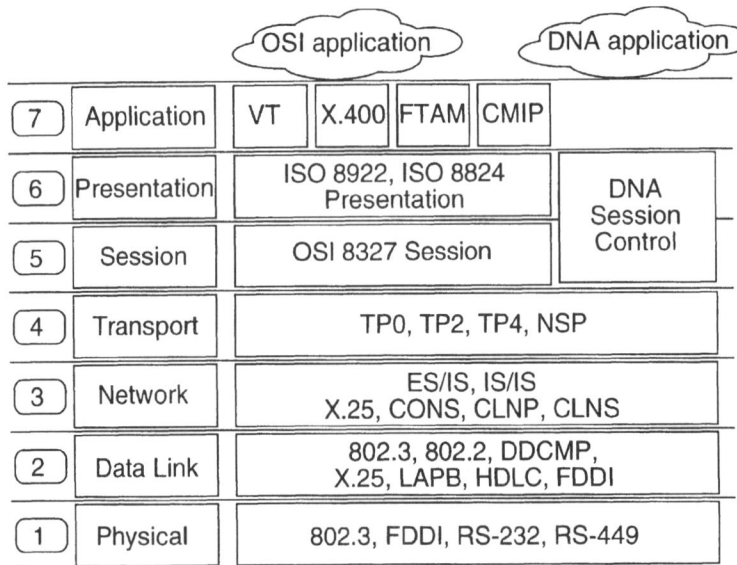

		OSI application	DNA application
7	Application	VT X.400 FTAM CMIP	
6	Presentation	ISO 8922, ISO 8824 Presentation	DNA Session Control
5	Session	OSI 8327 Session	
4	Transport	TP0, TP2, TP4, NSP	
3	Network	ES/IS, IS/IS X.25, CONS, CLNP, CLNS	
2	Data Link	802.3, 802.2, DDCMP, X.25, LAPB, HDLC, FDDI	
1	Physical	802.3, FDDI, RS-232, RS-449	

CLNS = connectionless network services
DDCMP = Digital Data Communications Message Protocol
NSP = Network Services Protocol

DNA protocols: DECNet Phase V. Learning Tree International

3-Mbits/sec Xerox Research Ethernet implementation. IEEE 802.3 was based on Ethernet Version 2 and is very similar, except for slight variations in frame format—a fact that makes them incompatible. Ethernet Version 2 is also sometimes referred to as ESPEC2.

High-Level Data Link Control (HDLC) is a data link protocol. Asynchronous and synchronous modes of transmission are both supported. Industry-standard modem protocols are used at the physical layer. Frame format and command structure are functions defined by HDLC.

Digital Data Communications Message Protocol (DDCMP) is similar to HDLC and was the original WAN data link protocol for DNA. Additionally, it implements full- and half-duplex point-to-point and multipoint communications. DDCMP numbers all its transmission messages (frames) and uses acknowledgments. It is also very efficient in that it can send message (frame) acknowledgments with other transmissions.

Connectionless Mode Network Services (CLNS) are provided at the network layer of DNA. They implement connectionless (OSI CLNS) and connection-oriented (OSI CONS) network services. DNA Phase V has implemented CLNS. Three ISO protocols provide CLNS support: ISO 8473 for connectionless mode network services, ISO 9542 for ES-IS routing exchange, and ISO 10589 for IS-IS intradomain routing. The latter protocols are reviewed under the OSI protocols section.

Network Services Protocol (NSP) was one of the original DNA protocols first introduced in 1974. A connection-oriented service, it also provides flow control through normal and high-level priority full-duplex channels.

ISO 8571 File Transfer, Access, and Management (FTAM) and Data Access Protocol (DAP) are file service protocols. File document types supported include text, binary, and hierarchical files. Service class functions include file transfer and management (file creation, deletion, retrieval, and others as implemented). While FTAM applications might appear different from different vendors, a core set of underlying file services are still provided.

Network Virtual Terminal Services (NVTS) provide for local terminal data formats to be converted for transmission over a network using its format before it is sent to the host.

MAILbus Product Family and X.400 Message Handling System compose the specifications for DECnet mail message services. MAILbus is a group of proprietary DEC products using the X.400 recommendations for message exchange. MAILbus is not a protocol specification.

Naming Services and X.500 Directory provide networkwide directory address to name resolution. X.500 specification recommends standards for directory services. While some differences remain between Naming Services and X.500, it is DEC's stated direction to comply fully with the OSI Directory standard.

Apple's AppleTalk protocol

AppleTalk was designed for Apple MacIntosh computers and is proprietary to Apple Computer Corporation. One of the most striking features of the protocol is that it is meant to be user friendly. It is generally transparent to the user. This aspect can best be highlighted by placing an AppleTalk-ready printer on the network; all users see the printer immediately and can access it right away. Access to the printer and the fact the printer is not directly connected to the user's workstation are transparent. AppleTalk works very well with small work groups that use only MACs. And finally, the protocol is built into the operating system so that there is no need to purchase additional network software. The resulting network is peer-to-peer based. AppleTalk deals with the topics and methods shown in Fig. 5-33. Also see Fig. 5-34.

There are three principal types of subnet (physical layer) protocol implementations: LocalTalk (LLAP), EtherTalk (ELAP), and TokenTalk (TLAP).

Local Talk is Apple's proprietary baseband CSMA/CA access protocol and is part of the MAC OS. EtherTalk provides Ethernet capability for MacIntosh computers and is IEEE 802.3 compatible.

EtherTalk is the subnet protocol of choice today for most MAC networks. TokenTalk provides Token Ring capability for MacIntosh computers and is IEEE 802.5 compatible. TokenTalk tends to be used in network environments that are dominated by IBM mainframe platforms but require MAC capabilities (desktop publishing).

Figure 5-33

Protocol	OSI Layer	Topic	Method
Local Talk	Physical	Connection Types	Multipoint
		Physical Topology	Bus
		Digital Signaling	State Transition
		Bit Synchronization	Synchronous
	Data Link MAC	Logical Topology	Bus
		Media Access	Contention
		Addressing	Physical Device
	Data Link LLC	Transmission Synchronization	Synchronous
		Connection Services	LLC Level Flow Control
			Error Control
AARP - AppleTalk Address Resolution Protocol	Data Link	Address Resolution or Physical and Device Address	Protocol Specific Resolution
DDP - Datagram Delivery Protocol	Network	Addressing	Logical Network Service
		Route Selection	Dynamic
		Interoperability	Network Layer Translation
RTMP - Routing Table Maintenance Protocol	Network	Route Discovery	Distance Vector
ZIP - Zone Information Protocol	Session	Protocol Specific	Arbitrary subdivision of network service providers in to zones
NBP - Name Binding Protocol	Transport	Address Resolution	Service Requested or Initiated
ATP - AppleTalk Transaction Protocol	Transport	Addressing	Transaction Identifier
		Segment Development	Division and Combination
		Connection Services	Error Control
ASP - AppleTalk Session Protocol	Transport	Connection Services	Segment Sequencing
			End-to-End Flow Control
	Session	Session	Connection

AppleTalk protocol topics and methods. Learning Tree International

Figure 5-33

		Administration	Establishment
			File Transfer
			Connection Release
PAP - Printer Access Protocol	Session	Session Administration	Connection Establishment
			File Transfer
			Connection Release
ADSP - AppleTalk Data Stream Protocol	Transport	Addressing	Connection Identifier
		Segment Development	Division and Combination
		Connection Services	Segement Sequencing
			Error Control
			End-to-End Flow Control
	Session	Session Administration	Connection Establishment
			File Transfer
			Connection Release
AFP - AppleTalk Filing Protocol	Session	Session Administration	Data Transfer
	Presentation	Translation	File Syntax (to some degree)
		Encryption	Public Key
AppleShare	Application	Network Services	File Print
		Service Advertisement	Active
		Service Used	Collaborative

Continued.

LocalTalk is an inexpensive LAN technology to connect Apple MacIntosh computers to each other, to printers, to PCs, and to file servers. LocalTalk is included with all versions of MAC OS, and hardware networking is built in. However, the protocol is used

Figure 5-34

7	Application	AppleShare Print Server, File Server, PC
6	Presentation	AppleTalk Filing Protocol (AFP)
5	Session	Printer Access Protocol (PAP) AppleTalk Session Protocol (ASP)
4	Transport	AppleTalk Transport Protocol (ATP)
3	Network	Datagram Delivery Protocol (DDP), Name Binding Protocol (NBP), Routing Table Maintenance Protocol (RTMP)
2	Data Link	AppleTalk Address Resolution Protocol (AARP)
1	Physical	LocalTalk EtherTalk TokenTalk

AppleTalk protocols. Learning Tree International

exclusively by Apple. IBM-compatible PCs require special network
interface adapters and software to function within this environment.
Because it is very easy and inexpensive to implement, it was initially
very popular with small businesses. However, as the business grows, a
faster underlying channel access methodology is required, and users
normally upgrade to EtherTalk for better performance.

⇨ LocalTalk channel access methodology

LocalTalk uses a Carrier Sense Multiple Access, Collision Avoidance
(CSMA/CA) channel access scheme at 230.4 Kbits/sec. Stations
access the cable medium in much the same way that Ethernet or IEEE
802.3 does. However, the protocol also implements a technique for
avoiding collisions. This is not to say that collisions do not
occasionally occur. It's just that they occur much less than in a
CSMA/CD network environment. The physical interface for LocalTalk
is RS-422 (balanced RS-449). It uses UTP voice-grade or better
cabling. The network is wired in a daisy-chain configuration. Figure
5-35 displays a typical LocalTalk network.

Figure 5-35

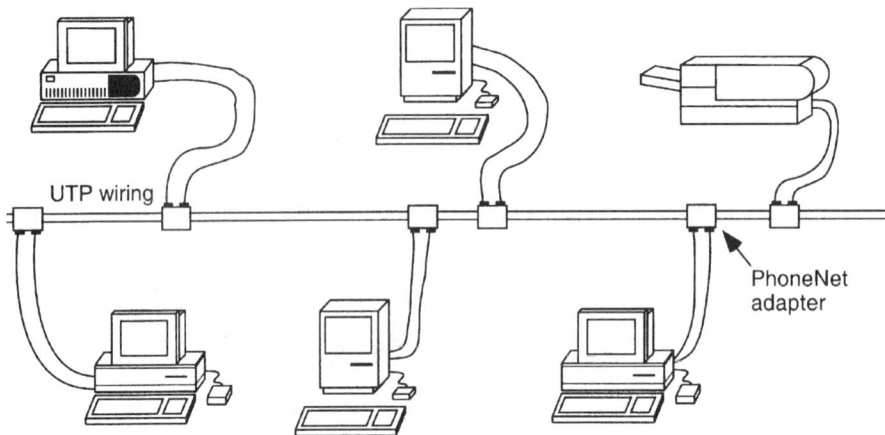

LocalTalk topology. Learning Tree International

In a CSMA/CA network, the sender senses (carrier sense) for a free channel. When the channel or cable is free of signals from other stations, it sends out a request to send (RTS) frame, which is addressed to the receiver to reserve the bus from other stations. If there is no response, a collision is assumed by the transmitting station. If there is no collision, the receiver sends a clear to send (CTS) frame back to the sender. The sender then puts data in a frame and transmits. Any collisions are resolved by upper-layer protocols. Broadcasts on this type of a network do not require CTS from all stations. The sending node simply issues an RTS with a broadcast node address of 255 and then sends the data frame.

⇨ LocalTalk frame structure

(See Fig. 5-36.)

Preamble is a two or more byte field with a value of 7Eh. The destination and source address denote the receive and sending stations respectively. The address is the one that is dynamically assigned when the station joins the network. Each address field is one byte (8 bits) in size. The frame types indicate data or control frames. Data frames have values of 1–127, which specify upper-layer protocols (like sockets or ports). The values 128–255 specify control frames types, of which

Data frame

Figure 5-36

Preamble flags	Destination address	Source address	Frame type	Length of data field	Data	CRC FCS	Flag	Abort sequence
>2 bytes 7E hex	1 byte	1 byte	1 byte 1–127 dec	10 low-order bits of 2 bytes	0–600 bytes	16 bits	1 byte 7E hex	18 bits

←————————————Frame————————————→ ←————————Trailer————————→

Control frame

Preamble flags	Destination address	Source address	Frame type	CRC FCS	Flag	Abort sequence
>2 bytes 7E hex	1 byte	1 byte	1 byte 128–255 dec	16 bits	1 byte 7E hex	18 bits

←————————Frame————————→ ←————————Trailer————————→

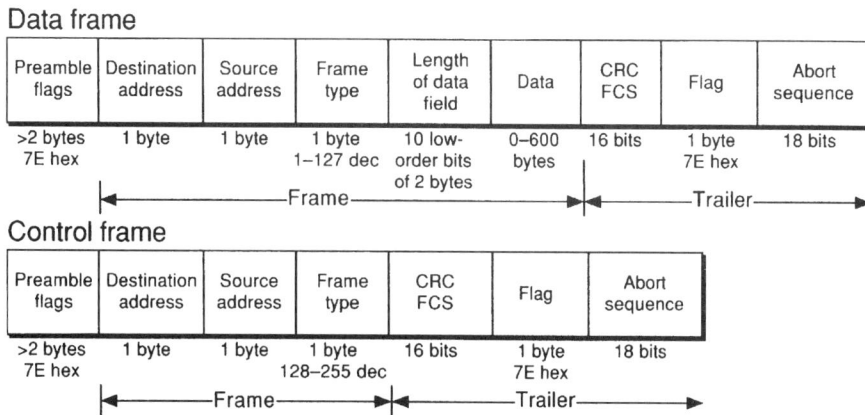

LocalTalk frame structure. Learning Tree International

only four are in use. Data fields can be up to 600 bytes in size and contain the protocol data unit of the upper layer. The frame check sequence is a 16-bit CRC field and is calculated based on all fields except the preamble. The trailer field denotes the end of the frame and has a value of 7Eh. A special abort sequence of 12 to 18 "1" bits marks the end of the frame and forces the receiver to lose synchronization.

⇨ LocalTalk characteristics

LocalTalk segment distances can be a maximum of 300 meters (approximately 900 feet) and support a maximum of 32 devices. LocalTalk devices automatically assign themselves addresses upon start-up and entry into the network. During this process, each device talks to other devices to determine and select a unique physical address.

EtherTalk and TokenTalk use IEEE Project 802 protocols to transport the higher-layer MAC protocols throughout the network. These protocols have been covered at the beginning of this chapter. Please refer to the IEEE Project 802 Specification section for more information on these protocols.

AppleTalk Address Resolution Protocol (AARP) provides a mapping between Ethernet and Token Ring physical network interface card addresses and AppleTalk physical addresses. AARP implements support for different types of data link layer protocols to be used by the upper-layer AppleTalk protocols.

⇨ Higher-layer protocols for AppleTalk

Datagram Delivery Protocol (DDP) is Apple's routing datagram (packet) creation protocol. Upper-level addresses are known as sockets. DDP delivers datagrams between sockets on peer applications. Sockets are dynamically assigned (DAS) by DDP as needed or statically assigned (SAS for the lower-level protocols).

DDP assigns 16-bit Apple Network IDs with the host physical node address as the host ID. A network might be assigned a range of network IDs by a network administrator. Network ID 0 and FF are reserved, 0 for transmission on the local network and FF for broadcasts. Routing Table Maintenance Protocol (RTMP), Zone Information Protocol (ZIP), and Name Binding Protocol (NBP) are closely associated with DDP. (See Fig. 5-37.)

Routing Table Maintenance Protocol (RTMP) is used by routers to broadcast their connectivity services (similar to RIP). RTMP uses a distance vector routing algorithm for route discovery.

Zone Information Protocol (ZIP) introduces the concept of zones to create logical network domains on large internetworks. This function is required in particular as the number of services on the Internetwork increases. Zones simplify user access to these services by limiting the number of services displayed. ZIP is also accessed by routers to provide additional functionality to manage relationships between zone and network names and designate service providers to zones.

Name Binding Protocol (NBP) is implemented to resolve the changing Network IDs to host names or entities. NBP translates between AppleTalk entity names and device network/host addresses. This service is required because a host's physical address can change each time it joins the network. This process is transparent to the end user.

Figure 5-37

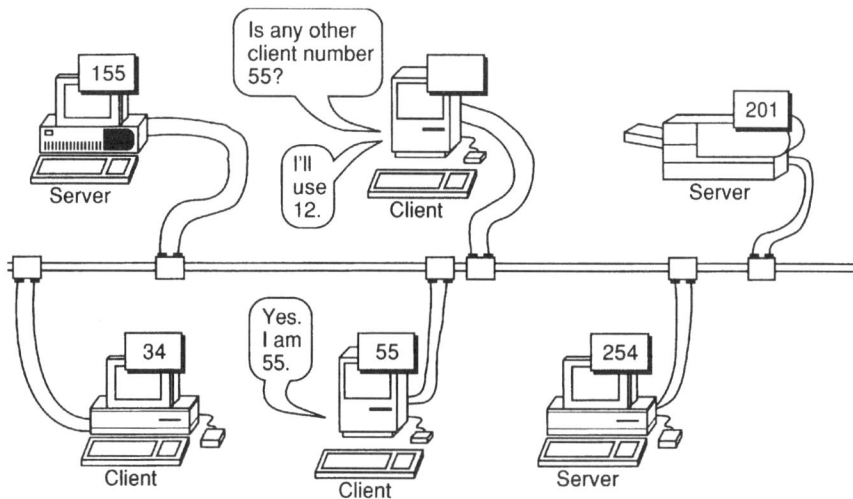

Server addresses: 128–254
Client addresses: 1–127
Broadcast address: 255

AppleTalk network IDs. Learning Tree International

AppleTalk Transaction Protocol (ATP) provides acknowledged transport-layer services. It is a transaction-based, connectionless-oriented delivery protocol. Common transport layer services are provided such as sequencing, acknowledgment, and recovery of lost transactions. Transactions are considered requests from a client workstation (peer) and replies from a server (peer). Finally, ATP also provides packet fragmentation and reassembly services for packets that are too large for the lower-level protocols.

AppleTalk Session Protocol (ASP) provides OSI session-layer protocol services and is responsible for optimizing file service functions. Like other session-layer protocols, ASP manages sessions or end-to-end links between computing entities. Functions include establishing, maintaining, and releasing sessions.

Printer Access Protocol (PAP) provides services similar to ASP in that it also functions at the session layer. The protocol was designed to work with shared network printers. Although the name implies that this protocol works with printers, it can actually be used to facilitate access to many types of servers (file, print, fax, database, etc.). Slight difference between PAP and ASP should, however, be noted. ASP is able to access multiple ATP transactions to reduce overhead on big data transfers. PAP allows either peer network device to initiate a session.

AppleTalk Data Stream Protocol (ADSP) is a connection-oriented transport services protocol for data streams. It is similar in functionality to TCP services. ADSP is different from ASP in that it can set up logical connections between two network device process sockets. ADSP is newer than ASP. Sequencing, fragmentation, and acknowledgment of data stream are all functions that ADSP provides. The protocol implements a 64-Kbyte window using sliding window flow control, also similar to TCP.

AppleTalk Filing Protocol (AFP) is an OSI application-layer service providing file sharing by extending the local file system functions to work with network file services. AFP provides transparent access, therefore, to remote file systems. As remote file systems become distributed, and the potential in a peer-to-peer network is that all users can access all other users file systems, AFP enforces secure access by authorized users to remote file systems. It does this through login names and passwords. Additional security is provided through encryption of this information before it is transmitted on the network. The protocol has functionality as NFS, XDR, and RPC. (See Fig. 5-38.)

AppleShare implements three main applications: AppleShare File Server, AppleShare Print Server, and AppleShare PC.

AppleShare File Server is a core network service—file sharing. It allows users to access remote file systems via AFP. The protocol registers users and maps users to server volumes and directories. Users log in to file servers and access network resources through this application protocol.

AppleShare Print Server is also a core network service—printer sharing. It allows users to access remote printers on the network in a transparent fashion. The protocol uses NBP and PAP to transmit

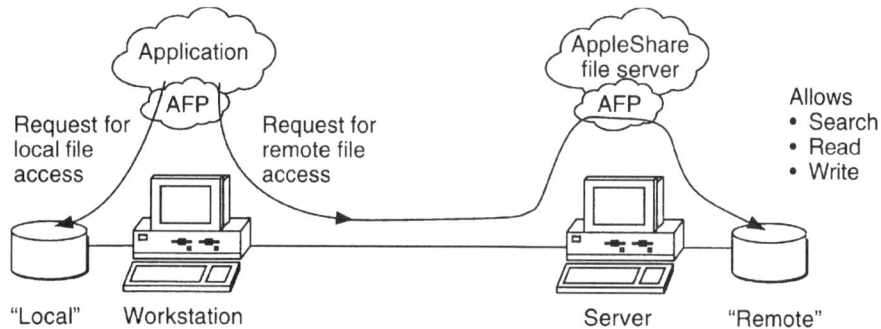

Figure 5-38

AppleTalk presentation protocols. Learning Tree International

information between AppleTalk network printers and network workstations. The AppleShare Print Server uses NBPs naming service to find the address of the designated AppleTalk printer. The print job is spooled into a queue and maintained by the AppleShare Print Server. It then establishes a session with the selected printer and transfers the print files to it for printing.

AppleShare services have also been extended to non-MacIntosh personal computers such as IBM-compatible systems running MS-DOS or PC-DOS. AppleShare PC provides the IBM-compatible personal computer with access to MacIntosh-based AppleShare file-sharing services. Additionally, it can access AppleTalk printers. AppleShare PC essentially makes MacIntosh remote file systems appear to be a local PC file system accessible via a DOS drive letter.

International Standards Organization's OSI protocols

The International Standards Organization (ISO) created the Open Systems Interconnection (OSI) reference model. Having done so, ISO felt that it could further simplify the networking industry by promoting a common set of protocols for network communications. The ISO has adopted some of the existing industry protocols as international standards and refers to the family of protocols as the OSI Suite. One could say that it is a conglomeration of protocols. Example protocols that have been selected include IEEE Project 802 and CCITT/ITU X.25 Recommendation. Where existing protocols were insufficient or not available, ISO created new ones to address the required functionality. Intermediate to Intermediate (IS-IS) is an example of an advance routing protocol developed by ISO committees. The problem with some of the new protocols, however, is that they have not been fully supported by industry and remain predominantly a paper protocol. Common Management Information Protocol (CMIP) is one such protocol that has not been able to supplant the *de facto* network management standard based on SNMP. (See Fig. 5-39.)

Figure 5-39

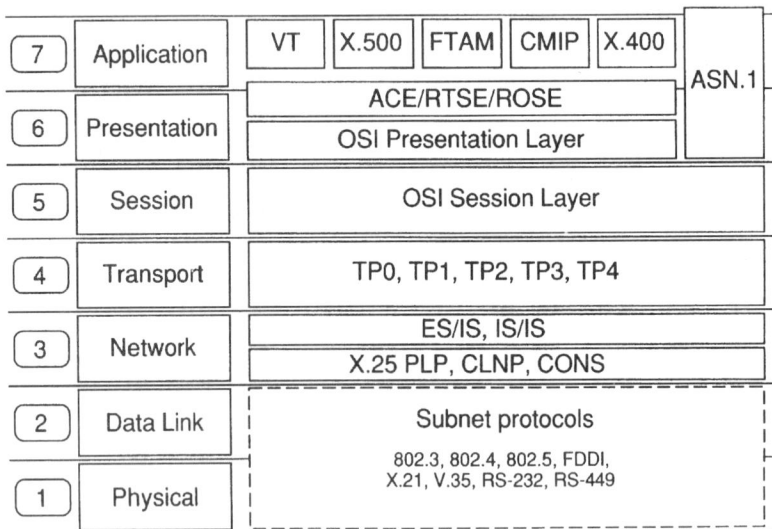

ACE = automatic cross-connection equipment   ROSE = remote operations service element
RTSE = reliable transfer service element   CONS = connection-oriented network services

OSI protocol suite. Learning Tree International

Given that the OSI protocol suite is made up of many industry protocols, a wide international audience has influence over how these protocols are implemented or adopted. Governments, industries, and commercial interest groups such as vendors all have a level of input into the protocol selection and standardization process. The resulting protocols are slow to be developed and implemented and might try to address too many issues to be practical. In general terms, the OSI protocols are meant for larger host-based network environments and not PC-based networks.

The U.S. government, in particular, has adopted only a subset of the OSI protocols called GOSIP (Government Open Systems Interconnect Profile). Acceptance throughout the industry has also been slow. TCP/IP is the main competitor protocol stack and really satisfies most users' requirements today. Large installed bases of proprietary protocols and the cost associated with migrating to OSI protocols is also a negative factor. However, OSI protocols promise to embody more functionality than currently available protocols provide, and as such, might be the future protocol of choice.

➪ OSI protocols description

➪ Subnet-layer protocols: (physical and data link)

The subnet section of the stack encompasses the physical and data link layers. Physical layer protocols implemented in the OSI suite are X.21, V.31, ISDN, RS-232, RS-449, and IEEE 802.3, 802.4, and 802.5. Data link layer protocols include IEEE 802.3, 802.4, and 802.5, High-Level Data Link Control (HDLC), and Link Access Procedure, Balanced (LAPB). The IEEE 802.2 specification is also included for logical link control.

➪ Network layer protocols

End System to Intermediate System (ES/IS) is used for local routing between hosts and routers. Intermediate System to Intermediate System (IS/IS) is a router-to-router internetworking protocol. Both ES/IS and IS/IS were derived to some degree from the TCP/IP suite of networking protocols. However, the addressing scheme implemented here goes well beyond the TCP/IP and the current limitations it faces. Additional network-layer protocols include X.25, Connection-Oriented Network Services (CONS), and Connectionless Network Protocol (CNLS).

⇨ Transport-layer protocols

Several protocols fit into the OSI's transport layer, and their use depends on the type of service that is required. There are five levels of service, and the protocols are referred to as *TP0, TP1, TP2, TP3, and TP4*. The transport layer functionality provides for fragmentation and reassembly, error recovery, connection, multiplexing and demultiplexing, flow control, and reliable service. Figure 5-40 highlights which of these services are provided by the five TP protocols.

Figure 5-40

Services	TP0	TP1	TP2	TP3	TP4
Fragmentation and reassembly	yes	yes	yes	yes	yes
Error recovery	no	yes	no	yes	yes
Connection multiplexing and flow control	no	no	yes	yes	yes
Sequencing acknowledgement	no	no	no	no	yes

OSI transport protocol functions. Learning Tree International

⇨ Session-layer protocols

The session layer is the beginning of interoperability services as the internetworking connection has already been established by the lower layer protocols. The main function of the protocols at this layer is to ensure that proper dialog is maintained between communicating applications or processes that are running on two network hosts. By doing so, the session layer ensures that all activities associated with the communication process are successfully completed. Checkpointing is a technique used for managing dialogs between communicating applications. Transactions or exchanges between the applications might involve multiple checkpoints during a session. Session-layer functionality is currently implemented by protocols working at upper layers of the OSI reference model.

⇨ Presentation-layer protocols

The main function of the presentation layer is to convert higher-layer characters (ASCII, EBCDIC) into bits that the computer can work with (bit stream). Here again, as with the session layer, this functionality is usually implemented by application-layer protocols. *Abstract Syntax Notation* (ASN.1) is a protocol implemented at this layer. ASN.1 originates from the CCITT/ITU X.409 standard. The protocol is used to provide data structures and formats that are independent of the underlying machine platform or hardware. ASN.1 employs a technique called *basic encoding rules* to facilitate communications between applications and the network.

⇨ Application-layer protocols

The main function of the application-layer protocols is to provide an interface between the end-user applications and application processes running on the hosts or servers, and the lower-layer protocols. *Application service elements* (ASEs) interact with the application-layer applications that provide the services available on the network.

Association Control Service Element (ACSE) allows OSI-based applications to communicate. ACSE identifies each OSI application with a unique title that is used throughout the communication process by other layer protocols.

Reliable Transfer Service Element (RTSE) provides a simple interface for applications and the session-layer reliable transfer delivery service. RTSE tells applications whether or not a transfer has been successful. Remote Operations Service Element (ROSE) implements Remote Procedure Call capability. ROSE allows applications to request operations from the remote host.

⇨ Application-layer applications

Application-layer protocols provide services to network users. File and print services are the most common. The following is a list of these services.

➤ *File Transfer, Access, and Management* (FTAM) provides remote file access and transfer services.

➤ *Message Handling System* (MHS) provides electronic mail delivery and is based on the CCITT/ITU X.400 specification.

➤ *Virtual Terminal* (VT) protocol provides terminal emulation. Because most large host systems employ centralized computing methods, a user needs to logon to the system in order to access its applications. VT is a widely used protocol and has been implemented on many different hosts platforms.

➤ *Directory Services* (DS) specifies networkwide host and services naming functions and is based on CCITT/IT X.500 specifications.

➤ *Common Management Information Protocol* (CMIP) is a network management facility for interaction between network management programs and network agents. Network agents can be hosts, nodes, or devices on the network. The protocol defines which objects on the network can be managed and the method for communicating status information. Status information is maintained in a management information base (MIB).

⇨ Additional protocols and standards

⇨ Fiber Distributed Data Interface (FDDI)

See Fig. 5-41.

FDDI is implemented at the physical and data link layers of the OSI reference model. It is the fastest of all current LAN technologies to interconnect personal computers and host systems, although it is usually referred to as a WAN protocol. A very high bandwidth allows transmissions of data, digitized voice, images, fax, and video all on the same cable system. It is also popular for high-bandwidth applications such as backbone rings and computer room networks (the network in the main computer room interconnecting all the primary hosts). Due

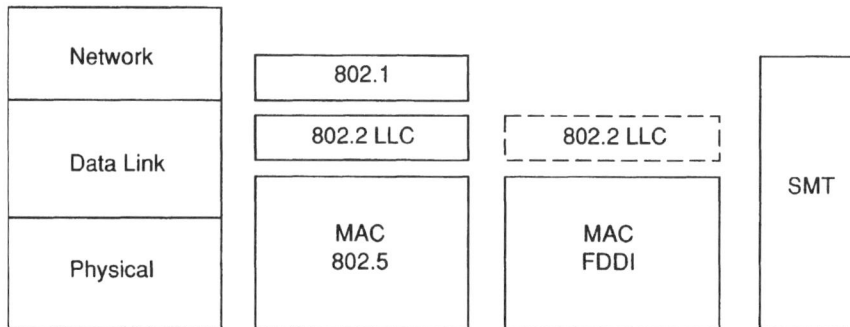

FDDI with IEEE protocols. Learning Tree International

Figure 5-41

to its ability to support large distances, the technology is also popular in metropolitan area network (MAN) installations. FDDI is an ANSI standard and was developed by its X3T9 committee. Subsequently it has been adopted by ISO as the 9314 standard.

FDDI protocols topics and methods

See Fig. 5-42.

FDDI characteristics

➢ Modeled after IEEE 802.5 Token Ring Technology.

➢ Works at the physical and data link layers.

➢ 100 Mbits/sec data rate.

➢ 500 stations (access points) per ring.
  • Doubles when ring has a failure.

➢ 100 km total cable length.
  • Will support 200 km if primary ring fails.
  • Repeaters are required every 2 km.
  • Operates in synchronous or asynchronous mode.
  • Fiber-optic cabling standard (see chapter 2).
  • Symbols denote 4 data bits using a NRZ 5-bit encoding.
  • Uses 16-bit or 48-bit station addresses.

Figure 5-42

Protocols	OSI Layer	Topics	Methods
FDDI	Physical	Conncetion Types	Point-to-Point
		Physical Topology	Star
			Ring (Dual)
		Digital Signaling	State Transition
		Bandwidth Used	Basedband
	Data Link MAC	Logical Topology	Ring
		Media Access	Token Passing

FDDI protocols topics and methods. Learning Tree International

The main setback today for implementing FDDI on every desktop is the cost. Network interface cards remain expensive, as does the expertise required to install the cable plant. However, based on the higher bandwidth demand that many applications are requiring of the network, necessity might drive the demand to the point where prices do become lower.

There are two possible topology configurations: Class A, which uses a logical and physical ring, and Class B, which uses a logical ring but implements a physical star cabling system. In the Class A topology, a counter rotating ring provides for very good cable redundancy and fault tolerance. The specification stipulates that the network and all devices connected to it must recover from a break in the cable very quickly. Class B provides a high level of fault tolerance in a manner similar to UTP hubs (concentrators). If the cable breaks between the one station and the hub, then only that station is affected. Inside the hub, the logical ring is closed as the faulty segment is removed from the ring. (See Fig. 5-43.)

In a Class A network, traffic flows on a primary ring until a failure or break in the cable occurs. When one or both fibers on the cable segment breaks, or if a stations network interface card fails, a beaconing technique is used to alert all stations on the network of the problem. The ring is then reestablished using primary and secondary rings. (See Fig. 5-44.)

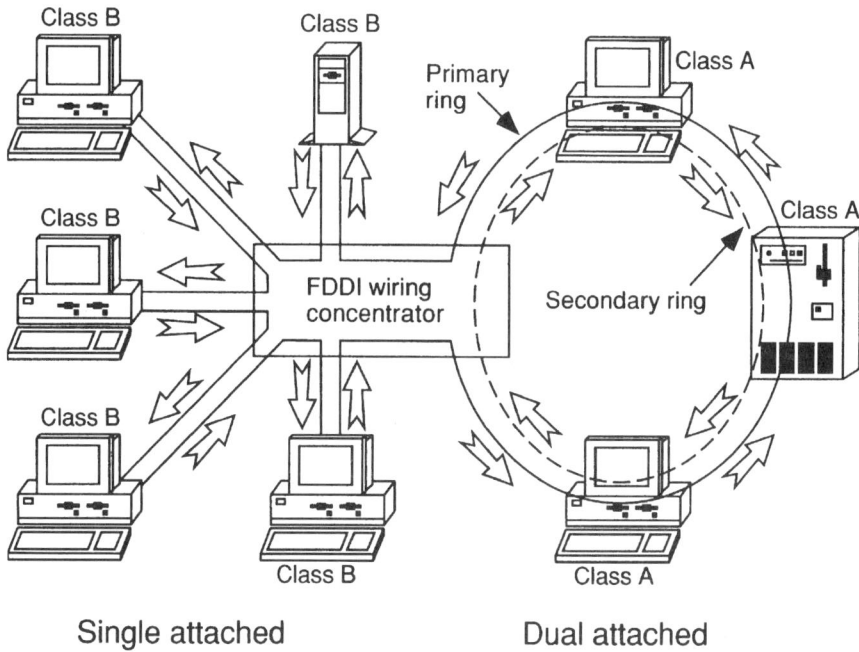

Figure 5-43

Class B

Class B

Primary ring

Class A

Class B

Class A

FDDI wiring concentrator

Secondary ring

Class B

Class B

Class A

Single attached

Dual attached

FDDI topology. Learning Tree International

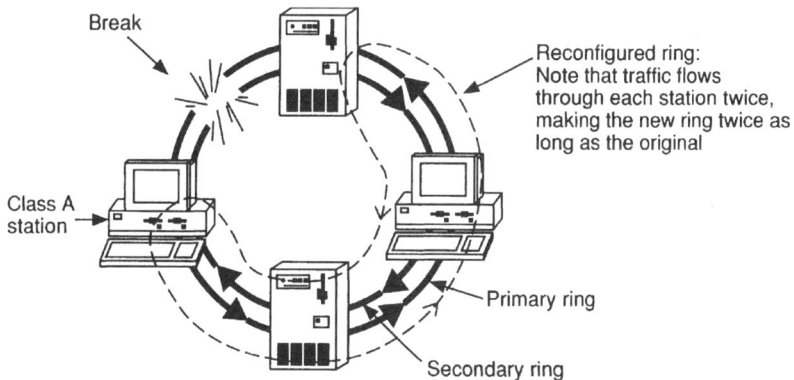

Figure 5-44

Break

Reconfigured ring: Note that traffic flows through each station twice, making the new ring twice as long as the original

Class A station

Primary ring

Secondary ring

- **Traffic flows on primary ring until failure occurs**
- **When one or both of the fibers on a segment breaks, or a station fails**
    - Stations begin beaconing to recover
    - Ring is re-established using primary and secondary rings
- **May be done only with Class A stations (dual attached)**

FDDI ring failure recovery. Learning Tree International

FDDI channel access methodology

As stated previously, FDDI was modeled after the IEEE 802.5 Token Ring technology and supports similar frame types—token and data/command. However, unlike Token Ring, the token (permission) frame is always released by the station immediately after the station finishes transmitting its data/command (information) frame. In this fashion, there can be several data/command frames on the ring at the same time. Intermediate stations circulate or repeat token and data/command frames. The receiving station copies the frame into its memory and forwards the frame back onto the ring, having modified the frame status field to acknowledge receipt of the frame to the transmitting station.

FDDI employs dynamic bandwidth allocation for traffic transmission. Traffic is classified into two categories: synchronous and asynchronous. Synchronous traffic is considered to be real time and continuous in nature. Video and voice are examples of synchronous traffic formats. Asynchronous traffic is more sporadic. Data and terminal transmissions are examples of asynchronous traffic. Due to the nature of the underlying transmission types, synchronous traffic is always given priority. Asynchronous has eight levels of priority depending on the underlying data format. Two stations holding an extended synchronous dialogue can restrict asynchronous traffic from being successfully transmitted. Station Management (SMT) is the protocol used to determine which traffic type gets the required bandwidth it needs. The protocol implements a bidding process among stations to determine the type of traffic they want to transmit.

FDDI frame structure

(See Fig. 5-45.)

FDDI has two frame types. Token or permission frames indicate to the station that it can begin to transmit an actual data. Data/command or information frames are the actual application data being sent over the

Data or command frame

Figure 5-45

Preamble	Start delimiter	Frame control	Destination address	Source address	Data	Frame check	End delimiter	Frame status
16 symbols	2 symbols	2 symbols	12 symbols	12 symbols	0 or more symbols	8 symbols	1 symbol	3 symbols

├─────────────────────Frame─────────────────────┤

Token frame

Preamble	Start delimiter	Frame control	End delimiter
16 symbols	2 symbols	2 symbols	2 symbols

FDDI frame structure. Learning Tree International

network by higher-level protocols. Similar to IEEE, FDDI frames use a preamble to separate frames from each other. Each station sends a series of IDLE symbols which have values of all ones (1). Five IDLE symbols that occur between frames. The maximum FDDI frame size is 4500 symbols.

The frame control indicates the type of frame or command being transmitted. As such, it denotes whether it is a synchronous or asynchronous transmission. It also carries address length information to indicate whether 16- or 48-bit addresses have been implemented.

The destination and source addresses are either 16 or 48 bits in length and indicate which station created the frame and which station is meant to receive the frame. The Information or Data field contains the protocol data unit of the upper-layer protocol. This can be many different protocols such as IPX or IP.

Frame Check is a 32-bit CRC field used to verify the completeness and integrity of the frame. The Frame Status field is used as an indication of the success or failure of the transmission it created. The transmitting station looks at the source address of frames it receives in order to determine if it in fact created the frame. If so, it then looks at the Frame Status field for acknowledgment that the destination station successfully received the frame.

⇨ ARCNET

Although not implemented by many organizations today, ARCNET was a very popular protocol in its time. Compared with other protocols when it was released, it was a fast and inexpensive LAN-based technology to connect PCs. The protocol was introduced by Datapoint Corporation in 1977 and was later adopted as a standard by ANSI. Mainly a manufacturing-based protocol solution, network interface cards were first introduced to the market by Standard Microsystems Corporation (SMC) in 1983. The protocol worked well in manufacturing environments because, like Token Ring, it is a deterministic protocol (we can predict how much time it will take before a given station has an opportunity to transmit information). Due to the relatively low price of network interface cards when compared to competing technologies (Ethernet, Token Ring), ARCNET it became very popular within small- to medium-sized business networks.

However, ARCNET specifications allow for it to cover a relatively large network installation. It is possible to have an ARCNET network spanning 20,000 feet from one end to the other. The American National Standards Institute adopted ARCNET as a standard in the 1980s. A higher-performance version of ARCNET operating at 20 Mbits/sec was available for a period of time but, due to implementation problems, did not capture a significant market share. Faster technologies have now surpassed this standard. (See Fig. 5-46.)

⇨ ARCNET characteristics

- ➤ 2.5 Mbits/sec baseband token-passing logical bus.
- ➤ 8-bit (256 potentials values) addresses that are user configurable.
- ➤ Can be wired with coaxial, UTP, and fiber-optic cable.
- ➤ Supports physical star or daisy-chain network topology.
- ➤ Basic star topology supports.
  - 100 feet between coax active hub (has power supply) to passive hub (no power supply) or passive hub to PC.
  - 2000 feet between coax active hub to active hub or active hub to PC.
  - 300 feet UTP cable between active hub and PC.

Figure 5-46

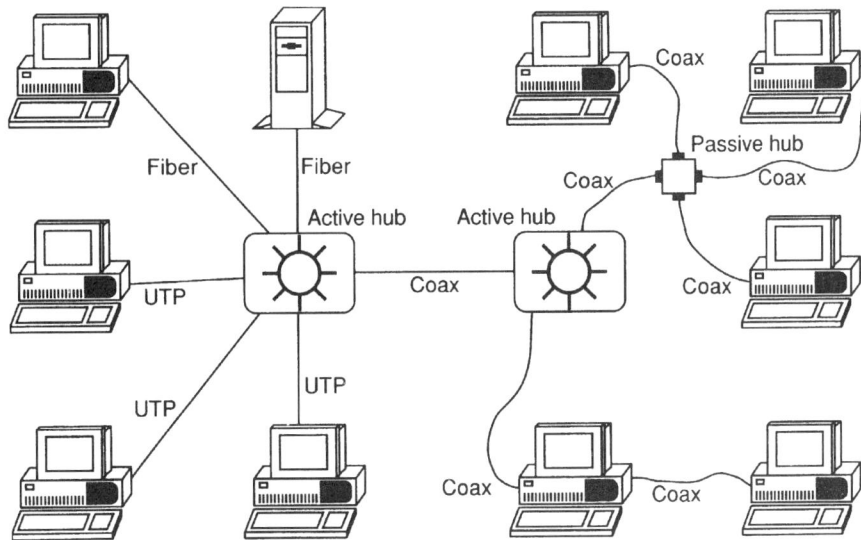

ARCNET topology. Learning Tree International

➡ ARCNET token-passing access methodology

ARCNET is similar to Token Ring or IEEE 802.5 in that it implements both permission and information tokens. However, a logical bus topology is used instead of a ring. (See Fig. 5-47.)

Each network interface card has an 8-bit (256 possibilities) address. Users select an address through dip switches or jumpers on the card. Nodes are assigned network addresses from 1 to 254. Address 0 and 255 are reserved. Token frames pass from one station to the next on the bus in a sequential order. Each station knows its address as the source identifier (SID). In turn, each station discovers the station address of the next identifier (NID) by broadcasting identification requests. A NID is the station with the next highest network interface card address.

A permission token is released on the bus, and the SID node then passes the permission token to the NID node. The node then has

Figure 5-47

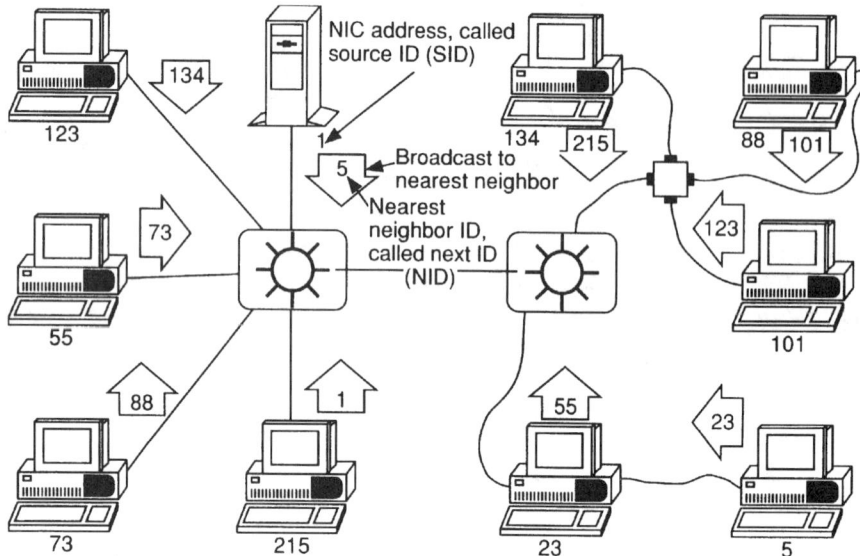

ARCNET channel access methodology. Learning Tree International

permission to begin to transmit an information frame as a SID. This node in turn sends the permission token to its NID. The station with the highest SID completes the loop by passing the permission token to the node with the lowest SID.

Finally, when stations want to join or leave the network, an autoreconfiguration is performed. A special transmission disrupts token passing. The station with the highest SID begins looking for a NID. As stations find their NIDs, they pass a token to that station to continue the process until all stations on the bus have discovered their NID. Normal token-passing operations are then resumed.

⇨ CCITT/ITU X.25

The International Telegraph & Telephone Consultative Committee (CCITT) originally defined Recommendation X.25 in 1974. A packet-switching protocol, X.25 became the basis for networks by Telenet, Tymnet, and Datapac. Today, CCITT is called the International Telecommunications Union (ITU). The protocol is implemented in wide area network (WAN) environments in particular public data networks.

Figure 5-48

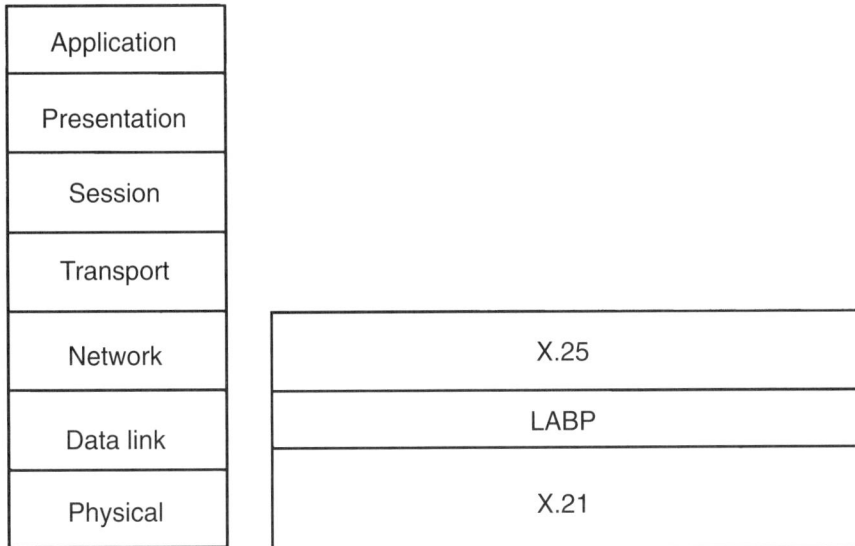

X.25 protocol stack. <small>Learning Tree International</small>

The X.25 Packet component of the protocol was no longer supported after 1984 because other high-level protocols provided that same functionality. (See Fig. 5-48.)

Three levels are associated with the X.25 protocol stack. Level 1 encompasses the physical layer, which is concerned with interface connectivity. X.21, X.21bis, and V.32 are some examples of the standards implemented at this level. Level 2 facilitates the mechanisms to establish connection-oriented data pathways. These mechanisms are specified as part of the Link Access Procedures-Balanced (LAPB) protocol. Level 3 specifies the manner in which packets are forwarded between data terminal equipment (DTE) and the data-circuit terminating equipment (DCE). Routing and switching methodologies are not specified within X.25 and are implemented on a vendor-independent basis, although most agree to a common format.

X.25 protocols topic and methods

See Fig. 5-49.

Figure 5-49

Protocols	OSI Layer	Topics	Methods
X.21	Physical	Connection Types	Point-to-Point
		Physical Topology	Mesh (hybrid)
		Bit Synchronization	Synchronous
LAPB	Data Link LLC	Connection Services	LLC Level Flow Control
			Error Control
X.25	Network	Addressing	Channel (per connection)
		Switching	Packet (virtual circuit)
		Connection Services	Network Layer Flow Control

X.25 protocol topics and methods. Learning Tree International

The X standards are subdivided into two categories: X.1 through X.39, and X.40 through X.199. The first category characterizes terminals, interfaces, service providers, and the facilities that offer them. The latter category specifies network architectures, transmission modes, and signaling methods.

The X.25 specification defines predominantly the Data Terminal Equipment (DTE) to Data Circuit-terminating Equipment (DCE). The protocol has been widely adopted throughout the world. The protocol was updated every four years until 1988, and thereafter updates were made as required. Most major upper-level protocols support X.25 directly.

X.25 protocol characteristics

The X.25 protocol uses standard interfaces for the physical layer. In Europe, the X.21 specification is implemented, whereas in North America, RS-232-C is used to connect to the network.

> ➤ Defines the Packet Level Protocol (PLP).

> ➤ Defines circuit-switching, connection-oriented technology.
>   - Permanent virtual circuits (PVC) using dedicated session links.
>   - Switched virtual circuits (SVC) using dial-up session links.
>   - Uses LAPB (similar to HDLC) for data link layer frame-level protocol.
>   - Implements a global addressing scheme defined by X.21.

(See Fig. 5-50.)

Figure 5-50

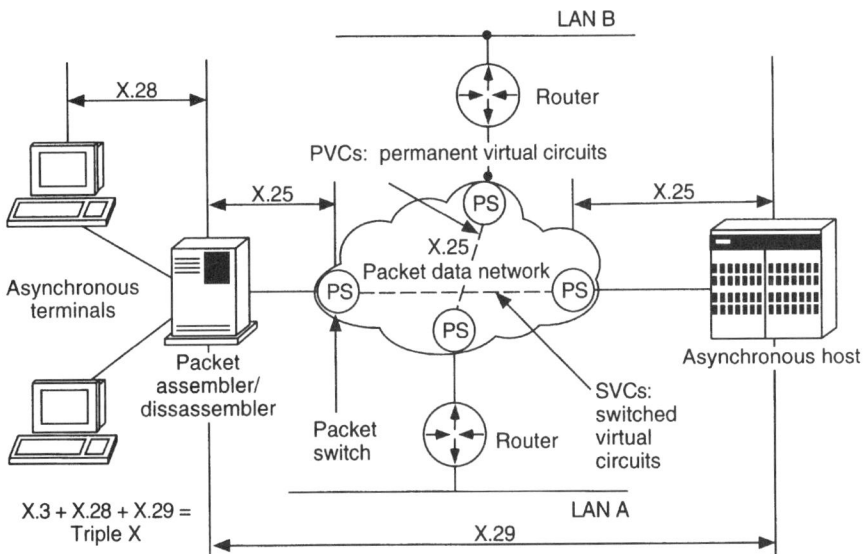

PS = packet switch

X.25 topology and devices. Learning Tree International

⇨ Synchronous Data Link Control (SDLC) protocol

SDLC is a bit-oriented synchronous data link layer protocol developed by IBM in 1975 for host/terminal (primary/secondary or master/slave) communications. The protocol is still widely used in many mainframe environments, but it is also implemented in LAN environments to facility gateway access to the mainframe using terminal emulation.

⇨ SDLC channel access methodology

In SDLC, the host/primary controls the communications process. The terminal/secondary responds to the primary or waits to be polled when it has something to transmit. The protocol was developed primarily for point to point communications between two entities or devices. (See Fig. 5-51.)

Figure 5-51

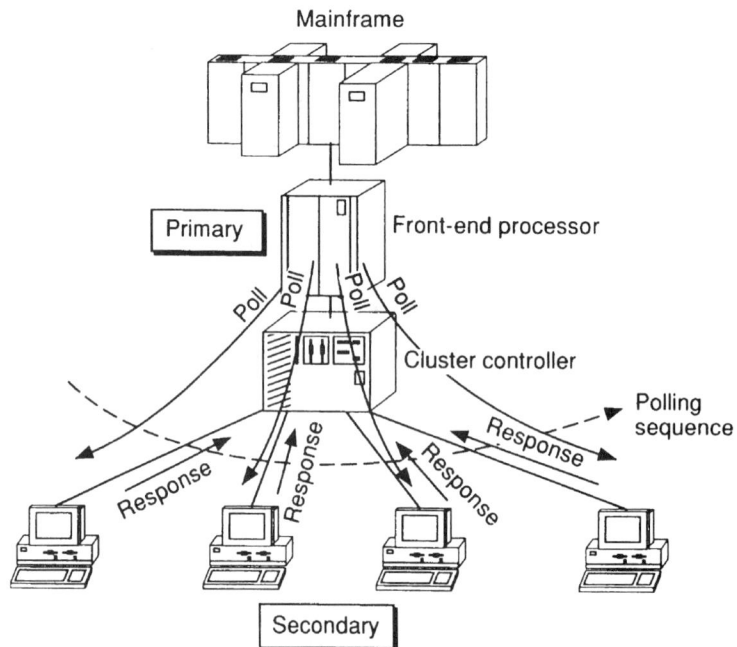

Polling device acts as primary
- Primary always controls communications

Terminals act as secondaries
- They communicate only when polled

SDLC access control. Learning Tree International

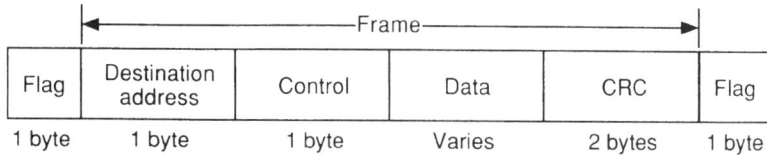

Figure 5-52

Frame types:

Information frame
- Frames that contain data

Supervisory frames
- Dataflow control frames

Unnumbered frames
- Frames used to establish the link

The SDLC frame structure. Learning Tree International

⇨ SDLC frame structure

(See Fig. 5-52.)

Start and end delimiters encapsulate the frame. SDLC generates a continuous bit stream so frames must have a method for denoting start and end points. A unique pattern of "01111110" bits is called a flag and is used for that purpose. The bit stuffing of data technique is used to enforce uniqueness of the flag to avoid misinterpretation of a similar bit pattern in the data portion of the frame.

Bit stuffing is the process whereby the sender adds a "0" bit after a series of five consecutive "1" bits found in any portion of the frame. The flag is then added, and the flag/frame combination are transmitted. The receiver removes the "0" bits out of the frame before processing it up the stack.

The Address field is a 1-byte field. It identifies the address of the terminal/secondary device that the frame is coming from or destined to. The Control field identifies three types of frames. Information frames transport upper-layer data and also provide some control functions. Supervisory frames hold information required to manage the flow of data, report status details, and acknowledge information frame processing. Unnumbered frames are another type of control frame. However, they provide services like diagnostics and station initialization. The Check Sum field is a 16-bit CRC field.

High Data Level Control (HDLC) and Link Access Procedure Balanced (LAPB) protocols

SDLC was modified and adopted by CCITT/ITU as a high-level data link control (HDLC) protocol in 1979. It is the data link layer protocol for packet-switched networks like X.25. HDLC implements full-duplexed, synchronous communications. Sixteen-bit CRC frame check sequences are normally used, but the protocol can support a 32-bit CRC as well if larger frame sizes are used. Data frame sizes are adjustable and are typically a maximum of 128 or 256 bytes in size.

Note: Some SDLC services are not provided in HDLC. Individual, group, and broadcast addresses, and certain commands to facilitate loop and go-ahead topologies, are not supported.

HDLC supports three types of control. Normal Response Mode (NRM), Asynchronous Response Mode (ARM), and Asynchronous Balanced Mode (ABM). Normal Response Mode (NRM) stipulates that the primary host always initiates the communication process with secondary devices on the network. This can be viewed as a master/slave, or host/terminal type of communication process where the master/host polls the slave/terminal to see if it has any information to transmit. Until it is polled, the slave/terminal cannot transmit any information.

Asynchronous Response Mode (ARM) allows the secondary device to initiate the communication process. And Asynchronous Balanced

Mode (ABM) allows either device to assume the primary (master) or secondary (slave) role during the communication process. The primary role is for transmission and the secondary role is for reception. The communication occurs in full-duplex mode.

Link Access Procedure, Balanced (LAPB) was adopted by CCITT/ITU for X.25 circuits in 1984. LAPB is a form of HDLC. The protocol implements HDLC in ABM mode.

⇨ Frame relay

(See Fig. 5-53.)

Figure 5-53

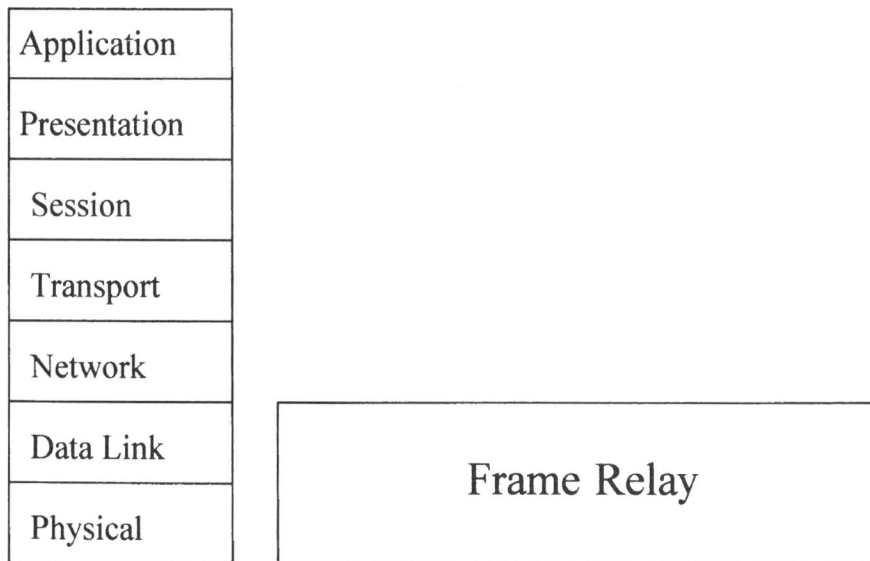

Frame Relay protocol stack. Learning Tree International

CCITT/ITU is the standards body responsible for the fast packet interface Frame Relay specification. The protocol was developed in order to address some of the inefficiencies of X.25 and to provide a better lower-level platform on which X.25 can function. Frame Relay implements a network architecture that provides a lower error rate than the current X.25 packet-switched network implementation. It does this by reducing the number of packets required to establish a call and transmit data. As such, X.25 can run faster in this format. Like X.25, it is often referred to as a WAN protocol. However, it can function in LAN environments as well and is being considered by several interconnection device manufacturers. (See Fig. 5-54.)

Figure 5-54   **X.25**

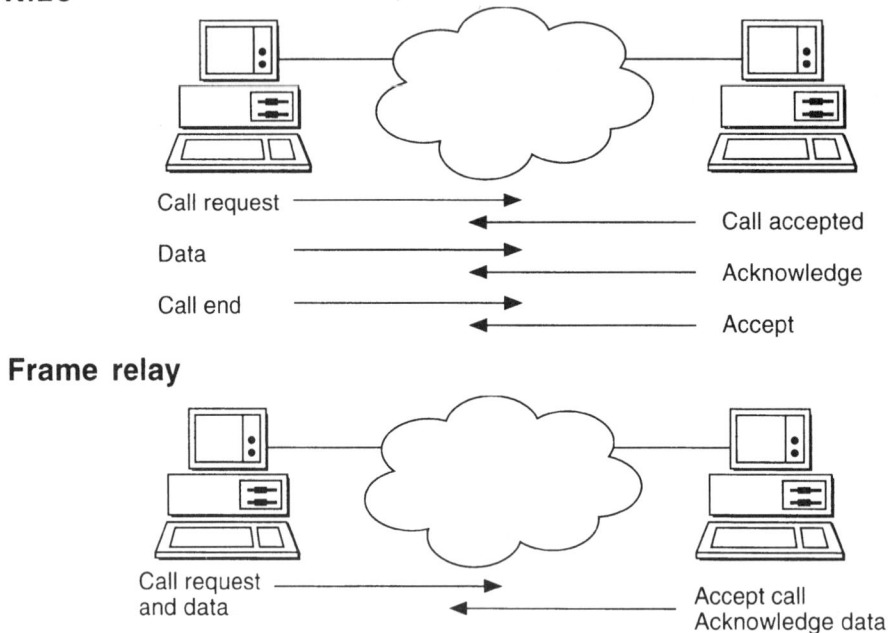

Frame relay

Comparison of X.25 and Frame Relay. Learning Tree International

Frame Relay protocols topics and methods

See Fig. 5-55.

Although Frame Relay provides some very good advantages, it is still only available in selected metropolitan regions and is not yet implemented in all the same places where X.25 can be found.

Protocol	OSI Layer	Topics	Methods
Frame Relay (CCITT/ITU I.451/Q931 & Q922)	Physical	Connection Types	Point-to-Point
		Physical Topology	Mesh (hybrid)
		Switching	Packet (virtual circuit)
	Data Link LLC	Connection Services	LLC Level Flow Control
			Error Control (detection only, no recovery)

Figure 5-55

Frame Relay protocol topics and methods. Learning Tree International

Integrated Services Digital Network (ISDN) and B-ISDN

ISDN is a group of international specifications created by CCITT/ITU that provides a common approach to integrating voice and data transmissions over digital telephone networks. B-ISDN is a broadband implementation for enhanced ISDN capability that provides faster data rates through 155 Mbits/sec instead of 64-Kbits/sec channels, using fiber-optic transmission media. Both ISDN and B-ISDN are viewed as WAN protocol standards. (See Fig. 5-56.)

ISDN topics and methods

ISDN is a very large undertaking. Because it is a digital-based telephone network, it would require that all existing telephone lines and equipment be replaced with fiber and digital-capable systems. Much of the traffic that would be sent over an ISDN network would originally be analog (voice), which would require conversion at both ends of the network. ISDN therefore defines the standards for integrating analog and digital transmissions over digital equipment. ISDN networks can function in circuit-switched or packet-switched connection configurations. (See Fig. 5-57.)

Figure 5-56

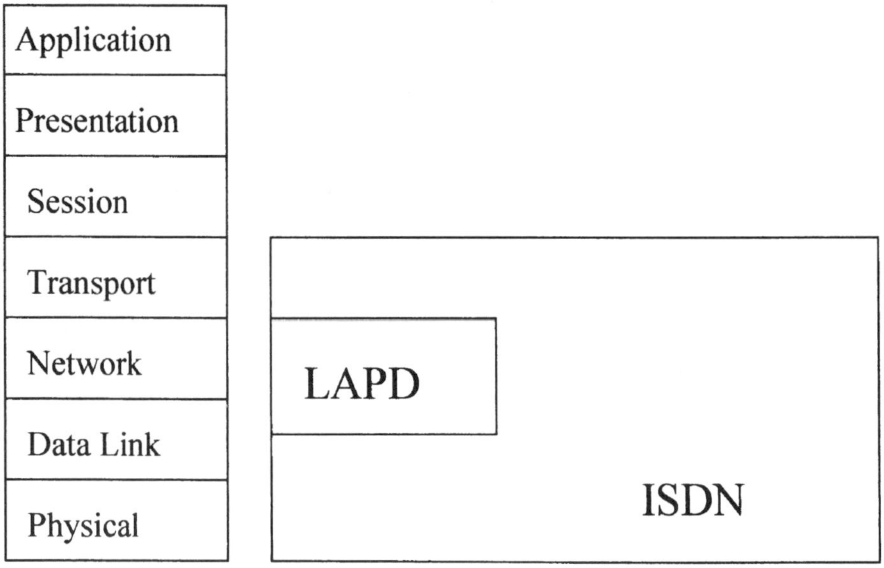

Application
Presentation
Session
Transport
Network
Data Link
Physical

ISDN protocol stack. Learning Tree International

Figure 5-57

Protocol	OSI Layer	Topics	Methods
ISDN	Physical	Multiplexing	TDM
LAPD (CCITT/ITU Q.920 & .921)	Data Link MAC	Addressing	Physical Device
	Data Link LLC	Connection Services	LLC Level Flow Control
			Frame Sequencing
ISDN (CCITT/ITU I.451/Q.930 & I.451/Q.931)	Network	Switching	Packet
			Circuit

ISDN protocols topics and methods. Learning Tree International

ISDN rate channels and characteristics:

> ➤ Channel A—4-kHz analog channel.

> ➤ Channel B—64-Kbits/sec digital channel.

> ➤ Channel C—8- or 16-Kbits/sec digital channel (normally used for out of band signaling).

> ➤ Channel D—16- or 64-Kbits/sec digital channel for out-of-band signaling with the following types.

- s—subchannel for signaling (call setup).
- t—subchannel for telemetry.
- p—subchannel for low-bandwidth data packets.

➢ Channel E—64 Kbits/sec digital channel for internal ISDN signaling.

➢ Channel H—384, 1536, 1920-Kbits/sec digital channel.

CCITT/ITU implements the following three channels as international ISDN services:

➢ Basic Rate:
  - 2 B Channels (64 Kbits/sec)
  - 1 D Channel (16 Kbits/sec).

➢ Primary Rate:
  - 1 D Channel (64 Kbits/sec).
  - 23 B Channels (North America and Japan) or 30 B Channels (Europe and Australia)

➢ Hybrid Rate:
  - 1 A Channel (4-kHz analog channel).
  - 1 C Channel (8- or 16-Kbits/sec digital).

Finally, it is important to remember that ISDN only specifies the transmission media service. The protocol uses LAPD on a separate D Channel to implement data link layer services with acknowledgments and connectionless oriented communications.

⇨ Asynchronous Transfer Mode (ATM)

The Asynchronous Transfer Mode (ATM) is a new standard way of implementing B-ISDN and cell relay-based network services. The protocol is currently still evolving and is being developed by ITU's Telecommunications Standards Sector (ITU-TSS), with additional input from the ATM Forum. ITU-TSS is responsible for assigning specifications for the protocol while the ATM Forum is concentrating on implementation issues. Primarily a WAN-oriented protocol, it is also being targeted at the LAN and MAN markets. (See Fig. 5-58.)

Figure 5-58

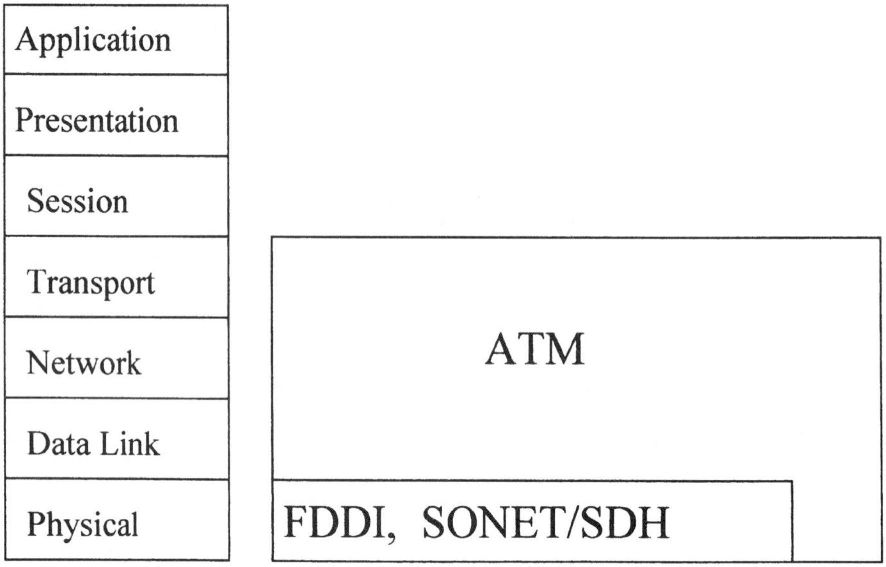

Application
Presentation
Session
Transport
Network
Data Link
Physical

ATM
FDDI, SONET/SDH

ATM protocol stack. Learning Tree International

➪ ATM protocol topics and methods

See Fig. 5-59.

The ATM standards are referred to as the I Series specification. The I Series denotes four types of services to be provided to upper-layer protocol stacks or suites:

> ➤ Connectionless data.

> ➤ Connection-oriented data.

> ➤ Constant-bit-rate traffic.

> ➤ Variable-bit-rate packet data using fixed delays.

The types of services were created to provide network transmission support for different types of protocols. For example, video uses constant bit rate service, whereas file transfers can use a connectionless type of service.

Figure 5-59

Protocol	OSI Layer	Topics	Methods
ATM	Data Link LLC	Transmission Synchronization	Isochronous
		Connection Services	Error Control
	Network	Switching	Packet (referred to as Cells)
		Route Selection	Static

ATM protocols topics and methods. Learning Tree International

The ATM protocol data unit is commonly referred to as a cell. Each cell is composed of a 53-byte packet with 5 bytes of type of service header information added to the packet.

⇨ Switched Megabit Data Service (SMDS) protocol (SMDS)

The Switched Megabit Data Service (SMDS) protocol was developed by Bell Communications Research in 1991. It is considered a form of ATM. SMDS has been designed for the MAN and WAN markets. SMDS is a data link layer protocol that can support different types of physical-layer specifications. (See Fig. 5-60.)

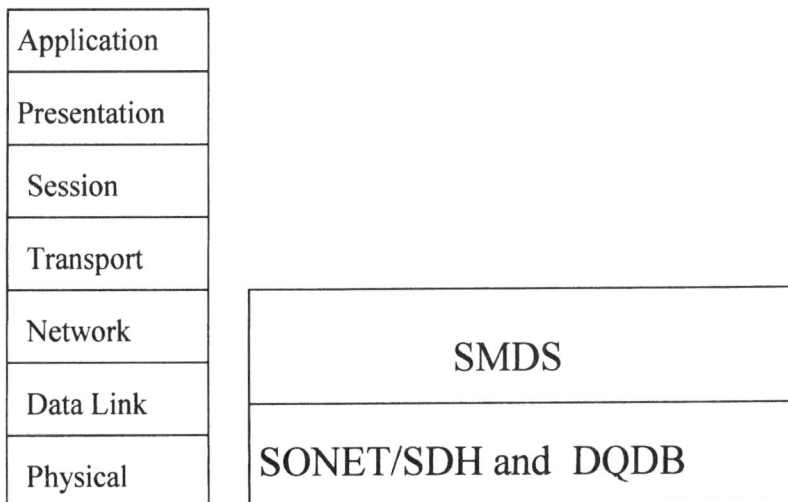

Figure 5-60

Application
Presentation
Session
Transport
Network
Data Link
Physical

SMDS
SONET/SDH and DQDB

SMDS protocol stack. Learning Tree International

⇨ SMDS protocol topics and methods

SMDS was designed as a connectionless service. It supports data transmission rates of 1544 Mbits/sec up to a very fast 45 Mbits/sec. (See Fig. 5-61.)

Figure 5-61

Protocol	OSI Layer	Topics	Methods
SMDS	Data Link LLC	Transmission Synchronization	Isochronous
	Network	Switching	Packet (referred to as Cells)

SMDS protocols topics and methods. Learning Tree International

⇨ Synchronous Optical Network (SONET) and Synchronous Digital Hierarchy (SDH) protocols

The Synchronous Optical Network (SONET) was developed by Bell Communications Research in 1984. (See Fig. 5-62.) It has been adopted as an ANSI protocol standard. Since then, CCITT/ITU has used SONET as the basis for its approved protocol standard, referred to as Synchronous Digital Hierarchy (SDH). Slight modifications were required when CCITT/ITU developed the new standard in order to address differences in the international community. As a result, the following types or implementations of the protocol have been created:

➢ SDH Europe with support for CEPT.

➢ SDH Japan.

➢ SDH SONET for North America.

Figure 5-62

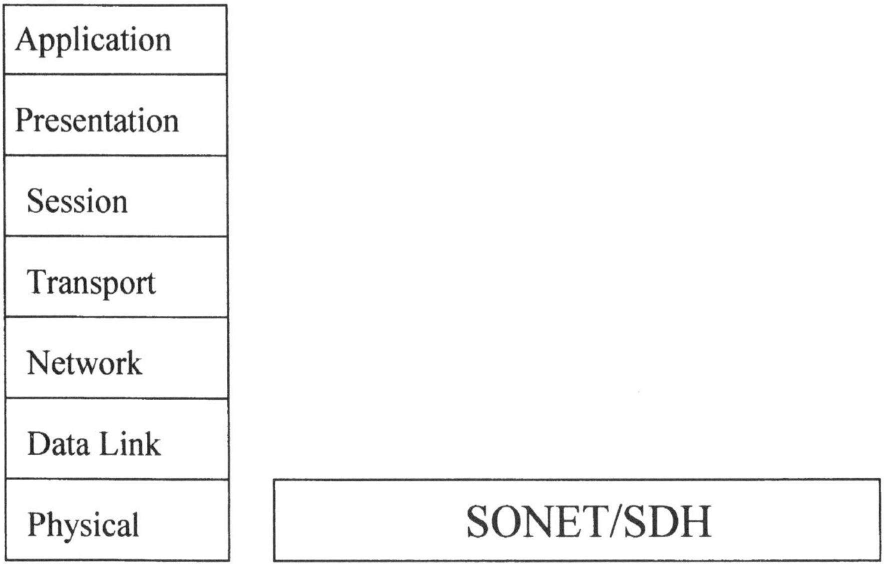

SONET/SDH protocol stack. Learning Tree International

SONET/SDH protocols topics and methods

The SONET/SDH standards have been accepted as practical physical layer implementations to support ATM, SMDS, DQDB, and FDDI. (See Fig. 5-63.) The following is a list of the documents that can be researched for extensive information and spec details on the two protocols.

➤ ITU G.707-709 SDH rates and formats.

➤ ITU G.774 management information model.

➤ ITU G.781-784 equipment and functions.

➤ ITU G.803 network architecture.

➤ ITU G.831 management capabilities.

➤ ITU G.957 optical interfaces.

➤ ITU G.958 line systems.

Figure 5-63

Protocol	OSI Layer	Topics	Methods
SONET/SDH	Physical	Connection Types	Point-to-Point
		Physical Topology	Mesh
			Ring
		Multiplexing	TDM

SONET/SDH protocols topics and methods. Learning Tree International

> ➤ ANSI T1.105 SONET rates and formats.

> ➤ ANSI T1.117 optical parameters for short reach.

> ➤ ANSI T1.118 OAM&P communications.

⇨ SONET and SDH capacity standards

See Fig. 5-64.

Figure 6-64

Data Rate in Mbits/sec	SONET OC and STS	SDH STM
51.84	1	
155.52	3	1
466.56	9	
622.08	12	4
933.12	18	
1244.16	24	8
1866.24	36	12
2488.32	48	16

SDH capacity standards table. Learning Tree International

⇨ Serial Line IP (SLIP) and Point to Point (PPP) protocols

See Fig. 5-65. Serial Line IP and the newer-version Point-to-Point Protocol were created to facilitate dial-up telephone links to IP-based networks. Although the last popular protocol covered in this chapter, it has probably captured a significant amount of the market over the last few years. The reason for this is the nonstop popularity of the

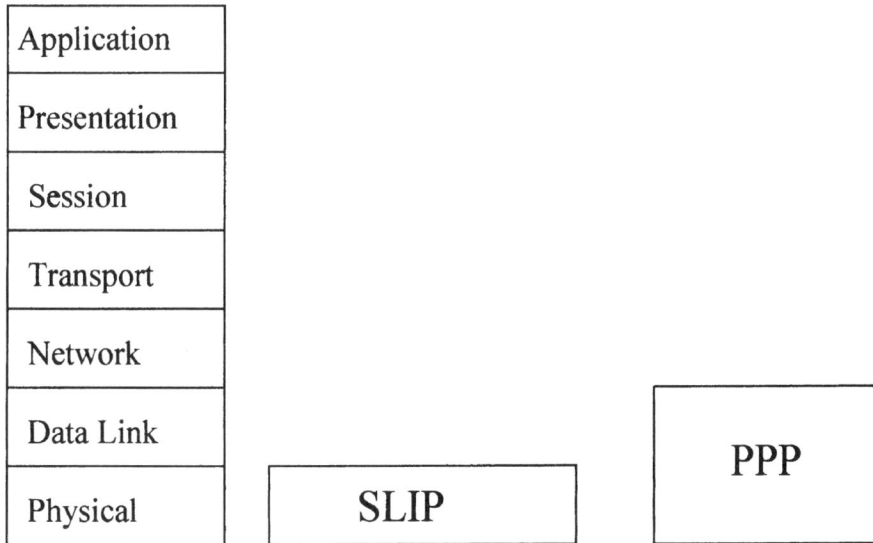

Figure 5-65

SLIP and PPP protocol stacks. Learning Tree International

Internet. Users that dial into an Internet service provider to browse or surf the Internet and World Wide Web (WWW) sites generally uses SLIP. However, SLIP and PPP can also interconnect two networks using routers. The networks are connected using modems through which one of the two protocols can be used.

Point-to-Point Protocol (PPP) was created by the Engineering Task Force (IEFT) to address the limitations of SLIP. PPP devices negotiate levels of service before data can be transmitted.

Serial Line IP and Point-to-Point protocols topics and methods

See Fig. 5-66.

SLIP protocol characteristics

> ➢ Designed to facilitate dial-up IP network connections.

> ➢ Limited functionally.

Figure 5-66

Protocol	OSI Layer	Topics	Methods
SLIP	Physical	Connection Types	Point-to-Point
PPP	Physical	Connection Types	Point-to-Point
	Data Link MAC	Addressing	Physical Device
	Data Link LLC	Connection Services	Error Control

SLIP and PPP protocols topics and methods. Learning Tree International

➤ It could not support multiple protocols at the same time.

➤ Standard was loosely implemented and varied among vendors.

PPP protocol characteristics

➤ Designed to address limitations of SLIP.

➤ Dynamic IP addressing capability.

➤ Multiple protocol support on the same connection.

➤ Password and login capability.

➤ Error control services.

⇨ Summary

While we have reviewed many different protocol stacks or suites, it is important to remember that in one way or another, they all achieve the same result. Likewise, each protocol suite can be referred or mapped to the OSI reference model, depending on the functionality and services the suite provides. Provided that you can identify what the protocol does, you can map it to the appropriate layer. From there, it is much easier to solve computer networking problems created by solution protocol suites.

⇨ Test your understanding

The purpose of this section is to help reinforce the information we have just reviewed. Proceed through the various sections and write down your answer to the questions. The answers are in appendix B.

1. Can you identify the category and the layer in which these protocols/programs belong?

	Transport/ network protocol	Remote program execution	File transfer	Database access	Remote terminal access	Distributed file system	PC NOS	E-mail	Network management	Directory services	Layer
TCP											
NetWare											
FTP											
NFS											
X.500											
X.25											
TELNET											
ROSE											
802.3											
TP4											
APPC											
DB2											
TFTP											
NCP											
HDLC											
Advanced server											
X.400											
RPC											
UDP											
IPX											
VT											
SNMP											
CMIP											
SMTP											
XDR											
IP											

The IEEE Project 802

2. The four basic MAC technologies defined by the IEEE 802 committee are:

   _____, _____, _____, _____

3. Name four types of 802.3 wiring schemes and their characteristics:

   _____, _____

   _____, _____

   _____, _____

   _____, _____

The Internet Protocols

4. Name three application protocols that are part of the TCP/IP protocol suite and one use of each protocol:

   _____, _____

   _____, _____

   _____, _____

5. What route advertising protocol is used in TCP/IP internets?

   _____

NetWare Protocols

6. Which NetWare protocol corresponds to the Application Layer of the OSI Model? _____

OSI Protocols

7. Who promotes the development of OSI protocols? _____

8. Name some OSI higher level protocols (Network Layer and above):

   _____

Additional Higher Level Protocols

9. Who promotes and develops SNA protocols? _____

10. In an IBM SNA network, what are the PU designations for:

    A 3270 terminal? _____

    A cluster controller? _____

    _____

    A front-end processor? _____

    The mainframe? _____

Additional Higher Level Protocols (continued)

11. Who promotes the development of AppleTalk protocols?

_____

12. DECnet Phase V is compatible with what protocol profile?

_____

Ansi FDDI

13. What is the FDDI data rate? _____

14. What cabling choices are availale for FDDI/?

_____ , _____

15. What access scheme does FDDI use? _____

Apple LocalTalk

16. What is the LocalTalk data rate? _____

17. What wiring type and topologies are employed in LocalTalk?

_____ , _____

Additional Data Link Protocols

What data link protocol is used with:

18. IBM SNA? _____

19. CCITT/ITU X.25/? _____

20. What does LAPB stand for? _____

21. What frame types are used with SDLC?

_____ , _____ , _____

(See Figs 5-67 to 87.)

Figure 5-67

Characteristic	Contention	Token passing	Polling
Description	Multiple access Listen before send Broadcast transmissions	Pass token Capture token and send a frame	Primary sends to or polls secondary, secondary sends when polled
Types	CSMA CSMA/CD CSMA/CA	Token Ring Token bus	Primary/secondary
Examples	Ethernet LocalTalk 802.3	802.5 FDDI 802.4	LAPB SDLC
Where used	PC LANS Enterprise networks	IBM mainframe networks PC LANs Backbones Industrial networks	X.25 WANs IBM mainframe networks
Advantages	Low overhead, simpler	Deterministic, performs well under load	Deterministic, efficient for terminal traffic
Disadvantages	Nondeterministic, degraded performance under heavy load	Added overhead due to token passing	High overhead

Reference: basic channel access techniques. Learning Tree International

Figure 6-68

Characteristic	Asynchronous	Synchronous
Transmission	Each character separately	Blocks of characters
Error check	Parity bit in each character	CRC at end of block
Framing	10 bits per character—start bit, 7 bits of data (ASCII encoded), parity bit and stop bit	Block SYN character, data characters, CRC character
Encoding scheme	Typically ASCII (7-bit)	Typically EBCDIC (8-bit)
Access scheme	I/O connection to host	SDLC, polling
Typical application	Terminal traffic PC-to-PC file transfer VT100 terminal connected to a VAX	IBM SNA networks 3270 terminal connected to an IBM mainframe
Synchronization	Derived from signal stream	Separate clock signal
Typical data rates	2400 bps, 9600 bps	19.2 Kbps
Advantages	Mature technology Universally employed Inexpensive hardware	More efficient Better error detection
Disadvantages	Poor error detection Inefficient use of channel bandwidth	More complex hardware

Reference: transmission types. Learning Tree International

Figure 5-69

Desig-nation	Common names	Data rate	Seg-ment length	Cable type	Wiring topology	Connect-ing devices	Charac-teristics
10BASE5	ThickNet	10 Mbps	500 m	50-ohm thick coax	Bus Baseband	MAU and AUI cables, repeaters	An OSI-standard, older technology. Uses SQE.
Ethernet Version 2	Ethernet ESPEC2 Ethernet 2	10 Mbps	500 m	50-ohm thick coax	Bus Baseband	Trans-ceivers, repeaters	Developed by DEC, Intel, and Xerox (DIX). Used with TCP/IP networks. Uses SQE.
10BASE2	ThinNet Cheapernet	10 Mbps	185 m	50-ohm thin coax	Bus daisy-chain Baseband	BNC Ts repeaters	Typical way to connect small Ethernet LANs.
10BASE-T	Twisted-pair Ethernet	10 Mbps	100 m	UTP 2 pairs	Star hierarchical Baseband	Concen-trators	Very popular way to wire 802.3 networks.
10BROAD36	Broadband Ethernet	10 Mbps	1800 m	75-ohm coax	Bus Broadband	MAU switch RF modems CATV components headend	Used in industrial networks as part of MAP installations.
1BASE5	StarLAN	1 Mbps	250 m	UTP	Star hierarchical Baseband	Hubs	Technology developed by AT&T. Not popular today.

Reference: 802.3 LANs. Learning Tree International

Figure 5-70

Frame component	Length	Use	Ethernet/802.3 differences
Preamble (not part of frame)	8 bytes (64 bits)	Start of frame delimiter. Alternating 0s and 1s. Last two bits are 1s.	Ethernet: Preamble. 802.3: last 8 bits are called start of frame.
Destination address	6 bytes (48 bits)	Physical address of receiver's NIC. All 1s mean broadcast.	Ethernet: 48 bits only. 802.3: allows alternative 16-bit definition
Source address	6 bytes (48 bits)	Physical address of sender's NIC. Stored in ROM.	Address space administered by the IEEE.
Type/length	2 bytes (16 bits)	Control field. ≤1500 dec: length >1500 dec: ethertype	Ethernet: **Type**. Specifies the network protocol using the frame. 802.3: **Length**. Specifies the length of the data field.
Data	Minimum 46 bytes (32 bits)	Frame payload	Ethernet: contains the packet or datagram. 802.3: may contain the 802.2 LLC or used without ("raw") as with NetWare IPX, then followed by packet.
Frame check sequence	4 bytes (32 bits)	32-bit Cyclic Redundancy Check (CRC) pattern for error checking	Same use in both specifications.

Reference: 802.3 and Ethernet frames. Learning Tree International

Figure 5-71

Characteristic	Description	802.5/IBM TRN differences
Access method	Baseband token-passing ring	—
Wiring topology	Star	802.5 does not specify
Wire types	Twisted pair: 2 pairs per station	802.5 does not specify
Data rates	1 Mbps, 4 Mbps, 16 Mbps	802.5: 1, 4 Mbps IBM TRN: 4, 16 Mbps
Signal encoding	Differential Manchester	—
Stations per ring	802.5: 250 IBM TRN: 260 for unmovable 72 for movable	As noted
Frame types	Data (LLC), control (MAC), token and abort frames	—
Frame lengths	Typical 4000 bytes. Maximum 8000 bytes. No minimum data field length.	—
Priority	Sophisticated mechanism	—
Failure recovery	Beaconing	—
CRC length	32 bits	—
Addresses	48 bits for source and destination stored in ROM or 16-bit user selectable.	—
Repeaters	Each NIC is a repeater. Ring length extender repeaters are available.	—
Connection devices	**Multistation Access Units** (MSAU) with relays to bypass stations removed from ring.	—
Promoter	Token Ring: IBM 802.5: IEEE	As noted

Reference: 802.5/IBM Token Ring characteristics. Learning Tree International

Protocol	Name	Characteristics and Uses
802.1	System Management and Internet-working	Specifies overview to all 802 standards and integrates them. Also defines Transport Spanning Tree algorithm for network bridging. Typically used in 802.3 LAN to resolve active loops in bridged networks.
802.2	**Logical Link Control** (LLC)	Defines additional fields in the data portion of 802 frames employed in multiplexing the use of one network card by multiple network (datagram) protocols. Employs two 8-bit destination and source service access points addresses (DSAP and SSAP) as well as one 8-bit control field for sequencing, acknowledgment, and flow control. Use of 802.2 with the addition of a 2-byte field containing the Ethertype is the basis of SNAP logical link control.
802.4	Token Bus	Token-passing multiple access scheme employed in broadband networks. Deployed in industrial and factory networks. Useful in low-delay, industrial controls situations. Part of the **Manufacturing Automation Protocol** (MAP) protocol suite.
802.6	Metropolitan Area Network	High-speed, long-distance access scheme for deployment in metropolitan areas. Scheme based on a **Distributed Queue, Dual Bus** (DQDB) proposal by University of Western Australia. Uses a dual fiber-optic bus with time slots.

Figure 5-72

Reference: additional IEEE protocols. Learning Tree International

Figure 5-73

Protocol	Name	Purpose
802.7	Broadband Technology Technical Advisory Group	Advises other 802 groups on installation and management of broadband cable plants and networks.
802.8	Fiber-Optic Technology	Advises other 802 groups on installation and maintenance of fiber-optic cable plants and networks.
802.9	Integrated Voice and Data LAN Working Group	Defines the use of ISDN-connected LAN devices. Uses unshielded twisted-pair wiring and 802.2 logical link control.
802.10	LAN Security Working Group	Defines standards for secure data exchange, encryption, and network management on a LAN.

Reference: additional IEEE protocols (continued). Learning Tree International

Figure 5-74

Characteristic	Description
Access method	Baseband, token-passing ring (similar to 802.5)
Wiring topology	Class B: Star wiring to concentrators—2 fibers Class A: Point to point to form a ring—4 fibers
Wiring type	Fiber optic, 62.5-micrometer core Some STP implementations, called CDDI or TPDDI
Data rate	100 Mbps
Address	48 bit and 16 bit allowed
Segment length	2 Km maximum point to point
Maximum ring length	100Km: Class A and B rings 200Km: Class A ring after failure of a segment
Maximum stations per ring	500 nodes : Class A and B rings 1000 nodes: Class A ring after failure of a segment
Ring types	Primary: Class A stations dual attached Secondary: Class B stations single attached
Priority	Sophisticated mechanism
Repeaters	Every 2 km required
Frame types	Token and data
CRC length	32 bit
Encoding	4 bits in 5 signals, NRZI
Bandwidth allocation	Synchronous: for continuous transmission Asynchronous: for other traffic Uses SMT protocol to assign bandwidth
Failure recovery	Uses beaconing similar to 802.5
Uses	Backbone rings, computer room interconnections, high-data-rate LANs.
Promoter	ANSI standard, adopted by ISO as an OSI protocol.

Reference: FDDI characteristics. Learning Tree International

Figure 5-75

Characteristic	Description
Access method	Baseband, token-passing bus
Wiring topology and wire types	Coax: Star using hubs or daisy chain TP: Star using hubs F.O.: Star using hubs
Data rate	2.5 Mbps for ARCNET 20 Mbps for ARCNET Plus
Data encoding	11-bit character: First three bits are "110" followed by 8-bit ASCII character
Addresses	8-bit user definable: 1–254 node addresses, 0 for broadcasts
Frame types	Data: PACket: PAC ACKnowledge: ACK Free buffer inquiry: FEB Invitation to transmit: ITT
Data frame size	512 bytes: data field variable from 1–508 bytes
Priority	No priority scheme
CRC length	16 bits
Repeaters	Active hubs are retransmitters. Passive hubs are signal splitters.
Uses	Small PC networks
Promoter	Datapoint was the developer and license holder, Standard Microsystems (SMC) the major chipset and NIC manufacturer

- **Although Novell suggests to use low addresses (1, 2, 3) for NICs in servers, it is recommended that as least one server have an address of 255 to expedite reconfigurations and network startup.**

Reference: ARCNET characteristics. Learning Tree International

Figure 5-76

Characteristic	Description
Access method	Baseband, CSMA/CA, bus
Wiring topology	Daisy-chain
Wiring type	UTP—1 pair: station to station Run 2 pairs to each station when wired through telephone wiring closet.
Data rate	230.4 Kbps
Segment length	300 meters
Max. nodes/segments	32
Physical interface	EIA RS-422 (balanced RS-449)
Physical addresses	Dynamically allocated on boot-up 1–127: client addresses 178–254: server addresses 255: broadcasts
Frame types	Control frames for protocol control Data frame to transfer data for upper layers
Data field size	0–600 bytes
CRC length	16 bits
Access detail	Sender uses a Request to Send (RTS) frame to reserve bus, receiver acknowledges reservation with a Clear To Send (CTS) frame. Only RTS needed for broadcasts.
Uses	Connect Apple Macintosh computers to each other, to Apple laser printers, to PCs, and to NetWare file servers. Used in small workgroup LANs.
Developer and promoter	Apple

Reference: LocalTalk characteristics. Learning Tree International

371

Figure 5-77

Access protocols	Access	Typical cable	Data rates	Frame sizes	Clocking/ CRC	Standards organizations responsible
Ethernet	Baseband CSMA/CD	Coax 50 ohm	10 Mbps	≥ 64 bytes ≤1518 bytes	Manchester 32-bit CRC	De facto, DIX
802.3	Baseband CSMA/CD	Coax or UTP	10 Mbps 1 Mbps	≥ 64 bytes	Manchester 32-bit CRC	IEEE
802.4	Broadband token bus	Coax 75 ohm	4 Mbps	—	32-bit CRC	IEEE
802.5	Baseband Token Ring	Not specified	1 Mbps 4 Mbps	≤ 8000 bytes	Differential Manchester 32-bit CRC	IEEE
Token Ring	Baseband Token Ring	STP	4 Mbps 16 Mbps	≤ 8000 bytes	Differential Manchester 32-bit CRC	Proprietary IBM
FDDI	Baseband token bus	Fiber optic	100 Mbps	≤ 4800 symbols	NRZ-I 32-bit CRC	ANSI
ARCNET	Baseband token bus	Coax 93 ohm	2.5 Mbps	512 bytes	16-bit CRC	ANSI
LocalTalk	Baseband CSMA/CA	UTPzz	230.4 kbps	600 bytes	16-bit CRC	Proprietary Apple

Reference: comparison of popular LAN access protocols. Learning Tree International

Figure 5-78

Characteristic	SDLC	HDLC	LAPB
Access method	Baseband polling	Baseband polling	Baseband polling
Topology	Point-to-point multidrop	Point-to-point	Point-to-point
Frame types	Information Supervisory Unnumbered	Information Supervisory Unnumbered	Information Supervisory Unnumbered
Control	Primary/ secondary polled	NRM ARM ABM	**Async Balanced Mode** (ABM) only
CRC length	16 bit	16 or 32 bit	16 bit
Reliability	Sequenced acknowledged flow control	Sequenced acknowledged flow control	Sequenced acknowledged flow control
Transparency	Bit stuffing	Bit stuffing	Bit stuffing
Use	IBM SNA	As a model protocol	CCITT X.25
Promoters and developers	IBM	CCITT, IEEE, ISO	CCITT

Reference: SDLC, HDLC, LAPB. Learning Tree International

Figure 5-79

OSI layer (TCP/IP layer)	Protocol	Characteristics
Network (Internet)	IP	**Internetwork Protocol:** used for routing. Connectionless datagram (packet) oriented.
	RIP	**Routing Information Protocol:** used to keep routing tables updated in routers and hosts by periodic broadcasts from routers.
	ARP	**Address Resolution Protocol:** broadcasts a request on subnet by host or router seeking physical node address for a given IP address.
	ICMP	**Internet Control Message Protocol:** messages for flow control, echo, and flow redirection. "Ping" is a popular use of ICMP echo messages.
Transport (Host to Host)	TCP	**Transport Control Protocol:** provides connection-oriented transport services host-to-host (end-to-end) across the internet. Sequencing, acknowledgment, and flow control are some of these services. Supports FTP, SMTP, and TELNET process services.
	UDP	**User Datagram Protocol:** provides connectionless transport services (no sequencing, acknowledgment, or flow control) for those process protocols that do not require these services. Supports SNMP and NFS processes, for example.

Reference: TCP/IP protocol suite. Learning Tree International

Figure 5-80

OSI layer (TCP/IP layer)	Protocol	Characteristics
Application Presentation Session (Process)	FTP	**File Transfer Protocol:** copy (files) from one host to another. User must work through established accounts on both hosts.
	SMTP	**Simple Mail Transfer Protocol:** host-to-host electronic mail transfer. Connects locally established E-mail systems.
	TELNET	**Remote Terminal Emulation:** user can log in to remote host from his/her current local session and run applications on the remote host.
	SNMP	**Simple Network Management Protocol:** specifies the management of network nodes that have agents running in them managed from nodes acting as network managers. Data is kept in **Management Information Base** (MIB) database.
	NFS	**Network File System:** logically attaches portions of file system on a remote NFS server to the local file system. Technology licensed by Sun. Uses RPC and XDR.
	RPC	**Remote Procedure Calls:** a redirector that filters calls by processes on one host to be executed on another. Local calls are passed to local operating system; network calls are sent via TCP/IP to remote system for execution.
	XDR	**eXternal Data Representation:** C language routines that allow machine-independent formatting of data, allowing sharing of information.

Reference: TCP/IP protocol suite (continued). _{Learning Tree International}

375

Figure 5-81

Layer	Protocol	Characteristics
Network	IPX	**Internetwork Packet eXchange:** derived from XNS. Routing protocol. Proprietary to Novell NetWare. Network addresses consist of logical network portion administered by network administrators; host portion is the physical node address. Uses a form of RIP for routing table updates.
Transport Session	SPX	**Sequenced Packet eXchange:** connection-oriented packet delivery. Sequenced, acknowledged, flow controlled. Establishes "virtual circuits." Used in RCONSOLE, remote printing, and SNA connections.
Application Presentation Session	NCP	**NetWare Core Protocol:** collection of file server functions for remote file access and printing on server as well as managing server security via the bindery. Contained in the SERVER.EXE program on the server and the NETX.COM shell on the DOS client.
	NetBIOS emulator	The emulator runs on a client workstation. Applications making NetBIOS-specific calls are supported by the emulator. It converts calls to NetWare and uses the Packet Exchange Protocol (PEP) to support sessions with the server.

Reference: NetWare IPX/SPC protocol suite. Learning Tree International

Figure 5-82

Layer	Protocol	Characteristics
Network	X.25	CCITT specification for packet-switched networks. Defines the **Packet Level Protocol** (PLP) for host-to-host (DTE-to-DTE) packet transfer. Connection-oriented. Uses LAPB at the frame level.
	CLNP	**ConnectionLess Network Protocol:** specifies datagram (connectionless) delivery similar to the IP protocol from TCP/IP. Uses 802.2 Type 1 services on LANs.
	ES-IS	**End System-Intermediate System:** routing protocol. Performs routing and routing advertising services from end host to routers in OSI networks.
Transport	TP0	**Transport Protocol 0:** connectionless transport services. Provides fragmentation and reassembly only. Used with X.25.
	TP1	**Transport Protocol 1:** same as TP0 with the addition of error recovery and acknowledgments.
	TP2	**Transport Protocol 2:** TP0 plus multiplexing of data streams over one virtual circuit.
	TP3	**Transport Protocol 3:** combined services of TP1 and TP2.
	TP4	**Transport Protocol 4:** reliable connection-oriented services. Sequencing, acknowledgments, and flow control. Used with the CNLP protocol.

Reference: OSI internetworking protocol. Learning Tree International

Figure 5-83

Layer	Protocols	Characteristics
Session	OSI Session Protocol	Specifies the management of application sessions or conversations. Full-duplex operation. May operate over any of the transport protocols.
Application	FTAM	**File Transfer and Access Management:** specifies a file transfer protocol as well as a remote file access method.
	CMIP	**Common Management Information Protocol:** specifies interactions between CMIP agents on subnets and the network management host. Defines a **Management Information Base** (MIB) database and MIB objects.
	MHS	**Message Handling System:** a subset of CCITT X.400 protocol for delivering electronic mail from host to host. Requires that MHS-based E-mail systems be operational on each host.
	ASN.1	**Abstract Syntax Notation 1:** specifies the language to use to define network objects (data types and structures) and data communications protocols.
	VT	**Virtual Terminal:** protocol for terminal emulation across the network, similar to TELNET.
	DS	**Directory Services:** based on CCITT/ITU X.500 protocol for networkwide host and services naming scheme.

Reference: OSI interoperability protocols. Learning Tree International

Figure 5-84

SNA Model Layer	SNA Protocols	Description
Physical	SDLC	**Synchronous Data Link Protocol**
	802.5 with 802.2	Token-passing ring access with logical link control.
Path Control	NCP	**Network Control Program**: resides in the host or front-end processor and performs routing, segmentation, and framing of data streams supporting sessions.
Transmission Control and Data Flow Control and Presentation Services	VTAM	**Virtual Telecommunications Access Method**: implements the **Network Addressable Units** (NAU) functions of sequencing, multiplexing sessions, data formatting, flow control, management and control, error recovery. Typically implemented in a program residing in the front-end processor.
	APPN	**Advanced Peer-to-Peer Networking**: the use of SNA networks to support peer-to-peer communications between two hosts, typically used for applications on a PC to communicate with applications on a mainframe. Uses LU 6.2 sessions and **Advanced Peer-to-Peer Communication** (APPC) conversations.
	NetView	Network-management architecture to manage problems, configuration information, performance, accounting, and change control in an SNA network.

Reference: IBM SNA protocol suite. Learning Tree International

379

Figure 5-85

Characteristics	Description
Access method	Baseband, polling, point-to-point links hierarchical
Access protocols	SDLC and 802.5 with 802.2 LLC
NAU	**Network Addressable Units:** units in an SNA network that perform unique functions to control and manage dataflow. NAUs have unique addresses. PUs and LUs are types of NAUs.
PU	**Physical Units:** hardware and software that manage the communication processes with a host. It resides in a host and other network devices. **PU 5**: host node, typically a mainframe. **PU 4**: communications controller node, typically a front-end processor. **PU 2**: peripheral node, typically cluster controllers **PU 2.1**: an active node, typically a PC supporting peer-to-peer LU 6.2 sessions over an SNA network.
LU	**Logical Units:** the logical connection into the network. LUs exchange information across the net. **PLU**: Primary Logical Unit; typically residing in a host, it initiates a session used by an application. **SLU**: Secondary Logical Unit, manages the session for the 3270 terminal or printer. **LU 2**: program-to-device (typically a 3270 terminal) session using primary/secondary transactions. **LU 3**: program-to-device (typically a printer) session using primary/secondary transactions. **LU6.2**: host-to-host, peer-to-peer sessions.

Reference: IBM SNA characteristics. Learning Tree International

Figure 5-86

Layer	Protocol	Description
Physical and Data Link	LocalTalk	Apple proprietary access protocol, baseband bus, CSMA/CA
	EtherTalk	Ethernet for Apple Macintosh computers 8002.3 compatible
	TokenTalk	Token Ring for Apple Macintosh computers 802.5 compatible
	AARP	**Apple Address Resolution Protocol**: translates between AppleTalk upper layer addresses and physical node addresses. Used by LocalTalk for dynamic address selection.
Network	DDP	**Datagram Delivery Protocol**: connectionless datagram (packet) delivery between sockets (upper layer addresses). Sockets are dynamically (DAS) or statically (SAS) assigned. SAS are used by lower level protocols; DAS are assigned by DDP as needed.
	RTMP	**Routing Table Maintenance Protocol**: maintains DDP routing tables from broadcasts received by node from router and servers.
	NBP	**Name Binding Protocol**: translates between AppleTalk names and addresses.
Transport	ATP	**AppleTalk Transport Protocol**: sequencing acknowledgment and fragmentation. Transaction based.
	ADSP	**AppleTalk Data Stream Protocol**: connection-oriented services, full duplex, reliable flow control above DDP. Manages connections between sockets. Uses sliding window flow control with 64-KB maximum window size.

Reference: the AppleTalk protocol suite. Learning Tree International

Figure 5-87

Layer	Protocol	Description
Session	PAP	**Printer Access Protocol:** primarily for workstation printer sessions supporting Apple Printing Services. May also be used for general session services between workstations and servers.
	ASP	**Apple Session Protocol:** works with ATP to provide logical session services.
Presentation	AFP	**Apple Filing Protocol:** manages access to remote files via remote procedure calls and implements access security to remote files.
Application	AppleShare File Server	Transparent remote access to file servers. Enforces secure access to remote files. Uses AFP for file access. Maps registered users to server volume and directories.
	AppleShare Print Server	Notifies users when remote printers become available. Keeps spool file of print requests, keeps list of available network printers.
	AppleShare PC	Allows MS-DOS computers to share remote Apple printers and files on AppleShare file servers.

Reference: the AppleTalk protocol suite (continued). Learning Tree International

⇨ Workshop

See Fig. 5-88.

Figure 5-88

Characteristic	San Jose Building 1 Network B	San Jose Building 1 Network C	San Jose Building 2 Network C	San Jose Building 4 Network A	San Jose Building 2 Network B
Protocol suite					
Layer 7					
Layer 6					
Layer 5					
Layer 4					
Layer 3					
Layer 2					
Layer 1					

Workshop. Learning Tree International

⇨ Practice exam questions

1. The IEEE 802 series standards were developed and are promoted by which standards organization?
   A. CCITT/ITU
   B. ISO
   C. IEEE
   D. ANSI

2. Which layer of the OSI reference model was not originally covered by Project 802 specifications?
   A. Physical layer
   B. Data link layer
   C. Network layer
   D. All of the above

3. What is the data rate for a 10BASE-T network?
   A. 1 Mbit/sec
   B. 10 Mbits/sec
   C. 16 Mbits/sec
   D. 100 Mbits/sec

4. IBM Token Ring Networks might operate at what data rate?
   A. 4 Mbits/sec
   B. 10 Mbits/sec
   C. 4 Mbits/sec and 16 Mbits/sec

5. The TCP/IP protocol suite was developed by which organization?
   A. IBM
   B. ANSI
   C. Department of Defense
   D. CCITT/ITU

6. Which layer of the OSI model characterizes IP?
   A. Data link
   B. Network
   C. Transport
   D. Session

7. What layer of the OSI model characterizes TCP?
   A. Data link
   B. Network

C. Transport

D. Session

8. Which protocol can be employed for file transfers across the Internet?

A. FTP

B. Telnet

C. DTP

D. ICMP

9. Novell's IPX protocol can be classified as functionally equivalent to which layer of the OSI model?

A. Data link

B. Network

C. Transport

D. Session

10. The OSI suite of networking protocols has been developed and/or adopted by which standards organization?

A. CCITT/ITU

B. ISO

C. ANSI

D. IEEE

11. Which is an example of an OSI transport protocol?

A. TP4

B. ES/IS

C. ASN.1

D. CMIP

12. Which is a protocol that performs network-layer functions?

A. TP4

B. ES/IS

C. HDLC

D. FTAM

13. The X.25 protocol is part of the OSI protocol suite.

A. True

B. False

14. Which protocol performs network management functions as part of the OSI protocol suite?

A. ASN.1

B. FTAM

C. CMIP

D. MHS

15. Which protocol is not part of the native NetWare protocol suite?
    A. IPX
    B. SPX
    C. NCP
    D. FTP

16. The X.25 protocol can be classified as functionally equivalent to which layer of the OSI Model?
    A. Physically
    B. Data link
    C. Network
    D. Transport

17. In an IBM SNA network, the host has which physical unit number?
    A. 1
    B. 2
    C. 4
    D. 5

18. In IBM SNA networks, a session connected to a 3270-type terminal is considered which type of logical unit (LU)?
    A. Type 0
    B. Type 1
    C. Type 2
    D. Type 4

19. Which organization developed and promotes the use of SNA?
    A. Digital Equipment Corp.
    B. International Business Machines
    C. Apple Computer
    D. Novell

20. In an IBM SNA network, a session is a logical connection between:
    A. Two network addressable units
    B. A logical unit and a physical unit
    C. A physical unit and a systems service control point
    D. Two physical units

21. Which DNA version is an implementation of OSI protocols?
    A. DECnet Phase III
    B. DECnet Phase IV
    C. DECnet Phase V
    D. Both DECnet Phase IV and Phase V

22. Which protocol is AppleTalk's implementation of the OSI network layer?
    A. AARP
    B. ATP
    C. DDP
    D. None of the above.

23. Which AppleTalk protocol supports printer access in an AppleTalk network?
    A. PAP
    B. ASP
    C. ATP
    D. Both PAP and ATP

24. Which AppleTalk protocol is employed by AppleTalk to translate between AppleTalk names and addresses?
    A. ARP
    B. AARP
    C. NBP
    D. RTMP

25. The organization that developed and promotes the use of the Fiber Distributed Data Interface (FDDI) access protocol is?
    A. ANSI
    B. IBM
    C. ISO
    D. CCITT/ITU

26. The data rate of an FDDI network is?
    A. 1 Mbit/sec
    B. 10 Mbits/sec
    C. 16 Mbits/sec
    D. 100 Mbits/sec

27. What is the data rate of the LocalTalk access protocol?
    A. 64 Kbits/sec
    B. 230 Kbits/sec

C. 1 Mbit/sec

D. 2.5 Mbits/sec

28. Which pair matches the data link layer protocol with the organization that has developed and promoted it?

A. IEEE/HDLC

B. ANSI/LAPB

C. IBM/SDLC

D. ISO/IP

29. Which is not a link access protocol?

A. SDLC

B. X.25

C. LAPB

D. HDLC

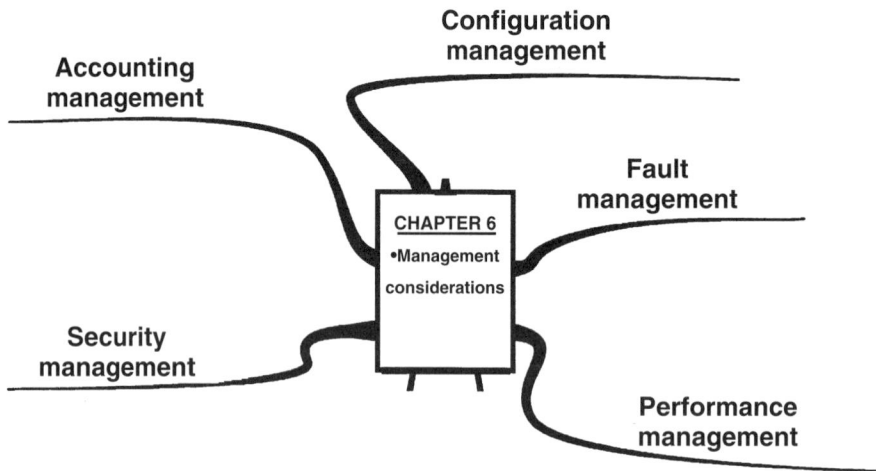

Accounting
management

Configuration
management

Fault
management

CHAPTER 6
•Management
considerations

Security
management

Performance
management

6

Network management

I N its bare essentials, network management is fire fighting at a distance. Some part of the network goes down, and the network administrator must identify the location of the outage and what to do to fix it. To accomplish this most-essential task well, a network administrator must have a wide variety of tools and techniques. Some activities, such as configuration and performance management, must be done well in advance of any outages. Other tasks, such as security and accounting, are often done after the fact. And the most important task, fault management, must be performed quickly and effectively at soon as an outage occurs. The models, the tools, the techniques, and the schemes for effective network management are considered in this chapter.

⇨ CNE exam objectives

➢ Identify the specific network-management functional areas.

➢ Describe the organizational issues involved with the following network-management functional areas:
  - Configuration management.
  - Fault management.
  - Performance management.
  - Security management.
  - Accounting management.

➢ Identify solutions, generic products, or strategies that address these network-management functional areas.

⇨ Network management functional areas

Distributed systems and multivendor networks present new and unique problems to the network manager. Traditional models of network management cannot be used. The classical role of the network manager as someone whose primary responsibility is to keep the network running is much too narrow a view to encompass the total set of duties required by enterprise systems.

In order to be successful, the network manager will have to implement a vendor-neutral strategy that can provide the information required to support the accounting, performance monitoring, configuration, security, and fault management of distributed multivendor networks. This can only be accomplished by careful planning and a commitment from high-level management.

⇨ The network management problem

Back in the good old days of vendor-specific, monolithic, terminal-host computing, network management was a complex but not impossible task. The network manager was mandated to deliver application systems from the host computer to the user's fingertips. This required control of equipment from the I/O port on the mainframe to the terminal on the user's desktop. In essence, the network manager provided a support service to the MIS director. As such the position was generally located within the MIS organization and frequently as a subgroup to the Technical Support or Operations department. In many ways, the Network Control Center (NCC) was equivalent to the Operations group. The operations manager was responsible for the efficient operation of the host computer, and the network manager had the same role with respect to the network. For many network managers, their job definition could be defined in a single sentence, "Keep the network up and running!" They approached this primarily as a technical task and, as such, most network managers took a very "hands-on" approach to their jobs with the emphasis on technical excellence.

To assist the network manager in fulfilling this mission, vendors provided the tools required to control their proprietary network systems. Each vendor had a set of tools unique to the company's product lines. Tightly coupled to the underlying network protocol, these network control systems provided information on both the logical and physical well being of the network. Training was also supplied by the vendor, and specialists could be called in to help optimize the system as required. While not perfect, the fact that network managers were operating within a set of rigid boundaries, defined by the proprietary nature of the protocol, provided a fair degree of control over the environment that allowed the network managers to accomplish their mandate.

As we have seen throughout this book, networks are no longer homogeneous. A variety of protocols, subnetworks, operating systems, and applications now guarantee that the network manager can no longer look to a single vendor to provide a solution for network management. In addition, as networks become more accessible, network security is becoming a rapidly growing concern. To add to this increasingly complex situation, the network manager is being called upon to deploy applications such as e-mail, directories, file transfer, distributed file systems, and gateway services that provide interoperability between heterogeneous environments. Many of these applications, such as groupware and multimedia systems, are being deployed without consultation by user groups who seem to assume that network bandwidth is free and unlimited.

To compound this problem, the tools that are required to handle the support and management of this complex environment are either immature, inadequate, incompatible, or unavailable. Network management staff has generally not been trained to handle this level of diversification. As LAN administrators create larger and larger subnetworks, the lines of authority and responsibility between the NCC and local support staff become less clear and lead to political situations that further complicate administrative issues. Finally, there is little appreciation at senior levels of the organization of these problems or the potential for disaster. In fact, within MIS, the NCC is still being viewed by the CIO in the same traditional role, so that funding required to handle these new tasks is generally not available.

We have often mentioned the concept of the "network as an organizational computer." If the backbone network represents the backplane of this new enterprise computer, then those who control the backbone by inference now control access to the entire set of information-processing assets available to the organization as a whole. The individual who has the responsibility to administer and manage these assets must have a senior role to play.

Earlier we stated that the traditional mandate of the network manager was to keep the network running. This mission statement will now have to be changed. We suggest a much more strategic view of network management. This new view might be best stated as, "How will network technology assist the organization in reaching its strategic objectives?" The answer to this question will be the primary responsibility of the network manager and the network control center.

⇨ A network management model

A model is required to define the various roles and duties that will have to be performed prior to determining the tools and staff required to implement a NCC. This model must be flexible enough to incorporate future services that the NCC will offer and capable of being inserted at various levels of the organizational chart. While a great deal of literature is available on the technical aspects of network management, the amount of material available on how to model the NCC is somewhat lacking.

⇨ The OSI network management model

As part of OSI, the ISO has defined the role of network management. This is illustrated in Fig. 6-1. There are five major areas defined.

Figure 6-1

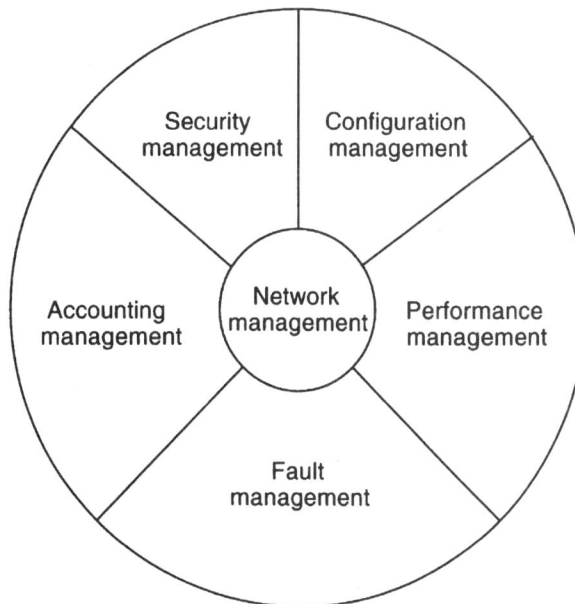

The OSI view on network management functions.

The defining ISO document for network management is Recommendation X.700: "Management Framework Definition For Open Systems Interconnection (OSI) for CCITT Applications."

❋ Configuration management

The ITU X.700 document defines the services of OSI configuration management as:

> Configuration management identifies, exercises control over, collects data from, and provides data to open systems for the purpose of preparing for, initializing, starting, providing for the continuous operation of, and terminating interconnection services. Configuration management includes functions to:
>
> a. set the parameters that control the routine operation of the open system;
>
> b. associate names with managed objects and sets of managed objects;
>
> c. initialize and close down managed objects;
>
> d. collect information on demand about the current condition of the open system;
>
> e. obtain announcements of significant changes in the condition of the open system;
>
> f. change the configuration of the open system.

Configuration management is that set of activities involved with the installation and modification of network elements. This includes both hardware and software such as bridges, routers, network interface cards, drivers, file systems, etc. Assignment of network addresses would also be included in this activity. An important element would be those activities involving change control. In a distributed environment, it will become increasingly difficult to retain any control over hardware and software once it has been released to the end-user community. Policies and procedures will not be enough. Some automated method of auditing changes will have to be made available. As a side aspect to change control, the task of software distribution must also be included as part of configuration management. How should new software be distributed, installed, and configured? There are numerous trade-offs between electronic distribution and the use of hard media such as diskettes or CD-ROMS. We will return to this subject a little later.

❊ Performance management

The ITU X.700 document defines the services of OSI performance management as:

> Performance management enables the behavior of resources in the OSIE and the effectiveness of communication activities to be evaluated. Performance management includes functions to:
>
> a. gather statistical information;
>
> b. maintain and examine logs of system state histories;
>
> c. determine system performance under natural and artificial conditions;
>
> d. alter system modes of operation for the purpose of conducting performance management activities.

Performance management refers to activities regarding the monitoring of the state of the network. These are required both to determine if the network is operating within specified metrics and to provide valuable input for capacity planning. Part of the problem regards the total volume of data available to the network manager. There is so much raw data available that the task of filtering and analyzing is a major undertaking. Further, the act of collection will place additional load on the network. In essence, performance management is a two-edged sword. To understand how the network is performing, we must collect data, but the act of collection impacts the network's performance! Resolving this dilemma has been a problem for network managers for many years. This problem has grown more complex as both the quantity and variety of network components have increased. Interpretation of the data is also challenging, since third-party software is required to integrate the various information sources.

❊ Fault management

The ITU X.700 document defines the services of OSI fault management as:

> Fault management encompasses fault detection, isolation, and the correction of abnormal operation of the OSI environment. Faults cause open systems to fail to meet their operational objectives and they may be persistent or transient. Faults manifest

themselves as particular events (e.g., errors) in the operation of an open system. Error detection provides a capability to recognize faults. Fault management includes functions to:

a. maintain and examine error logs;

b. accept and act upon error detection notifications;

c. trace and identify faults;

d. carry out sequences of diagnostic tests;

e. correct faults.

Fault management refers to activities involved in isolating and correcting network errors. Of all network management activities, this area can be the most complex. Any network error can cause a cascade of fault reports. For example, a fault in a modem will probably cause reported errors from modem, router, and session monitoring systems. Where should the network technician begin in isolating the problem? In complex systems, this fault isolation activity will require sophisticated software systems that can interpret the incoming fault reports and isolate the original error. Fault recovery must also be managed. The total set of activities required to restore a system to a viable state include fault reporting, response time, isolation time, diagnostic effort, the correction process, the restart process, recovery time, and user sign-off. At each step of the process, proper management procedures are required in order to ensure that a successful recovery is accomplished.

The fault management system will also have to collect information so that the network manager can estimate both the mean time between failure (MTBF) and the mean time to repair (MTTR) of network components. This information is valuable because it allows the network manager to take a more proactive role in the maintenance of network components. Having this information will also allow the network manager to calculate the cost of network outage. LANs are particularly vulnerable to outage, since the potential productivity loss is the product of the number of users and the length of the outage. Does the network manager have the time to collect all this information? Not without the assistance of sophisticated tools.

Assigning a value to the outage is difficult. Much depends on the nature of the work being performed on the LAN. However, as mission-critical applications migrate to LAN-based client/server systems, the cost of this outage is sure to rise. Fault management should also provide expert system or automatic diagnostic capabilities so that problems can be corrected without the need for human operator intervention. While this capability is still beyond many of today's system, it is found in sophisticated telecommunication systems and is likely to migrate into the data communication world.

✳ Security management

The ITU X.700 document defines the services of OSI security management as:

> The purpose of security management is to support the application of security policies by means of functions, which include:
>
> a. the creation, deletion, and control of security services and mechanisms;
>
> b. the distribution of security-relevant information;
>
> c. the reporting of security-relevant events.

A very important area of network management that must be considered is security. The security system will require the capability to handle all aspects of network authentication, authorization, access control, and validation. The security system must also be responsible for the integrity of data that is in transit between source and destination. The problems associated with network security, particularly with LAN-based networks, are obvious. At any point in the communication system, information might be tapped, disrupted, or usurped. While encryption techniques might solve some of these problems, encryption cannot solve all of them. One security problem deserves special mention. As application services are distributed, it is likely that a user (i.e., client) will have to contact many servers in order to accomplish a particular task. Sending authentication information, such as passwords, to each server will increase the likelihood of a security breach. Later in this chapter, we will discuss one possible solution to this problem.

✳ Accounting management

The ITU X.700 document defines the services of OSI accounting management as:

> Accounting management enables charges to be established for the use of resources in the OSIE [Open Systems Interconnect Environment], and for costs to be identified for the use of those resources. Accounting management includes functions to:
>
> a. inform users of costs incurred or resources consumed;
>
> b. enable accounting limits to be set and tariff schedules to be associated with the use of resources;
>
> c. enable costs to be combined where multiple resources are invoked to achieve a given communication objective.

Accounting will rapidly become an important requirement for distributed networks. At the current time, many local departments and users consider corporate network bandwidth to be free and unlimited. New applications are added without any consideration of capacity use. Network managers are faced with an increasingly heavy load of traffic and no way to determine the responsible parties or applications. Until such time as users can be made aware of the cost of transmission, we can anticipate that the load will continue to increase at an escalated pace. This is especially true as multimedia and groupware applications become more available, not to mention real-time video conferencing. The network management system must have the capability to charge users for bandwidth use. By doing this, users will become more sensitive to how they use the networks, and network managers will be able to perform between capacity planning. As an additional benefit, the use of an accounting system will provide the basis for the NCC to be viewed as a profit center rather than a cost center. This is important if network managers expect to have the budgets required to deploy more sophisticated, high-speed networks that will be required in the future. Sadly, this capability is one of the last considered by network managers who are trained to think in terms of reliability, serviceability, and availability rather than accountability.

⇨ Network management schemes

There are many proprietary schemes for managing network devices on a LAN. Cabling manufacturers have their cable management schemes. Bridge manufacturers have their proprietary bridge managing schemes. So do concentrator and hub manufacturers. Network operating systems have their own utilities to manage the server, which adds to the variety. And variety is the spice of life for a network administrator, isn't it?

Definitely not! It is most desirable to have one and only one all-encompassing management scheme that integrates information about all network devices in one clear display on one workstation on the network. Wouldn't that be nice? Today that dream can almost be realized. The question is not so much how or whether it can be done, but should it be done at all for small PC networks. More about that later. Let's tackle the how first and then ponder the why and come up with our rule of thumb for deployment of a management scheme.

⇨ Simple Network Management Protocol (SNMP)

SNMP is the industry-standard network management protocol. SNMP means the Simple Network Management Protocol and has become the standard for network management in the industry. The acronym SNMP means both the protocol SNMP used for conversations between manager stations and network agents and the entire set of components supporting SNMP, including the agent, the manager, the database of information, and the architecture.

SNMP is part of the TCP/IP protocol suite and actually requires that the UDP protocol at the transport level and the IP protocol at the network level, both from the TCP/IP suite, be operational for SNMP to work.

❋ Components of SNMP

The SNMP architecture is composed of five components: the management station, the network agents, the conversation protocol, the collection of data objects, and the underlying TCP/IP network.

✳ The management station

The management station is the brains behind the management operation. It is constantly polling SNMP agents on the network, inquiring as to their health and well being. The management station occasionally asks the agents to take some corrective action. It keeps all information about network status and device parameters and network statistics in a database called the MIB (see below). It makes the information available to a network manager in a colorful display of network status. The manager is also able to write reports from the database of network information and remotely manipulate agent parameters. There might be more than one management node on a network.

✳ The SNMP protocol

SNMP is the conversation protocol for management. It has four verbs in its vocabulary. A management station has the ability to read the value of a variable under an agent's management by using the GET command. If the information is in the table, the GET NEXT command allows the management node to retrieve all the values in that table. An agent's parameter can be changed with the SET command. It is by changing a parameter that the management node can effect a change of state in the network. Finally, the agent itself can alert the manager about the change of status of a crucial parameter via the TRAP verb. Newer versions of SNMP have added more commands and better security features but are not in widespread use yet.

The protocols in the SNMP protocol stack are: IP for addressing and routing, UDP for transport (connectionless), and SNMP for management queries and conversations.

✳ Agents

Agents are programs that run in the devices being managed and keep track of the value of parameters relating to those devices or relating to nearby LANs. Agents also take action when a local MIB parameter is changed by the management node. Agents alert the management node when crucial parameters exceed set values.

❋ The MIB

The MIB, or management information base, is a collection of
network-parameter information being collected by the management
node and being observed and reported on by the agents. The MIB is a
database of thousands of network parameters. The database residing
at the network manager is the complete collection of all values for all
devices, whereas the MIB at the agents is a smaller version, or subset,
related to the local device or LAN itself only.

❋ The TCP/IP network

SNMP has been designed to work over a TCP/IP internet. In
particular, it requires the transport of IP packets from the
management stations to the agents and back. Any other protocol will
not do. TCP/IP is used exclusively for this task.

Figure 6-2 shows all of these components in action. Notice that there
are agents for bridges, routers, and file servers. The network manager
appears next to the network management, not at the network control
center as it should be.

Figure 6-2

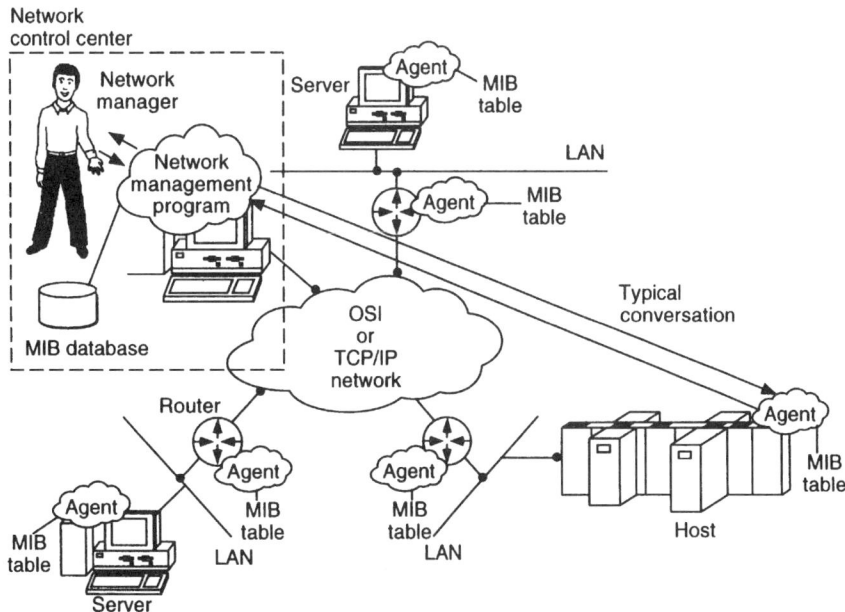

The SNMP network management architecture and components. Learning
Tree International

401

By and large, the SNMP system described previously can be deployed in today's networks. There are some significant areas of concern, such as security, with the early version of SNMP. These are addressed by the new version of SNMP being proposed and adopted as the next-generation network manager protocol. It will have authentication and several new conversation verbs, making it more robust in functionality.

Novell NetWare file servers have a version of TCP/IP, an SNMP agent, and network manager that come standard with the product. It has very few practical features for managing the server. It appears that Novell put it there so that a NetWare file server could participate in SNMP network management, and not so much as the platform for a network management station.

There is no question that SNMP is preferred over proprietary schemes as a network management architecture and protocol. It is definitely superior to proprietary schemes, especially as a network becomes heterogeneous to a larger degree and you have to grapple with the multivendor dimension of LANs. On the other hand, SNMP network management requires a lot of effort to set up and get working efficiently and productively. And it might definitely be overkill for the simpler situation of a couple of departmental PC networks with a limited number of servers, bridges, and routers. As networks get complex and become enterprisewide networks, you will need the sophistication of SNMP to know what is going on around the nets. But for smaller nets, it is not necessary.

As a rule of thumb, sophisticated SNMP network management schemes are not needed for small PC nets (20–50 PCs and a couple of file servers). These schemes are more useful in large, multivendor networks that have a wide variety of internetworking devices in place.

Troubleshooting tools

Troubleshooting tools might be considered fault management systems. That's what they are—devices and techniques for identifying types of faults, pinpointing location, checking component operation, and isolating the faults until a repair can be effected. Troubleshooting tools, or fault management systems, help us to see the nature and location of the problem so we can come up with a solution.

⇨ Fault management systems

Problems might occur anywhere on the network. Figure 6-3 demonstrates a few possible places. The locations and situations are so varied, we need an array of devices and methods. Some devices and methods are global in scope, i.e., they check on global parameters. Others are extremely local and check on minute details. Figure 6-3 gives some idea of the magnitude of the troubleshooting problem.

Figure 6-3

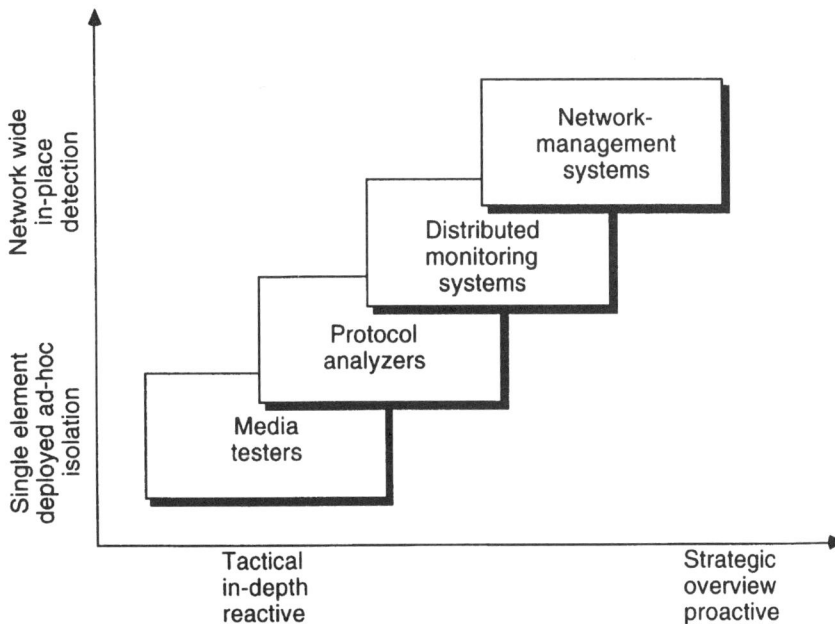

Faults can occur anywhere on the network, and a network manager must have an array of global and local troubleshooting tools ready to identify and locate these faults. Learning Tree International

❊ Type of tools

Troubleshooting tools range from very detailed and specific devices to global tools such as SNMP-based network management systems. The following is a list of troubleshooting tools ranging from the detailed, local tool to a more global system:

1 Media testers.

2 Protocols analyzers.

3 Distributed monitoring systems.

4 Network management systems.

Figure 6-4 graphically positions these tools and devices in a hierarchy from tactical in-depth tools to the more strategic ones. Also, they are categorized as to their deployment, ranging from single-element, local, isolated, ad-hoc placement to networkwide, in-place systems. Courtesy of Learning Tree International.

Figure 6-4

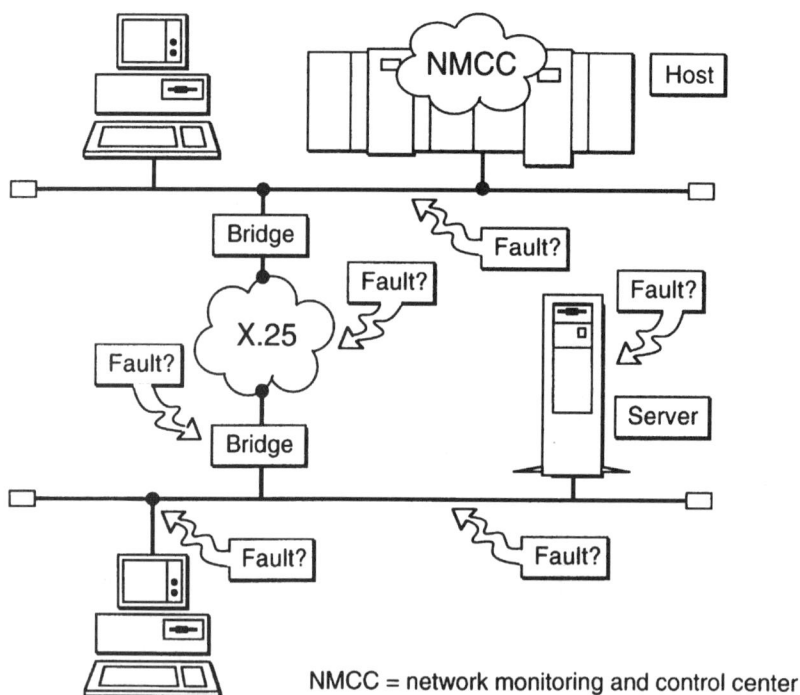

NMCC = network monitoring and control center

Fault management systems ranked by whether they are tactical strategic devices, whether they help with a single problem and are used ad-hoc, or whether they are employed to monitor systemwide parameters from stationary management stations. Learning Tree International

☀ Deployment

The deployment of strategic and tactical troubleshooting tools is only successful when we carefully consider where they should be placed and what the reasons are for each placement. Also, a mixed tool type is needed to be successful in troubleshooting. You will have a wide variety of tactical tools and some of the more complex local tools such as protocol analyzers. Depending on the size of your network, you will have some type of networkwide strategic monitoring system. Unless you have a very large network, you might not be deploying very high-end management systems. In the next sections, we consider each type of system in detail.

⇨ Media testers

Cable problems can be investigated with a variety of cable testers. They range from simple ohmmeters to test continuity to sophisticated TDR (time domain reflectometer) devices. The purpose here is to isolate the exact cause of a problem on a cable segment. Included in this category, we have programs that check whether a network card is defective.

☀ Types of media testers

Most cable testers are media specific. There are testers for copper cables and for fiber cables. For copper cables, one might begin troubleshooting with a simple ohmmeter to check continuity. Usually, measuring resistance is just one function of a multimeter, so one would not buy an ohmmeter per se, but typically one would buy a multimeter.

There is a very sophisticated device called a time domain reflectometer that is used to check a cable. The instrument essentially shoots a short electrical pulse down a cable and looks for echoes. Echo pulses occur when there are shorts or opens in a cable. If an echo is found, then the time it took for the echo to return is a measure of where the short or open is located. This tool can be used to locate faults in cables and to measure cable length (using the proper terminator at the other end of a cable).

There is a version of the TDR that works for fiber-optic cables. It is called and OTDR (Optical TDR). Rather than shooting an electrical pulse down the cable, it shoots an optical pulse down the fiber while looking for echoes.

❈ Types of media testers to get

Simple testers are sufficient for small networks. Buy a DMM (digital multimeter) with an ohmmeter function. You can also get a simple continuity tester in its place, but the DMM is more versatile. Larger networks with a correspondingly larger cable plant require more sophistication. A TDR makes more sense as an additional device. There are wire testers for specific technologies, and these are sometimes appropriate. IBM makes a Token Ring cabling wire tester that is very useful in troubleshooting Type 1 and Type 2 cable problems.

Manufacturers of network cards make available programs that test their NICs. Avail yourself of one of these for each type of network card you have. The programs will test whether the NIC is responding to drivers in the computer and whether it is attached to the network and working properly. Often these programs can be used between two network cards to send a frame between them to test a cable segment, thus testing the continuity of the cable between two stations. In TCP/IP networks, you can use the PING function to make this station-to-station test.

⇨ Protocol analyzers

Protocol analyzers are very sophisticated tools. They provide a great deal of information and need experienced interpretation. They are best used by trained technicians who know what they are looking for and can use the tool to its best advantage. If you buy a protocol analyzer, we recommend that you invest in training, or the tool will be nothing more than a bookend on your technician's shelf. They are invaluable for larger networks. Smaller networks (less than 100 nodes) might benefit from them, but it is better to invest the money in more-needed items in smaller nets.

Essentially, a protocol analyzer is a computer with a network card that accepts, stores, and displays the details of all frames on the LAN segment to which it is attached. Protocol analyzers differ in sophistication by how much filtering they can do in choosing which frames to display, collection of statistics on frame parameters, frame types they can decode, and troubleshooting intelligence built into them. They work at the frame level typically, but they can decode most of the protocols encoded into a frame. They are specific to frame technology. In other words, Token Ring, Ethernet, FDDI, and X.25 protocol analyzers are different from each other, mostly because they have a different network card in them.

Some protocol analyzers can generate frames and emulate them as originating from a specific address. The frames can be generated with specific characteristics. They can be short frames or long frames, data frames or information frames, for example. This function is typically available in the more expensive, hardware-based models.

❊ Use of protocol analyzers

Protocol analyzers are used to look for frames with error—such as frames with a bad CRC—and to identify the sending station. Also, they can be used to troubleshoot an exchange of frames between a workstation and server, especially when that station has problems logging on. Protocol analyzers can monitor frame parameters, collect statistics, and periodically report the collected data to a network management station.

❊ Types of protocol analyzers

There are two types of protocol analyzers: software based and hardware based. The software-based device is nothing more than a program that runs on a PC that has been outfitted with a network card. The NIC has to be of a type that is able to accept all frames. Normally, NICs only accept either broadcast frames or frames that contain the NIC address in the destination field. The software-based programs are often limited in functionality, but they are low cost and are an easy starting place for a technician just learning to use one of these tools.

The hardware-based devices are more sophisticated and handle multiple protocols. They are often programmed to collect statistics dynamically, but these are more expensive. They collect more information and decode the frames and the upper-level protocols with more intelligence, but they require more training to be useful.

There is also a vast difference between LAN protocol analyzers using NICs and WAN protocol analyzers. The former can be either hardware or software based. The latter are strictly hardware based and are more dedicated devices.

⇨ Distributed monitoring systems

Distributed monitoring systems are typically in-place monitoring programs based on a server or other network computer. They are event driven. When a certain crucial event occurs on the system, they take either a corrective action or, more likely, sound an alarm. They can be used ad-hoc to inspect the network at a certain time or can be permanently installed to continuously monitor the network. They can also take some action, for example, causing routers to switch the packet flow to an alternate route, or they can shut down ports on a hub to isolate a troublesome NIC or LAN segment.

✳ Types of distributed monitoring systems

Typically these are proprietary systems. There are two types: the functionality that comes with the server operating system in the form of system management utilities, and those produced by third parties as add-on products to manage PC networks. By and large, monitoring systems sit on a server, watch for crucial events to occur, and then sound the alarm. They can be watching for security-related events, disks getting full, or network traffic reaching crucial levels. Often, monitoring systems collect statistics that can be summarized in network reports.

✳ Use of distributed monitoring systems

These tools are very useful for PC networks. For small nets, we do not recommend purchasing expensive add-on products. Instead, use the utilities that come with the network operating system. As you add more servers to your network and the network gets larger, you might want to acquire and install some add-on products.

⇨ Network management systems

Network management systems are employed for networkwide monitoring. Although there are many proprietary products that will do this job, we typically use SNMP-based systems for universality. The details of an SNMP-based network management system is explored earlier in this chapter. They are much more useful for large networks with many servers and different types of computers.

❊ Use of network management systems

Typically there will be one or more network management nodes on the network, with the manager version of the network management program running on the nodes. This program will check on the status and receive periodic updates from agent programs on the devices— such as servers, routers and bridges—on the network being managed.

❊ Types of network management systems

There are two types of networkwide managers: those based on the SNMP standard, and proprietary products. Also, there are some products that work very well for telephone-circuit-based wide area networks. One such product is AT&T's ACCUNET. Then there are other products that are based on the SNMP standard, such as HP's OpenView, and they have become so popular that they are the basis for many OEM management products. There are some management systems that are so proprietary that they only manage one type of network. Such is the case with IBM's NetView, which is popular for IBM mainframe environments.

In general, it is not recommended to deploy elaborate network management systems for small nets. It is most useful when nets get above 500 nodes and many servers with many bridges and routers. Several staff members are needed to support an elaborate network management system, putting such a system out of the reach of the small network administrator.

⇨ Deployment of troubleshooting tools

So how many of these tools should a network manager have, and where should they be placed to be prepared to troubleshoot network problems? Your troubleshooting kit, which doubles as your maintenance kit, should have some kind of a media tester. Consult chapter 8 for the components of a technician's troubleshooting/maintenance kit. Definitely you should have software to check the network cards in your system. Often the software is free and comes from the NIC manufacturer.

Should you have a protocol analyzer? The authors have been involved with many small PC networks and have seldom found a need for a protocol analyzer. They are very useful, and often we wished we had one to troubleshoot a problem. It would have made the job easier and cut down the amount of time we spent at it. But our experience and knowledge helped us find ways around not having that tool. If you have a small net, skip it. As the network gets larger, consider getting the software-only version of a protocol analyzer. Get familiar with using it. If you decide you need the more sophisticated hardware-based protocol analyzer, then don't forget to get training. It is really needed. And purchase a protocol analyzer with very specific problems in mind that it will solve. Don't buy it with a general notion that it will help with troubleshooting, because it will most likely sit on a shelf unused.

Use every available utility that came with the server NOS to do some distributed network management. We always found these to be sufficient as a first cut. As the number of servers increases, consider a third-party utility for alarms and monitoring purposes. Only for very large and complex networks should a sophisticated networkwide management system be considered. In that case, make sure it is based on the SNMP standard and that the system is easy to use. You will need to allocate some serious staff time to install, monitor, and run this sophisticated system.

Test your understanding

To see how much you have learned about the concepts presented in chapter 6, take five minutes to answer the following questions. What are the five areas of network-management concern as defined by ISO, their characteristics, and some of the tools that might be used to perform this management task? Turn to appendix C for typical answers to these questions.

1. Area: _____

   Characteristic: _____

   _____

   Tools: _____

2. Area: _____

   Characteristic: _____

   _____

   Tools: _____

3. Area: _____

   Characteristic: _____

   _____

   Tools: _____

4. Area: _____

   Characteristic: _____

   _____

   Tools: _____

5. Area: _____

   Characteristic: _____

   _____

   Tools: _____

7
Building the network

I N chapter 7 we bring all the technologies we have studied in earlier chapters together as we build a network from the ground up. While it is important to look at components individually and develop an understanding of their functionality, it helps if we can acquire an appreciation of when we might use a specific technology. The application of the technology is what this chapter tries to demonstrate.

⇨ Chapter outline

- ➤ Chapter objective
- ➤ CNE exam objectives
- ➤ Creating a small department network
  - The single segment network
  - Extending the segment with repeaters, hubs or concentrators
  - Managing segment traffic load with bridges
- ➤ Growing to an enterprise network
  - Supporting multiple protocols
  - Making the network even bigger with routers
  - Extending the LAN to other platforms with gateways
- ➤ Keeping the enterprise network running
  - Using network management to be alerted to potential network problems on the network

⇨ Chapter objective

The objective of this chapter is to create a network from scratch by starting with a single physical network segment and adding appropriate network components and enabling technologies as the network grows into an enterprise network with global connections.

⇨ CNE exam objectives

Although this chapter does not address any CNE exam objectives as defined by Novell, we believe it will help you develop a better understanding of how the different network components are used to create and keep a network up and running. Also, developing a larger perspective will give you a better understanding of the individual components' capabilities and limitations.

⇨ Creating a small department network

⇨ The single-segment network

Our story starts with our old friend, International Technologies. The company didn't always have a worldwide enterprise network interconnecting various disparate computer platforms. It started out in one office with a small group of stand-alone personal computers. Eventually, the day came when they had to implement a multiuser database application and share an expensive color printer. While sharing the printer could have easily been accomplished with a low-cost print-sharing switch box, the multiuser database application was going to require a network for implementation. One of the IT research engineers had always shown interest in networks and stand-alone personal computers and so was given the job of putting the network in place (on top of performing regular job duties).

It was decided that the network to be implemented would be a client/server file-server-based system with a central server providing file- and print-sharing services. The network operating system selected by the company was NetWare 3.x. The main reason NetWare 3.x was chosen was because the multiuser database application the company would begin to rely on for business crucial functions had already been tested on this NOS. Novell's IPX/SPX was the network layer protocol that would be implemented at the workstations in order to facilitate file server access. None of the current personal computers was powerful enough at this time to even run the network operating system. A file server with lots of RAM and hard disk drive storage space was purchased as to ensure future expansion capacity.

One must always start by looking at what applications a business requires to accomplish its business goals. That should always be the crucial selection criteria for any network architecture or product, and not the other way around. Choosing a network architecture first can later limit the potential application list that can be reviewed to meet the business requirement.

The resulting network configuration then became one file server and three computers in one small office area where the desks were all close together. Ethernet technology was about 20% of the cost of Token Ring at the time, so Ethernet got the nod. Ethernet coax cable was purchased instead of using unshielded twisted pair because there weren't that many stations on the network. The network was wired in 10BASE2 daisy-chain configuration. UTP also required a separate concentrator to be purchased, which added to the cost of the network. The IEEE 802.2 frame type was used because this was the default frame type for NetWare 3.12, which was the NOS version to be installed. Figure 7-1 is a diagram of the resulting single-segment network.

Figure 7-1

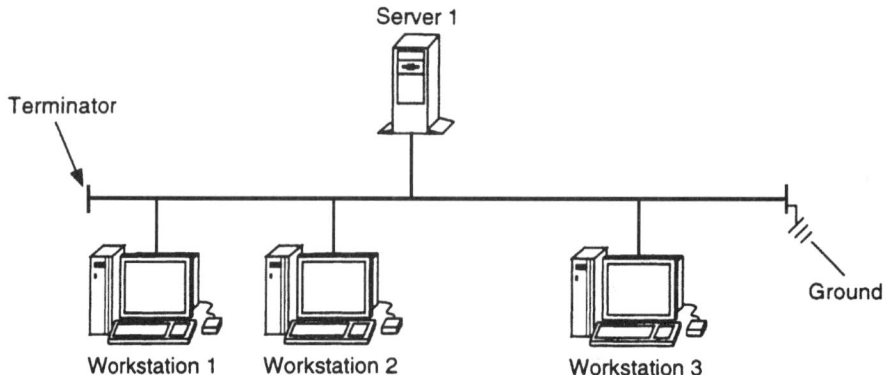

Single-segment network using coax. Learning Tree International

The network configuration was very productive and managed to handle many additional new stations as the company grew. The file server was used to store main office applications like word processing, spreadsheet, electronic mail and calendaring, and the original multiuser database application the network was purchased for. However, two problems arose that caused the research engineer to eventually rethink the original network design. The main problem with the coax cable was that every time someone moved the cable, the whole network would no longer be accessible by anyone. It sometimes took a long while to locate the problem section of cable. The second problem was one of growth. The company was expanding quickly and had just leased more office space on the upper floor of the building.

⇨ Extending the segment with repeaters, hubs, or concentrators

Before running the Ethernet coax cable to the new office space, the research engineer discovered that this would exceed the allowable length of the cable for a single physical segment. At this stage there were two possible choices. The first option was to purchase a repeater to interconnect the two coax cable segments. However, this idea was dropped because of the initial problems experienced with coax cable taking the whole network down. It was therefore decided that UTP cabling and hubs (also called concentrators) would be installed. The research engineer explained to the budgeting committee that UTP would be more fault tolerant when people moved their workstations. One station could be disconnected without affecting anyone else. Someone raised the concern that there was still the problem of the distance between the two offices, as the research engineer had stated that UTP has a limitation of 100 meters per individual cable segment. It was explained that a fiber-optic repeater link would be used between the two hubs so that this would not be a problem. Further, the fiber-optic link would not be susceptible to electromagnetic interference from the fluorescent lights or other equipment in the telephone company room interconnecting the two floors. Everyone unanimously agreed that this would be a better network design to go with, and the budget resources were made available. Figure 7-2 is a diagram of the new network design for the two offices.

As the years passed, the new network design allowed the company to expand significantly. But as new stations were continually added to the network, performance began to suffer and users complained that the network was getting slower. The company had simply added new hubs in each office to the original hub. The current network now had about

Figure 7-2

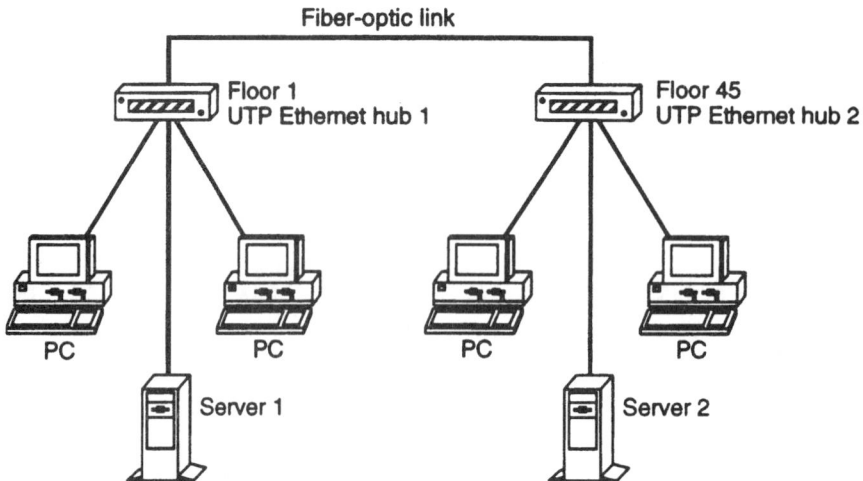

Ethernet UTP network design. Learning Tree International

50 attached stations and one file server in each office. Users accessed mainly the file server in their own office environment and only occasionally needed to access information on the other office's file server. Also, each server was the focal point for a post office for electronic mail exchange. The two servers communicated with each other to exchange mail.

The research engineer, who by this time had almost returned to regular research duties, was brought back into the picture to find a solution to the performance problem. The research into how Ethernet worked, coupled with some late-night reading on IEEE specifications (doesn't everyone?) showed him what was wrong with the company's existing network architecture. The offices were connected by hubs (hubs work at the physical layer of the OSI reference model, remember). A hub functions in the same way as a repeater; it simply repeats each and every bit that is sent to it. It is not aware of logical groupings of bits. The framing of bits is done at the data link layer. It was concluded that with the existing network design and layout, all traffic from one office was being repeated to the other office's physical network segment. Network traffic was going from one office to the other even when it was not required. For example, if a workstation in Office B attached to the file server in the same office sent a frame, the network in Office A would still see all the electrical signals or bits generated from that conversation, even though it did not need to. The additional load of traffic on a network segment where the traffic was not required was causing the degradation in network performance.

⇨ Managing segment traffic load with bridges

The research engineer concluded that a different device—a bridge— was needed to keep traffic on its own network segment. A bridge is a filter/forward device that works at the data link layer of the OSI reference model. This device is used to connect two or more physical network segments together. A bridge will build a frame from a series of bits received from the physical layer. Once a frame is constructed, the bridge analyzes the addressing information inside the frame to determine whether it should filter the frame out or forward it onto the other segment. Therefore, the bridge would solve the current problem by keeping traffic local to its particular segment, while keeping the two segments connected for cross-segment traffic. Figure 7-3 demonstrates the same network, only now a bridge is interconnecting to the office network segments.

Figure 7-3

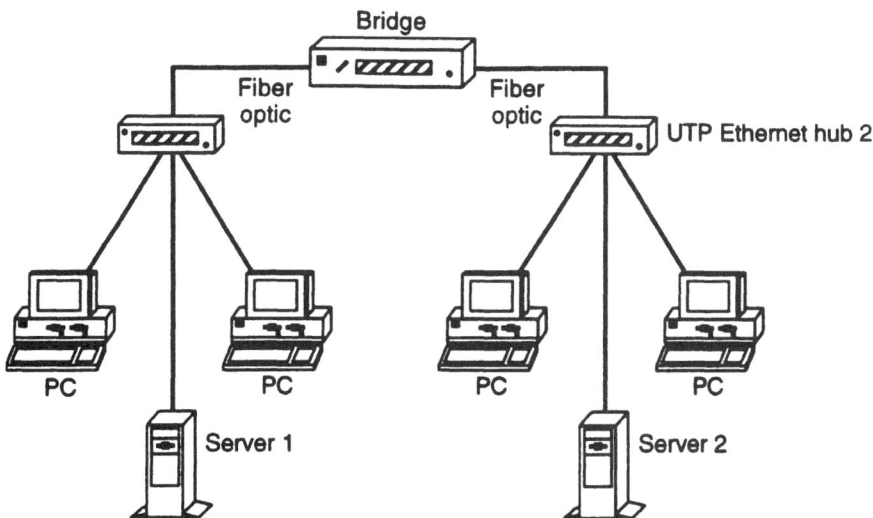

A bridge is used to interconnect network segments. Learning Tree International

It is important to note that even though the bridge will keep traffic destined for stations on the local network segment from going onto other network segments, it will not limit local network devices from accessing servers on other network segments. In this manner, when a workstation tries to attach to another office file server, the bridge will read the destination address of the frame, determine if that station is on the other network, and then forward it onto that physical network segment. The same process occurs when the server responds to the workstation device requesting the service.

With the bridge installed, the performance on each local network segment became very acceptable for a short time. However, the company continued to expand, and it didn't take long before even the local network segments in each office became bogged down with traffic once again. Each office expanded to two file servers and over 200 users in each office. In addition to a greater amount of traffic on each local network, the bridge also had to track over 500 network devices located in both offices.

Despite the hope of returning to a regular research engineering job, the research engineer became dedicated full time to keeping the network up and running. Trying to keep up-to-date on the changes in technology was also a full-time job for him. However, at this point the research engineer discovered a new solution to the current problem of traffic overload experienced in each office. Intelligent hubs were introduced by several manufacturers, and articles in the literature detailed how these new hubs could isolate traffic within particular physical areas of the network, much in the same manner that a bridge does. Additionally, the intelligent hubs would support high-speed network interface card links on some of the ports. The technology used in the new intelligent hubs is also sometimes referred to as Ethernet switches. As frames enter the switch, the address is analyzed to determine which port of the hub the device is connected to. Many devices can be connected to one hub port via a concentrator off that port. In this scenario, a frame is only transferred to the hub port that the device is located on. Other ports on the hub do not see the frame. The end result is that each port of the hub looks like it has its own 10-Mbit/sec Ethernet segment, although cross port communications are still supported.

A review of the current network design, shown in Fig. 7-3, showed our engineer that by purchasing only two intelligent hubs, a reconfiguration to the network could be done to take advantage of this new technology. Figure 7-4 is the new network layout after installing a new intelligent hub (switch) in each office. You can see that the old hubs, which did not support this capability, are now connected to the new intelligent hub. Also notice that the two file servers in each office are connected directly to the intelligent hub. Once again, network performance increased as traffic was further isolated to each area of the network. Another problem was solved.

Figure 7-4

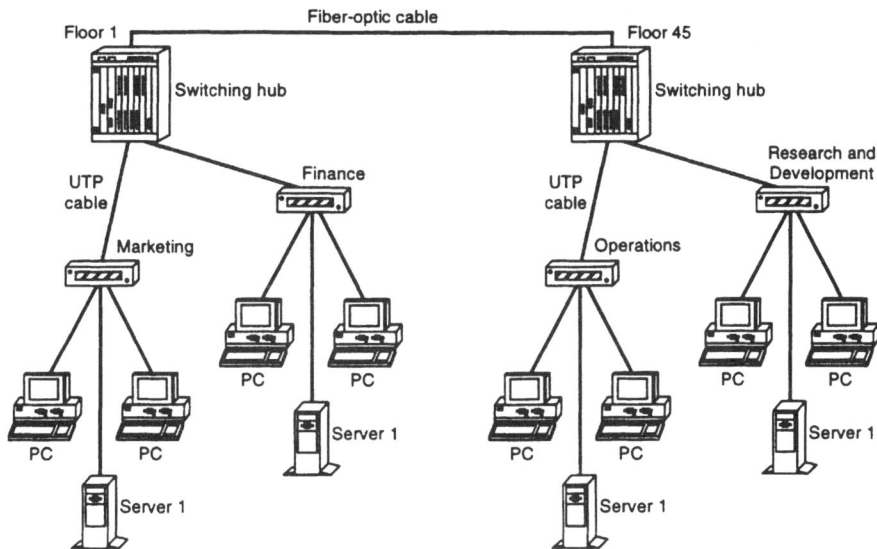

Intelligent hub network design. Learning Tree International

Occasionally, though, the remote office file servers disappeared for periods of time and could not be seen by local users (annoying, to say the least). Since the only device in between the two interconnected networks was the bridge, it was assumed that this was potentially the problem. Calls to the bridge manufacturer met with an explanation that the particular model was only designed to handle up to 500 network device addresses. It was determined that the current architecture was probably exceeding this number when salespeople brought their notebooks into the office and connected them to the LAN. The manufacturer also explained that the bridge was no doubt taking much longer to process frames because the table it had to look through for filter and forwarding decisions was reaching its maximum limit. Problems just don't seem to end, do they? Ah, the joys of technology!

A new, more powerful bridge was installed with more memory and a bigger processor to handle the problem. It was recognized as only a temporary measure, and another solution would eventually need to be found.

⇨ Growing to an enterprise network

Our research engineer was becoming quite adept at managing the two office networks by now. Starting from three workstations and one file server located in one office, the network had grown to over 500 workstations, printers that were connected directly to the network transmission medium (cable), and four file servers spread over two offices. Things, however, weren't going too badly. The most recent network interconnection problem had been solved, and it looked like the research engineer might be able to do a little less fire fighting and more proactive planning. After all, there was the all-important network documentation and procedures that needed to be created but had been set aside to solve crises. Now maybe these tasks would get done.

It was not to be. The workstation desktop needed to be better standardized throughout the organization. Our research engineer had been promised some relevant training courses by management once things settled down. Furthermore, a recent audit of the company revealed that it was potentially vulnerable to a disaster because it did not store backups of its data off site, and there was no disaster plan in place yet. Yes, there are always many other things to do . . .

But alas, our engineer friend's plans were foiled again. At a Monday morning management meeting (it always happens on a Monday morning, doesn't it?) the research-engineer-cum-network-administrator was told that a new group was going to be added to the company shortly. Almost 200 new devices would be added to the network. The research engineer at first did not see this to be a particular problem. After all, the brilliant intelligent hub design could be duplicated for the new office section. The bridge interconnecting both networks would begin to be strained but should be able to handle the additional demand. Additionally, there would be one experienced UNIX networking person joining the research engineer to manage the new network configuration.

Then the other shoe dropped. A description of the new devices to be added to the network was discussed at that fateful meeting. While some of the new devices would be DOS and Windows-based workstations, there would also be a significant number of UNIX-based hosts and workstations using TCP/IP as the networking protocol. The new devices to be added were located in both offices. Due to some of the business applications running on some of the new UNIX hosts, all workstations throughout the organization were going to need access to hosts using TCP/IP and Telnet terminal emulation. Additionally, a new NetWare file server was added at each office to provide the new users with access to corporate applications and electronic mail. Although the UNIX-based systems use Ethernet network interface cards over UTP, they use the Ethernet_II or ESPEC2 frame format instead of IEEE 802.2. It was, however, determined that the NetWare file servers would not have to support TCP/IP because there was currently no requirement for it. So much for plans to catch up on ongoing projects like training, network documentation, or that disaster recovery plan! It was back on the shelf for our research engineer.

We are making light of the latter issues not because they are not important, but because all too often they are placed at the bottom of the priority list. This despite the fact that these issues should be considered a mandatory requirement. In a properly run Management Information Systems (MIS) department, with an appropriate budget, they would get equal attention. What is amazing is that some organizations come to depend upon weak networking architectures and information management systems for their crucial business applications. When they are denied these applications due to a disaster, they lose a competitive advantage and risk going out of business.

So at the end of the Monday morning meeting, the research engineer was given the task of integrating the new systems gracefully into the existing network environment. Not an easy task based on the fairly large difference between the two networks.

⇨ Supporting multiple protocols

Interestingly enough, the initial integration stage seemed to go relatively well. Because the UNIX hosts and workstations use Ethernet over UTP, the intelligent hub-based system was in fact able to be duplicated. The intelligent hubs and the bridge supported up to four potential Ethernet frame formats, so supporting Ethernet_II and IEEE 802.2 did not prove to be a problem. However, the bridge was becoming a bottleneck, and some solution would need to be found to address this in the near future (it happened sooner than they realized).

However, getting the UNIX-based systems physically connected to the network was only the first phase of the project and turned out to be the easiest part. At this stage they had two network environments (one NetWare and one UNIX) accessing the same physical network cabling plant. Workstations using IPX/SPX over IEEE 802.2 frames could access NetWare file-server applications. Workstations using TCP/IP over Ethernet_II frames could access UNIX host-based applications using terminal emulation. But the network was not yet interoperable. Our research engineer and the new UNIX networking guru still needed to provide corporatewide access from all workstations to the UNIX host-based applications. In turn, the new workstations, which were currently configured with TCP/IP, would also need to access the NetWare file servers simultaneously in order to access corporate applications. The opportunity to further standardize the workstation desktop had arrived! Figure 7-5 highlights the new network configuration once the UNIX-based hosts and additional workstations were added.

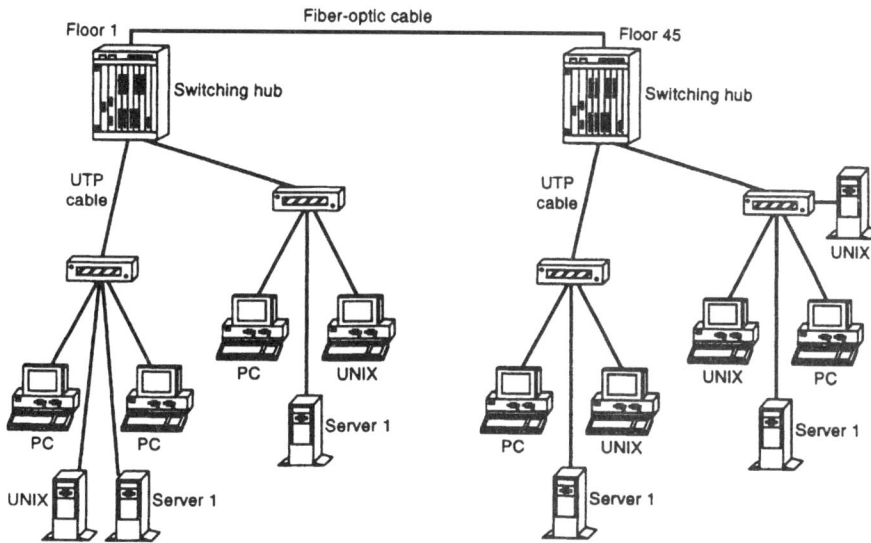

Figure 7-5

UNIX devices added to network. Learning Tree International

It was determined that the original workstations would be configured first to communicate with both the NetWare file servers and UNIX-based hosts, although the situation could have been tackled from either end. The original NetWare workstations were already using Novell's Open Data Link (ODI) interface, which provided support for multiple data link layer frame types (Ethernet_II and IEEE 802.2) and multiple network layer networking protocols (IP and IPX). Consideration was given to using Microsoft's Network Device Interface Specification (NDIS), but it was rejected mainly because the network standard was Novell, and not because it could not have provided a similar solution. It was the old, "If it ain't broke, don't fix it" approach.

A new workstation configuration was created supporting both frame types and network protocols. A memory manager was used at the workstations to make more conventional memory available after all the protocols were loaded. Several terminal emulation packages were tested, and one was selected based on its support of business applications that required very high graphics capability. The new configuration was then implemented at all of the original NetWare-based workstations (over the weekend, of course). Users on the original NetWare workstations now had access to both the NetWare file servers (which they already had access to before) and the new UNIX-based hosts. Access to the UNIX hosts (user login name and password) was provided. Users now had to be trained on how to use the UNIX-based applications, but that was another group's challenge. Our engineer could rest . . .

The new workstations were using Ethernet_II with TCP/IP packet drivers with stand-alone applications. The new corporate workstation desktop standard was now ported to these workstations. The users in questions were added to the appropriate NetWare servers (user login names and passwords) and given required rights to corporate applications. They had access to the UNIX hosts just as they always had through the new terminal emulation package, but they also now had access to the mainstay of corporate desktop applications, including the all-important electronic mail.

The project to provide corporatewide access to all host platforms was going well. However, network performance was once again starting to suffer despite the use of intelligent hubs. Also, the bridge was becoming overloaded once again now that the network workstations and directly connected printers surpassed 600 (even though the marketing brochure said it would handle 750). The UNIX networking guru proposed that the bridge be replaced with a router. Aha! You always knew we would eventually get around to the router solution. You probably wonder why it wasn't thought of sooner. A thorough study of the difference between the two types of devices, bridges versus routers, convinced the research engineer to give routers a try.

⇨ It's time to implement network routers

One of the main advantages for using a router over a bridge was the router's ability to work at the network layer of the OSI reference model. The current network was considered very flat. This means that there was one IPX and one IP network address for the entire network, which was located in both offices. Despite having intelligent hubs and a bridge to split up network traffic, broadcast frames, and packets are transmitted across the entire network. Under the bridge configuration, these broadcasts were allowed to cross the bridge and were further replicated on every port of the intelligent hubs. The broadcasts were raising network segment use and reducing overall network performance.

It was proposed that a routed network would further isolate network layer packet-based traffic to each logical segment. Furthermore, because the routers are concerned only with logical network addresses (there were going to be two network addresses under the proposed configuration), its routing table would be much smaller than the bridge table of the physical network interface card addresses (600 and increasing). Therefore, routers would be much faster since they could make a route selection decision much faster than the bridge could. Also, routers would afford more flexibility in the future should they need to integrate networks that support other frame types such as Token Ring or IEEE 802.5. (See Fig. 7-6.)

Figure 7-6

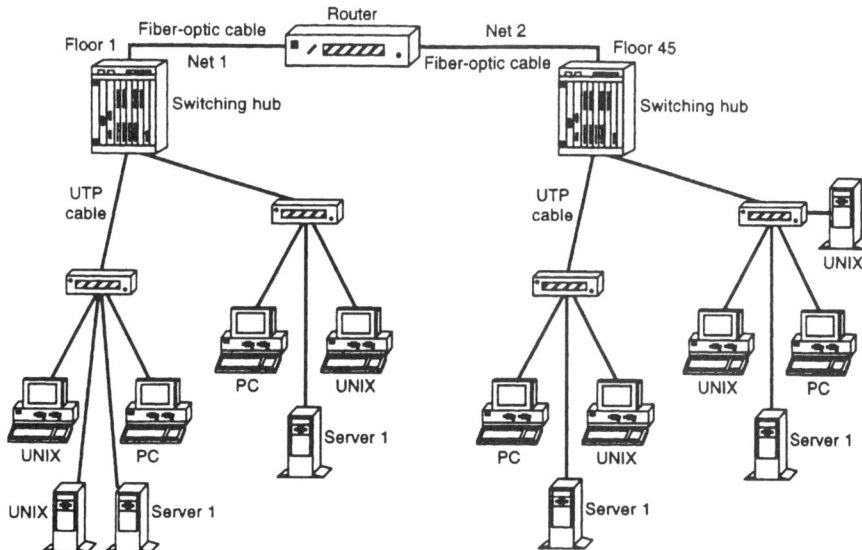

A router replaces a bridge as an internetwork device. Learning Tree International

A router was installed to replace the bridge. The router was configured to support both IPX and IP because both network-layer protocols were in use. Network addressing standards were also enforced. The router solution worked well and subsequently allowed the organization to expand rapidly as it added new offices on other floors. But they soon ran out of available leasable space in the existing building and needed to set up additional locations in other parts of the city. Additionally, the organization acquired several smaller companies in other countries that also required access to headquarter's UNIX-based applications. A larger TCP/IP network was required, and the implementation of the routers was a leading success factor during this phase of network growth.

It was during this phase that the organization moved from a LAN-based to a WAN-based internetwork. The routers were now connecting both Ethernet LANs to Ethernet LANs and to other network topologies such as Token Ring. Some of these networks were interconnected through WAN links using both high-speed asynchronous transmission media (ATM) and slower fractional T1 and 56-Kbits/sec leased lines supporting the TCP/IP protocol stack. Once the internetwork was established, it was determined by management that some of the NetWare-based applications should also be accessible from all workstations on the enterprise network. The support for IPX on the internetwork created a significant amount of additional WAN link traffic. (See Fig. 7-7.)

As the networks grew, so too did the number of network addressees supported on the entire enterprise network for IP and IPX. While initially this did not create a problem, the routing table broadcast size and frequency began to take up too much of the WAN link channel bandwidth, especially on the slower links. For TCP/IP, static links were set up to ensure better use of the Internet WAN links. For IPX/SPX, Service Advertising Protocol (SAP) filtering was implemented at all the routers connected to the internetwork. Both of these measures helped reduce the WAN link traffic associated with maintaining routers and server-based information. However, it was realized that this also was only a temporary measure.

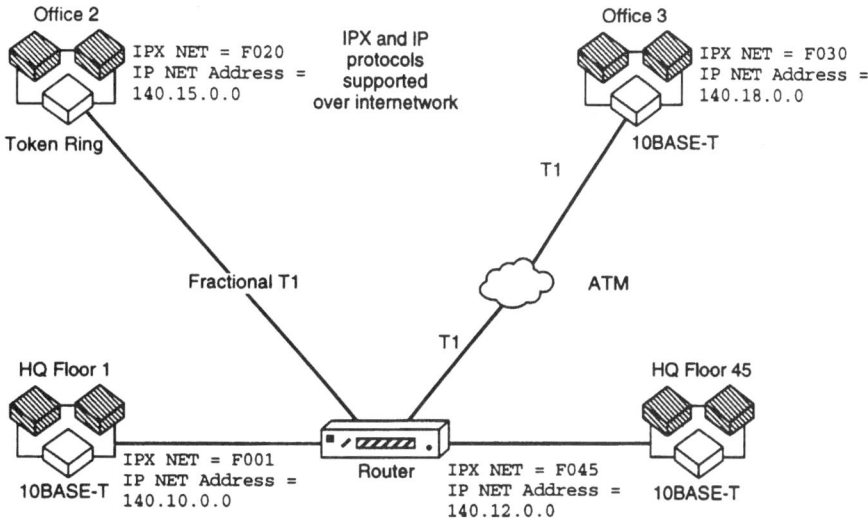

Figure 7-7

Multisite internetwork. Learning Tree International

The network was functioning sufficiently well at this point that the network administration staff, which had now reached five, was able to start addressing some issues that had been sitting on the back burner for some time. It was also during this period that our research engineer became Director of Networking Infrastructure (about time, don't you think?) and was able to report some progress at one of the Monday morning management meetings. The news was greeted with much enthusiasm. Parties were organized and much merriment abounded.

Unfortunately, at the same meeting the issue of accessing the Internet from workstations was put forward by the Marketing Department. The proposal was that the company could make all of its marketing and sales information available over the Internet. (Isn't marketing always the source of technical nightmares?) It was also put forward that Internet access would provide the entire organization with worldwide electronic mail access. Unfortunately, the Finance Department rejected the proposal on the grounds that it would open up the organization's network to Internet hackers (ah, eventually we were going to get around to these lovely creatures—the bane of any self-respecting network

engineer). They could place the organization at serious risk. The Director of Network Infrastructure (our former research engineer and now a whiz at internetworking) proposed that the financial systems could be set up on an IPX-only network connected to one of the routers. This network configuration would mean that only IPX-based stations throughout the corporation's internetwork could access the financial systems. As the Internet connection was IP based, this should not create so much of a security risk. Furthermore, a fire wall would be set up between the corporate network and the Internet to provide a higher level of access security. Ha! A technical solution can always be trotted out at these Monday meetings.

The proposal sounded very good, except that the Finance Department staff also needed access to the UNIX-based TCP/IP host applications. The solution was to set up the NetWare file server holding the finance applications on its own IPX network while the workstations remained on another logical IPX and IP-based network. With this configuration, the finance staff could access both the IPX based finance NetWare file server and the TCP/IP-based UNIX host applications. Figure 7-8 shows this new configuration. Please note that with a bridge, this solution would not have been feasible unless workstation addresses were hard coded into the bridge table (static entries), which is a somewhat inflexible approach.

The proposal was accepted and an Internet access provider was engaged. The Internet link was established at the corporation's headquarters using a router connected to a main network backbone using Ethernet with Ethernet_II frame format and to the Internet provider's 64 Kbit/sec ISDN link. Network users were now able to Telnet to corporate and to Internet-based UNIX hosts. Additionally, they could use the File Transfer Protocol (FTP) to download research papers and other files from hosts on the Internet. However, transparent electronic mail access had yet to be implemented.

⇨ When a router does not fulfill the requirement

And this was not the only challenge that our fearless Director of Network Integration was about to face. The company, in its surge of

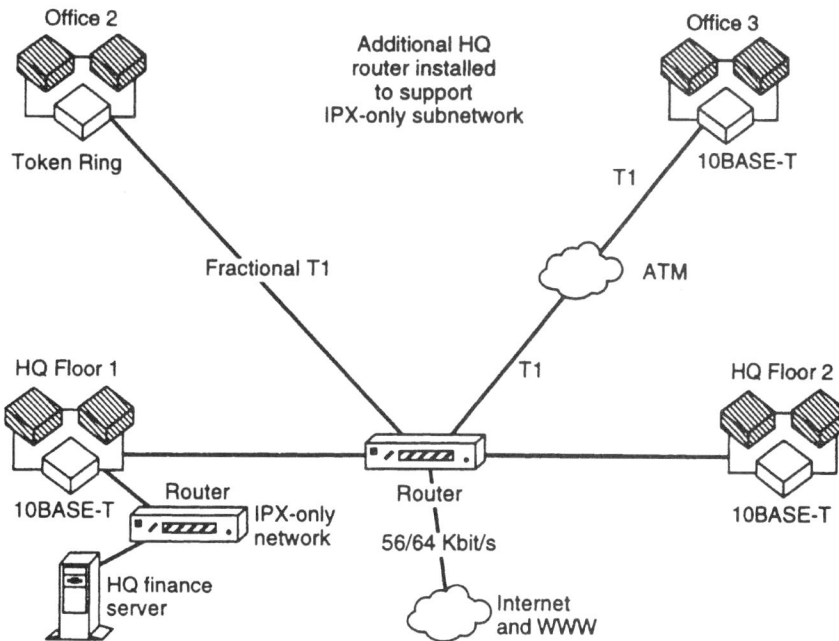

Figure 7-8

Selective network-layer protocol routing. Learning Tree International

growth, had just acquired an organization whose entire information system was based on a DEC VAX using DEC LAT protocol. DEC LAT is a higher-layer protocol that does not have any network layer functionality such as logical network addressing or routing. Unfortunately for our Director, the applications on the DEC VAX were going to need to be accessed by the entire corporation. The suggestion was put forward to convert the application to a client/server-based system that would fit into the current network architecture, but this was deferred by management due to the estimated costs of conversion. The challenge was for our Director to determine how the DEC LAT protocol and subsequent DEC VAX services would be made accessible throughout the enterprise.

Once again, our Director hit the books and found that the routers that had been implemented as the corporatewide standard were also capable of acting as bridges when a certain higher-level protocol was used. The brouter solution! In the case of DEC LAT, the routers could be configured to function as a bridge and work at the data link layer level, thereby passing the FRAME along with the higher-layer LAT protocol encapsulated inside of it onto another physical network segment. Because this service was not required too often, the routers were able to handle the additional bridge-level processing quite well. When reconfigured in this fashion, the routers were now called brouters because of their ability to route certain protocols and bridge others on an as-needed basis. (See Fig. 7-9.)

Figure 7-9

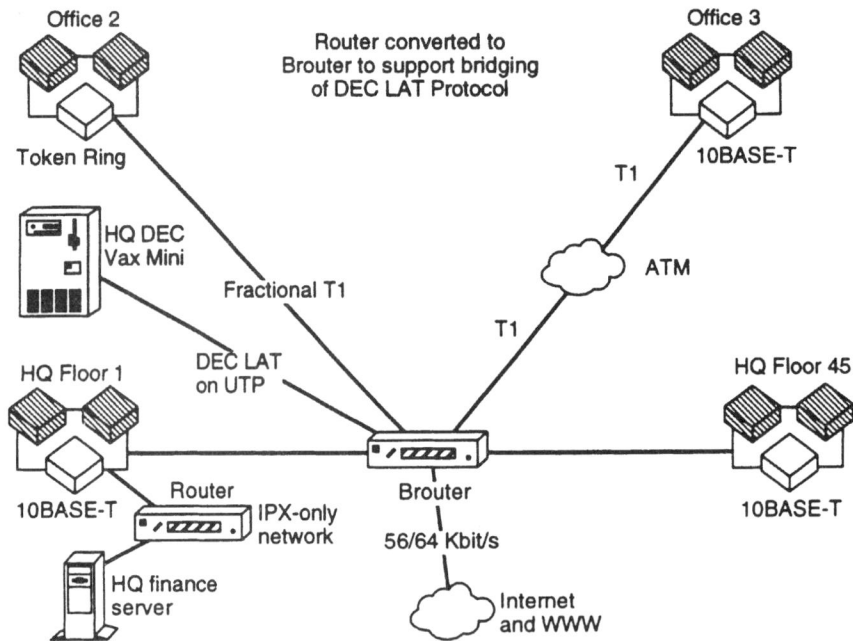

Brouter replaces router to provide protocol specific bridging as needed. Learning Tree International

Extending the LAN to other platforms with gateways

The network continued to grow and now required seamless integration of electronic mail. The company's management was very clear in stating the corporate goal that there should be only one electronic mail system supported throughout the organization. It was up to the network integration staff to figure out how to make this happen. The corporate standard was Microsoft Mail (despite it being a predominantly Novell environment), which was included with the Microsoft Office Suite of applications. Microsoft Mail post offices were in place and running at each NetWare file server. The Internet standard, however, was SMTP-based electronic mail. A device was required to integrate and translate between the two disparate application formats or protocols, and an electronic mail gateway was implemented to resolve this problem. Figure 7-10 demonstrates the process that occurs when mail is transferred between network systems.

This, however, was not to be the last implementation of gateway devices on the network. Some of the company's inventory processing had reached the stage where management was required to find a corporate application to respond to the new demand. Subsequent analysis determined that a centralized mainframe-based application was the only one currently available to meet the demands today yet provide for additional growth. As was the corporation's policy, a company with existing technology was purchased to meet the requirement. And an IBM 370 mainframe computer with a centralized processing host was introduced into the network.

Although the IBM mainframe was capable of supporting TCP/IP connections, several SDLC links existed at different locations of the company that was just purchased. These locations already had NetWare networks installed and used SNA gateways to connect to the mainframe located at the central site. The strategy was to use both SDLC-based SNA gateways and TCP/IP internetworks until the SDLC-based SNA gateways could be converted or phased out. Both the SDLC SNA gateways and TCP/IP connections would be supported in the interim. (See Fig. 7-11.)

Figure 7-10

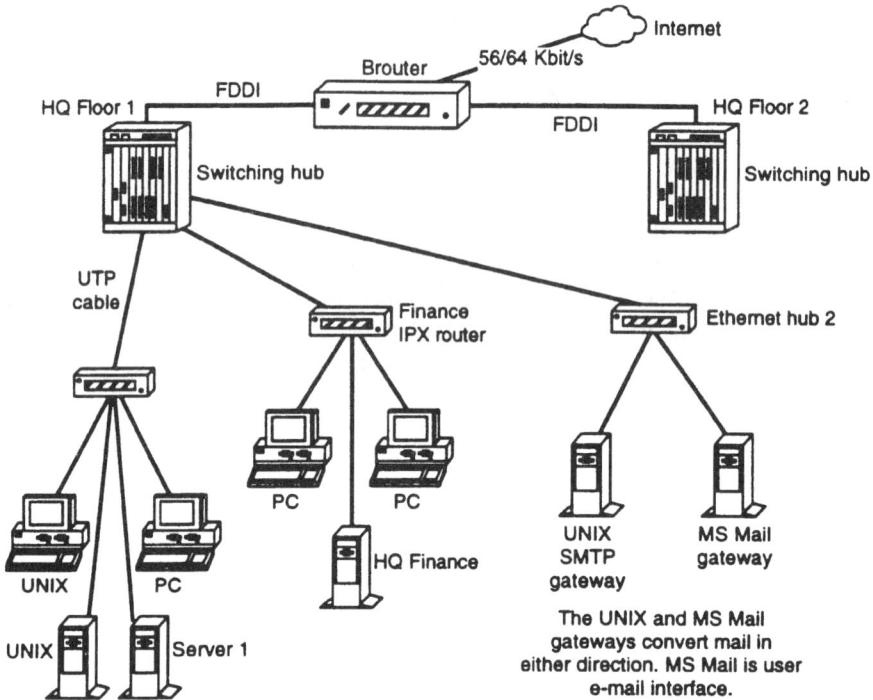

MS Mail to UNIX SMTP gateway for messaging services. Learning Tree International

At this point management became concerned with certain issues regarding the future expansion of the corporate internetwork. It required some potential solutions to be put forward. There were two main areas under question. It had been suggested by outside consultants that the organization move to one protocol throughout the corporate internetwork (TCP/IP) because of the level and volume of routing and service traffic associated with supporting multiple protocols. The second area concerned better network management.

Although NetWare requires IPX/SPX, recent advancements by Novell allow workstations to use the NetWare Core Protocol (NCP) to be encapsulated within TCP/IP. The resulting protocol combination provides workstations with full NetWare and UNIX host access. However, this was a new configuration, and the network integration

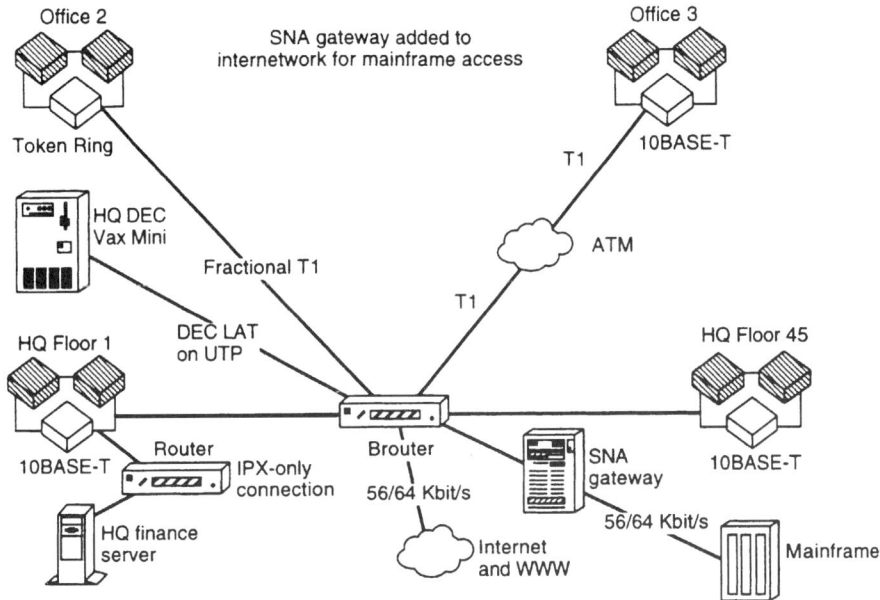

Figure 7-11

SDLC SNA mainframe gateway. Learning Tree International

team stated that it would take some time to test and implement, should the test prove successful.

The network management issues were strongly pushed by our Director of Network Infrastructure because of a belief that they had been sorely neglected and a solution was long overdue. Additionally, it was believed that the extra network management support tools would allow the network administration group to be more proactive in resolving network-related problems.

⇨ Keeping the enterprise network running

The International Technologies corporate network has grown significantly. It now boasted support for almost every platform, including DOS-based personal computers, UNIX-based hosts, DEC VAX minicomputers, and IBM mainframe systems. However, with such growth, it had become almost impossible for the small network administration staff to be at all places at the same time. In addition to the concerns regarding traffic levels and errors on individual network segments, the issue of hackers was also brought forward after Internet access was introduced.

Under the new network strategy, the five key network management issues ware addressed. (You didn't think all that stuff in chapter 6 was wasted on our research-engineer-turned-director, did you?):

> Configuration management.

> Performance management.

> Fault management.

> Accounting management.

> Security management.

Under this program, a network management station was installed at the corporation's networking headquarters. Network management agents were installed throughout the internetwork to monitor various areas of the network. The areas to be monitored included: the performance and status of individual network segments (detect, isolate, and diagnose network segment problems); the performance of file and print servers; monitoring of proper authorized access to network resources; proper accounting of network resource access; and finally configuration management of network-connected devices.

The network management team was now able to provide senior management with ongoing statistics on the health and function of the internetwork. But more than this, the network management systems alerted the team to potential problems on the internetwork before the problems began to affect users. (Isn't technology wonderful?) Our research engineer's biggest problem now was finding someone else to take the server message pager, which called whenever any of the file servers went down!

Summary of building a network

Please note that many of the same problems would have arisen with Token Ring networks. Additionally (and this is the beauty of the network industry), other solutions might also have solved the problems encountered by International Technologies while it was expanding its network. Ultimately, it comes down to what technology is in place, what the mandate or objective is for the new network, and what budget or resources are available to solve the networking problem. Your challenge is always how to get the different aspects and resources to work together to find a workable solution at the lowest cost! We wish you the best of luck in your own networking efforts.

A

LAN cabling rules

⇨ Acknowledgment

The following information and diagrams are reproduced here with the kind permission of South Hill Datacom Spring/Summer 1995 "Solutions" catalog. It is a wonderful catalog with pictures and descriptions of all manner of networking devices and tools. We highly recommend that you obtain such a catalog to have a ready reference to solutions and a source of prices. South Hill Datacom can be reached at:

760 Beechnut Drive
Pittsburgh, PA 15205
800-245-6215

⇨ Ethernet

⇨ General rules

The Ethernet local area network was co-developed by Digital Equipment Corp (DEC), Intel, and Xerox. In 1983, the IEEE committee adopted the original specification, creating the 802.3 standard. It is by far the most widely installed and supported network to date.

The IEEE 802.3 standard defines how a device accesses the network and the speed at which the network operates. The accessing scheme dictated for Ethernet is Carrier Sense Multiple Access with Collision Detection (CSMA/CD):

➤ *Carrier Sense (CS)*. A device first listens for a clear channel before transmitting. If the channel is in use (or a carrier is sensed), the device will delay its transmission.

➤ *Multiple Access (MA)*. Many pieces of equipment can be interconnected to a single or common cable, and all have equal access to the cable when the channel is clear.

➤ *Collision Detection (CD)*. Since it is possible for more than one device to sense a clear channel and begin transmitting at the same time, data collisions will occur. When they do, the devices sense this and stop their transmissions. At this point, each device waits a random length of time and then attempts to retransmit.

The following standards call for a data rate of 10 Mbps. New standards are emerging for 100 Mbps Ethernet. The original 10 Mbps 802.3 standards also define the types of cabling which should be used as follows:

➤ 10Base-5   Ethernet over RG-8 type coax, 50-ohm impedance (sometimes called thick Ethernet)

➤ 10Base-2   Ethernet over RG-58 type coax, 50-ohm impedance (also known as ThinWire or Thinnet)

➤ 10Base-T   Ethernet over 22-24 AWG unshielded twisted pair, 100-ohm impedance, EIA/TIA Category 3 or higher

➤ 10Base-FL   Ethernet over optical fiber

⇨ Standard thick Ethernet (10Base-5) wiring rules

➤ A standard thick Ethernet cable can have a maximum length of 500 meters (1640 feet).

➤ Up to 100 transceivers can be attached to a 500-meter cable length.

➤ Transceivers must be spaced at least 2.5 meters (8.2 feet) apart. To ensure proper spacing, a standard Ethernet cable is premarked every 2.5 meters.

➤ A transceiver cable is required for each transceiver on the network.

➤ A standard transceiver drop cable can have a maximum length of 50 meters (165 feet). Be advised that some devices may have an internal cable equivalency and this should be taken into consideration. To find this internal equivalency, it would be best to consult the user's manual.

➤ When using the more flexible office transceiver cabling, the maximum cable length is 12.5 meters.

➤ In a standard Ethernet network, you are limited to 101 segments (one backbone and 100 branch segments).

➤ The maximum number of stations on a thick Ethernet network is 1024.

➤ Both ends of a standard Ethernet cable segment must be terminated with a 50-ohm terminator.

➤ Repeaters are used to continue the signal from one segment to another. This allows the overall cable segment length to be increased. However, data should not pass through more than two repeaters before reaching its final destination.

⇨ ThinWire Ethernet (10Base-2) wiring rules

➤ A ThinWire cable segment should not exceed 185 meters (606 feet).

➤ External transceivers must be spaced at least 0.5 meter 1.6 feet) apart.

➤ Both ends of a ThinWire cable segment must terminate with a 50-ohm terminator.

➤ When directly attaching to a station rather than using a transceiver, it is imperative that the "T" connector be used at the workstation.

➤ Up to 30 devices can be attached directly to a 185-meter cable segment.

➤ When using multiport repeaters, up to 29 devices can be attached to each port of the repeater.

➤ A local repeater may be attached to the ThinWire cable to extend the distance.

➤ Data may not pass through more than two repeaters before it reaches its destination.

➤ Each ThinWire cable segment should have one end grounded. Never configure the cable in a closed loop.

⇨ Twisted Pair Ethernet (10Base-T) wiring rules

➤ Since 10Base-T is wired as a star topology, an active concentrator or hub is required.

➤ You can connect your network devices to the hub in one of two ways: (1) direct connection with a 10Base-T patch cable, provided your network device has a built-in 10Base-T transceiver and an RJ-45 jack; or (2) via a 10Base-T transceiver, which has an RJ-45 jack and an AUI DB-15 male connector for attachment to the AUI port on a standard Ethernet device.

➤ Although unshielded twisted-pair (UTP) cabling is a reliable transmission medium, it is inherently sensitive to electromagnetic and radio frequency interference (EMI/RFI), so try to install it as far as possible from fluorescent lights. And to avoid the possibility of induced spikes or noise, do not install UTP in a conduit with electrical wiring.

➤ 10Base-T is wired according to the AT&T 258A (EIA/TIA 568B) cabling specification; however, only pins 1 and 2 and pins 3 and 6 are used.

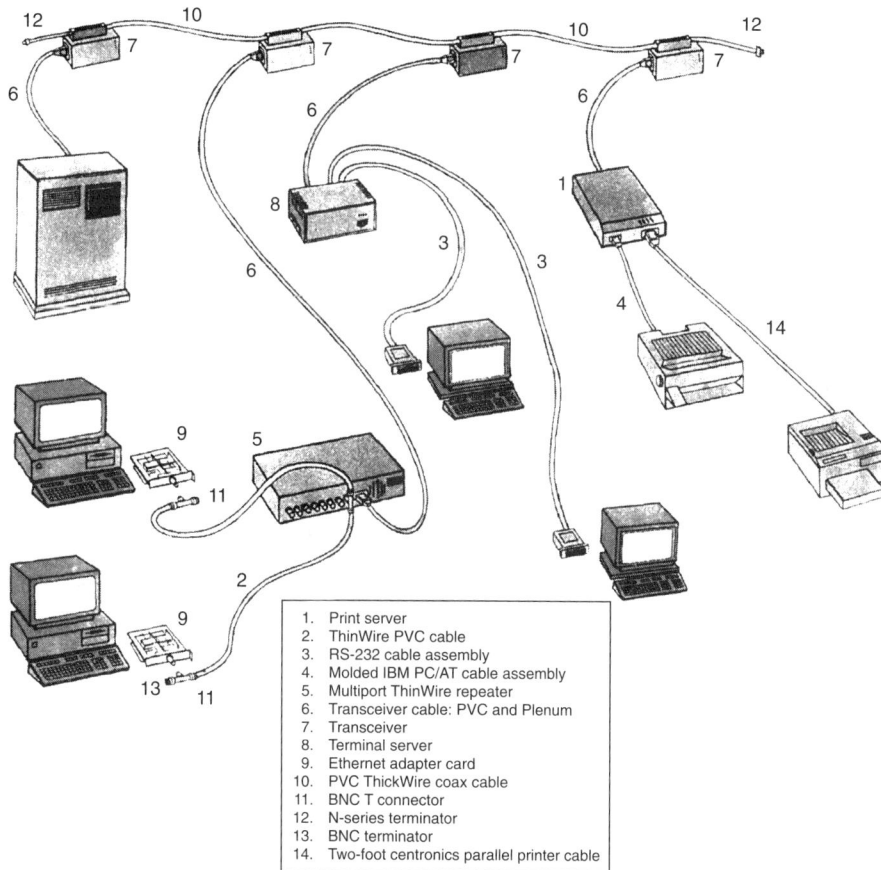

1. Print server
2. ThinWire PVC cable
3. RS-232 cable assembly
4. Molded IBM PC/AT cable assembly
5. Multiport ThinWire repeater
6. Transceiver cable: PVC and Plenum
7. Transceiver
8. Terminal server
9. Ethernet adapter card
10. PVC ThickWire coax cable
11. BNC T connector
12. N-series terminator
13. BNC terminator
14. Two-foot centronics parallel printer cable

Thick Ethernet (10Base-5) typical cabling layout.

> ➤ As a general rule, never try to operate more than one station on any cable drop. Also, it is not recommended to pass both voice and data on any single cable drop.

> ➤ 10Base-T cable drops can be a maximum of 100 meters (330 feet).

> ➤ No flat satin telephone cable should be used anywhere in the network.

> ➤ Concentrators or hubs may be daisy chained together via UTP cabling. They may also be attached to optical fiber or standard thick or ThinWire coax backbones.

Figure A-2

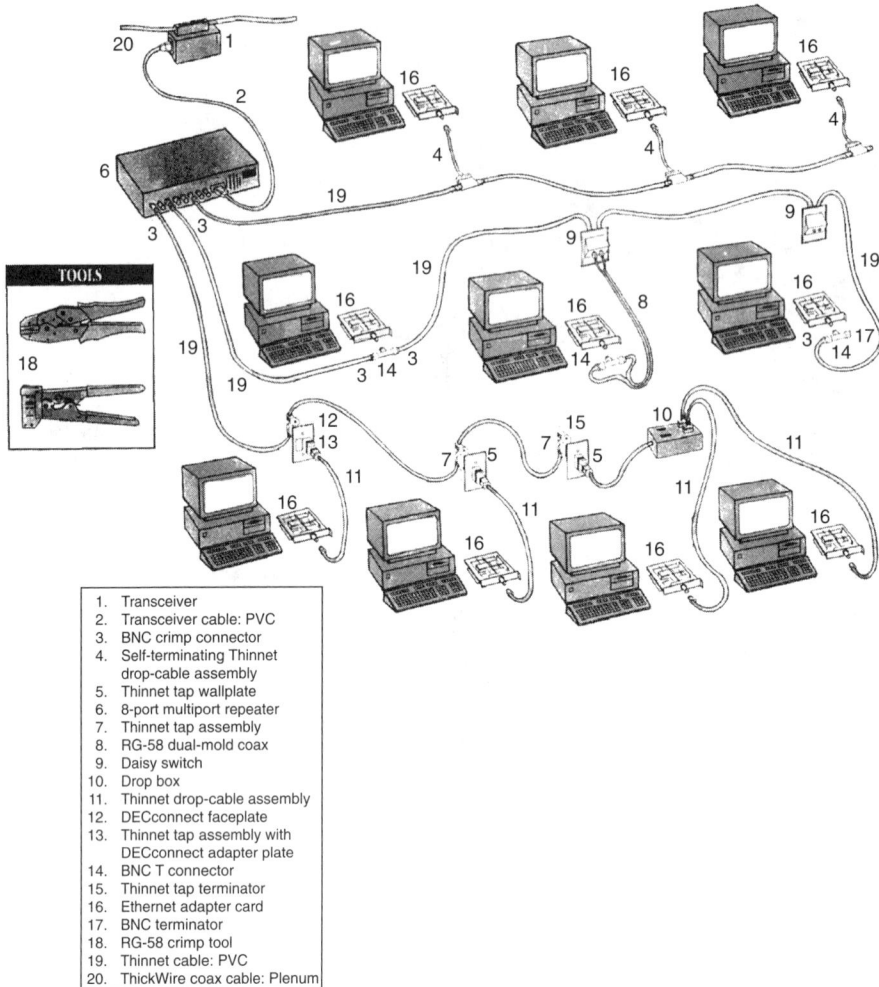

1. Transceiver
2. Transceiver cable: PVC
3. BNC crimp connector
4. Self-terminating Thinnet drop-cable assembly
5. Thinnet tap wallplate
6. 8-port multiport repeater
7. Thinnet tap assembly
8. RG-58 dual-mold coax
9. Daisy switch
10. Drop box
11. Thinnet drop-cable assembly
12. DECconnect faceplate
13. Thinnet tap assembly with DECconnect adapter plate
14. BNC T connector
15. Thinnet tap terminator
16. Ethernet adapter card
17. BNC terminator
18. RG-58 crimp tool
19. Thinnet cable: PVC
20. ThickWire coax cable: Plenum

Thin Ethernet (10Base-2) typical cabling layout.

⇨ Fiber-optic links (10Base-FL) wiring rules

➤ A pair of fiber-optic repeaters can be used to establish a fiber-optic link for connecting a remote location to the local network.

➤ When using a pair of fiber-optic repeaters, the fiber link between the repeaters should not exceed 2 km in length.

➤ A pair of fiber-optic repeaters counts as only one repeater in the two-repeater restriction.

➤ When choosing fiber-optic cable, it is advisable to consider a cable that will operate in both current and future applications, such as 62.5/125 micron fiber that will meet the ANSI FDDI specification.

Figure A-3

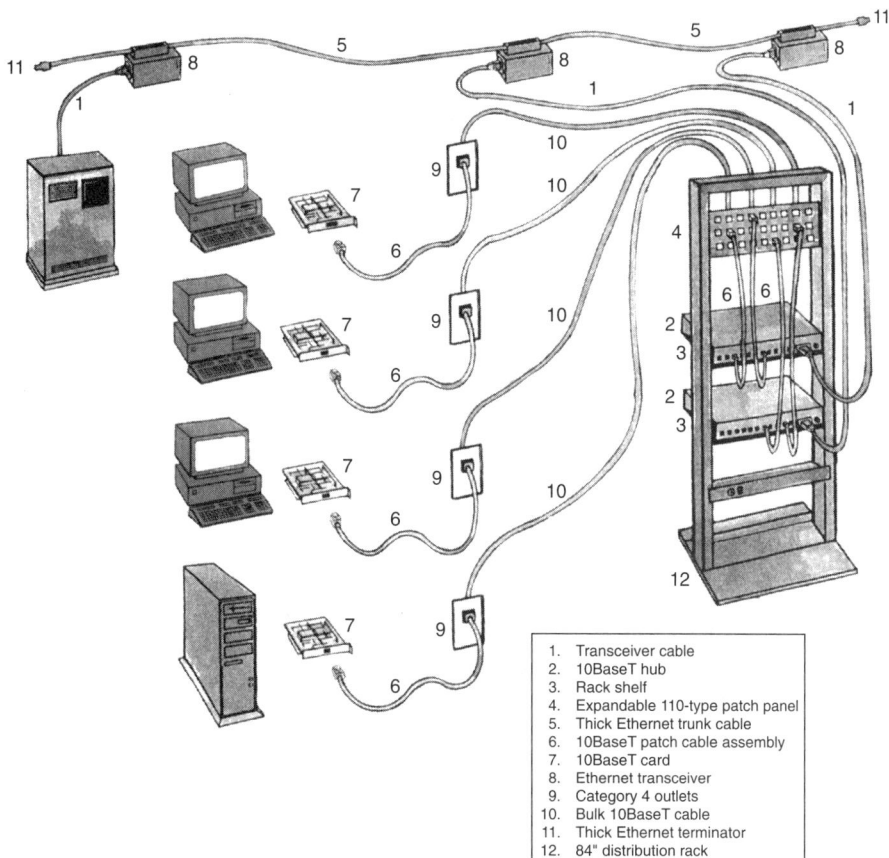

1.	Transceiver cable
2.	10BaseT hub
3.	Rack shelf
4.	Expandable 110-type patch panel
5.	Thick Ethernet trunk cable
6.	10BaseT patch cable assembly
7.	10BaseT card
8.	Ethernet transceiver
9.	Category 4 outlets
10.	Bulk 10BaseT cable
11.	Thick Ethernet terminator
12.	84" distribution rack

Twisted-pair Ethernet (10Base-T) typical cabling layout.

⇨ Bridges

Bridges are used to link two or more IEEE 802.3 networks, creating a much larger network. By using bridges, you can exceed the limits imposed by the 802.3 standards.

In addition to growth capabilities, bridges provide some means of data traffic management. First, an algorithm allows the bridge to self-learn the address of each device attached to the networks on both sides of it. Once this learning process is complete, the bridge will only pass information which is destined for the other opposite network. All other information will be stopped or filtered out, creating a more efficient network. Changes to the network (adding or removing devices) will not affect the bridge in any way, since the learning process is automatic.

Bridges operate at the data link layer and are protocol-transparent. This means that any protocol that operates over Ethernet can be used with a bridge. Some of the more popular protocols include TCP/IP, LAT, XNS, and DECnet. The bridge can pass one or more of these protocols across the networks.

The bridging process works the same way whether in a local bridge or in a remote bridge. The only difference is a local bridge operates individually to interconnect two LANs in the same location, while remote bridges operate in pairs with CSU/DSUs or modems over some type of telephone line to interconnect remotely spaced networks.

⇨ Token Ring

⇨ General rules

The Token Ring network, which IBM has adopted as its internetworking standard, is the fastest growing network for new installations. In addition to being supported by IBM, the Token Ring network features a 4 or 16 Mbps data rate, a relatively easy physical topology to install and a very reliable accessing scheme.

This network uses a physical star, logical ring topology which benefits you in several ways:

1 The cabling all goes to a central hub or location called a multistation access unit (MSAU). The MSAU is the device that actually creates the physical star and logical ring.

2 Since all of the cabling is brought to a single location and starred out, locating a defective cable is relatively simple. All one needs to do is a simple continuity test.

3 The MSAU provides the network with some fault protection. Should a device on a port or lobe on the MSAU fail, the MSAU will automatically remove that device from the ring.

4 The accessing method in this network is a token-passing arrangement, which means that every bit of information travels from one station to the next, and so on. In this process of passing the bit, the information is completely regenerated by each station and passed along. This results in good clean data everywhere on the network.

5 Simply put, all information to be sent is given a destination address and placed on the network, passing from device to device. When it reaches the device with the destination address, the device removes the information. All other information continues on the network.

⇨ Token Ring installation

1 Up to 260 devices can be connected to a local Token Ring network using Type 1 or Type 2 cable. With UTP cable, the limit is 72 devices.

2 By using proper formulas and charts below, you can rapidly calculate the maximum allowable lobe lengths and the adjusted ring length when using Type 1 and 2 cable. These distances are very important to track when initially installing your network.

3 To determine the allowable lobe length (distance between MSAU and station), look up [on Table A.1] the number of MSAUs being used. Next, look up the number of wiring closets being used. Where the two columns meet is the total of the longest lobe in the network plus the adjusted ring length (ARL). Adjusted ring length (ARL) is equal to the sum of all the cable lengths between wiring closets minus the shortest of those lengths in multiple wiring closet applications.

Now calculate your adjusted ring length (ARL):

ARL = Sum of all cables − the shortest of these runs

Subtract your ARL from the number on the chart and you will now have the longest allowable length for your lobes.

4 Remember that even if your lobe length exceeds 100 meters (330 feet), you should try to stay within this parameter to allow for future expansion.

5 If you use Type 6 or Type 9 cable in place of Type 1 or Type 2 cable, determine the maximum allowable lobe length for Type 6 or 9 by using the formula above to calculate the longest length for Type 1 or 2, and dividing it by 1.333.

6 If you use Type 8 cable in place of Type 1 or Type 2 cable, determine the maximum allowable lobe length for Type 8 by using the formula above to calculate the longest length for Type 1 or 2 and dividing by 2.

7 The number of copper and optical repeaters used must be subtracted from the total of 260 stations the ring will support on Type 1 or 2 cable or the total of 72 stations on Type 3 cable.

8 Bridges will let you build networks with more than 260 attaching units per ring.

9 A maximum of 16 parallel bridges are allowed between any two rings.

10 Surge suppressors can't be used between an attached device and an MSAU.

11 Rings using surge suppressors in the main path can only pass through two wiring closets.

12 You are limited to 16 MSAUs in a ring when surge suppressors are used.

13 In a single-wiring-closet application, up to 33 MSAUs can be used to attach up to 260 devices, each of which can have a drop length of 100 meters from the distribution panel to the faceplate.

14 When using surge suppressors, add 200 feet to your adjusted ring length (ARL) to account for signal loss.

15 Add 100 feet to your adjusted ring length (ARL) when using surge suppressors and copper repeaters.

16 Maximum length for Type 1 or Type 2 cable from the faceplate or floor monument connector and the connector in the distribution panel should not exceed 100 meters (330 feet).

17 Maximum recommended length of cable between two wiring closets is 200 meters (660 feet) for Type 1 and Type 2 cable and 133 meters (437 feet) for Type 9 cable. Type 5 fiber-optic cable length can be up to 2000 meters (6600 feet).

NOTE: The distances shown in the following charts are applicable only to networks using passive, nonpowered MSAUs. If you are using active, powered MSAUs, check the manufacturers' specifications for distances.

Table A-1

Unshielded Twisted-Pair (UTP)
Cable Configuration for Token Ring Networks

4 Mbps Token Ring Network Multiple Wiring
Closet Distances in Feet for UTP Cable

Number of wiring closets

		1	2	3	4
	1	730			
	2	711	678		
	3	692	659	642	
N	4	673	640	623	606
U	5	654	621	604	587
M	6	635	602	585	568
B	7	616	583	566	549
E	8	597	564	547	530
R	9	578	545	528	511
	10	559	526	509	492

16 Mbps Token Ring Network Multiple Wiring
Closet Distances in Feet for UPT Cable

Number of wiring closets

		1	2	3
	1	180		
	2	148	128	
	3	116	96	76
	4	84	64	
	5	52		

(Left margin vertical letters: N U M B E R   O F   M S A U S)

Assumptions:

RI and RO are terminated at a patch panel in each closet with 8 foot patch cords.

Multiple MSAUs in one closet are connected with 3 foot, UTP patch cords.

Shielded Twisted-Pair (STP) Cable Configuration for Token Ring Networks Using Type 1 and Type 2 Cables

Table A-2

4 Mbps Token Ring Network Multiple Wiring
Closet Distances in Feet for Type 1 & 2 Cable

Number of wiring closets

		2	3	4	5	6	7	8	9	10	11	12
	2	1192										
	3	1163	1148									
	4	1135	1120	1104								
	5	1106	1091	1076	1061							
N	6	1078	1062	1047	1032	1017						
U	7	1049	1034	1019	1004	989	974					
M	8	1020	1005	990	975	960	945	930				
B	9	992	977	962	947	932	916	901	886			
E	10	963	948	933	918	903	888	873	858	843		
R	11	935	920	905	890	874	859	844	829	814	799	
	12	906	891	876	861	846	831	816	801	786	770	755
	13	878	863	848	833	817	802	787	772	757	742	727
O	14	849	834	819	804	789	774	759	744	729	713	698
F	15	821	806	791	775	760	745	730	715	700	685	670
	16	792	777	762	747	732	717	702	687	671	656	641
	17	764	749	733	718	703	688	673	658	643	628	613
M	18	735	720	705	690	675	660	645	629	614	599	584
S	19	707	691	676	661	646	631	616	601	586	571	556
A	20	678	663	648	633	618	603	587	572	557	542	527
U	21	649	634	619	604	589	574	559	544	529	514	499
S	22	621	606	591	576	561	545	530	515	500	485	470
	23	592	577	562	547	532	517	502	487	472	457	441
	24	564	549	534	519	503	488	473	458	443	428	413
	25	502	520	505	490	475	460	445	430	415	399	384
	26	474	492	477	461	446	431	416	401	386	371	356
	27	445	463	448	433	418	403	388	373	357	342	327

Table A-2

Continued
16 Mbps Token Ring Network Multiple Wiring
Closet Distances in Feet for Type 1 & 2 Cable

Number of wiring closets

		2	3	4	5	6	7	8	9	10
	2	530								
N	3	509	492							
U	4	487	471	454						
M	5	465	449	432	416					
B	6	443	427	411	394	378				
E	7	422	405	389	372	356	340			
R	8	400	383	367	350	344	318	301		
	9	378	361	345	329	312	296	279	263	
O	10	356	340	323	307	290	274	258	241	225
F	11	334	318	301	285	269	252	236	219	203
	12	312	296	279	263	247	230	214	197	181
M	13	270	253	236	220	204	188	171	155	138
S	14	227	211	194	178	161	145	129	112	96
A	15	184	168	152	135	119	102	86	69	53
U	16	142	125	109	92	76	60	43	27	10
S	17	99	83	66	50	33	17	—	—	—
	18	56	40	24	—	—	—	—	—	—

Figure A-4

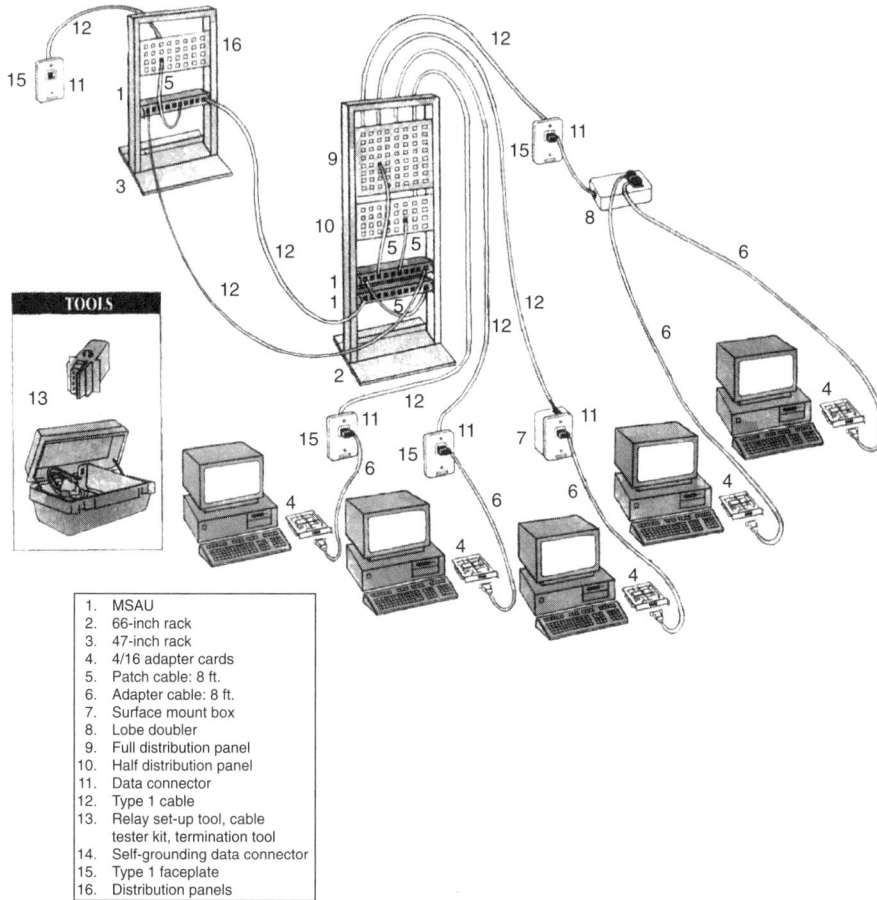

1.	MSAU
2.	66-inch rack
3.	47-inch rack
4.	4/16 adapter cards
5.	Patch cable: 8 ft.
6.	Adapter cable: 8 ft.
7.	Surface mount box
8.	Lobe doubler
9.	Full distribution panel
10.	Half distribution panel
11.	Data connector
12.	Type 1 cable
13.	Relay set-up tool, cable tester kit, termination tool
14.	Self-grounding data connector
15.	Type 1 faceplate
16.	Distribution panels

Standard Token Ring cabling layout using STP cables for 4 or 16 Mbps network cards.

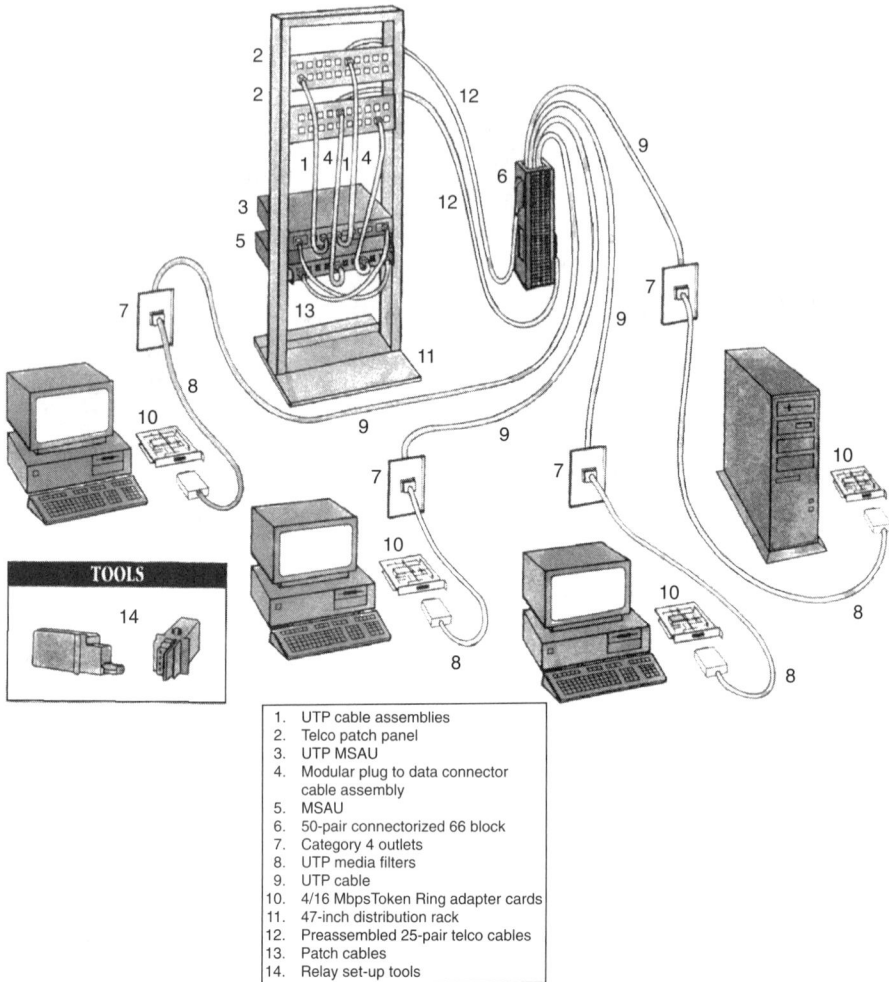

1. UTP cable assemblies
2. Telco patch panel
3. UTP MSAU
4. Modular plug to data connector cable assembly
5. MSAU
6. 50-pair connectorized 66 block
7. Category 4 outlets
8. UTP media filters
9. UTP cable
10. 4/16 Mbps Token Ring adapter cards
11. 47-inch distribution rack
12. Preassembled 25-pair telco cables
13. Patch cables
14. Relay set-up tools

Token Ring cabling for 4 Mbps network cards using unshielded twisted-pair (UTP) wiring.

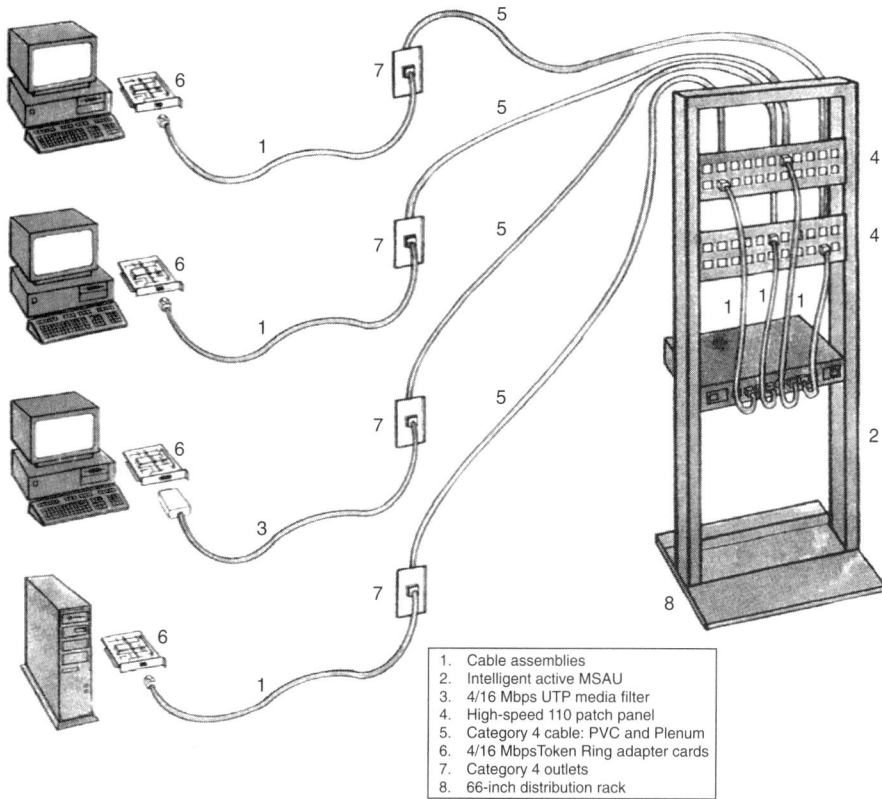

1. Cable assemblies
2. Intelligent active MSAU
3. 4/16 Mbps UTP media filter
4. High-speed 110 patch panel
5. Category 4 cable: PVC and Plenum
6. 4/16 MbpsToken Ring adapter cards
7. Category 4 outlets
8. 66-inch distribution rack

Token Ring cabling for 16 Mbps network cards using unshielded twisted-pair (UTP) wiring.

B

Answers to "Test your understanding" sections

⇨ Chapter 1

1. Describe:
   - Centralized computing: All processing done on central computer
   - Distributed computing: Processing on individual computers, file servers
   - Cooperative computing: Application code distributed over several hosts

2. Describe the characteristics of:
   - Local area networks: High data rates, short distances, user owned
   - Wide area networks: Longer distances, third-party service
   - Metropolitan area networks: Within a city, high data rates

3. What are the elements of computer networks?

- Sharing network services, rules protocols, pathway media and signals

4. What is the difference between enterprise networks and global networks?
   - Enterprise networks, connecting all computers with a company; global networks, between companies

5. Describe the characteristics of:
   - Servers: Support shared file, print, and application services
   - Clients: Consumers of network services, run applications
   - Peers: End-user computers that may also provide network services

6. What is the difference between file-server-based nets and peer-to-peer nets?
   - File-server centric versus distributed services

7. What are the popular types of network services and their characteristics?
   - File: File transfer from server to clients
   - Print: Client printing via server queues
   - Message: Message passing, e-mail, faxing
   - Application: Sharing processing power, distributed cycle
   - Database: Query processing, SQL

⇨ Chapter 2

1. List the types, characteristics, one advantage, and one disadvantage of the following types of media:

Media	Types	Characteristic and use	Bound or unbound	Advantage and disadvantage
Twisted pair	UTP	Copper pairs, building wiring, most popular	Bound	Installed for voice, cheaper, more noisy, easier to install
	STP			
	Cat. 1-5			

Media	Types	Characteristic and use	Bound or unbound	Advantage and disadvantage
Coax	50 Ω 75 Ω 93 Ω		Bound	Older installations, less EMI problems, more expensive
Fiber optic	Multimode Single mode	Used in some building wiring, more popular between buildings	Bound	Very expensive, no EMI problems
Satellite	--	Long data path causes delay, Point-to-point WAN links	Unbound	Need license
Radio	UHF VHF	Point-to-point WAN links	Unbound	Need license

2. List the types of telephone links that may be used for data, the data rate, and the device that is needed to attach to the phone network.

Phone link	Data rate	Device needed to attach
Voice grade line	Up to 28.8 Kbps Typical 14.2 Kbps	Modem and RS-232 port
Leased line	56 Kbps (64 Kbps)	DSU/CSU and RS-232 port
T1 leased line	1.54 Kbps	DSU/CSU and RS-232 port
ISDN (2B+D)	64 Kbps Up to 128 Kbps	ISDN Interface

3. What is the Internet?

A worldwide network of networks, supports company-to-company e-mail, file transfers, and remote program execution, based on the TCP/IP protocol suite, was created by the U.S. DoD.

4. Describe the function and application of the following network devices:

Device	Function	Application
NIC	Network card attaches PC to network	Data Link and Physical Layer protocol implementation. Framing and access control

459

Device	Function	Application
Transceiver	Media attachment unit	Converts signals to proper type for media being used, detects collisions
RJ-45	Adapter jack cable	10Base-T and Token Ring wiring using UTP
Concentrator	Connects individual cables into one physical network	10Base-T, ARCNET, FDDI all use concentrators in a star wiring configuration
Bridge	Connects two LANs at the data link level	Filter/forward/floods frames from one LAN to another
MUX	Multiplexes slow data streams into a faster one	Used for sending terminal traffic on a leased line between two remote sites
Router	Routes packets Connects networks at the Network Layer	Used in routed internets such as IP and IPX networks
CSU/DSU	Channel attach unit	Connects digital leased line to communicating device serial port

⇨ Chapter 3

1. Name the layer of the OSI model, what it manages, some of its functions, and an example protocol:

	Layer name	What it manages	Functions	Examples
1	Physical	Bits	Signal levels	RS-232-C
2	Data Link	Frames	Channel access, creation of frames	Ethernet Token Ring
3	Network	Packets	Routing of datagrams or packets	X.25, IP, IPX
4	Transport	Connections	End-to-end reliable transfer	TCP, TP4
5	Session	Session dialogue	Manages the dialogue between applications	SPX, RPC
6	Presentation	Data representation	The way the data is presented	XDR
7	Application	Messages	Interface between use application and network	X.400, FTP, NFS

2. The protocol bits added by any layer to the front of the data are called the header.

3. Name the three different types of protocols standards: *de jure*, *de facto*, *proprietary*

4. Name one proprietary, one *de jure*, and one *de facto* protocol: IBM SNA, ISO TP0, ARPAnet IP

⇨ Chapter 4

⇨ The physical layer

1. Network topologies: bus, star, ring

2. Switching modes: packet, circuit, message

3. Encoding protocols: ASCII, EBCDIC

⇨ Signals and multiplexing

4. Transmission modes: simplex, half duplex, full duplex

5. Signal types: analog, digital

6. Signaling technologies: AM, FM, PM

7. Multiplexing techniques: FDM, TDM, STM

8. Modulation types: ASK, FSK, PSK

⇨ Modems and codecs

9. Analog device used to send digital information over analog phone lines: Modem

10. Popular modem protocols: Bell 212A, CCITT/ITU V.29

11. The RS-232 protocol is used for: DTE-DCE Interface

12. Digital device used to send analog voice signals over digital lines:
Codec

⇨ The data link layer

1. The services provided by the data link layer are: framing, error
check, access scheme

2. Three types of data communications transmissions are:
synchronous, asynchronous, and isochronous

3. IBM employs what types of data link protocols?
SDLC and Token Ring

4. What are the three popular types of channel access technologies?
contention, token passing, polling

⇨ Internetworking devices

1. In what layer of the OSI model do the following internetworking
devices operate?
   • Gateways: Network layer and above (4–7)
   • Routers: Network (3)
   • Bridges: Data link (2)
   • Repeaters: Physical (1)

2. How does a bridge accomplish its function?
Filters/forwards frames based on physical addresses

3. What address does a bridge use to perform frame forwarding?
Destination physical (frame) address

4. What address must a router use to perform packet forwarding?
Destination network address

5. How does a router accomplish its function?
Routes packet based on network address

6. What is the key feature of using bridges?
Simple to deploy, transparent

7. What is the most important decision to be made in using routers?
   The protocol to route

8. When should you use a router over a bridge?
   Whenever possible

9. Name some popular types of gateways: SNA, e-mail, X.25

10. When should you use a gateway?
    When there is no other choice

⇨ Chapter 5

1. Can you identify the category and the layer in which these protocols/programs belong?

	Transport/ network protocol	Remote program execution	File transfer	Database access	Remote terminal access	Distributed File System	PC NOS	E-mail	Network management	Directory services	Data Link Layer
TCP	√										
NetWare							√				
FTP			√								
NFS						√					
X.500										√	
X.25	√										
TELNET					√						
ROSE											
802.3											√
TP4	√										
APPC	√										
DB2				√							
NCP						√					
HDLC											√
Advanced Server							√				
X.400								√			
RPC		√									
UDP	√										
IPX	√										
VT					√						
SNMP									√		
CMIP									√		
SMTP							√				
IP	√										

⇨ The IEEE Project 802

2. The four basic MAC technologies defined by the IEEE 802 committee are:
   - 802.3 CSMA/CD
   - 802.4 token bus
   - 802.5 Token Ring
   - 802.6 MAN

3. Name four types of 802.3 wiring schemes and their characteristics:
   - 10Base-2, bus topology, baseband 50W thin coax, 185-m segment
   - 10Base-5, bus topology, baseband 50W thick coax, 500-m segment
   - 10Base-T, star topology, baseband UTP wiring, 100-m segment
   - 10Broad-36, bus topology, broadband 75W coax, 1800-m segment

⇨ The Internet protocols

4. Name three application protocols that are part of the TCP/IP protocol suite and one use of each protocol:
   - SMPT, e-mail transfer
   - Telnet, remote terminal access
   - FTT, host-to-host file transfer

5. What is the route advertising protocol used in TCP/IP internets?
   - RIP

⇨ NetWare protocols

6. Which NetWare protocol corresponds to the application layer of the OSI model?
   - NetWare Core Protocol (NCP)

OSI protocols

7. Who promotes the development of OSI protocols?
   - ISO

8. Name some OSI higher-level protocols (network layer and above):
   - X.25
   - TP0
   - P4
   - FTAM
   - DS

⇨ Additional higher-level protocols

9. Who promotes and develops SNA protocols?
   - IBM

10. In an IBM SNA network, what are the PU designations for:
    - A 3270 terminal: None
    - A cluster controller: PU 2
    - A front-end processor: PU 4
    - The mainframe: PU 5

11. Who promotes the development of AppleTalk protocols?
    - Apple

12. DECnet Phase V is compatible with what protocol profile?
    - OSI

13. Who promotes the development of AppleTalk protocols?
    - Apple

14. DECnet Phase V is compatible with what protocol profile?
    - ISO OSI,
    - GOSIP

⇨ ANSI FDDI

15. What is the FDDI data rate?
    - 100 Mbps

16. What cabling choices are available for FDDI?
    - F.O.,
    - T.P/

17. What access scheme does FDDI use?
    - Token passing

⇨ Apple LocalTalk

18. What is the LocalTalk data rate?
    - 230 Kbps

19. What wiring type and topologies are employed in LocalTalk?
    - UTP, daisy-chain

⇨ Additional data link protocols

What data link protocol is used with:

20. IBM SNA?
    - SDLC

21. CCITT X.25?
    - LAPB

22. What does LAPB stand for?
    - Link access procedure, balanced

23. What frame types are used with SDLC?
    - Information, supervisory, unnumbered

⇨ Chapter 6

1. Area: Security

   Characteristic: Access control, passwords, accounts, encryption, authentication

   Tools: Audits, protocol analyzers, encryption/decryption tools

2. Area: Configuration

   Characteristic: Keep track of changes, document network, inventory

   Tools: Physical walkthroughs, configuration/inventory programs

3. Area: Performance

   Characteristic: Monitor and evaluate performance of network

   Tools: Protocol analyzers, standard network tests

4. Area: Fault

   Characteristic: Detect, isolate, fix network problems

   Tools: Protocol analyzers, cable tester, VOM

5. Area: Accounting

   Characteristic: Cost charge back for network usage

   Tools: Accounting software

C

Answers to practice exams

➡ Chapter 1

1. Networks that connect virtually all parts of an organization are called:
   Ans: A. Enterprise networks
        B. Global networks
        C. Wide area networks
        D. Local area networks

2. Networks that span organizational and geographical boundaries are called:
        A. Enterprise networks
   Ans: B. Global networks
        C. Wide area networks
        D. Local area networks

3. Database services provide what additional functionality to networks?
        A. Salability
        B. File transfers
        C. Print queuing
   Ans: D. Query processing

4. Which function may not be considered part of printing services of a network?
   - A. Fax services
   - Ans: B. File transfers
   - C. Queuing
   - D. Printing

5. Which is not a characteristic of a local area network?
   - A. A variety of cabling media is used
   - B. Data rates are in the range of 1 to 100 Mbits/sec
   - C. Distances spanned are short, typically within a building or campus
   - Ans: D. It uses very few protocols

6. Which of the following is an aspect of database services?
   - A. File transfer
   - Ans: B. Replication
   - C. Electronic Mail
   - D. Image processing

7. Which of the following is not considered an aspect of message services?
   - A. Work-flow management
   - B. Electronic mail
   - C. Directory services
   - Ans: D. Fax services

8. Print services provide which two the following features?
   - A. Fax services
   - Ans: B. Queuing
   - Ans: C. Limited access specialized printers
   - D. Store-and-forward services

9. File services support mobile (nomadic) computing: True or False:
   - Ans: A. True
   - B. False

10. In peer-to-peer networks:
   - A. A computer can be a client or a server, but not both
   - Ans: B. Security and management of resources is difficult
   - C. A centralized server provides services clients
   - D. Is intended to be used by large groups of users

⇨ Chapter 2

1. The data rate of a T1 digital transmission link is:
   A. 64 Kbits/sec
   B. 128 Kbits/sec
   Ans: C. 1.54 Mbits/sec
   D. 2.048 Mbits/sec

2. Which is an example of a bounded type of media?
   A. Twisted pair
   B. Coaxial
   C. Fiber optic
   Ans: D. All of the above

3. Which is not a characteristic of fiber-optic cables?
   A. They are immune from electromagnetic interference
   B. They are much smaller than coaxial cables
   C. Attenuation is much less than that of signals on conductors
   Ans: D. They have extremely narrow bandwidths

4. Which unbounded transmission media type does not require FCC or governmental approval before operating?
   A. Terrestrial microwave
   B. Satellite microwave
   Ans: C. Laser
   D. Radio

5. The ISDN protocol has been developed and promoted by which standards organization?
   A. IEEE
   B. ISO
   Ans: C. CCITT/ITU
   D. ANSI

6. In local telephone service, the responsibility of the service provider extends to:
   A. The central office
   B. The local loop
   Ans: C. The demarcation point
   D. The subscriber location

⇨ Chapter 3

1. In a peer-to-peer network, the control information inserted into a protocol data unit by a peer layer making a request is called:
    Ans: A. Header
        B. Frame
        C. Packet
        D. Message

2. The information units produced by the data link layer of the OSI model are called:
        A. Bits
    Ans: B. Frames
        C. Datagrams (packets)
        D. Segments

3. The information units produced by the network layer of the OSI model are called:
        A. Bits
        B. Frames
    Ans: C. Datagrams (Packets)
        D. Segments

4. Which best describes the function of the network layer of the OSI model?
        A. It defines the electrical and mechanical specifications for the interface hardware to the network.
        B. It frames the data stream into logical groups of information.
    Ans: C. It moves information across a network made up of multiple network segments.
        D. It provides error control and data-flow control between two endpoints of the network.

5. Which is not an example of the implementation of the application layer of the OSI model?
        A. NFS
        B. FTAM
    Ans: C. ES/IS
        D. FTP

6. Which is not a standards-making organization?
   A. CCITT/ITU
   B. ISO
   C. IEEE
   Ans: D. ASCII

7. Which organization is most responsible for the production and promotion of the OSI model?
   A. CCITT/ITU
   Ans: B. ISO
   C. IEEE
   D. ANSI

8. Models are concepts for communicating while protocols are actual solutions to a communication process:
   Ans: A. True
   B. False

9. Protocols are _____ components:
   A. Hardware
   B. Software
   Ans: C. Hardware and software
   D. None of the above

⇨ Chapter 4

1. Which factor contributes to the attenuation of electrical signals as they propagate over copper wires?
   A. Capacitance of the wires
   B. Resistance of the wires
   Ans: C. Both A and B
   D. None of the above

2. The difference between analog and digital data is:
   Ans: A. Analog data can take any value in a range; digital data is discrete and can have only a limited number of values.
   B. Analog data is discrete and can have only a limited number of values, whereas digital data can take any value within a range.
   C. Both A and B
   D. None of the above

3. Which is an example of analog signals carrying analog data?
   A. The use of modems and voice-grade lines
   Ans: B. Music transmitted by commercial radio stations
   C. A terminal directly connected to a host computer
   D. Music encoded in compact disks (CDs)

4. Which digital encoding scheme is not self-clocking?
   Ans: A. Bipolar
   B. Biphase
   C. Manchester
   D. Differential Manchester

5. A voice telephone switch employs which type of switching technology?
   A. Packet switching
   B. Message switching
   Ans: C. Circuit switching
   D. Both packet switching and circuit switching

6. Which technique is used to recover unused bandwidth in conventional TDM systems?
   A. Signal regeneration
   Ans: B. Statistical multiplexing
   C. Broadband signaling
   D. None of the above

7. Which network type employs twisted-pair cabling?
   A. Token Ring networks
   B. Ethernet networks
   C. ARCNET networks
   Ans: D. All of the above

8. The RS-232-C interface was standardized by which standards organization?
   A. ANSI
   B. CCITT/ITU
   Ans: C. EIA
   D. IEEE

9. Which is not a characteristic of a DCE?
   A. It connects a DTE to a communication channel.
   B. Its function is to convert a DTE's data format to a signal suitable for the media.

C. A modem is an example of it.

Ans: D. The user interfaces with it.

10. Which statement about modems is not true?

A. A modem modulates an analog signal with digital data for transmission.

B. A modem on the receiving end demodulates the analog signal, extracting digital data for the destination DTE.

Ans: C. A modem is used for transmitting digital voice.

D. A null modem is a cable that connects the transmit circuit of one DTE to the receive circuit of another DTE.

11. Which is not specified by the RS-232 standard?

A. The mechanical characteristics of the interface

B. The electrical characteristics of the interface

C. The functional characteristics of the interface

Ans: D. The framing characteristics of the interface

12. In which communication mode is the transmission two-way simultaneous?

A. Simplex

B. Half duplex

Ans: C. Full duplex

D. Both half duplex and full duplex

13. Which statement is not true of asynchronous transmissions?

A. Each character being sent is transmitted separately.

B. There is a random interval between transmissions.

Ans: C. The transmitter and receiver clocks are continually synchronized.

D. A bit may be added at the end of the character to detect errors in transmission.

14. Which protocol employs a token-passing method of sharing a common channel?

A. 802.4

B. 802.5

C. FDDI

Ans: D. All of the above

15. Which protocol employs a collision-detection mechanism?
    Ans: A. 802.3
    B. 802.4
    C. 802.5
    D. LocalTalk

16. What technique is employed in block transmissions to ensure that the frame does not contain the unique pattern of bits representing a flag?
    Ans: A. Manchester encoding
    B. Zero-bit stuffing
    C. Nonreturn to zero (NRZ) encoding
    D. None of the above

17. A repeater operates at which layer of the OSI model?
    Ans: A. Physical
    B. Data link
    C. Network
    D. All layers

18. A bridge operates at which layer of the OSI model?
    A. Physical
    Ans: B. Data link
    C. Network
    D. Transport

19. A router operates at which layer of the OSI model?
    A. Physical
    B. Data link
    Ans: C. Network
    D. Transport

20. Which device reconstructs and retransmits a signal from one part of a network to another as an exact duplicate of the originally transmitted signal?
    Ans: A. Repeater
    B. Bridge
    C. Router
    D. Gateway

21. What address does a bridge use in forwarding frames in a linked network?
    A. Node logical address
    B. Station network address

Ans: C. Station physical address
    D. All of the above

22. Which device uses filtering/forwarding as a technique for linking two networks?
Ans: A. Bridge
    B. Repeater
    C. Router
    D. Gateway

23. Which is not a type of bridge?
    A. Transparent
    B. Source routing
    C. Remote
Ans: D. Asynchronous

24. In a network that uses routers for linking subnetworks, the logical network addresses of nodes are assigned by:
    A. The router manufacturer
    B. The network card manufacturer
Ans: C. The network administrator
    D. They are automatically configured by the routers.

25. Which statement best describes the function of a gateway?
Ans: A. It translates between incompatible protocol implementations.
    B. It acts as a router for various protocols implemented in the gateway.
    C. It connects two different types of networks.
    D. None of the above.

⇨ Chapter 5

1. The IEEE 802 series standards were developed and are promoted by which standards organization?
    A. CCITT/ITU
    B. ISO
Ans: C. IEEE
    D. ANSI

2. Which layer of the OSI reference model was not originally covered by Project 802 specifications?
    A. Physical layer
    B. Data link layer
Ans: C. Network layer
    D. All of the above

3. What is the data rate for a 10BASE-T network?
    A. 1 Mbit/sec
Ans: B. 10 Mbits/sec
    C. 16 Mbits/sec
    D. 100 Mbits/sec

4. IBM Token Ring Networks can operate at what data rate?
    A. 4 Mbits/sec
    B. 10 Mbits/sec
Ans: C. 4 Mbits/sec and 16 Mbits/sec

5. The TCP/IP protocol suite was developed by which organization?
    A. IBM
    B. ANSI
Ans: C. Department of Defense
    D. CCITT/ITU

6. Which layer of the OSI model characterizes IP?
    A. Data link
Ans: B. Network
    C. Transport
    D. Session

7. What layer of the OSI model characterizes TCP?
    A. Data link
    B. Network
Ans: C. Transport
    D. Session

8. Which protocol can be employed for file transfers across the Internet?
Ans: A. FTP
    B. TELNET
    C. DTP
    D. ICMP

9. Novell's IPX protocol can be classified as functionally equivalent to which layer of the OSI model?

        A. Data link

Ans: B. Network

        C. Transport

        D. Session

10. The OSI suite of networking protocols has been developed and/or adopted by which standards organization?

        A. CCITT/ITU

Ans: B. ISO

        C. ANSI

        D. IEEE

11. Which is an example of an OSI transport protocol?

Ans: A. TP4

        B. ES/IS

        C. ASN.1

        D. CMIP

12. Which is a protocol that performs network-layer functions?

        A. TP4

Ans: B. ES/IS

        C. HDLC

        D. FTAM

13. The X.25 protocol is a part of the OSI protocol suite.

Ans: A. True

        B. False

14. Which protocol performs network management functions as part of the OSI protocol suite?

        A. ASN.1

        B. FTAM

Ans: C. CMIP

        D. MHS

15. Which protocol is not part of the native NetWare protocol suite?

        A. IPX

        B. SPX

        C. NCP

Ans: D. FTP

16. The X.25 protocol can be classified as functionally equivalent to which layer of the OSI model?
    A. Physical
    B. Data link
    Ans: C. Network
    D. Transport

17. In an IBM SNA network, the host has which physical unit number?
    A. 1
    B. 2
    Ans: C. 4
    D. 5

18. In IBM SNA networks, a session connected to a 3270-type terminal is considered which type of logical unit (LU)?
    A. Type 0
    B. Type 1
    Ans: C. Type 2
    D. Type 4

19. Which organization developed and promotes the use of SNA?
    A. Digital Equipment Corp.
    Ans: B. International Business Machines
    C. Apple Computer
    D. Novell

20. In an IBM SNA network, a session is a logical connection between:
    Ans: A. Two network addressable units
    B. A logical unit and a physical unit
    C. A physical unit and a systems service control point
    D. Two physical units

21. Which DNA version is an implementation of OSI protocols?
    A. DECnet Phase III
    B. DECnet Phase IV
    Ans: C. DECnet Phase V
    D. Both DECnet Phase IV and Phase V

22. Which protocol is AppleTalk's implementation of the OSI network layer?
    A. AARP
    B. ATP

Ans: C. DDP
      D. None of the above.

23. Which AppleTalk protocol supports printer access in an AppleTalk network?
Ans: A. PAP
      B. ASP
      C. ATP
      D. Both PAP and ATP

24. Which AppleTalk protocol is employed by AppleTalk to translate between AppleTalk names and addresses?
      A. ARP
      B. AARP
Ans: C. NBP
      D. RTMP

25. The organization that developed and promotes the use of the fiber distributed data interface (FDDI) access protocol is?
Ans: A. ANSI
      B. IBM
      C. ISO
      D. CCITT/ITU

26. The data rate of an FDDI network is?
      A. 1 Mbit/sec
      B. 10 Mbits/sec
      C. 16 Mbits/sec
Ans: D. 100 Mbits/sec

27. What is the data rate of the LocalTalk access protocol?
      A. 64 Kbits/sec
Ans: B. 230 Kbits/sec
      C. 1 Mbit/sec
      D. 2.5 Mbits/sec

28. Which pair matches the data link layer protocol with the organization that has developed and promoted it?
      A. IEEE/HDLC
      B. ANSI/LAPB
Ans: C. IBM/SDLC
      D. ISO/IP

29. Which is not a link access protocol?
    A. SDLC
Ans: B. X.25
    C. LAPB
    D. HDLC

D

Online services, Internet, and CD-ROM vendor resources

The information in this appendix is updated and maintained at the following Internet Web site: http://www.hookup.net/~infomen/

Many vendors make information available in electronic form, and four key vendor sources of information are:

1. Online service forums—The most popular is CompuServe.
2. Internet—Anonymous FTP and World Wide Web servers on the Internet. These are becoming increasingly popular.
3. CD-ROM—Many vendors make available copious amounts of technical and product information in CD-ROMs. They are available to qualified customers.
4. A bulletin board—In addition to the services just listed, some vendors maintain a private bulletin board for patches, fixes, and a place to answer questions from customers.

We highly recommend that a multivendor network manager obtain an account on both CompuServe and the Internet. The Internet account should be a slip or PPP account, if it is a dial-up account, or set it up through your company's network. But it must be more than just a Telnet access or e-mail-only account. It has to have FTP access at minimum, or better yet, full WWW access. It is very useful to access the Internet via the graphics interface of the Web via Mosaic or an equivalent interface. It is also important to have an e-mail account both on CompuServe and the Internet.

The following list is sorted alphabetically by vendor. We have tried to get as much information as possible about each vendor's offering. Many new services are springing up all the time, so use this list as a starting point in your search.

Association for Computing Machinery

URL: http://info.acm.org/

The ACM is the oldest and most influential of all computer organizations. Most of its work is academic, but ACM provides a valuable resource for research on the cutting edge of the industry. Join up! They deserve your support.

Apple

URL: http://www.apple.com/
CompuServe: GO APPLE

Stick to the Mac Communications Forum for information about networks and the Mac. It is worthwhile going there for technical solutions to your Mac connectivity problems.

ATM forum

Looking for information on ATM? Check out the ATM forum's Web server. Download their White Paper for information on how to decide if ATM meets your needs.

URL: http://atmforum.com/

⇨ AT&T

URL: http://www.att.com/

AT&T provides WAN services and other networking products. It is worth a peek at AT&T's site to check out the company's products and information. The site has links to the Bell Labs server as well.

⇨ Banyan

URL: http://www.banyan.com/
CompuServe Forum: GO BANYAN

The name of the forum you want is BANFORUM. It contains a wealth of information, tech notes, and product news—enough to satisfy any Banyan fan or network integrator needing to deal with Banyan servers.

⇨ Bay Networks

URL: http://www.baynetworks.com/
CompuServe Forum: GO BAYNETWORKS

This is a useful Web site and forum for information on new products, updates, and general information on Bay Networks' internetworking products. The Synoptics and the Wellfleet companies merged to form Bay Networks.

⇨ Cisco Systems

URL: http://www.cisco.com/

This is a useful Web site for information on new products, updates, and general information on Cisco's internetworking products.

⇨ Compaq

URL: http://www.compaq.com/

There is lots of information here about Compaq's products and services.

⇨ Computer Associates International

CA is a major player in the software field, especially for mainframes. Check out their offerings on CompuServe.

CompuServe: GO CAI

⇨ Digital

URL: http://www.digital.com/
CompuServe Forum: GO DEC

Digital maintains its computer catalog online at either location (CompuServe or the Web server). Digital also has a service for integrators that can be reached through the CompuServe forum GO DECNIDEV. There are several DEC forums dealing with the issues of networking.

CD-ROM Digital makes available a wonderful CD-ROM. It is called DEC Direct Interactive. The CD is Digital's entire catalog and has a great deal of information on it. Call 1-800-344-4825 to get your copy. It is a subscription, so you will get one every month. Or order by e-mail: converge@world.std.com.

⇨ Disaster recovery

The group Binomial International maintains a Web page on disaster recovery and contingency planning at:

URL: http://www.binomial.com/links.html

Binomial maintains links to other disaster recovery resources on the Internet through that URL. You can subscribe to the company's newsletter by sending the message:

SUBSCRIBE DISASTER-RECOVERY in the body of the message. Send it to: majordome@magmacom.com.

Disaster Recovery Journal

CompuServe forum: GO DRJNRL

The Disaster Recovery Journal (DRJ) is a journal dedicated to business continuity and news gathering. DRJ has been a primary force in the disaster recovery arena for over eight years and is published quarterly by Systems Support, Inc. Subscriptions are free to all qualified personnel in the United States and Canada who are involved in managing, preparing, or supervising contingency planning. The DRJ also hosts two annual conferences. One is in the spring in San Diego, California, and one is in the fall in Atlanta, Georgia.

Ethernet information

Dan Kegel's Fast Ethernet Page There is good information here on the status of Fast Ethernet, 100Base-X, 100VG AnyLAN, and much more! You can jump from here to many other sites of similar interest.

URL: http://alumni.caltech.edu/~dank/fe/

The Ethernet Page On this page there is information on 10-Mbps Ethernet and the 100-Mbps varieties. It has original papers and a great deal more. Many vendor sites are listed with jumps to their servers. It is worthwhile checking it out.

URL: http://wwwhost.ots.utexas.edu/ethernet/

⇨ IBM

URL: http://www.ibm.com/
CompuServe Forum: GO IBM
Gopher Sites: www01.ny.us.ibm.net

This site contains entry into many IBM public-domain files that cover various areas, including new technology, client/server networks, product announcements, and case studies. The files are available for a free download.

CD-ROM The OS/2 Developer's Connection is a CD-ROM series. A yearly subscription brings about six CD-ROMs per quarter containing product demos, LAN connection tools, developer's tools, and other useful files. The low price makes it attractive to anyone interested in OS/2 development. It also includes a migration system to facilitate migrating programs from MS-Windows to OS/2.

⇨ Intel

URL: http://www.intel.com/

Intel has several networking products, and they keep information about these at the Web server just listed.

⇨ InformationWeek

Abstracts of articles in the *InformationWeek* magazine can be read online on the Web.

URL: http://techweb.cmp.com/iwk

⇨ Hewlett-Packard

URL: http://www.hp.com/
CompuServe Forum: GO HP

Check out the HP Systems Product Forum under the main menu. There is a great deal of information on OpenView and other networking products.

Internet Society

URL: http://www.isoc.com/
FTP server: ftp.isoc.org

There is a great deal of information at these servers about the Internet, Internet providers, RFCs, the process of creating a protocol, copies of the protocols and many more important facts about TCP/IP as well. One interesting URL contains information on Internet providers and it is well worth the visit. The Network Service Providers Around the World (NSPAW) file , courtesy of Mr. Barry Raveendran Greene may be found at:

URL: http://www.isoc.org/~bgreene/nsp-index.html

Institute for Electrical and Electronic Engineers (IEEE)

URL: http://www.ieee.com/

The IEEE maintains a very active computer group that publishes many magazines of interest. Membership also gains you access to a vast array of specifications and standards of interest.

Learning Tree International

URL: http://lrntree.com/

Learning Tree International has a full range of educational opportunities for the network professional. The company produces and runs short courses (three- to five-day seminars) in high technology—everything from datacom and networks to databases to technical management. The company also has a full line of CBTs that parallel instructor-led courses. Learning Tree International will customize courses to fit a company's requirements. The company also does full Novell CNE and Microsoft MSE training, has over 90 courses in its catalog, and runs over 2000 courses a year worldwide. It is worth a visit if you are looking for technical education.

⇨ Lotus

URL: http://www.lotus.com/
CompuServe: GO LOTUS

You are welcome to peruse the entire forum, but we recommend you stick to network products: Notes and cc:Mail. Be sure to choose Lotus Comm Forum under the main menu.

⇨ Microsoft

URL: http://www.microsoft.com/

Microsoft maintains a collection of product information and other resources on this Web site. The server features Windows NT Server Evaluation kits that can be downloaded, as well as many white papers. The site includes information on the use of Windows NT as an Internet server. Network integrators can use this Web site to search the Microsoft Software Library and Microsoft TecNet. You can get Developer Network News as well as Windows News online. The Web site provides access to ftp.microsoft.com as well.

CompuServe Forum: GO MSNETWORKS

This forum deals with networking out of a larger collection of forums known as The Microsoft Connection. There is a great deal of information here, including how to hook up a Windows NT workstation to a network and all of Microsoft's server products.

CD-ROM There are several CD-ROMs available from Microsoft. The Windows NT Resource Guide comes with a CD-ROM loaded with technical information on networking Windows NT. It is well worthwhile. Also, Microsoft makes available a CD called Network Developer's CD (the word network has nothing to do with data networking but with people networking between developers). You get a few free copies before you have to sign up and pay for the subscription. The networking information is not worth the price of a subscription. Get a few sample copies and see for yourself.

⇨ National Aeronautics and Space Administration (NASA)

URL: http://epims1.gsfc.nasa.gov/engineering/engineering.html

NASA maintains a virtual library staffed with volunteer "maintainers." It contains a comprehensive list of links to dozens of subjects, including engineering topics ranging from aerospace and control to nuclear and power engineering. There are dozens of categories and lists such as information resources, manufacturers/vendors, and educational and research institutions.

⇨ Novell

URL: http://www.novell.com/
CompuServe Forum: GO NETWIRE

Netwire is a comprehensive forum that has been around for many years. This has traditionally been a NetWare technician's resource of last resort. If you could not find the answer to your question here, you simply gave up. And the Novell staff always promptly answer questions. If you have anything to do with Novell products, getting a CompuServe account is a must.

CD-ROM Novell makes a lot of information available on CD. You can get a free subscription to Novell's Market Messenger CD-ROM. It contains a complete description of Novell's entire product line and a lot of technical information on both NetWare and UNIX. Then there is the NetWare Support Encyclopedia, which is full of good technical information. You get a free copy when you become a CNE (Certified

NetWare Engineer). After that, it costs several thousands of dollars for a yearly subscription. You can subscribe, even though you don't have a CNE. Most NetWare manuals these days come on CD so you can get an inexpensive copy to carry around or access from your CD-ROM player. It is easier to carry than the bookshelf of red-bound books you could be carrying around!

⇨ National Computer Security Association

CompuServe forum: GO NCSA

The National Computer Security Association is an organization that provides educational materials, training, testing and consulting services to improve computer and information security, reliability, and ethics. Training is delivered through public and in-house seminars, and NCSA's annual security conference provides a meeting ground for members and nonmembers to share experiences and learn about current technology and solutions. NCSA manages this CompuServe forum dedicated to computer security and ethics (GO NCSAFORUM or NCSA). NCSA can also be reached via e-mail at 75300.2557@compuserve.com.

⇨ Oracle

URL: http://www.oracle.com/
CompuServe Forum: GO ORACLE

This is run by the Oracle user group called the IAOG.

⇨ Retix

URL: http://www.retix.com/

⇨ Silicon Graphics

URL: http://www.sgi.com/

Silicon Graphic's server is called Silicon Surf, and it is a lot of fun to visit. The company makes great workstations.

⇨ Software.net

URL: http://software.net/

This company sells over 7800 software products online. Many of these products can be sampled online. If you are looking for communication products, you can check them out.

⇨ Sun

URL: http://www.sun.com/
CompuServe Forum: GO SUNSOFT

Don't confuse this forum with GO SUN, or you will wind up buying sunglasses. There are lots of demos of all of their products.

CD-ROM Sun makes Solaris demonstrations available on CD-ROM for Windows workstations. The demo also runs on Solaris 2.2 Sparcstations. There is some limited information there. If you are considering buying Sun Sparcstations, then this might be of use to you. Sun's e-mail address is: cdtimes@sun.com.

⇨ Thomas-Conrad

URL: http://www.tci.com/

You'll find lots of information on all of their products. There are manuals and drivers for FTP download and technical information.

There are also white papers and many other tidbits of Fast Ethernet and 100VG AnyLAN.

⇨ 3COM

URL: http://www.3com.com/
CompuServe Forum: GO ASKTHREECOM

⇨ Xerox

URL: http://ww.xerox.com/
CompuServe: GO XEROX

This site has a great deal of information on printers and office products. It also has some limited information on software products that work over a network.

⇨ Other resources

⇨ 800 directory

AT&T maintains an 800 directory service for U.S. toll-free numbers on the Web.

URL: http://att.net/dir800

⇨ Windows NT resource

You'll find Windows NT information at this site. Dave Baker, a Windows NT consultant and software architect in Beverly Hills, California, has set up a Web resource related to Windows NT. It includes links to Windows NT information databases and a list of Windows NT consultants. It is located at:

URL: http://www.bhs.com/winnt/resources.html

CD-ROMs A wonderful set of CD-ROMs with standards and other utilities can be obtained from InfoMagic. The company has the complete set of Internet, CCITT, IEEE, ANSI, and ISO standards on CD. It even has the complete set of RFCs in Hypertext. The company's phone number is 1-602-526-9565.

⇨ Job and career server

JobTrack Corporation of Los Angeles, California, USA, maintains a job-tracking server on the Web. It keeps employer listings for part-time and full-time positions. It is used by more than 150,000 small and large employers for want-ad placement. If looking for a job, check it out!

URL: http://www.career.com/

⇨ Yahoo server

The Yahoo server is a wonderful general reference on the Web. It breaks down the Web into categories. Check out the computers section.

URL: http://www.yahoo.com/computers/

⇨ Networth server

This is a hypertext listing of public companies that have home pages on the Net. It has a search engine to allow you to locate the home page by keyword. Once you find the listing on this server, it will take you to that home page if you so wish.

URL: http://networth.galt.com/www/home/info/insider/publicco.htm

E

International Technologies case study information

⇨ **International Technologies at a glance**

International Technologies is a company that manufactures computer equipment. It is headquartered in San Jose, California, with offices and facilities in Paris, Hong Kong, Toronto, and Mexico City. The headquarters campus consists of four multistory buildings. The offices in France, Hong Kong, and Canada are each housed in three-story buildings. The new repair facility in Mexico occupies one floor of rented space. Each department and office has independently developed its internal computing resources, as described in the network blueprints in the following diagrams.

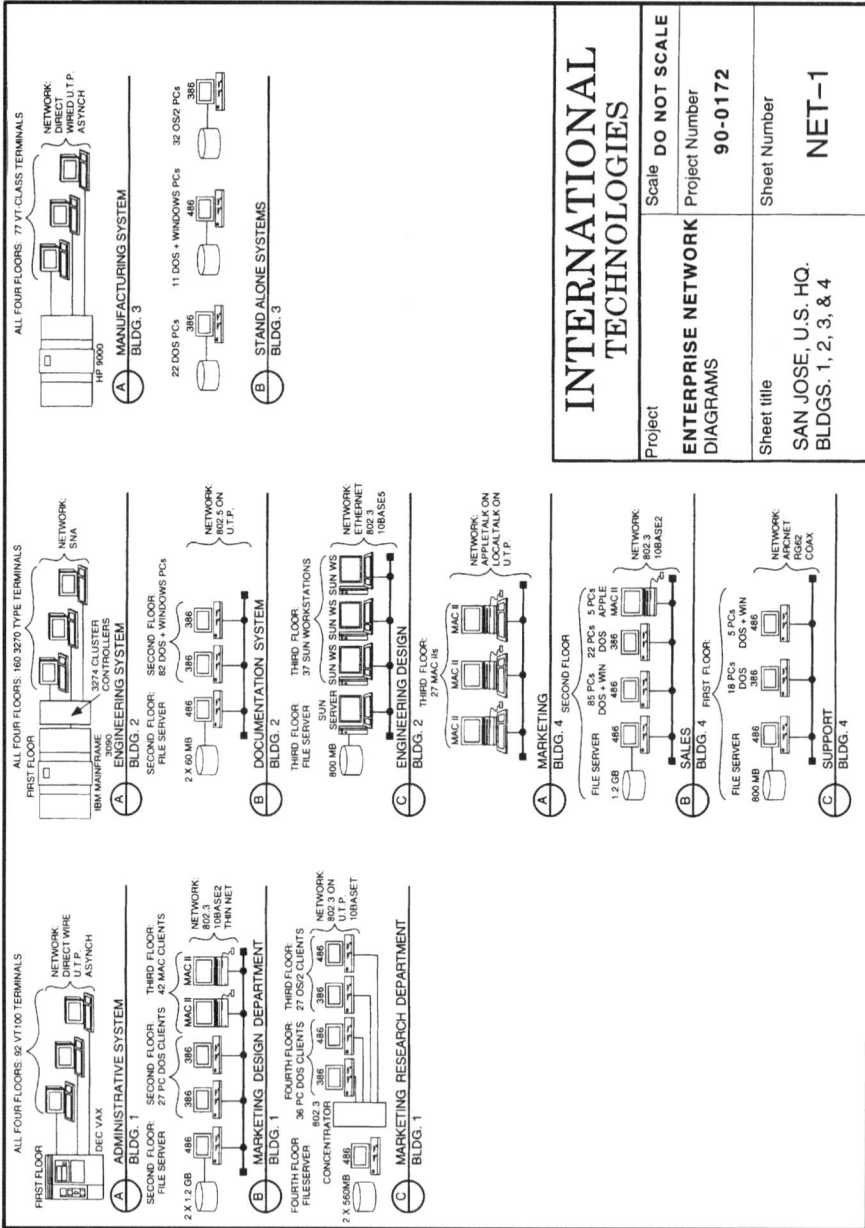

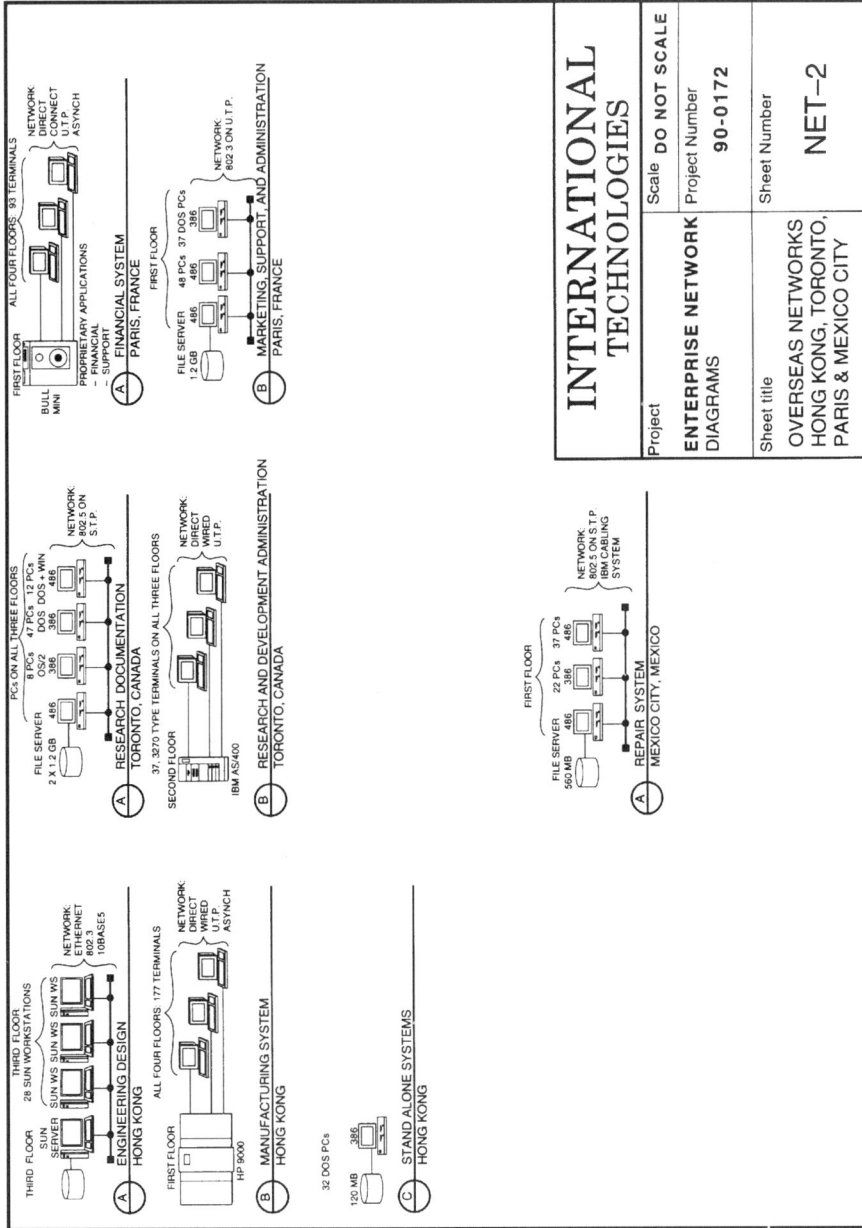

INTERNATIONAL TECHNOLOGIES

Project	Scale **DO NOT SCALE**
ENTERPRISE NETWORK DIAGRAMS	Project Number **90-0172**
Sheet title	Sheet Number
OVERSEAS NETWORKS HONG KONG, TORONTO, PARIS & MEXICO CITY	**NET-2**

OS: VMS
DB: INGRESS
EMAIL: ALL-IN-ONE

FIRST FLOOR

ALL FOUR FLOORS: 92 VT100 TERMINALS

NETWORK:
DIRECT
WIRE
U.T.P.
ASYNCH

DEC VAX

(A) ADMINISTRATIVE SYSTEM

NOS: NOVELL NETWARE 3.11
DB: DBASE
EMAIL: CCMAIL
WP: WORD PERFECT
APP: ALDUS PAGEMAKER
GUI: WINDOWS 3
MAC

SECOND FLOOR:
FILE SERVER

2 X 1.2 GB

SECOND FLOOR:
27 PC DOS +
WINDOWS CLIENTS

THIRD FLOOR:
42 MAC CLIENTS

386   486   MAC II   MAC II

NETWORK:
802.3
10BASE2
THIN NET

(B) MARKETING DESIGN DEPARTMENT

NOS: OS/2 AND
MS LAN MAN 2.1
DB: SQLSERVER
EMAIL: MICROSOFT MAIL
WP: MICROSOFT WORD
APP: MICROSOFT EXCEL
GUI: WINDOWS 3
MAC

FOURTH FLOOR
FILESERVER

2 X 560 MB

802.3
CONCENTRATOR

486

FOURTH FLOOR:
36 PC DOS +
WINDOWS CLIENTS

THIRD FLOOR:
27 OS/2 CLIENTS

386   486   386   486

NETWORK:
802.3 ON
U.T.P.
10BASET

(C) MARKETING RESEARCH DEPARTMENT

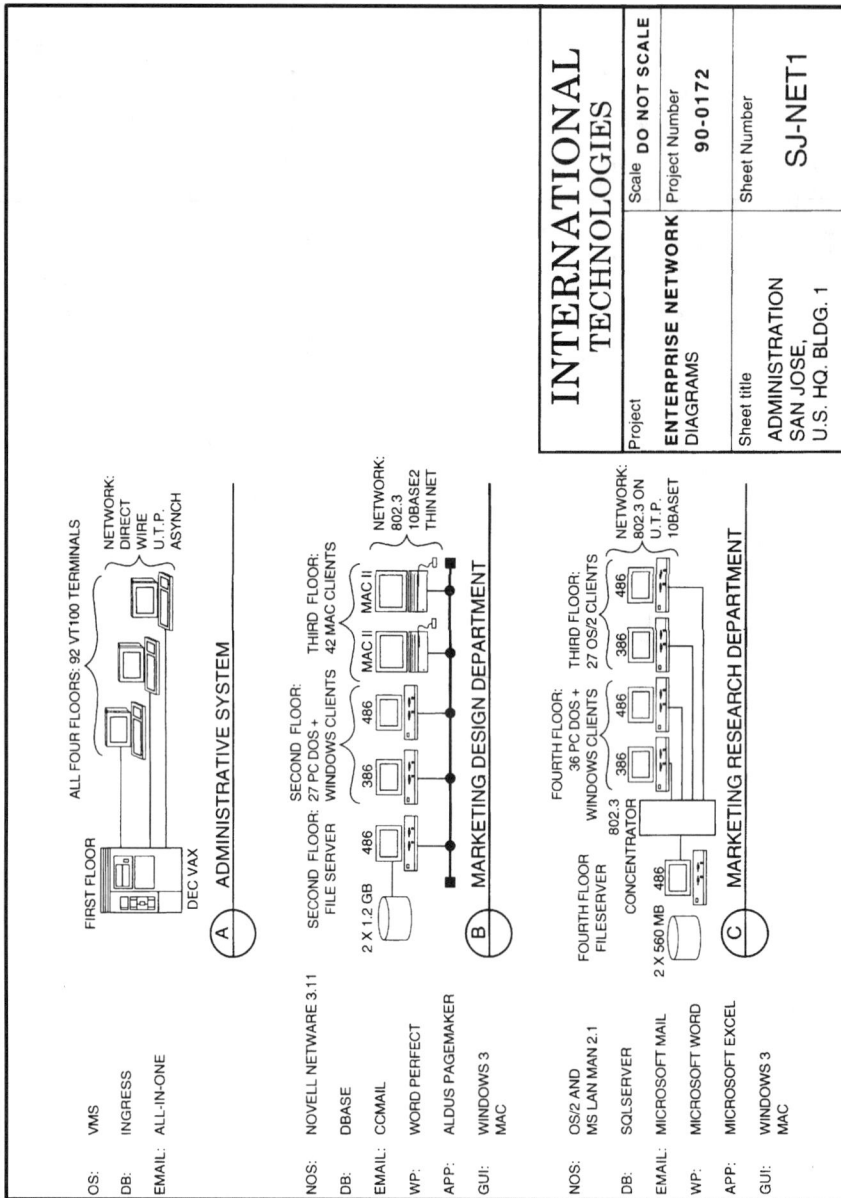

INTERNATIONAL
TECHNOLOGIES

Project

ENTERPRISE NETWORK
DIAGRAMS

Scale **DO NOT SCALE**

Project Number
90-0172

Sheet title

ADMINISTRATION
SAN JOSE,
U.S. HQ. BLDG. 1

Sheet Number

SJ-NET1

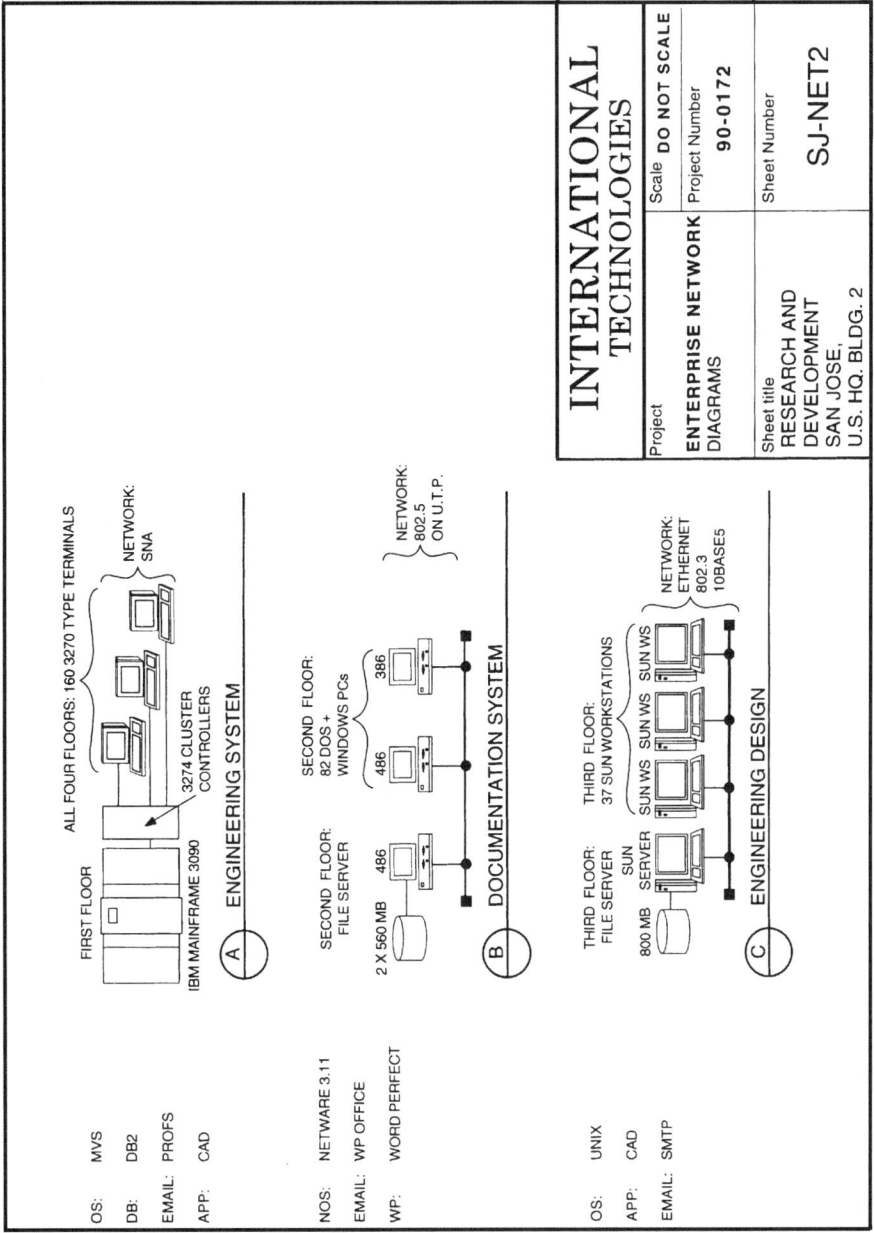

INTERNATIONAL
TECHNOLOGIES

| Project | Scale DO NOT SCALE | Project Number |
| ENTERPRISE NETWORK DIAGRAMS | | 90-0172 |

| Sheet title | | Sheet Number |
| RESEARCH AND DEVELOPMENT SAN JOSE, U.S. HQ. BLDG. 2 | | SJ-NET2 |

ALL FOUR FLOORS: 160 3270 TYPE TERMINALS

NETWORK: SNA

3274 CLUSTER CONTROLLERS

FIRST FLOOR

IBM MAINFRAME 3090

(A) ENGINEERING SYSTEM

OS: MVS
DB: DB2
EMAIL: PROFS
APP: CAD

SECOND FLOOR: 82 DOS + WINDOWS PCs

386
486
486

NETWORK: 802.5 ON U.T.P.

SECOND FLOOR: FILE SERVER

2 X 560 MB

(B) DOCUMENTATION SYSTEM

NOS: NETWARE 3.11
EMAIL: WP OFFICE
WP: WORD PERFECT

THIRD FLOOR: 37 SUN WORKSTATIONS

SUN WS   SUN WS   SUN WS   SUN WS   SUN WS

NETWORK: ETHERNET 802.3 10BASE5

THIRD FLOOR: FILE SERVER SUN SERVER

800 MB

(C) ENGINEERING DESIGN

OS: UNIX
APP: CAD
EMAIL: SMTP

501

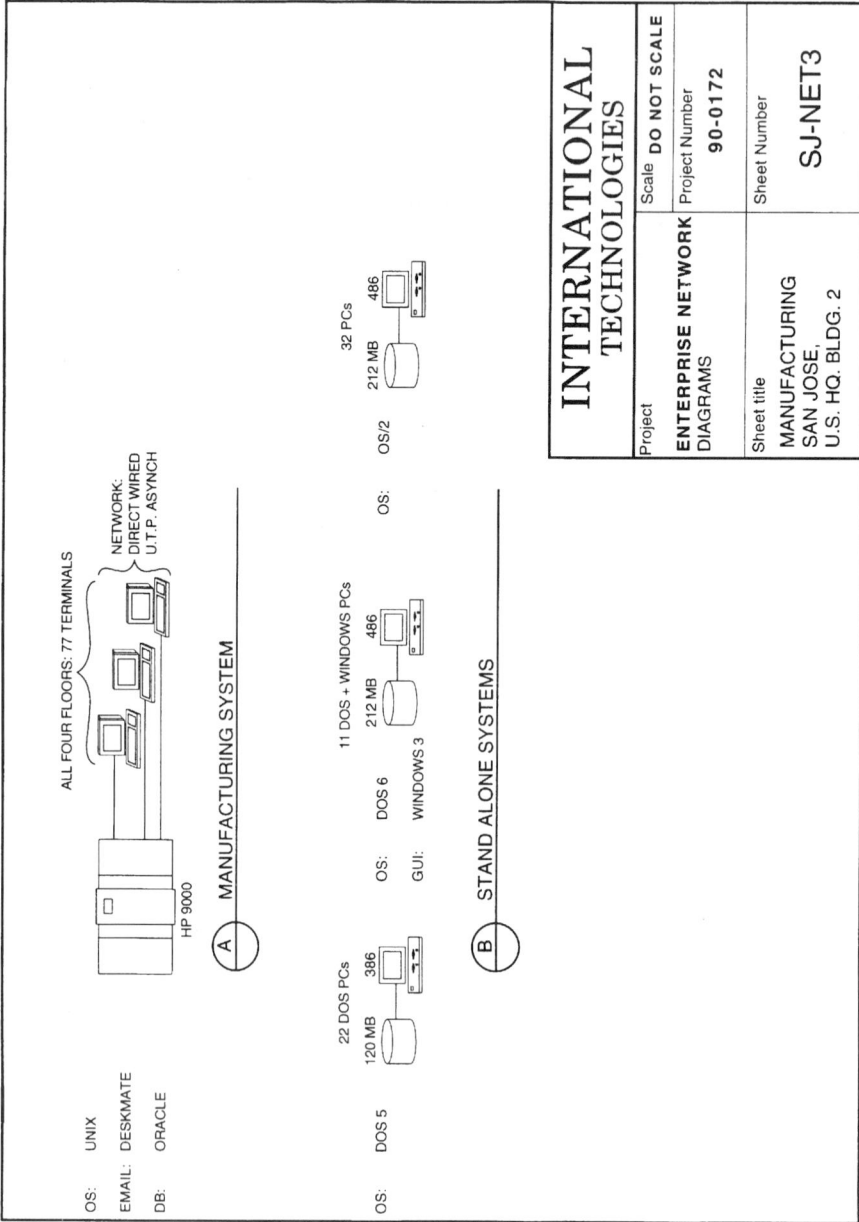

INTERNATIONAL TECHNOLOGIES

Project	Scale **DO NOT SCALE**	Project Number
ENTERPRISE NETWORK DIAGRAMS		**90-0172**
Sheet title	Sheet Number	
MANUFACTURING SAN JOSE, U.S. HQ. BLDG. 2		SJ-NET3

ALL FOUR FLOORS: 77 TERMINALS

NETWORK: DIRECT WIRED U.T.P. ASYNCH

HP 9000

(A) MANUFACTURING SYSTEM

OS: UNIX
EMAIL: DESKMATE
DB: ORACLE

22 DOS PCs
120 MB   386

11 DOS + WINDOWS PCs
212 MB   486

32 PCs
212 MB   486

OS: DOS 5

OS: DOS 6
GUI: WINDOWS 3

OS: OS/2

(B) STAND ALONE SYSTEMS

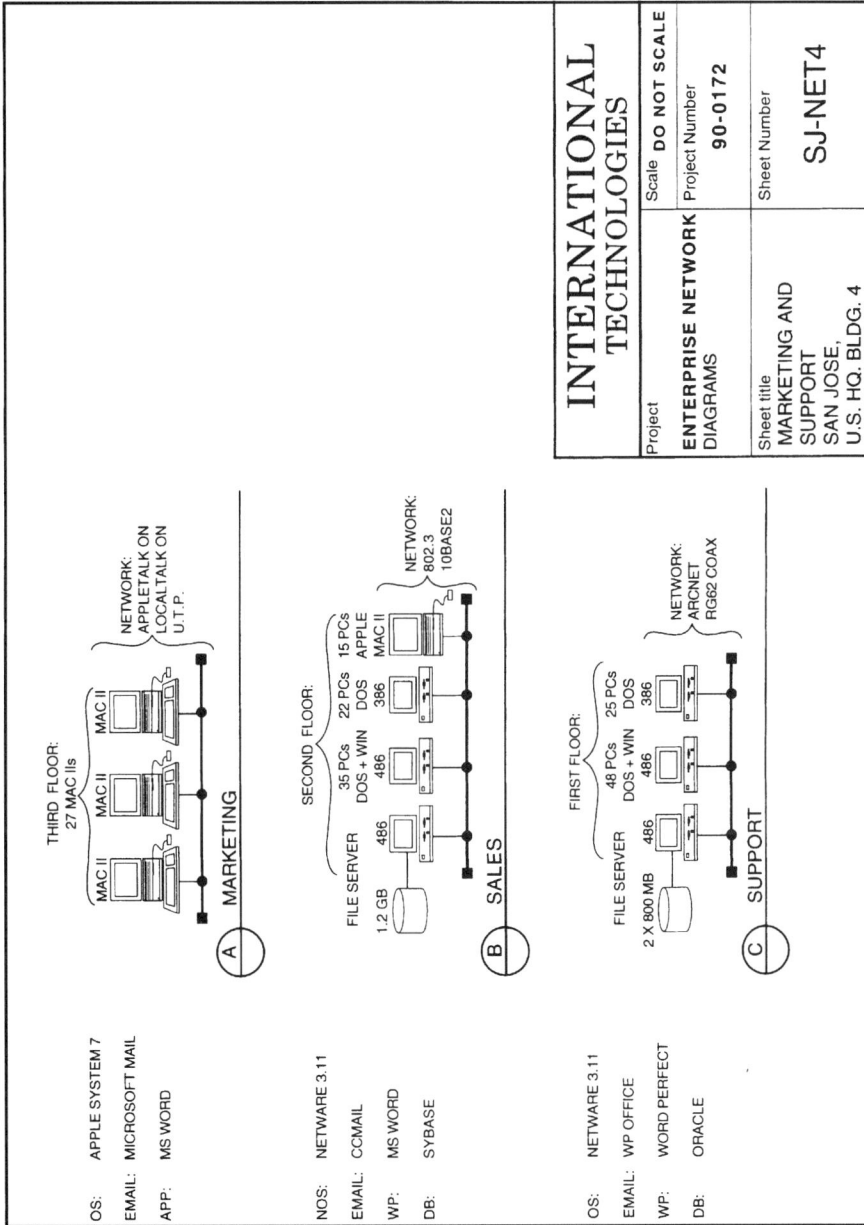

INTERNATIONAL TECHNOLOGIES

Scale **DO NOT SCALE**

Project Number **90-0172**

Sheet Number **SJ-NET4**

Project **ENTERPRISE NETWORK DIAGRAMS**

Sheet title **MARKETING AND SUPPORT** SAN JOSE, U.S. HQ. BLDG. 4

A — MARKETING

THIRD FLOOR: 27 MAC IIs

MAC II   MAC II   MAC II

NETWORK: APPLETALK ON LOCALTALK ON U.T.P.

OS: APPLE SYSTEM 7
EMAIL: MICROSOFT MAIL
APP: MS WORD

B — SALES

SECOND FLOOR:

FILE SERVER 486   1.2 GB

35 PCs DOS + WIN 486

22 PCs DOS 386

15 PCs APPLE MAC II

NETWORK: 802.3 10BASE2

NOS: NETWARE 3.11
EMAIL: CCMAIL
WP: MS WORD
DB: SYBASE

C — SUPPORT

FIRST FLOOR:

FILE SERVER 486   2 X 800 MB

48 PCs DOS + WIN 486

25 PCs DOS 386

NETWORK: ARCNET RG62 COAX

OS: NETWARE 3.11
EMAIL: WP OFFICE
WP: WORD PERFECT
DB: ORACLE

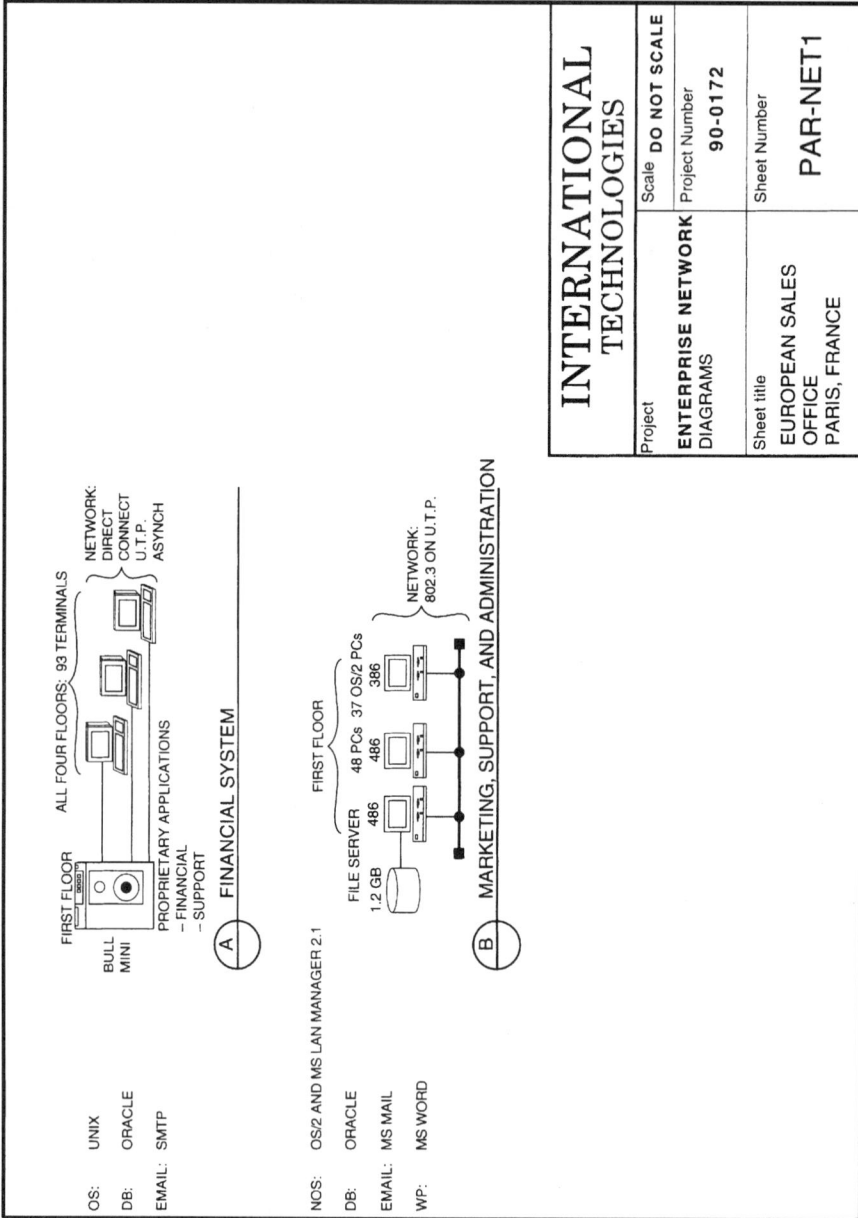

INTERNATIONAL TECHNOLOGIES

Project
ENTERPRISE NETWORK DIAGRAMS

Scale **DO NOT SCALE**

Project Number
90-0172

Sheet title
EUROPEAN SALES OFFICE
PARIS, FRANCE

Sheet Number
PAR-NET1

FIRST FLOOR   ALL FOUR FLOORS: 93 TERMINALS

NETWORK:
DIRECT
CONNECT
U.T.P.
ASYNCH

BULL
MINI

PROPRIETARY APPLICATIONS
– FINANCIAL
– SUPPORT

(A)   FINANCIAL SYSTEM

OS: UNIX
DB: ORACLE
EMAIL: SMTP

FIRST FLOOR

FILE SERVER   48 PCs 37 OS/2 PCs
1.2 GB   486   486   386

NETWORK:
802.3 ON U.T.P.

(B)   MARKETING, SUPPORT, AND ADMINISTRATION

NOS: OS/2 AND MS LAN MANAGER 2.1
DB: ORACLE
EMAIL: MS MAIL
WP: MS WORD

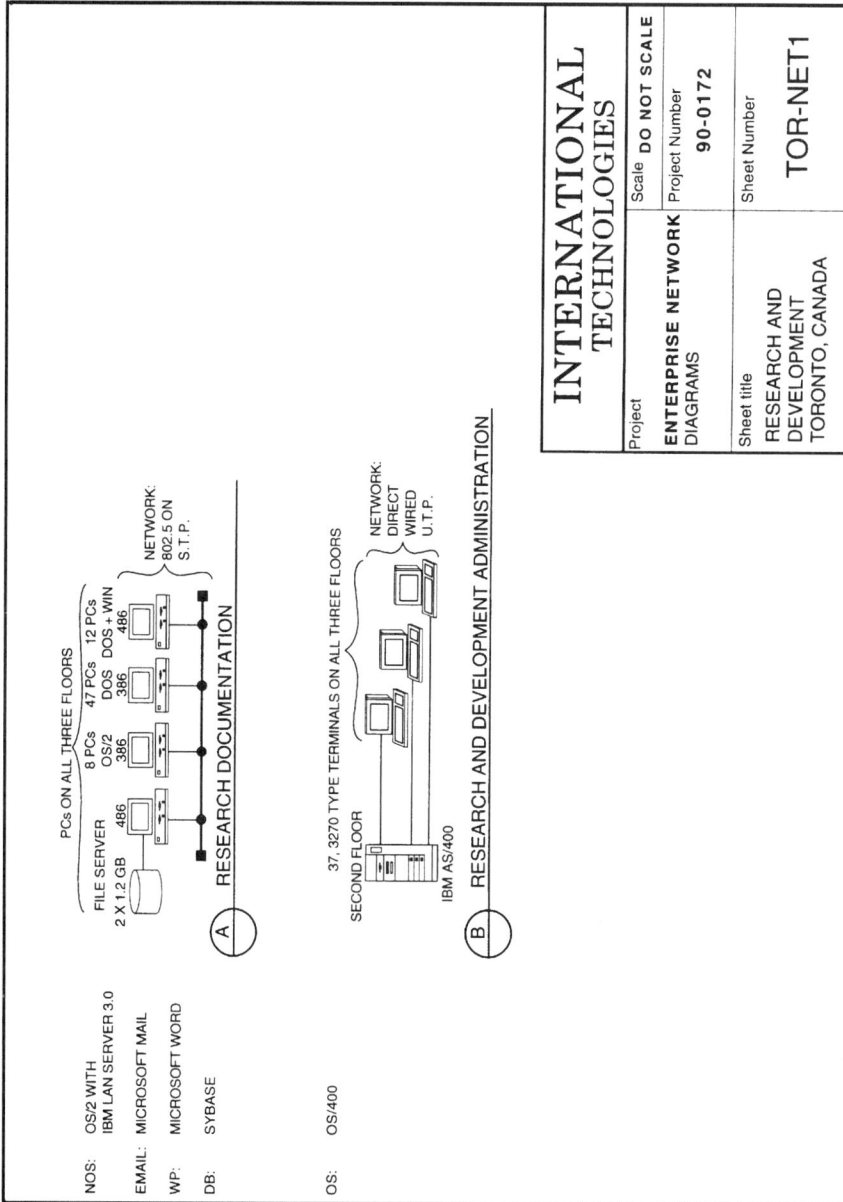

NOS: OS/2 WITH
IBM LAN SERVER 3.0

EMAIL: MICROSOFT MAIL

WP: MICROSOFT WORD

DB: SYBASE

OS: OS/400

PCs ON ALL THREE FLOORS

FILE SERVER   8 PCs   47 PCs   12 PCs
2 X 1.2 GB   OS/2   DOS   DOS + WIN
486   386   386   486

NETWORK:
802.5 ON
S.T.P.

(A) RESEARCH DOCUMENTATION

37, 3270 TYPE TERMINALS ON ALL THREE FLOORS

SECOND FLOOR

IBM AS/400

NETWORK:
DIRECT
WIRED
U.T.P.

(B) RESEARCH AND DEVELOPMENT ADMINISTRATION

INTERNATIONAL
TECHNOLOGIES

Project	Scale **DO NOT SCALE**	Project Number
ENTERPRISE NETWORK DIAGRAMS		**90-0172**
Sheet title		Sheet Number
RESEARCH AND DEVELOPMENT TORONTO, CANADA		TOR-NET1

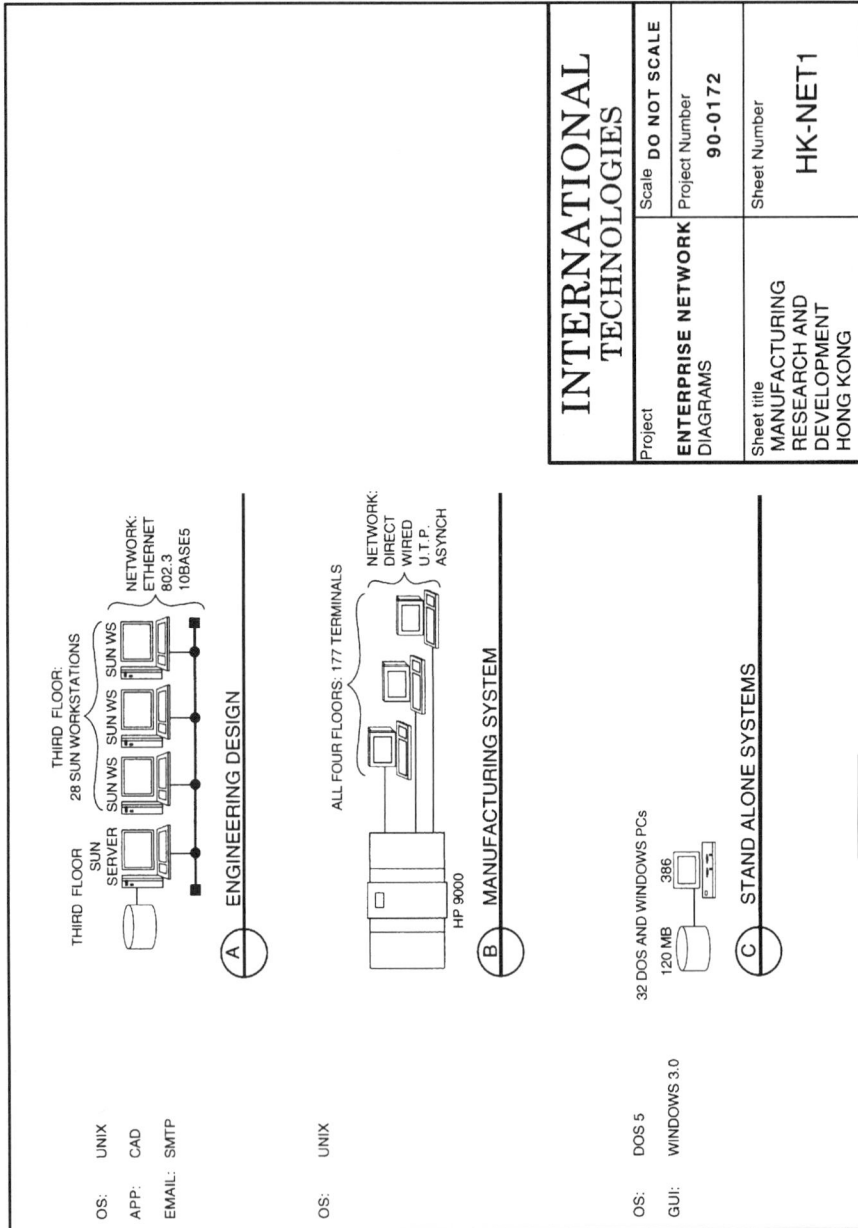

INTERNATIONAL
TECHNOLOGIES

Project
ENTERPRISE NETWORK
DIAGRAMS

Scale DO NOT SCALE
Project Number
90-0172

Sheet title
MANUFACTURING
RESEARCH AND
DEVELOPMENT
HONG KONG

Sheet Number
HK-NET1

THIRD FLOOR:
28 SUN WORKSTATIONS

THIRD FLOOR
SUN
SERVER   SUN WS   SUN WS   SUN WS

NETWORK:
ETHERNET
802.3
10BASE5

A ENGINEERING DESIGN

OS: UNIX
APP: CAD
EMAIL: SMTP

ALL FOUR FLOORS: 177 TERMINALS

NETWORK:
DIRECT
WIRED
U.T.P.
ASYNCH

HP 9000

B MANUFACTURING SYSTEM

OS: UNIX

32 DOS AND WINDOWS PCs

120 MB   386

C STAND ALONE SYSTEMS

OS: DOS 5
GUI: WINDOWS 3.0

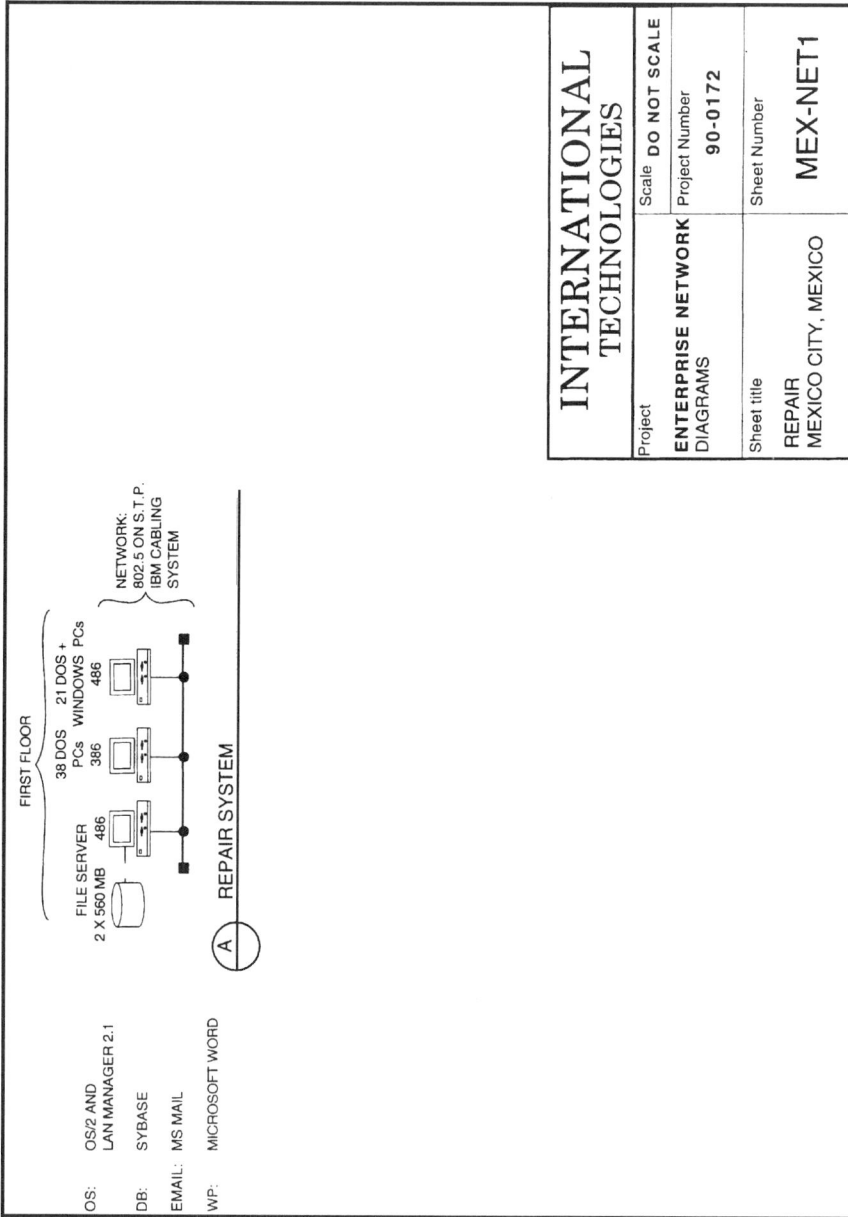

FIRST FLOOR

FILE SERVER 486
2 X 560MB

38 DOS PCs 386

21 DOS + WINDOWS PCs 486

NETWORK:
802.5 ON S.T.P.
IBM CABLING
SYSTEM

A — REPAIR SYSTEM

OS: OS/2 AND LAN MANAGER 2.1
DB: SYBASE
EMAIL: MS MAIL
W.P.: MICROSOFT WORD

INTERNATIONAL
TECHNOLOGIES

Project	Scale DO NOT SCALE
ENTERPRISE NETWORK DIAGRAMS	Project Number 90-0172
Sheet title	Sheet Number
REPAIR MEXICO CITY, MEXICO	MEX-NET1

F

Standards organizations and addresses

⇨ Sources for standards

All CCITT standards are available from:

International Telecommunications Union (ITU)
Sales Department
Place des Nations
1211 Geneva 20
Switzerland
Voice: (022) 730-52-85
Fax: (022) 730-51-94

⇨ CCITT/ITU standards agents

United States
United States Department of Commerce
National Technical Information Service
5285 Port Royal Road
Springfield, VA   22161
USA
Voice: (703) 487-4650
Fax: (703) 321-8547

Canada
Standards Council of Canada
Attn: Sales Division
350 Sparks Street
Suite 1200
Ottawa, Ontario   K1P 6N7
Canada
Voice: (613) 238-3222
Fax: (613) 995-4564

⇨ United Kingdom

London Information
Index House
Ascot, Berkshire   SL5 7EU
UK
Voice: (0344) 87-4343
Fax: (0344) 29-1194

Japan
The ITU Association of Japan
Nihon Chemical Building, 7th Floor
15-12 Nishi-Shimbashi
Minato-ku 3C
Tokyo   105
Japan
Voice: (3) 435-1931
Fax: (3) 435-1935

France
AFNOR
French Association for Standardization
Tour Europe
CEDEX 7
92080 Paris La Defense
France
Voice: (01) 42-91-5555
Fax: (01) 42-91-5656

Sweden
Swedish Telecom
Technology Department
Economy Office
PAE Room E 146
123 86 Fagersta
Sweden
Voice: (021) 90-250
Fax: (021) 11-1636

⇨ Additional standards organizations

American National Standards Institute (ANSI)
1430 Broadway
New York, NY   10018
USA
Voice: (212) 642-4900
Fax: (212) 302-1286

AT&T Technologies Commercial Sales
P.O. Box 19901
Indianapolis, IN   46219
USA
Voice: (317) 352-8461
Fax: (317) 352-8484

Bell Communication Research
Information Management Services
60 New England Ave., DSC 1B-252
Piscataway, NJ   08854-4196
USA
Voice: (800) 521-2673
Fax: (908) 336-2551

British Telecom International
150 East 52nd Street
New York, NY   10022
USA
Voice: (212) 319-6518
Fax: (212) 297-2727

British Telecom International
Holburn Center
120 Holburn
London EC1 A2TE
UK
Voice: (071) 492-2000
Fax: (071) 831-9959

Electronic Industries Association (EIA)
Standards Sales
2001 I Street, NW
Washington, D.C. 20006
USA
Voice: (202) 457-4966
Fax: (202) 457-4985

European Computer Manufacturers Association (ECMA)
114, Rue de Rhone
CH-1204 Geneva
Switzerland
Voice: (022) 735-3634
Fax: (022) 786-5231

Institute of Electrical and Electronics Engineers (IEEE)
445 Hoes Lane
P.O. Box 1331
Piscataway, NJ 08855
USA
Voice: (201) 562-3800
Fax: (201) 562-1571

International Electrotechnical Commission (IEC)
3, Rue de Varembe
1211 Geneva 20
Switzerland
Voice: (022) 734-0150
Fax: N/A

International Standards Organization (ISO)
Central Secretariat
1, rue de Varembe
CH-1211 Geneva
Switzerland
Voice: (022) 734-1240
Fax: (022) 733-3430

Omnicom International Ltd.,
Forum Chambers, First Floor
The Forum
Stevenage, Hertfodshire   SG1 1EL
UK
Voice: (0438) 742-424
Fax: (0438) 740-154

Omnicom PBI
1201 Seven Locks Road, Suite 300
Potomac, MD   20854
USA
Voice: (301) 340-1520
Toll Free: (800) 777-5006
Fax: (301) 309-3847

G

List of acronyms

This list of terms is reprinted with permission from Mr. Frank Walther.

A Acknowledgment (ARCNET)

AAL ATM Adaption Layer

ABM Asynchronous Balanced Mode

ACK Acknowledgement

ACSE Association Control Service Element

ADE Above Decks Equipment

ADMD Administrative Management Domain (X.400)

AFP AppleTalk Filing Protocol

AI Application Interface

AIP ATM Interface Processor

AIS Alarm Indication Signal

AL Attention Line

AMP Active Monitor Present (Token Ring)

AMPS Advanced Mobile Phone Service

ANSI American National Standards Institute

AOCD Advise of Charge D (ISDN)

AOCE Advise of Charge E (ISDN)

APL Active Path Length

APPC Advanced Program-to-Program Communication (IBM SNA)

APPN Advanced Peer-to-Peer Networking (IBM SNA)

ARCNET Attached Resource Computer NETwork

ARL Adjusted Ring Length

ARP Address Resolution Protocol (DoD)

ARPA Advanced Research Project Agency (DoD)

ASCII American Standard Code for Information Interchange

ASIC Application-Specific Integrated Circuit

ASN.1 Abstract Syntax Notation 1

AT Advanced Technology (IBM)

AT ATtention (Hayes Modems)

ATM Adobe Type Manager

ATM Asynchronous Transfer Mode

ATM Automatic Banking and Teller Machine

AU Access Unit

AU Administrative Unit

AUI Attachment Unit Interface

AWG American Wire Gauge

BBN Bolt, Beranek and Newman Inc.

BEB Binary Exponential Backoff

BECN Backward Explicit Congestion Notification (Frame Relay)

BER Bit Error Rate

BERT Bit Error Rate Test

BGP Border Gateway Protocol

B-ICI Broadband Inter Carrier Interface

BIP Bit-Interleaved Parity

B-ISDN Broadband ISDN

BIT Binary digIT

BIU Basic Information Unit (SNA)

BNC Baby N Connector

BOOTP Boot Protocol (DoD)

BPDU Bridge Protocol Data Unit

BSD Berkeley System Distribution

BTAM Basic Telecommunication Access Method (IBM SNA)

BTU Basic Transmission Unit (Token Ring)

CAN Customer Access Network

CAPI Common ISDN Application Programming Interface

CAR Carrierless Amplitude Modulation, Phase Modulation

CBDS Connectionless Broadband Data Service

CBE Certified Banyan Engineer

CBS Certified Banyan Specialist

CBS Constant Bitrate Service

CCF Cross Correlation Function

CCITT Comité Consultatif International Télégraphique et
Téléphonique

CCN Cluster Controller Node (IBM SNA)

CDDI Copper Distributed Data Interface (FDDI, TPDDI)

CDMA Code Division Multiple Access (Wireless)

CDPD Cellular Digital Packet Data (Wireless)

CDV Cell Delay Variation

CEO Chief Executive Officer (USA)

CEPT Conférence des Administrations Européennes des Postes et
Télécommunications

CF Call Forwarding (ISDN)

CGW Customer Gateway

CICS Customer Information Control System (IBM SNA)

CIDR Classless InterDomain Routing

CIF Common Intermediate Format

CIO Customer Information Online (Cisco)

CIR Committed Information Rate

CLIP Calling Line Identification Presentation (ISDN)

CLIP Calling Line Identification Restriction (ISDN)

CLP Cell Loss Priority

CLS ConnectionLess Server

CMIP Common Management Information Protocol

CMIS Common Management Information Service

CMOL CMIP on LLC

CMOS Complementary Metal-Oxide Semiconductor

CMOT CMIP on TCP/IP

CN Corporate Network

CNA Certified NetWare Administrator (Novell)

CNE Certified NetWare Engineer (Novell)

CNI Certified NetWare Instructor (Novell)

CODEC CODierung/DECodierung

COLR COnnected Line Identification Restriction (ISDN)

CP Control Point (IBM SNA)

CPCS Common Part Convergence Sublayer (ATM/AAL)

CPDP Cellular Digital Packet Data

CPE Customer Premises Equipment

CPSS Control Packet Switching System

CPT Cooperative Programming Tool

CPU Central Processing Unit

CRC Cyclic Redundancy Check

CS Convergence Sublayer (ATM/AAL)

CSCW Computer Supported Cooperative Work

CSE Cooperative Software Engineering

CTP Configuration Test Packet

CUG Closed User Group (ISDN)

CW Call Waiting (ISDN)

D/A Digital/Analog

DAP Digest Authorization Protocol

DARPA Defense Advanded Research Projects Agency (DoD)

DAS Dual Attached Station (FDDI)

DASD Direct Access Storage Device

DAT Duplicate Address Test (Token Ring)

DC Data Communication

DCC Data Communication Channel

DCE Data Circuit-Terminating Equipment

DCE Data Communication Equipment

DCE Distributed Computing Environment

DCT Discrete Clock Transmitter

DDV Datendirektverbindung (früher: HfD)

DEC Digital Equipment Corporation

DECnet DEC Network Architecture

DES Data Encryption Standard

DHSD Duplex High Speed Data

DID Destintation IDentification (ARCNET)

DIS Draft International Standard

DISC Disconnect (LLC Command)

DIX DEC, Intel, Xerox

DLC Data Link Control

DLM Distributed LAN Monitoring

DLSw Data Link Switching (IBM)

DM Disconnected Mode (LLC Response)

DME Distributed Management Environment

DNA Digital Network Architecture

DNA Downstream Neighbour's Address

DNS Domain Name Service

DoD Department of Defense

DQDB Distibuted Queue Dual Bus

DSAP Destination Access Point

DSU Data Service Unit

DTE Data Terminal Equipment

DXI Data eXchange Interface

ECNE Enterprise CNE

EDI Electronic Data Interchange

E-DSS1 European Digital Subscriber Signalling System

EGP Exterior Gateway Protocol

EGW Edge Gateway

EIA Electronic Industries Association

EISA Extended Industry Standard Architecture

EMI ElectroMagnetic Interference

ENL European Network Laboratory

ENQ Enquiry (ARCNET)

EoB End of Bus

EOF End Of Transmission (ARCNET)

EPROM Erasable and Programmable Read Only Memory

ESIG European SMDS Interest Group

ETSI European Telecommunications Standards Institute

EVE European Videophone Experiment

FBE Free Buffer Enquiry (ARCNET)

FCS Frame Check Sequence

FDCT Forward Discrete Cosine Transformation

FDDI Fiber Distributed Data Interface (CDDI, TPDDI)

FDM Frequency Division Multiplexing

FEC Forward Error Correction

FECN Forward Explicit Congestion Notification (Frame Relay)

FEP Front End Processor

FERF Far End Receive Failure

FFOL FDDI Follow On LAN

FOIRL Fiber-Optic Inter-Repeater Link

FRMR FRaMe Reject (LLC Response)

FRS Frame Relay Service

FTAM File Transport, Access, and Management

FTP File Transport Protocol (DoD)

GAN Global Area Network

GDSS Group Decision Support Systems

GFC Generic Flow Control

GGP Gateway-to-Gateway Protocol

GNS Get Nearest Server

GPS Global Positioning System

HDLC High-Level Data Link Control

HEC Header Error Control

HLPI Higher Layer Protocol ID

HoB Head of Bus

HOPTE High Order Path Terminating Equipment

HPR High Performance Routing (IBM)

HSD High Speed Data

HSSI High Speed Serial Interface

I Information (LLC)

ICI Inter-Exchange Carrier Interface (SMDS)

ICMP Internet Control Message Protocol

IDCT Inverse Discrete Cosine Transformation

IDN Integrated Digital Network

IDNX Integrated Digital Network eXchange

IEEE Institute of Electrical and Electronics Engineers

IETF Internet Engineering Task Force

IMS Information Management System (IBM SNA)

INMERSAT International Maritime Satellite Organization

IOS Internetwork Operating System (Cisco)

IP Internet Protocol (DoD)

IP Internetworking Port (ISDN)

IPX Internetwork Protocol eXchange

IS International Standard

ISA Industry Standard Architecture

ISDN Integrated Services Digital Network

IS-IS Intermediate System to Intermediate System Routing Protocol (ISO 10589)

ISO International Standardization Organization

IT Invitation to Transmit (ARCNET)

ITU-TSS International Telecommunications Union-Telecommunications Standards Sector

JPEG Joint Photographic Experts Group

JTAM Job Transfer and Management

kb Kilobit

KB KiloByte

KBPS KiloBit Per Second

LAA Locally Administered Address (Token Ring, IBM)

LAN Local Area Network

LANCE LAN Controller for Ethernet

LAPB Link Access Procedure for Balanced Mode

LAPD Link Access Procedure for D-Channels

LC Late Counter (FDDI)

LCP Link Control Protocol

LLC Logical Link Control

LMI Local Management Interface (Frame Relay)

LOF Loss of Frame (SDH)

LOP Loss of Pointer (SDH)

LOS Loss of Signal (SDH)

LP Layer Protocol

LPDU LLC-PDU

LSB Least Significant Bit (MSB)

LU Logical Unit (IBM SNA)

MAN Metropolitan Area Network

MAU Multistation Access Unit

MBPS MegaBit Per Second

MBS Maximum Burst Size

MCA MicroChannel Architecture

MDBS Mobile Data Base Stations (Wireless)

MDIS Mobile Data Intermediate Systems (Wireless)

MHS Message Handling System

MIB Management Information Base

MIC Medium Interface Cable

MIC Medium Interface Connector

MIPS Millions Instructions Per Second

MISTER COOL Multimedia ISDN Terminal for Cooperation over Long Distances

MLL Maximum Lobe Length

MLT Multi Level Transmit

MNP Microcom Network Protocol

MODEM MOdulator/DEModulator

MoU Memorandum of Understanding

MPEG Motion Pictures Experts Group

MPR MultiProtocol Router

MS Message Store (X.400)

MS AIS Multiplexer Section Alarm Indication Signal (SDH)

MSB Most Significant Bit (LSB)

MSN Multiple Subscriber Number (ISDN)

MSOH Multiplexer Section Overhead

MSP Multiplexer Section Protection (SDH)

MSS MAN Switching System

MSTE Multiplexer Section Terminating Equipment (SDH)

MTA Message Transfer Agent (X.400)

MTD Maximum Transmission Distance

MTSO Mobile Telephone Switching Office

MUX Multiplex

MVS Multiple Virtual Storage (IBM)

NA Negative Acknowledgement (ARCNET)

NAEC Novell Authorized Education Center

NAK Negative Acknowledgement

NAS Network Application Support (DEC)

NASC Novell Authorized Service Center

NCB Network Control Block (NetBIOS)

NCCF Network Communication Control Facility (IBM SNA)

NCP NetWare Core Protocol

NCP Network Control Program

NE Network Elements (SONET/SDH)

NEMA National Electrical Manufacturers Association

NetBEUI NetBIOS Extended User Interface

NetBIOS Network Basic Input/Output System

NEXT Near End CrossTalk

NFS Network File System

NII National Information Infrastructure (USA)

NIS Network Information Services (Yellow Pages)

NIU Network Interface Unit

NLM NetWare Loadable Module

NLP Network Layer Protocol

NLSP NetWare Linked Services Protocol (Novell)

NM Network Management

NMC Network Management Center

NMF Network Management Forum

NMS Network Management Station

NNI Network-Node Interface (ATM)

NPSI Network Packet Switch Interface (IBM SNA)

OAM Operation, Administration, and Maintenance

OCE Open Collaborative Environment

OFTEL Office of Telecommunications

OOF Out of Frame (SDH)

OSF Open Software Foundation

OSI Open Systems Interconnection

OSS Operations Support System

P Packet (ARCNET)

PAD Packet Assembler/Disassembler

PC Personal Computer (IBM)

PCI Peripheral Component Interconnect

PCI Protocol Control Information

PCM Pulse Code Modulation

PCMCIA Personal Computer Memory Consortium International Association

PCR Peak Cell Rate

PDA Personal Digital Assistant

PDH Plesiochronous Digital Hierarchy

PDS Packet Driver Specification (FTP)

PDU Protocol Data Unit

PEP Packetized Ensemble Protocol

PIN Personal Identification Number

PIN Processor Independent NetWare (Novell)

PL Physical Layer

PLCP Physical Layer Convergence Procedure

PLL Phase Locked Loop

PLS Physical Signalling (OSI-Schicht 1)

PLT Payload Type (ATM)

PMD Physical Medium Dependent

PN Peripheral Node (IBM SNA)

POH Path Section Overhead (SDH)

PPP Point-to-Point Protocol

PRMD Private Management Domain (X.400)

PT Payload Type

PTO Public Telecommunications Operator

PTT Poste, Téléphonique & Télégraphique

PU Physical Unit (IBM SNA)

PVC Permanent Virtual Channel

QCIF Quarter Common Intermediate Format

QLLC Qualified Logical Link Control (IBM SNA)

QoS Quality of Service

RACE Research on Advanced Communications in Europe

RAI Remote Alarm Indication (SDH)

RARP Reverse ARP (DoD)

RBOCs Regional Bell Holding Companies

REJ Reject (LLC)

RF Radio Frequency

RFC Request for Comments

RFI Radio Frequency Interference

RIP Routing Information Protocol

RIPL Remote Initial Program Load

RL Ring Latency (FDDI)

RMON Remote MONitoring (MIB)

RNR Receive Not Ready (LLC)

RPC Remote Procedure Call

RPS Redundant Power Supply

RR Receive Ready (LLC)

RS Recommended Standard

RSOH Regenerator Section Overhead (SDH)

RSTE Regenerator Section Terminating Equipment (SDH)

RU Request/Response Unit (SNA)

RUA Remote User Agent (X.400)

SAA System Application Architecture (IBM SNA)

SAAL Signalling AAL

SABME Set Asynchronous Balanced Mode Extended (LLC Command)

SAP Service Access Point (LLC)

SAP Source Address Protocol

SAP Service Advertisement Protocol

SAR Segmentation and Reassembly (AAL)

SARM Set Asynchronous Response Mode

SAS Single Attached Station (FDDI)

SBA Synchronous Bandwith Allocator (FDDI)

SBP AppleTalk SideBand Protocol

SCR Sustainable Cell Rate

SDDI Shielded Distributed Data Interface

SDH Synchronous Digital Hierarchy

SDLC Synchronous Data Link Control

SDXC Synchronous Digital Cross Connect (SONET/SDH)

SGMP Simple Gateway Monitoring Protocol

SID Source IDentification (ARCNET)

SINIX Siemens UNIX

SIP SMDS Interface Protocol

SIR Sustained Information Rate (SMDS)

SLIP Serial Line Interface Protocol

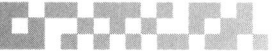

SMDS Switched Multimegabit Data Service

SMFA Specific Management Functional Areas

SMI Structure of Management Information

SMP Simple Management Protocol

SMP Standby Monitor Present (Token Ring)

SMT Station ManagemenT (FDDI)

SMT Surface Mounted Device

SMTP Simple Mail Transfer Protocol (DoD)

SN Subarea Node (IBM SNA)

SNA System Network Architecture (IBM)

SNI Siemens-Nixdorf Informationssysteme

SNI Subscriber Network Interface

SNMP Simple Network Management Protocol

SNRM Set Normal Response Mode

SOH Section Overhead (SDH)

SOH Start Of Header (ARCNET)

SONET Synchronous Optical Network

SR Source Routing

SRI SIP Relay Interface

SRT Source Routing Transparent

SSAP Source Service Access Point

SSCF Service Specific Coordination Function (ATM/AAL)

SSCOP Service Specific Connection Oriented Protocol (ATM/AAL)

SSCP System Services Control Point (IBM SNA)

SSCS Service Specific Convergence Sublayer (ATM/AAL)

STDA StreetTalk Directory Assistant [Service, Program]

STM Synchronous Transport Mode (SDH)

STM Synchronous Transport Modul (STM-1, STM-4, STM-16)

STP Shielded Twisted Pair

STS Synchronous Transport Signal

SVC Switched Virtual Circuit

SVID System V Interface Definition (UNIX)

SYN Synchronize/Synchronous

TA Terminal Adapter (ISDN)

TAC Technical Assistant Center (Cisco)

TAE Teilnehmer-Anschluß-Endeinrichtung

TCAM TeleCommunication Access Method (IBM SNA)

TCP Transmission Control Program (DoD)

TCU Trunk Coupling Unit

TDM Time Division Multiplex

TDR Time Domain Reflectometer

TE Terminal Equipment

TELNET Teletype Network [Protocol]

TEST Test (LLC Command/Response)

TFTP Trivial FTP (DoD)

THT Token-Holding Timer (FDDI)

TIC Token-Ring Interface Coupler (IBM)

TK Telecommunication

TLA Three-Letter Acronym

TMN Telecommunications Management Network (SONET/SDH)

TNT Timer No Token

TP Twisted Pair

TPDDI Twisted Pair Distributed Data Interface (FDDI,CDDI)

TP-PMD Twisted Pair Physical Medium Dependent

TR Token Ring

TRN Token Ring Network

TRT Token-Rotation Timer (FDDI)

TSA Technical Support Alliance (Novell)

TSM Timer Standby Monitor

TSO Time Sharing Option (IBM SNA)

TTRT Target Token-Rotation Time (FDDI)

TU Tributary Unit (SDH)

TUG Tributary Unit Group (SDH)

TVSt Teilnehmer-Vermittlungsstelle (ISDN)

UA Unnumbered Acknowledgement (LLC Response)

UA User Agent (X.400)

UDC Universal Data Connector

UDP User Datagram Protocol

UI Unnumbered Information (LLC Command)

UI User Interface

ULP Upper Layer Protocol

UNA Upstream Neighbour's Address

UNC Universal Naming Convention

UNI User(-to-)Network Interface

UPC User Parameter Control

UTP Unshielded Twisted Pair

UUCP Unix-to-Unix Copy Protocol

VC Virtual Channel

VC Virtual Container

VC-4 Virtual Container Level 4

VCC Virtual Channel Connection

VCI Virtual Channel Identifier

VESA Video Electronics Standards Association

VIM Vendor Independent Messaging

VLB VESA Local Bus

VLM Virtual Loadable Module (Novell)

VM Virtual Machine (IBM SNA)

VNA Virtual Network Application

VNA Virtual Network Architecture (Ungermann-Bass)

VP Virtual Path

VPC Virtual Path Connection

VPI Virtual Path Identifier

VSAM Virtual Storage Access Method (IBM SNA)

VSAT Very Small Aperture Terminal

VSE Virtual Storage Extension (IBM SNA)

VSPC Virtual Storage Personal Computing (IBM SNA)

VTAM Virtual Telecommunication Access Method (IBM SNA)

WAN Wide Area Network

WDM Wavelength Division Multiplexing

WYSIWIS What You See Is What I See

WYSIWYG What You See Is What You Get

X.25 CCITT Specification

X.400 CCITT Specification

X3T9.5 ANSI-Standard for FDDI

XID eXchange IDentification (LLC Command/Response)

XNS Xerox Network System

XPG X/Open Portability Guide

XT eXtended Technology (IBM)

H

CD-ROM listing

We are very pleased to provide you with the attached, information-packed CD-ROM. Over 100 megabytes of application and data files provide a fast amount of supplementary information to topics discussed in the book. Many of the applications can be run right from the CD-ROM itself, without using any of your computer's hard disk drive space.

While many of the applications run under Microsoft Windows, several may also be run under DOS. The many data files, including Request for Comment-RFCs, can be accessed from either Windows or DOS text editors. There is a Windows-based menuing system that provides access to both Windows- and DOS-based applications and data files.

Those of you who are preparing to write your CNE exam will also be delighted to know that Novell's Certification Assessment Test is on the CD-ROM. A text file explaining the current CNE and Master CNE program is provided as well. Additionally, a demonstration version of the Cyber Pass NetWare certification tests has also been included. Finally, an electronic version of the Networking Technologies Chapter Quiz questions is available and can be run right from the CD-ROM.

Other software includes an OSI Tutorial with interactive review questions after each layer section, a Windows version of the Netware Frequently Asked Questions (120 pages of NetWare-related text files), a multivendor HTML page with Web links to all the major vendor sites, as well as several hundred Request For Comment files relating to the world of networking technologies.

Finally, we have included a working demo copy of the BANalyzer© Protocol Reference Database application. BANalyzer© is a text-based database system with complete information on over 100 network-related protocols, including actual protocol decodes and trace files, so you can see what it actually looks like. You can access the wealth of information—over 35 megabytes in size—directly from the CD-ROM itself. There is too much in this application to list it here, so just try it. As you work in the networking industry, remember it and you will have a fantastic reference that you can easily carry with you wherever you go.

CD-ROM installation and access instructions

The easiest way to access the CD-based applications and data files is through Microsoft Windows. In the root of the CD-ROM directory, you will find the **NTMENU.EXE** file. This file presents a Windows menu application that provides access to or runs the CD-ROM applications. Several of the applications can be run directly from the CD-ROM itself. However, you should be aware that the Novell NetWare Certification Assessment Sampler and the Cyber Pass Certification demonstration test can only be run from your computer's hard disk and, as such, will require hard disk drive space. (See Fig. H-1.)

CD-ROM listing of applications and data files

A: Novell's NetWare Certification Assessment Sampler software
  • Directory: \CNETEST
  • Must be installed on computer hard disk drive.
  • Requires 5 megabytes of disk space.

B: Novell's NetWare CNE and CNE Master program Documentation and FAQ.
  • Directory: \CNEDOC

NETWORKING TECHNOLOGIES CD ROM DISK MENU

Previous	Main	Next

Contents	** READ ME FILES **	** PROGRAMS **
OSI Tutorial	CNE Program Text	Access CNE DOC
BANalyzer Read Me	CNE Program FAQ	Access CNE Q_A
BANalyzer Install Doc.	CNE Test Read Me	Install CNE Sampler
BANalyzer Ready Install	CNE Quizer	Install CNEQuizer
BANalyzer New Install	NetTech Quizer	Run NetTech Quizer
RUN BANalyzer C: Drive	NetWare FAQ	Run NetWare FAQ
RUN BANalyzer CD ROM	Request For Comment	Access RFCs
	MultiVendor HTML	Network Technologies

CD-ROM menu.

- Can be accessed directly from the CD-ROM.
- Does not require any hard disk space.

C: Cyber Pass Monster CNE Certification demonstration software
- Directory: \MONSTER
- Must be installed on computer hard disk drive.
- Requires 8 megabytes of disk space.

D: Networking Technology Chapter Quiz Questions, Electronic Version
- Directory: \NTQUIZ
- Can be run directly from CD-ROM drive.
- Does not require any computer disk drive space.

E: NetWare Frequently Asked Questions—Windows Version
- Directory: \NWFAQ
- Can be run directly from CD-ROM drive.
- Does not require any computer disk drive space.

F: OSI Tutorial—DOS Version
- Directory: \OSITEACH
- Can be run directly from CD-ROM drive.
- Does not require any computer disk drive space.

G: Multivendor HTML
- Directory: \ENTRENET
- Can be run directly from CD-ROM drive.
- Does not require any computer disk drive space.

H: Request For Comments
- Directory: \RFC
- Data files. Can be accessed directly from CD-ROM drive.
- Does not require any computer disk drive space.

I: BANalyzer
- Directory: \!BANAL
- Can be run directly from CD-ROM drive.
- Does not require any computer disk drive space.

We hope you will find the CD-ROM we have compiled very helpful and informative. We believe it makes a great companion in your CD-ROM collection.

Index

About the authors

Dr. Andres Fortino received his B.E., M.S., and Ph.D. degrees in Electrical Engineering from the City University of New York with a major concentration in semiconductor device design and manufacture. He spent four years working for IBM Corporation in solid-state device research and development, contributing to the development of the 256-Kbyte RAM chip. In that period he was awarded several patents and ten invention disclosures. He has written three textbooks on semiconductor device design and manufacturing and a book on local area networks and dBase III Plus.He authors and edits seminars for Learning Tree International and has consulted with major international corporations, including Xerox, Phillips, and IBM. Currently he is part of the engineering staff of Royal Teton Engineering in Montana.

Arnold Villeneuve is an independent consultant based out of Orleans, ON, Canada. He has over 12 years experience in the computer industry and has achieved Novell, Banyan, Microsoft, and related industry certifications. He also authors and teaches courses for Learning Tree International, a world leader in technology-related training and education.

PURCHASER REGISTRATION FORM

Dear Networking Technologies Purchaser/Reader:

The authors, Dr. Andres Fortino and Arnold Villeneuve, would like to thank you for purchasing this book. We welcome your comments and feedback so that we may improve the book in future revisions. As a special bonus for registering the purchase of this book and providing any feedback we will send you the following applications absolutely FREE:

1. a Windows based OSI Tutorial
2. an HTML version of the Mind Maps found at the beginning of each chapter
3. the most recent version of the NetWare FAQ.

Once again, thank you for buying this book. We look forward to hearing from you and hope you will take us up on our offer.

Yours Truly

Dr. Andres Fortino and Arnold Villeneuve

NAME: _____

STREET: _____

CITY: _____ STAT/PROV: _____

COUNTRY: _____ ZIP/PC: _____

EMAIL (optional):_____ PHONE: _____

COMMENTS: _____

Please forward your completed registration to the following address:

Networking Technologies Registration
c/o Infomentat Inc.,
Convent Glen Mall
P.O. Box 62034
Orleans, Ontario Canada
K1C 7H8

CD-ROM WARRANTY

This software is protected by both United States copyright law and international copyright treaty provision. You must treat this software just like a book. By saying "just like a book," McGraw-Hill means, for example, that this software may be used by any number of people and may be freely moved from one computer location to another, so long as there is no possibility of its being used at one location or on one computer while it also is being used at another. Just as a book cannot be read by two different people in two different places at the same time, neither can the software be used by two different people in two different places at the same time (unless, of course, McGraw-Hill's copyright is being violated).

LIMITED WARRANTY

McGraw-Hill takes great care to provide you with top-quality software, thoroughly checked to prevent virus infections. McGraw-Hill warrants the physical CD-ROM contained herein to be free of defects in materials and workmanship for a period of sixty days from the purchase date. If McGraw-Hill receives written notification within the warranty period of defects in materials or workmanship, and such notification is determined by McGraw-Hill to be correct, McGraw-Hill will replace the defective CD-ROM. Send requests to:

> McGraw-Hill
> Customer Services
> P.O. Box 545
> Blacklick, OH 43004-0545

The entire and exclusive liability and remedy for breach of this Limited Warranty shall be limited to replacement of a defective CD-ROM and shall not include or extend to any claim for or right to cover any other damages, including but not limited to, loss of profit, data, or use of the software, or special, incidental, or consequential damages or other similar claims, even if McGraw-Hill has been specifically advised of the possibility of such damages. In no event will McGraw-Hill's liability for any damages to you or any other person ever exceed the lower of suggested list price or actual price paid for the license to use the software, regardless of any form of the claim.

McGRAW-HILL, SPECIFICALLY DISCLAIMS ALL OTHER WARRANTIES, EXPRESS OR IMPLIED, INCLUDING, BUT NOT LIMITED TO, ANY IMPLIED WARRANTY OF MERCHANTABILITY OR FITNESS FOR A PARTICULAR PURPOSE.

Specifically, McGraw-Hill makes no representation or warranty that the software is fit for any particular purpose and any implied warranty of merchantability is limited to the sixty-day duration of the Limited Warranty covering the physical CD-ROM only (and not the software) and is otherwise expressly and specifically disclaimed.

This limited warranty gives you specific legal rights; you may have others which may vary from state to state. Some states do not allow the exclusion of incidental or consequential damages, or the limitation on how long an implied warranty lasts, so some of the above may not apply to you.